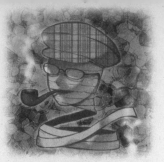

池田晃久
AKIHISA IKEDA

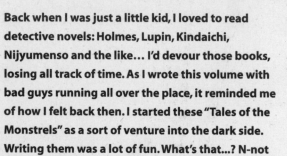

Back when I was just a little kid, I loved to read detective novels: Holmes, Lupin, Kindaichi, Nijyumenso and the like… I'd devour those books, losing all track of time. As I wrote this volume with bad guys running all over the place, it reminded me of how I felt back then. I started these "Tales of the Monstrels" as a sort of venture into the dark side. Writing them was a lot of fun. What's that…? N-not enough *hotness*…? There'll definitely be some in the next volume! (*laugh*)

Akihisa Ikeda was born in 1977 in Miyazaki. He debuted as a mangaka with the four-volume magical warrior fantasy series *Kiruto* in 1999, which was serialized in *Monthly Shonen Jump*. *Rosario+Vampire* debuted in *Monthly Shonen Jump* in March of 2002, and is continuing in the new magazine *Jump Square* (Jump SQ). In Japan, *Rosario+Vampire* is also available as a drama CD. In 2008, the story was released as an anime.

Ikeda has been a huge fan of vampires and monsters since he was a little kid.

He says one of the perks of being a manga artist is being able to go for walks during the day when everybody else is stuck in the office.

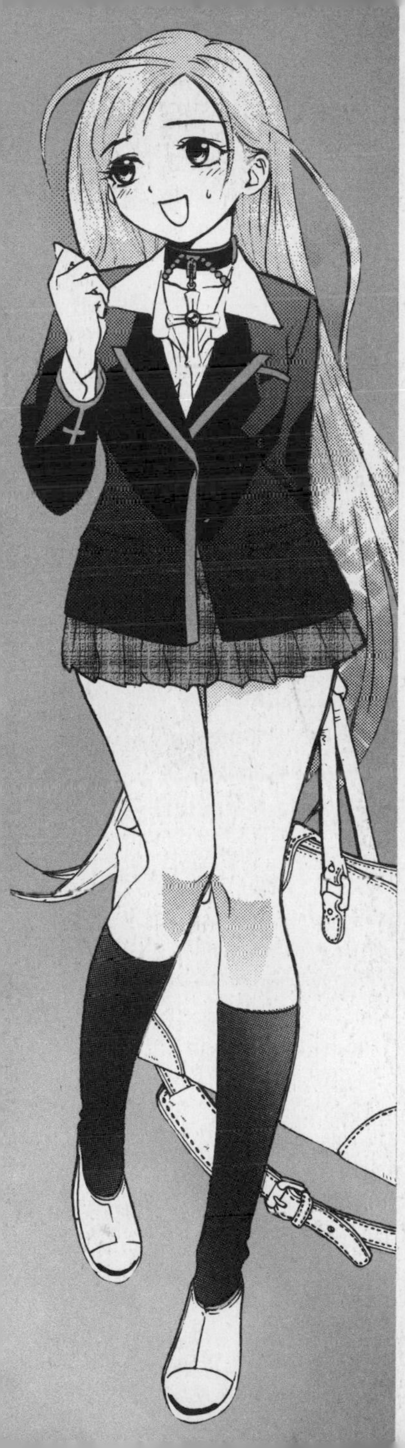

ROSARIO+VAMPIRE 8
The SHONEN JUMP ADVANCED Manga Edition

STORY & ART BY AKIHISA IKEDA

Translation/Kaori Inoue
English Adaptation/Gerard Jones
Touch-up Art & Lettering/Stephen Dutro
Design/Ronnie Casson
Editor/Annette Roman

VP, Production/Alvin Lu
VP, Publishing Licensing/Rika Inouye
VP, Sales & Product Marketing/Gonzalo Ferreyra
VP, Creative/Linda Espinosa
Publisher/Hyoe Narita

The rights of the author(s) of the work(s) in this publication to be so identified have been asserted in accordance with the Copyright, Designs and Patents Act 1988. A CIP catalogue record of this book is available from the British Library.

Printed in the U.S.A.

Published by VIZ Media, LLC
P.O. Box 77010
San Francisco, CA 94107

10 9 8 7 6 5 4 3 2 1
First printing, August 2009

www.viz.com

www.shonenjump.com

PARENTAL ADVISORY
ROSARIO+VAMPIRE is rated T+ for Older Teen and is recommended for ages 16 and up. It contains suggestive situations and graphic violence.

RATED T+ FOR OLDER TEEN

ratings.viz.com

ROSARIO+VAMPIRE
SHIKIGAMI
8

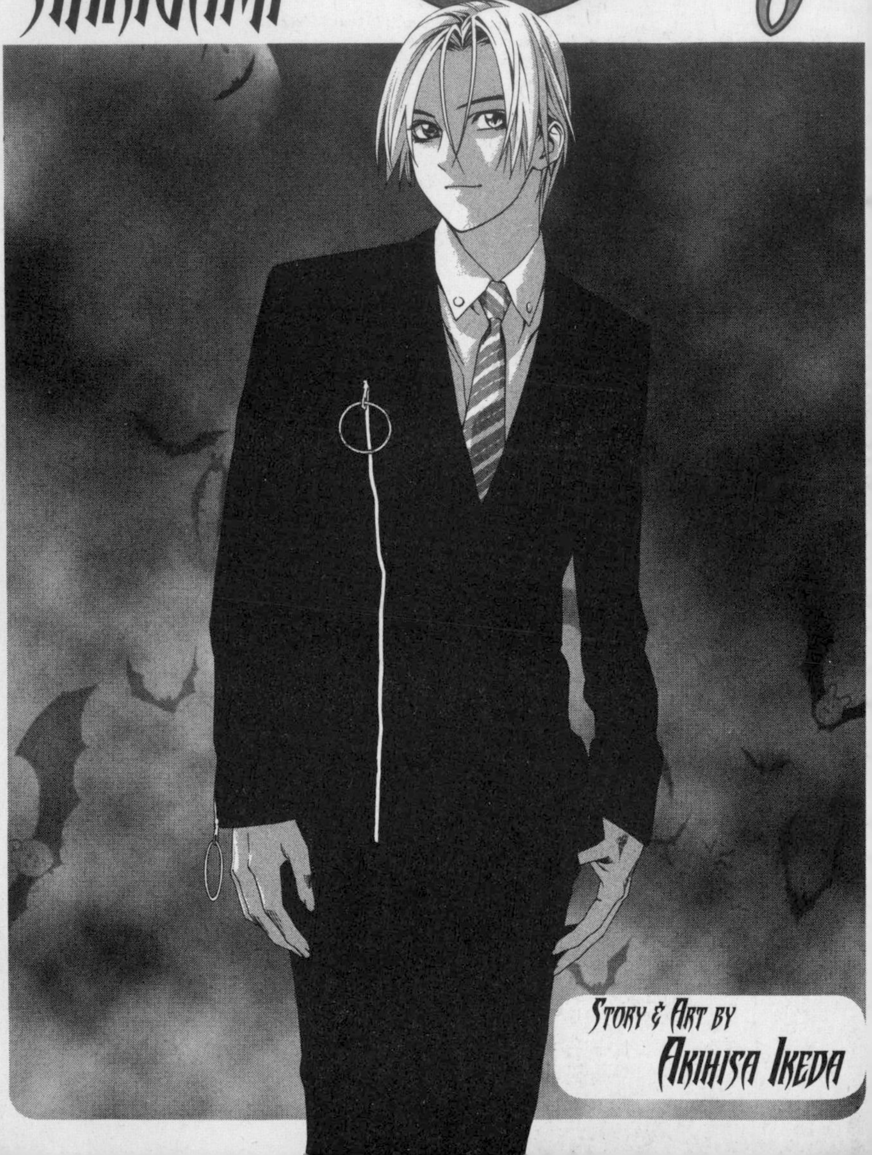
STORY & ART BY
AKIHISA IKEDA

Horror Story Thus Far

Tsukune Aono unsuspectingly enrolls in Yokai Academy—a private school for monsters! When beautiful Moka Akashiya befriends him, Tsukune is determined to stay...despite the rule that any humans who learn of Yokai's existence must be slain!

After joining the school News Club with Moka, Tsukune's life is pure bliss...unless you count being attacked by 1.) the school "Enforcers," 2.) a witch living in the human world, and 3.) a gang of "monstrels." Fortunately, Moka saves Tsukune's life repeatedly by infusing him with her own blood, which briefly transforms him into a butt-kicking vampire! Unfortunately, the side effects of Moka's blood eventually turn poor Tsukune into a flesh-craving ghoul and send him on a mindless rampage!

Tsukune's humanity is restored through a "spirit lock" chained to his wrist by the school headmaster, who then expels him on suspicion of being a monstrel "Anti-Schooler"! Tsukune may stay on one condition...that he join the School Festival Committee! What could be scarier than that...?!

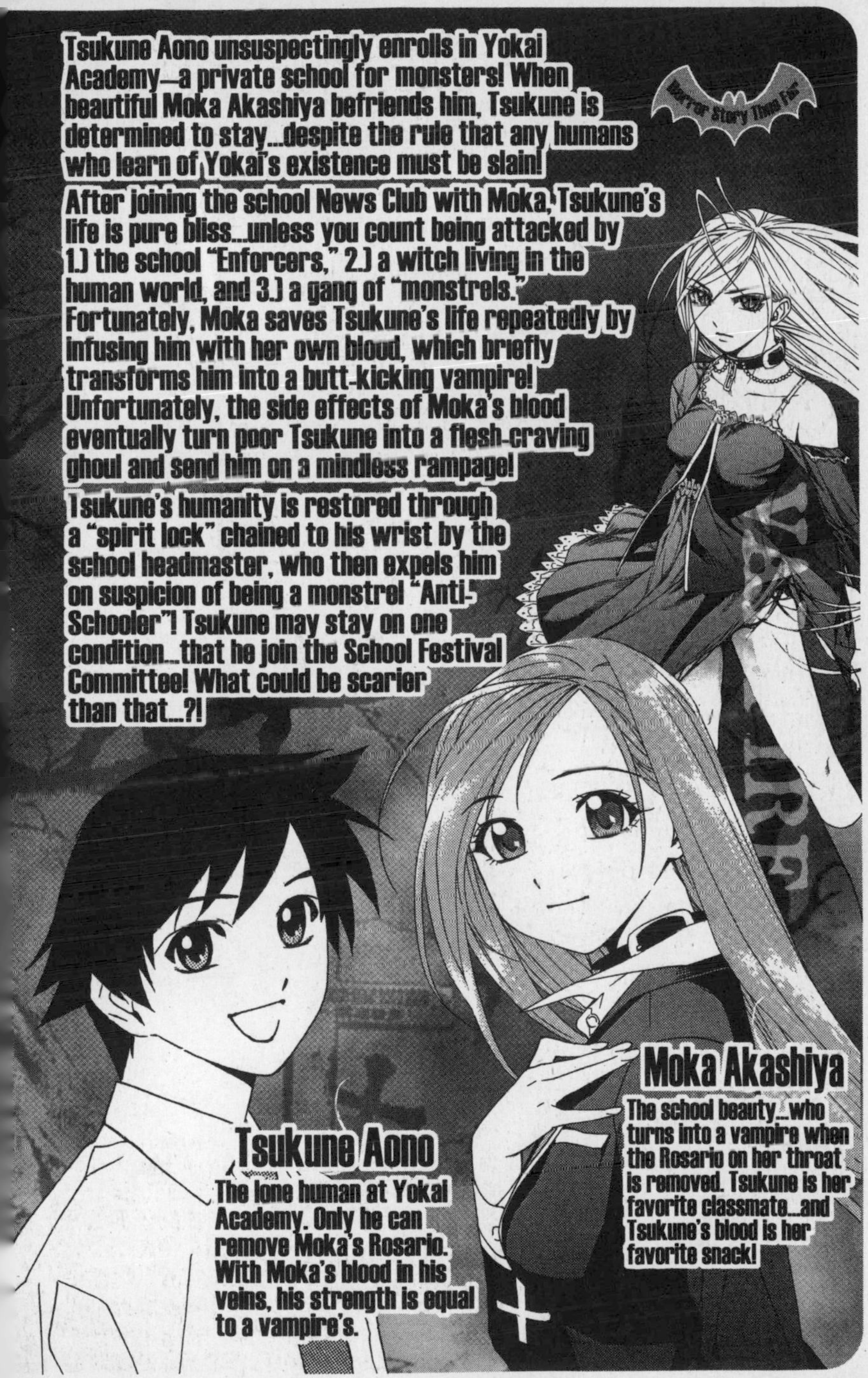

Moka Akashiya

The school beauty...who turns into a vampire when the Rosario on her throat is removed. Tsukune is her favorite classmate...and Tsukune's blood is her favorite snack!

Tsukune Aono

The lone human at Yokai Academy. Only he can remove Moka's Rosario. With Moka's blood in his veins, his strength is equal to a vampire's.

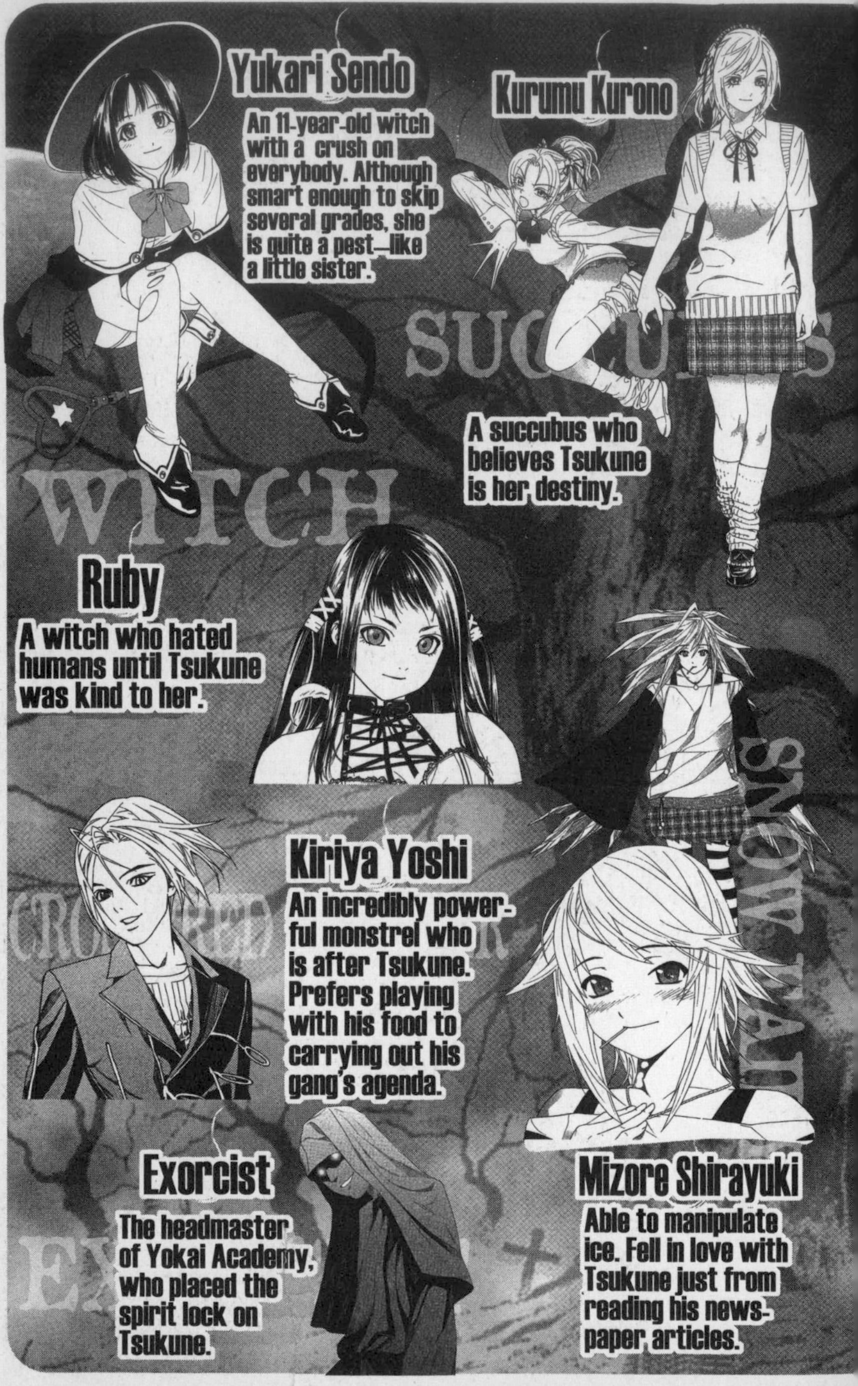

Yukari Sendo

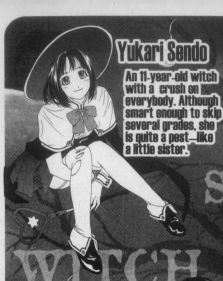

An 11-year-old witch with a crush on everybody. Although smart enough to skip several grades, she is quite a pest—like a little sister.

Kurumu Kurono

A succubus who believes Tsukune is her destiny.

Ruby

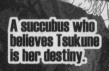

A witch who hated humans until Tsukune was kind to her.

Kiriya Yoshi

An incredibly powerful monstrel who is after Tsukune. Prefers playing with his food to carrying out his gang's agenda.

Exorcist

The headmaster of Yokai Academy, who placed the spirit lock on Tsukune.

Mizore Shirayuki

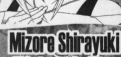

Able to manipulate ice. Fell in love with Tsukune just from reading his newspaper articles.

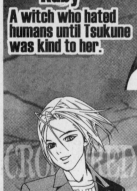

CONTENTS

Volume 8: Shikigami

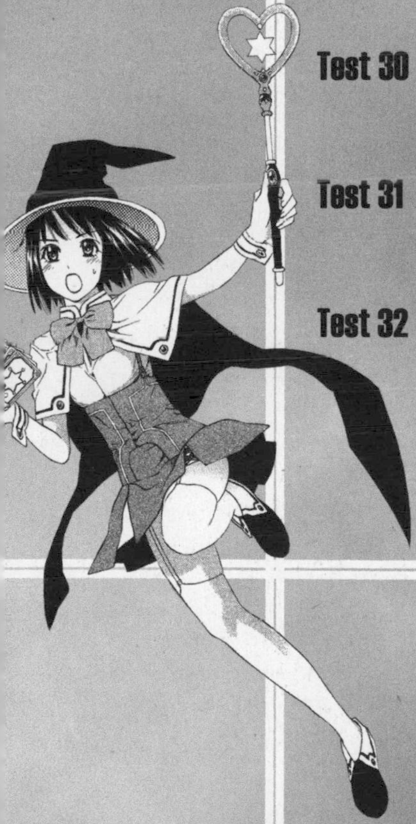

READ THIS WAY

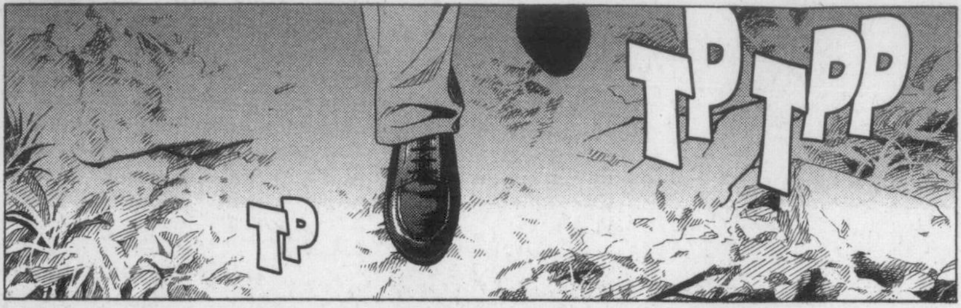
TPTPP
TP

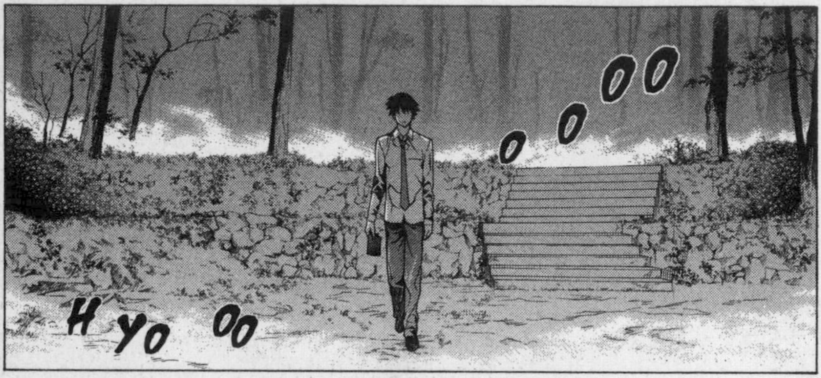
OOOOO
HYOOO

29: The Dark Heart of the School

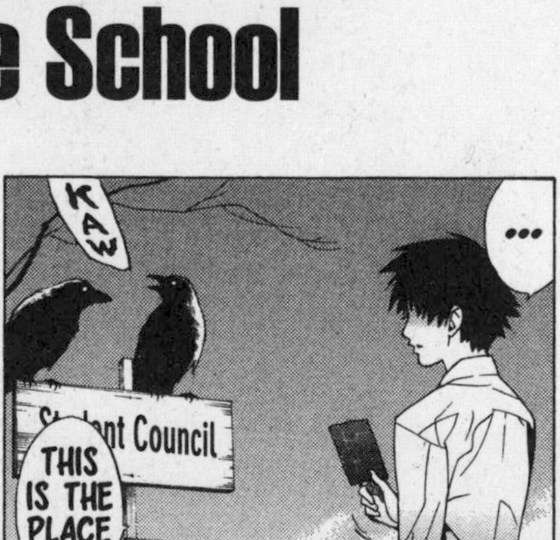
...
KAW
THIS IS THE PLACE ...
HOOOOO

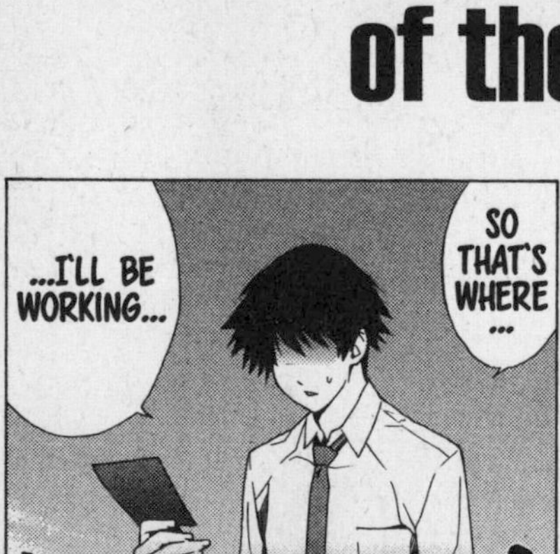
SO THAT'S WHERE ...
...I'LL BE WORKING...
HYOOO

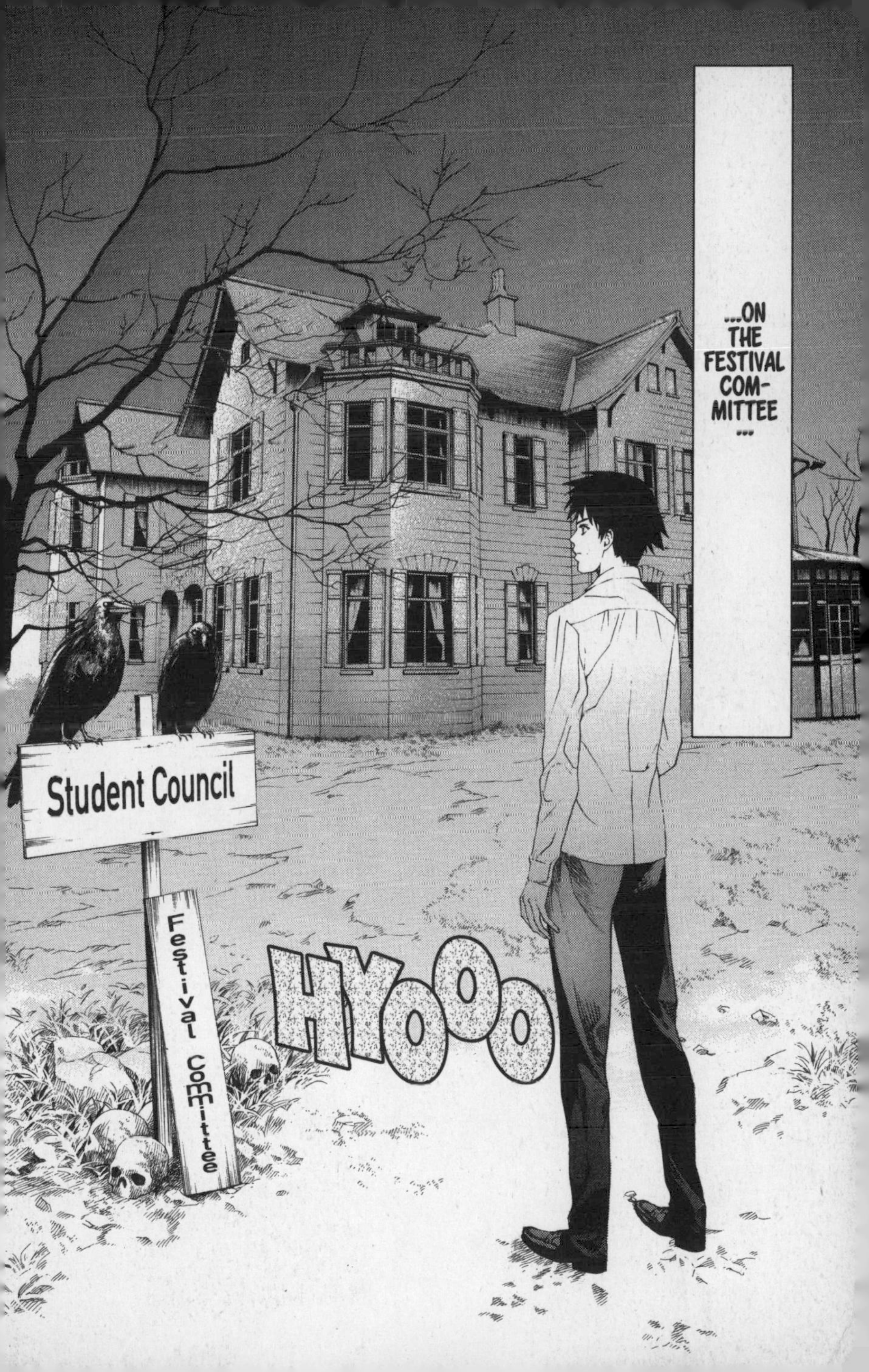
...ON THE FESTIVAL COM-MITTEE ...
Student Council
Festival Committee
HYOOO

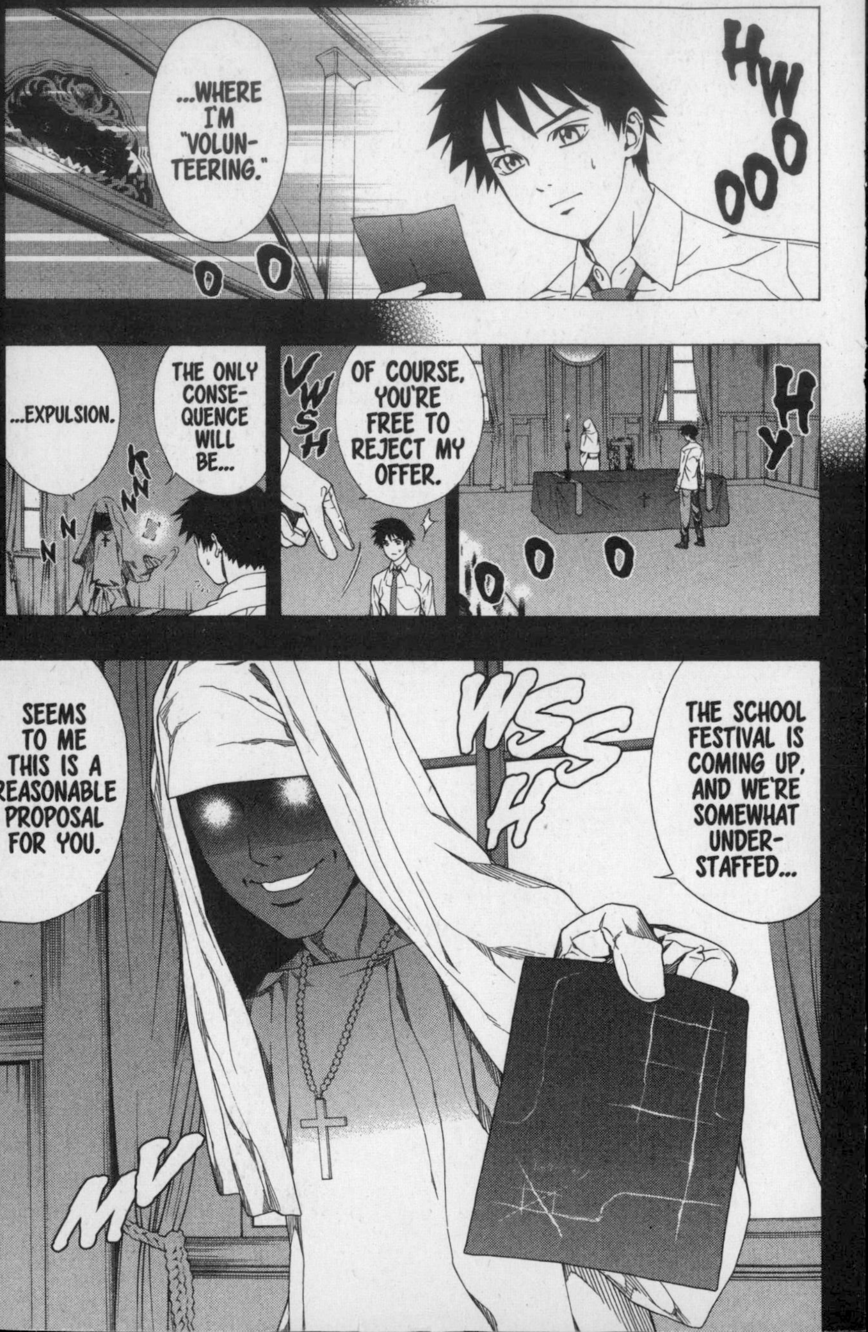
HWOOOO
...WHERE I'M "VOLUN-TEERING."
VWSH
OF COURSE, YOU'RE FREE TO REJECT MY OFFER.
THE ONLY CONSE-QUENCE WILL BE...
...EXPULSION.
THE SCHOOL FESTIVAL IS COMING UP, AND WE'RE SOMEWHAT UNDER-STAFFED...
WSSH
SEEMS TO ME THIS IS A REASONABLE PROPOSAL FOR YOU.
MV

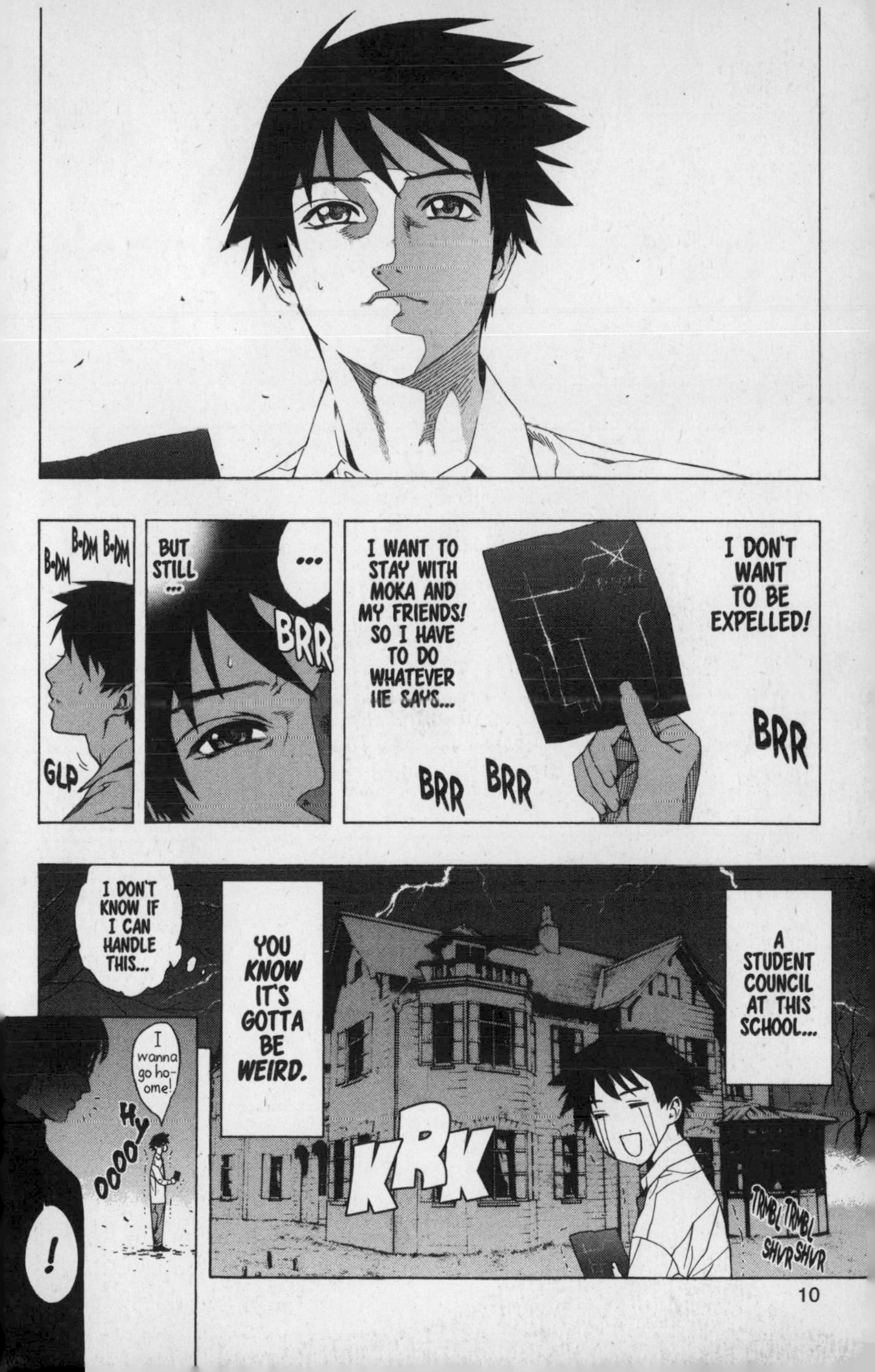

I DON'T WANT TO BE EXPELLED!
I WANT TO STAY WITH MOKA AND MY FRIENDS! SO I HAVE TO DO WHATEVER HE SAYS...
BRR
BRR
BRR
...
BRR
BUT STILL ...
B-DM B-DM
B-DM
GLP
A STUDENT COUNCIL AT THIS SCHOOL...
TRMBL TRMBL
SHVR SHVR
KRK
YOU KNOW IT'S GOTTA BE WEIRD.
I DON'T KNOW IF I CAN HANDLE THIS...
I wanna go ho-ome!
HYOOOO
!

READ THIS WAY

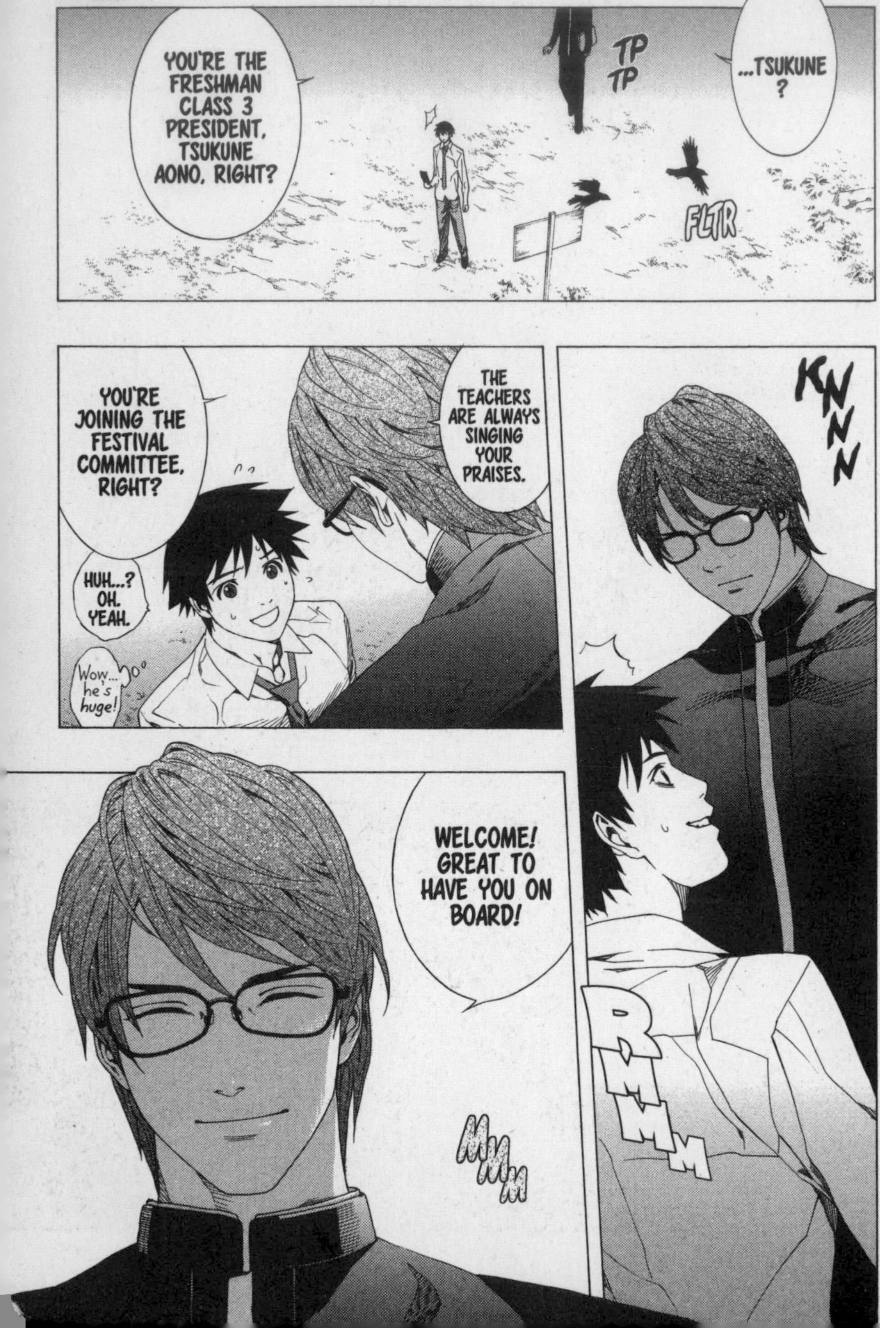

...TSUKUNE?
TP TP
FLTR
YOU'RE THE FRESHMAN CLASS 3 PRESIDENT, TSUKUNE AONO, RIGHT?
KNNN
RMMMM
THE TEACHERS ARE ALWAYS SINGING YOUR PRAISES.
YOU'RE JOINING THE FESTIVAL COMMITTEE, RIGHT?
HUH...? OH. YEAH.
Wow... he's huge!
WELCOME! GREAT TO HAVE YOU ON BOARD!
MMM

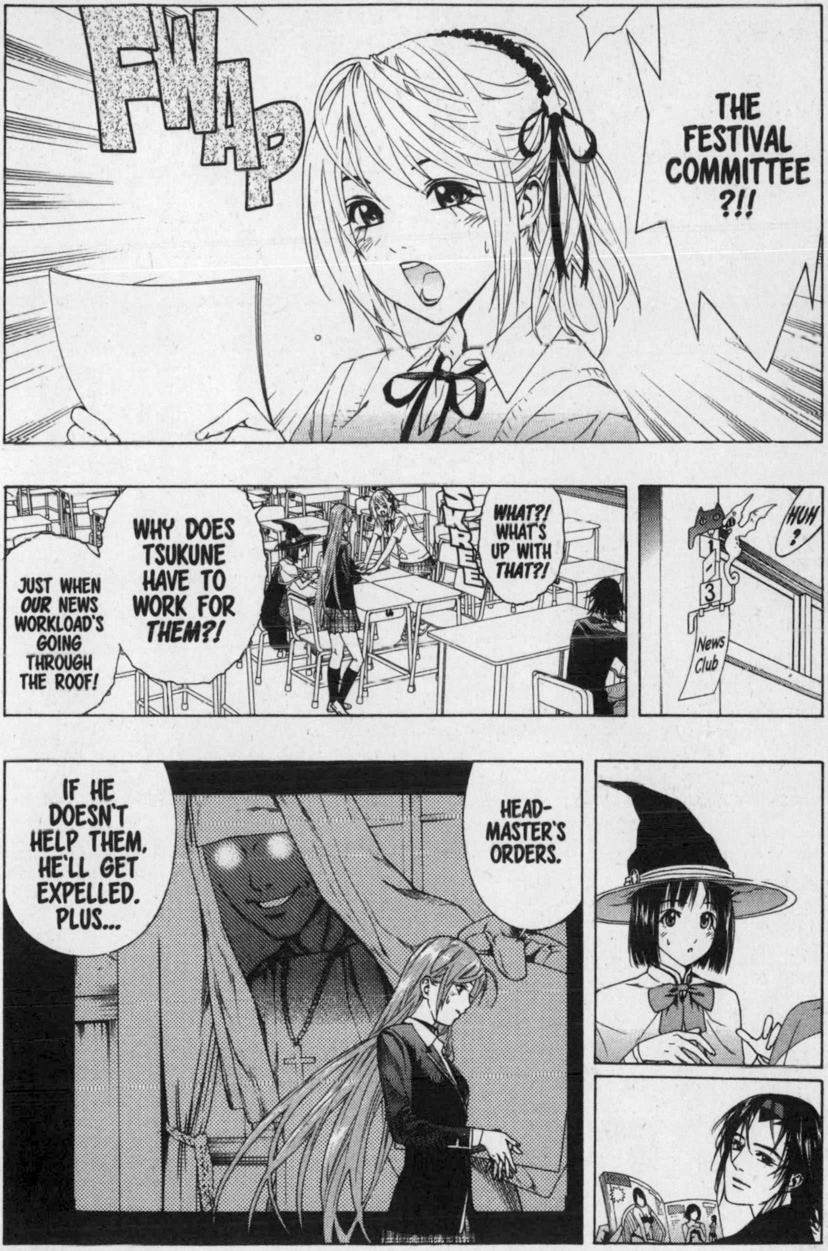
FWAP
THE FESTIVAL COMMITTEE ?!!
HUH ?
News Club
WHAT?! WHAT'S UP WITH THAT?!
WHY DOES TSUKUNE HAVE TO WORK FOR THEM?!
JUST WHEN OUR NEWS WORKLOAD'S GOING THROUGH THE ROOF!
HEAD-MASTER'S ORDERS.
IF HE DOESN'T HELP THEM, HE'LL GET EXPELLED. PLUS...

READ THIS WAY

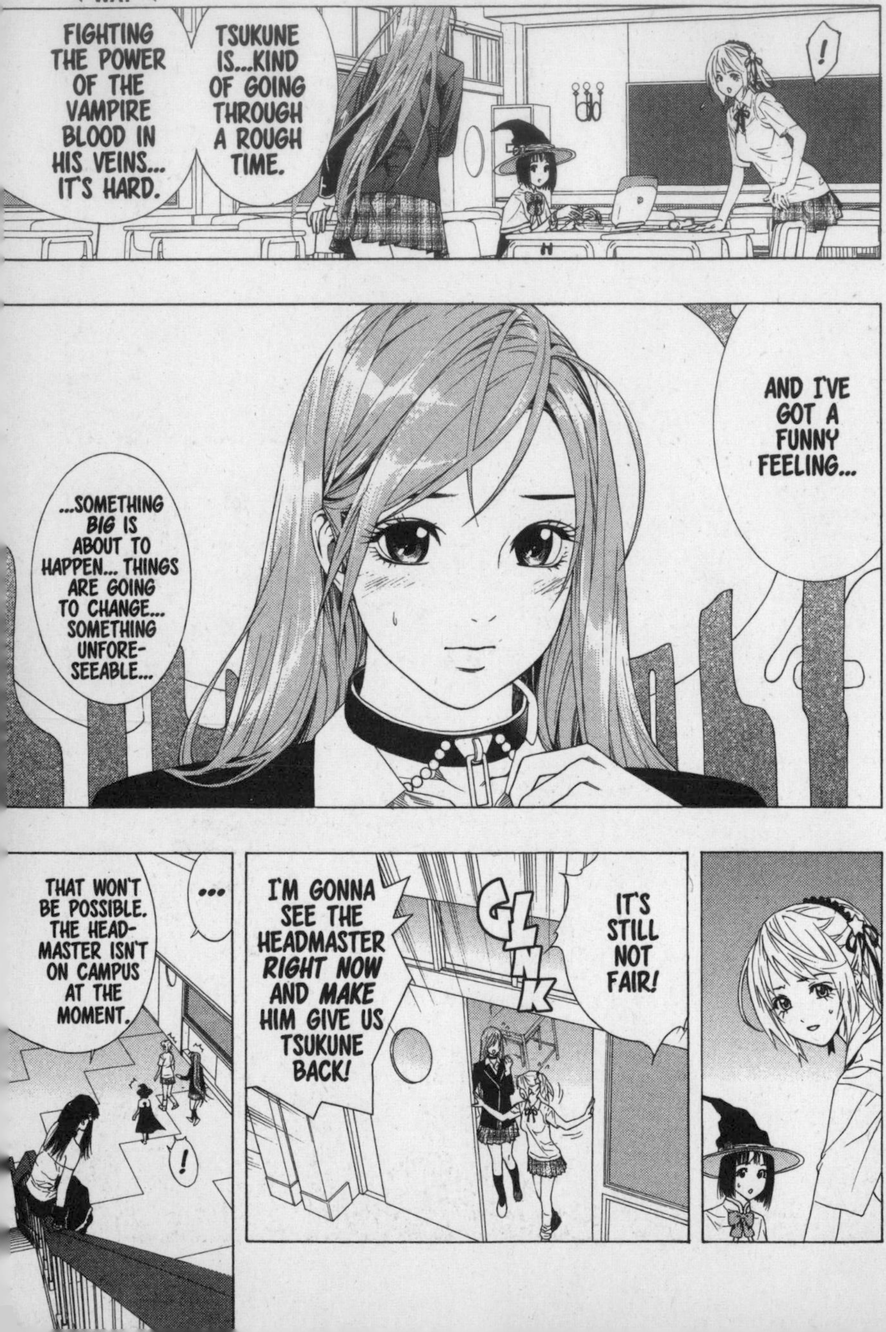
!
TSUKUNE IS...KIND OF GOING THROUGH A ROUGH TIME.
FIGHTING THE POWER OF THE VAMPIRE BLOOD IN HIS VEINS... IT'S HARD.
AND I'VE GOT A FUNNY FEELING...
...SOMETHING *BIG* IS ABOUT TO HAPPEN... THINGS ARE GOING TO CHANGE... SOMETHING UNFORE-SEEABLE...
IT'S STILL NOT FAIR!
GLINK
I'M GONNA SEE THE HEADMASTER *RIGHT NOW* AND *MAKE* HIM GIVE US TSUKUNE BACK!
...
THAT WON'T BE POSSIBLE. THE HEAD-MASTER ISN'T ON CAMPUS AT THE MOMENT.
!

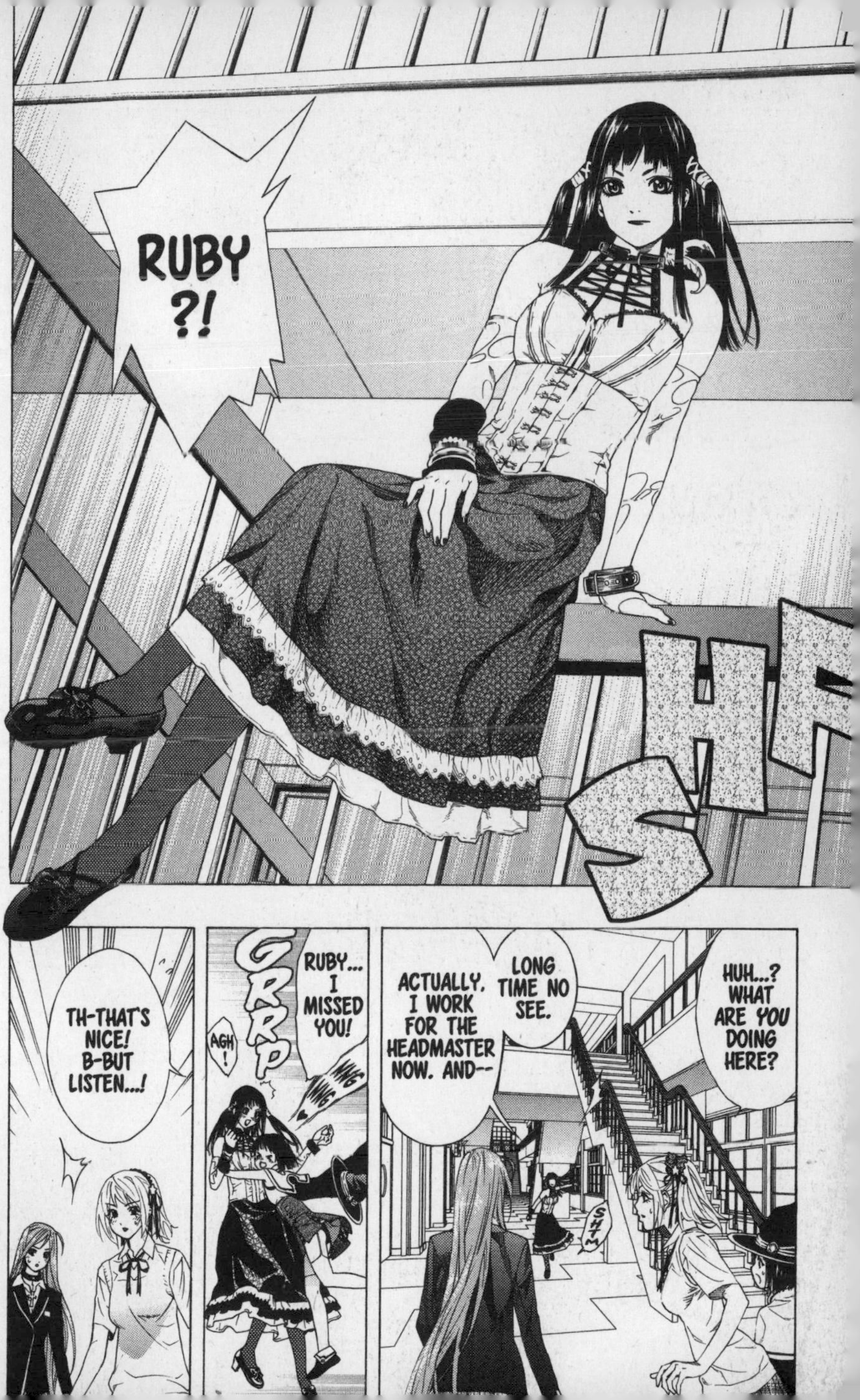
RUBY ?!
HUH...? WHAT ARE YOU DOING HERE?
SHTM
LONG TIME NO SEE.
ACTUALLY, I WORK FOR THE HEADMASTER NOW. AND--
RUBY... I MISSED YOU!
GRRP
AGH!
TH-THAT'S NICE! B-BUT LISTEN...!

READ THIS WAY

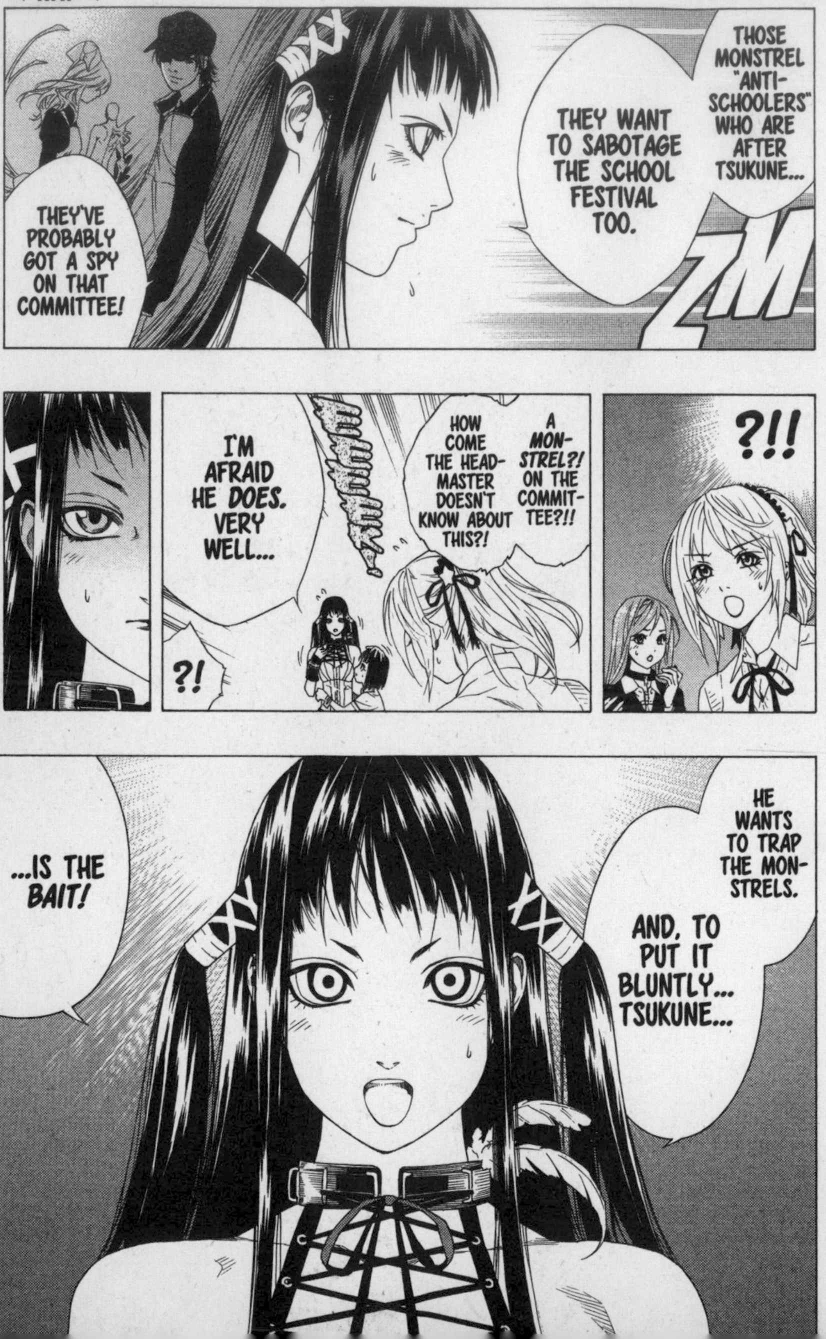
THOSE MONSTREL "ANTI-SCHOOLERS" WHO ARE AFTER TSUKUNE...
THEY WANT TO SABOTAGE THE SCHOOL FESTIVAL TOO.
ZM
THEY'VE PROBABLY GOT A SPY ON THAT COMMITTEE!
?!!
A MONSTREL?! ON THE COMMITTEE?!!
HOW COME THE HEADMASTER DOESN'T KNOW ABOUT THIS?!
I'M AFRAID HE DOES. VERY WELL...
?!
HE WANTS TO TRAP THE MONSTRELS.
AND, TO PUT IT BLUNTLY... TSUKUNE...
...IS THE BAIT!

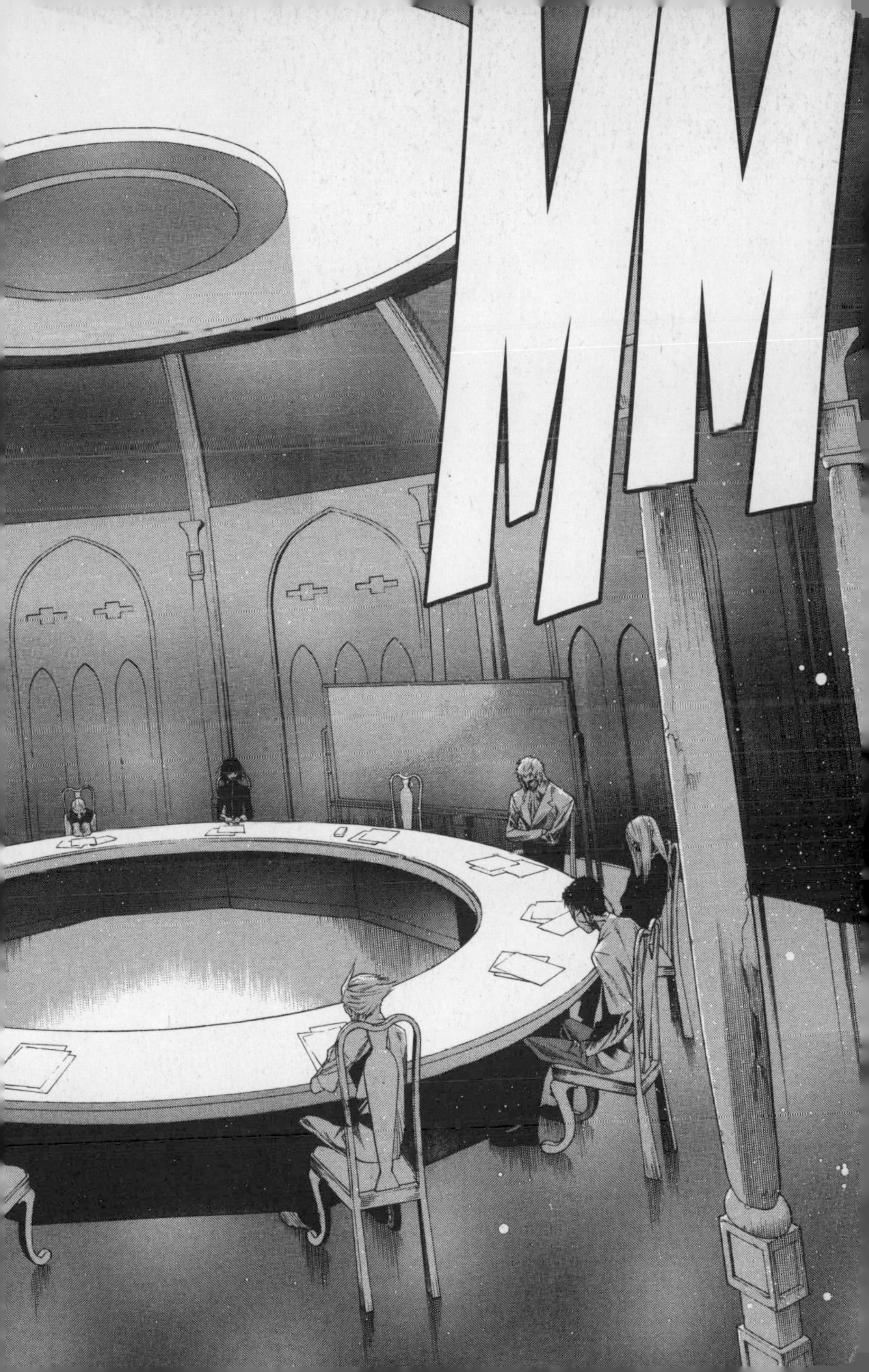
MMM

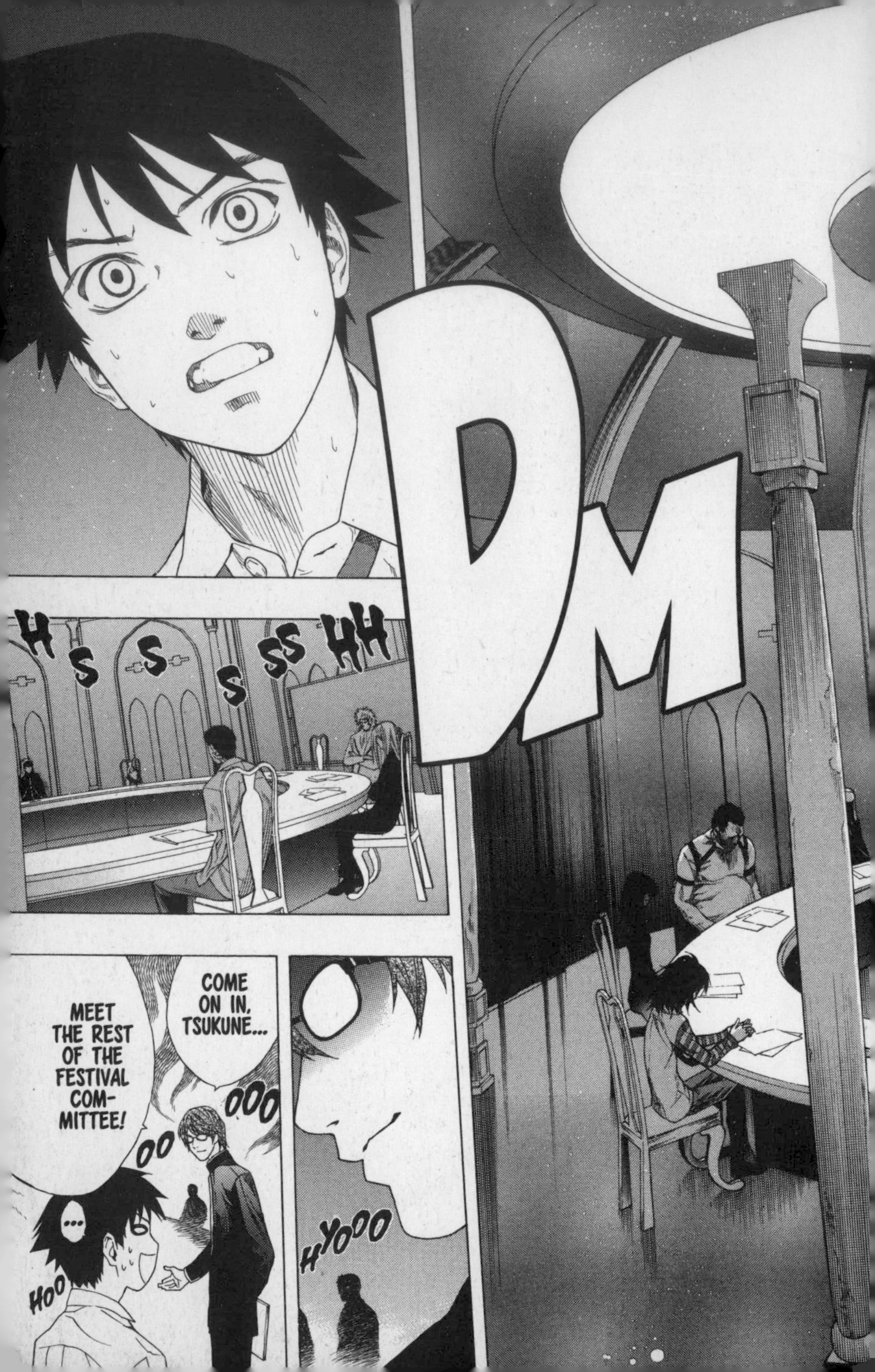
DM
HSSSSSHH
HYOOO
COME ON IN, TSUKUNE...
MEET THE REST OF THE FESTIVAL COM-MITTEE!
OOO
OO
HOO
...

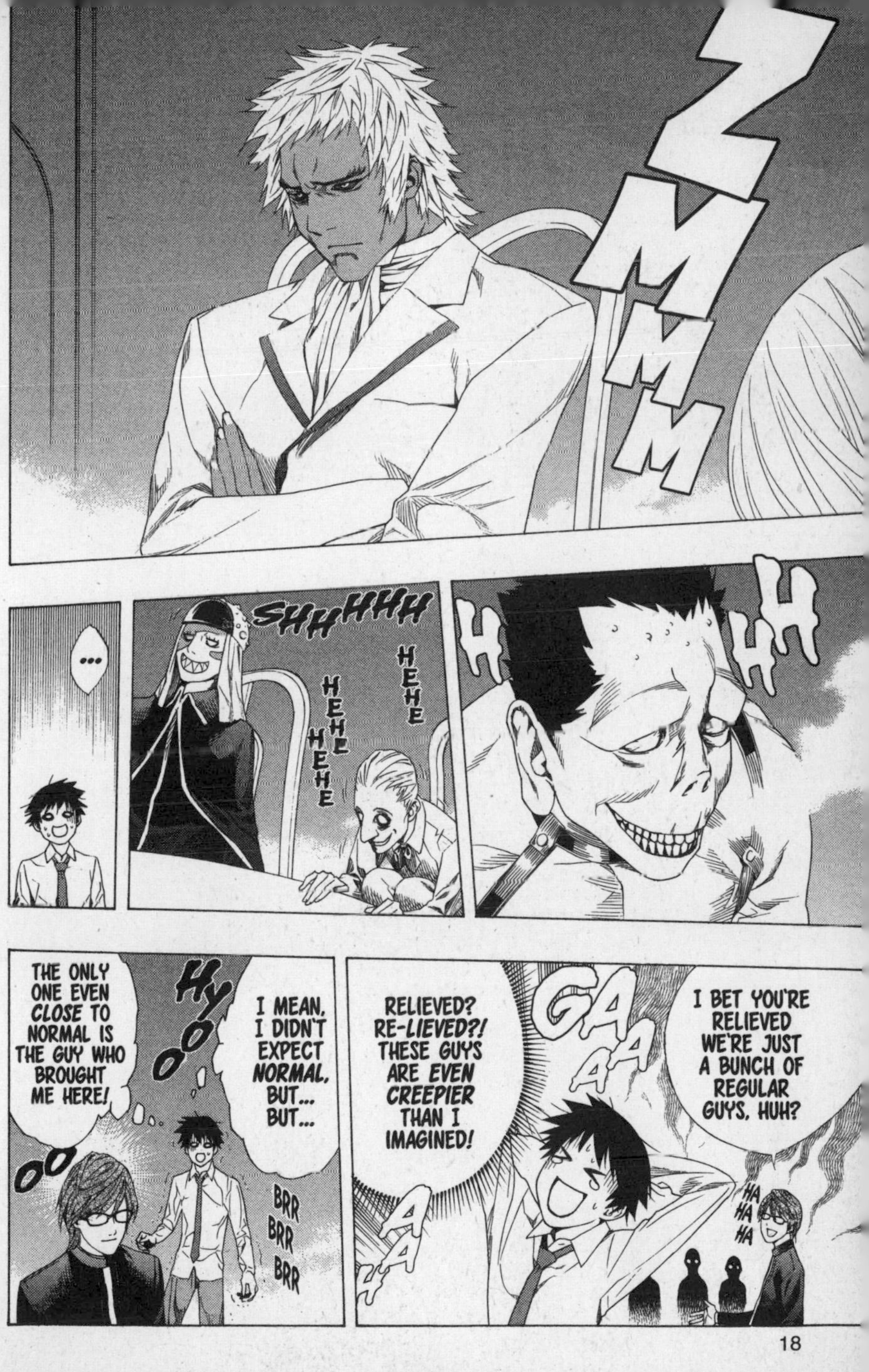
ZMMMM
HHHHH
SHHHHHH
HEHE
HEHE
HEHE
HEHE
...
I BET YOU'RE RELIEVED WE'RE JUST A BUNCH OF REGULAR GUYS, HUH?
HA HA HA HA
GAAAA
RELIEVED? RE-*LIEVED*?! THESE GUYS ARE *EVEN CREEPIER* THAN I IMAGINED!
I MEAN, I DIDN'T EXPECT *NORMAL*, BUT... BUT...
BRR BRR BRR
THE ONLY ONE EVEN *CLOSE* TO NORMAL IS THE GUY WHO BROUGHT ME HERE!

READ THIS WAY

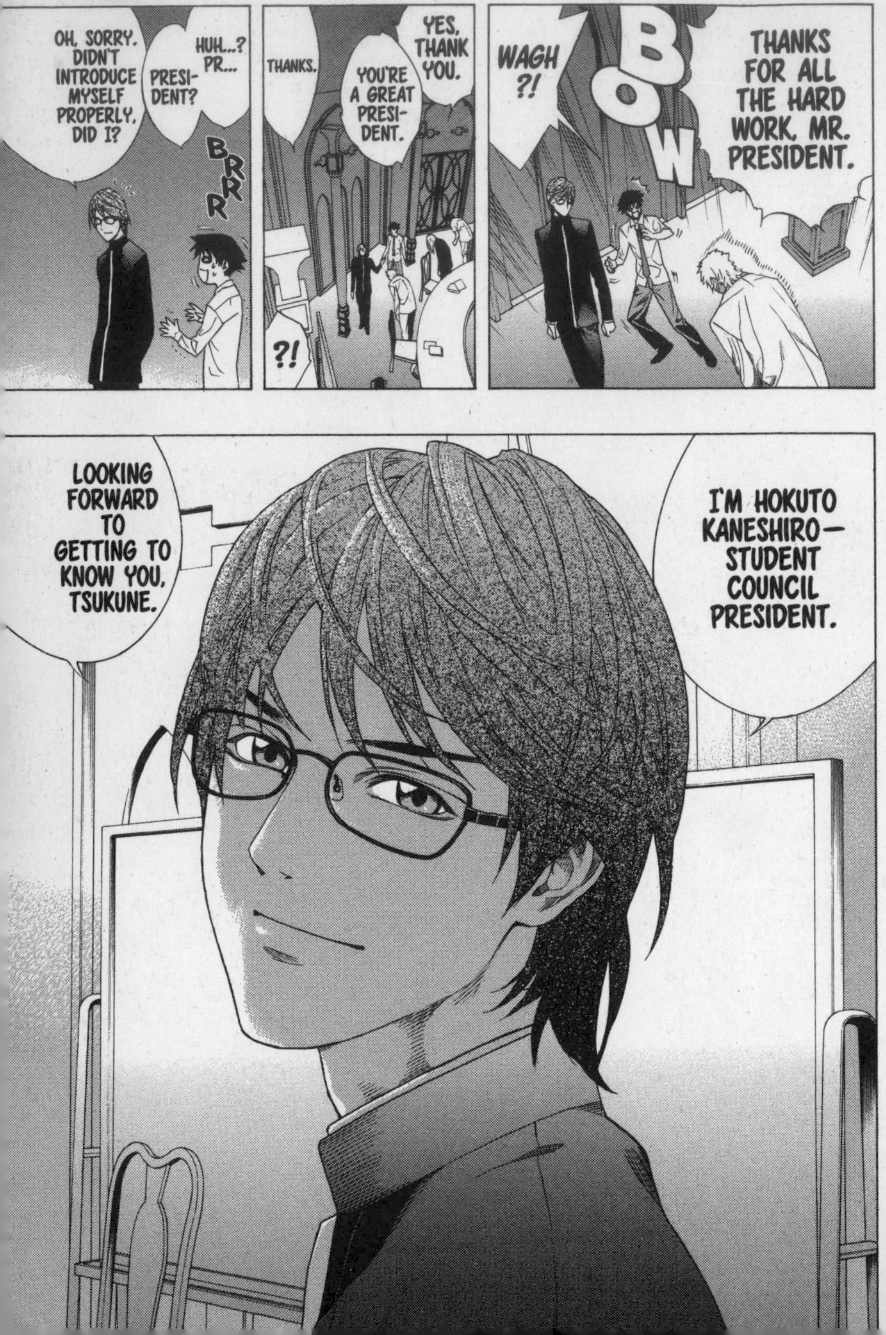
THANKS FOR ALL THE HARD WORK, MR. PRESIDENT.
BOW
WAGH ?!
YES, THANK YOU.
YOU'RE A GREAT PRESIDENT.
THANKS.
?!
HUH...? PR...
PRESIDENT?
BRRR
OH, SORRY. DIDN'T INTRODUCE MYSELF PROPERLY, DID I?
I'M HOKUTO KANESHIRO— STUDENT COUNCIL PRESIDENT.
LOOKING FORWARD TO GETTING TO KNOW YOU, TSUKUNE.

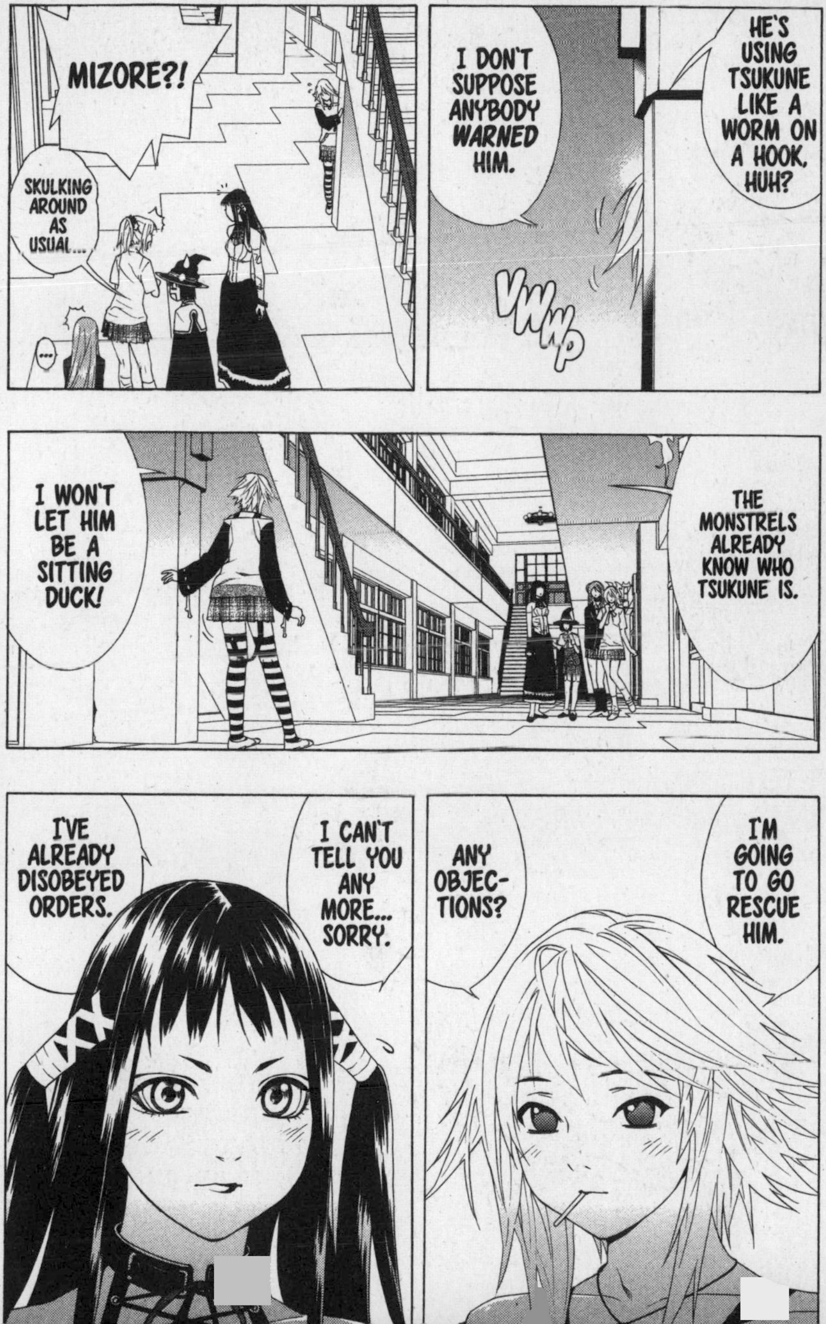
HE'S USING TSUKUNE LIKE A WORM ON A HOOK, HUH?
I DON'T SUPPOSE ANYBODY WARNED HIM.
VWWP
MIZORE?!
SKULKING AROUND AS USUAL...
...
THE MONSTRELS ALREADY KNOW WHO TSUKUNE IS.
I WON'T LET HIM BE A SITTING DUCK!
I'M GOING TO GO RESCUE HIM.
ANY OBJECTIONS?
I CAN'T TELL YOU ANY MORE... SORRY.
I'VE ALREADY DISOBEYED ORDERS.

READ THIS WAY

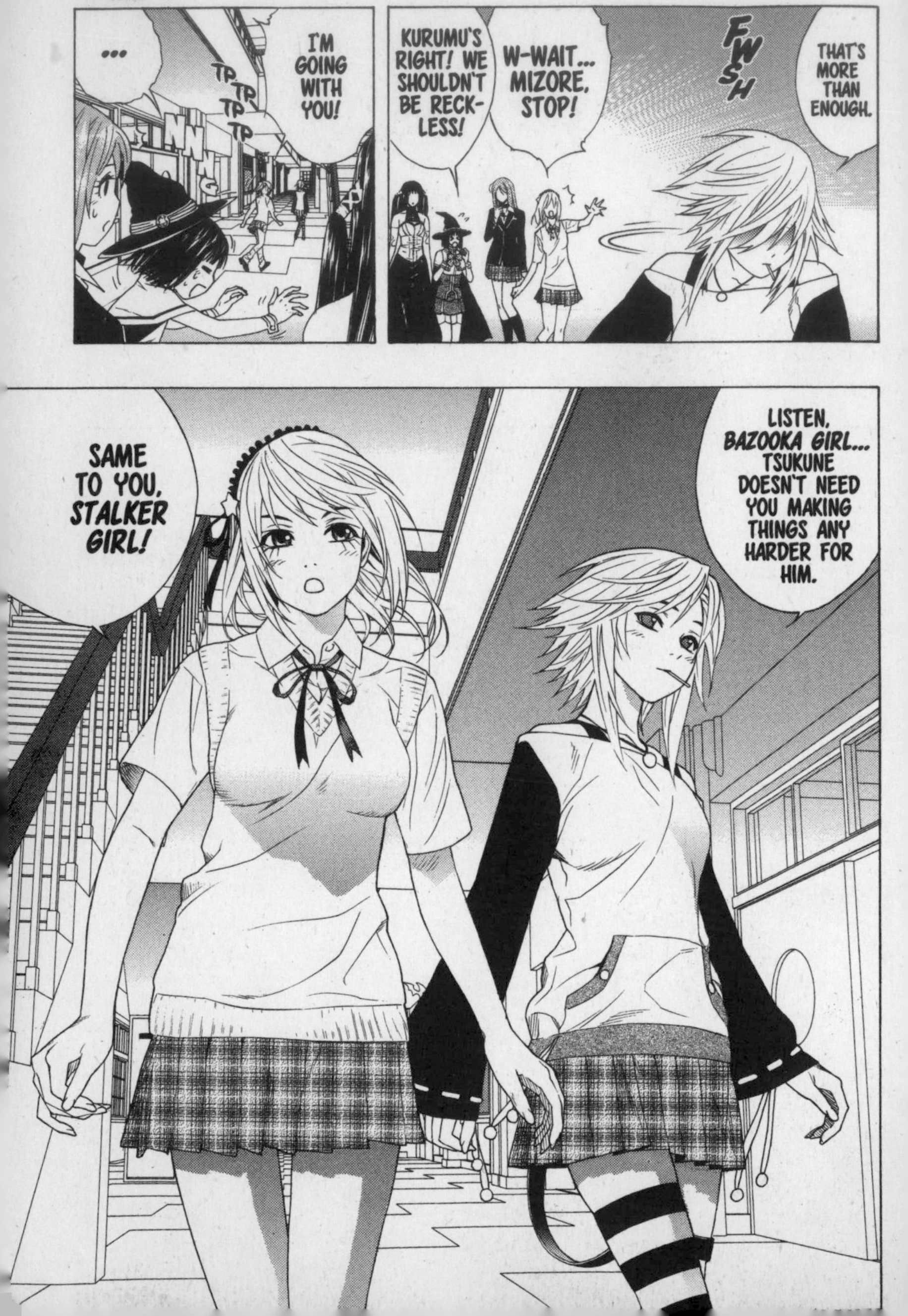
THAT'S MORE THAN ENOUGH.
FWSH
W-WAIT... MIZORE, STOP!
KURUMU'S RIGHT! WE SHOULDN'T BE RECK-LESS!
I'M GOING WITH YOU!
...
TP TP TP TP
NNNG
LISTEN, BAZOOKA GIRL... TSUKUNE DOESN'T NEED YOU MAKING THINGS ANY HARDER FOR HIM.
SAME TO YOU, STALKER GIRL!

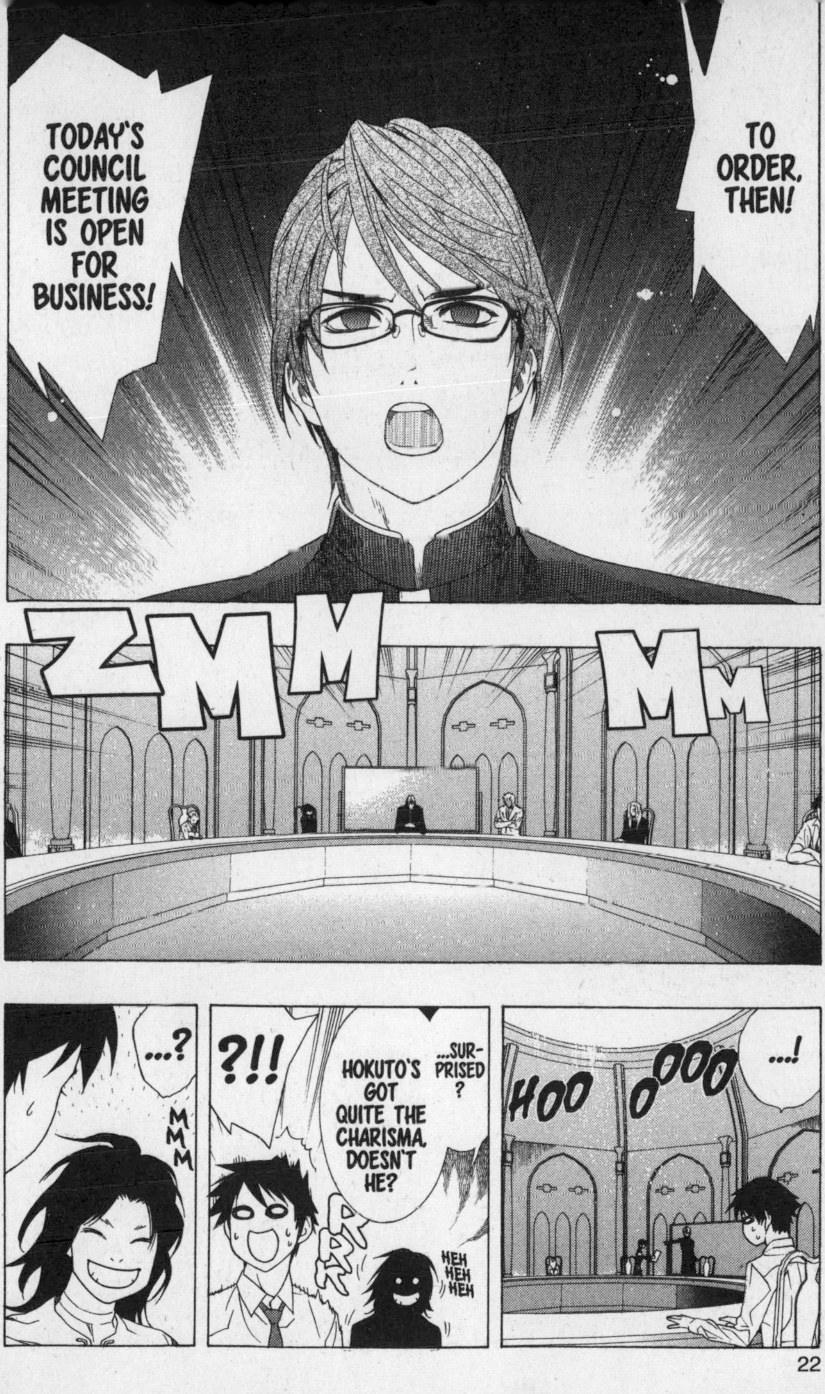
TO ORDER, THEN!
TODAY'S COUNCIL MEETING IS OPEN FOR BUSINESS!
ZMMM MMM
...!
HOO OOOO
...SUR-PRISED?
HOKUTO'S GOT QUITE THE CHARISMA, DOESN'T HE?
?!!
HEH HEH HEH
...?
MMM

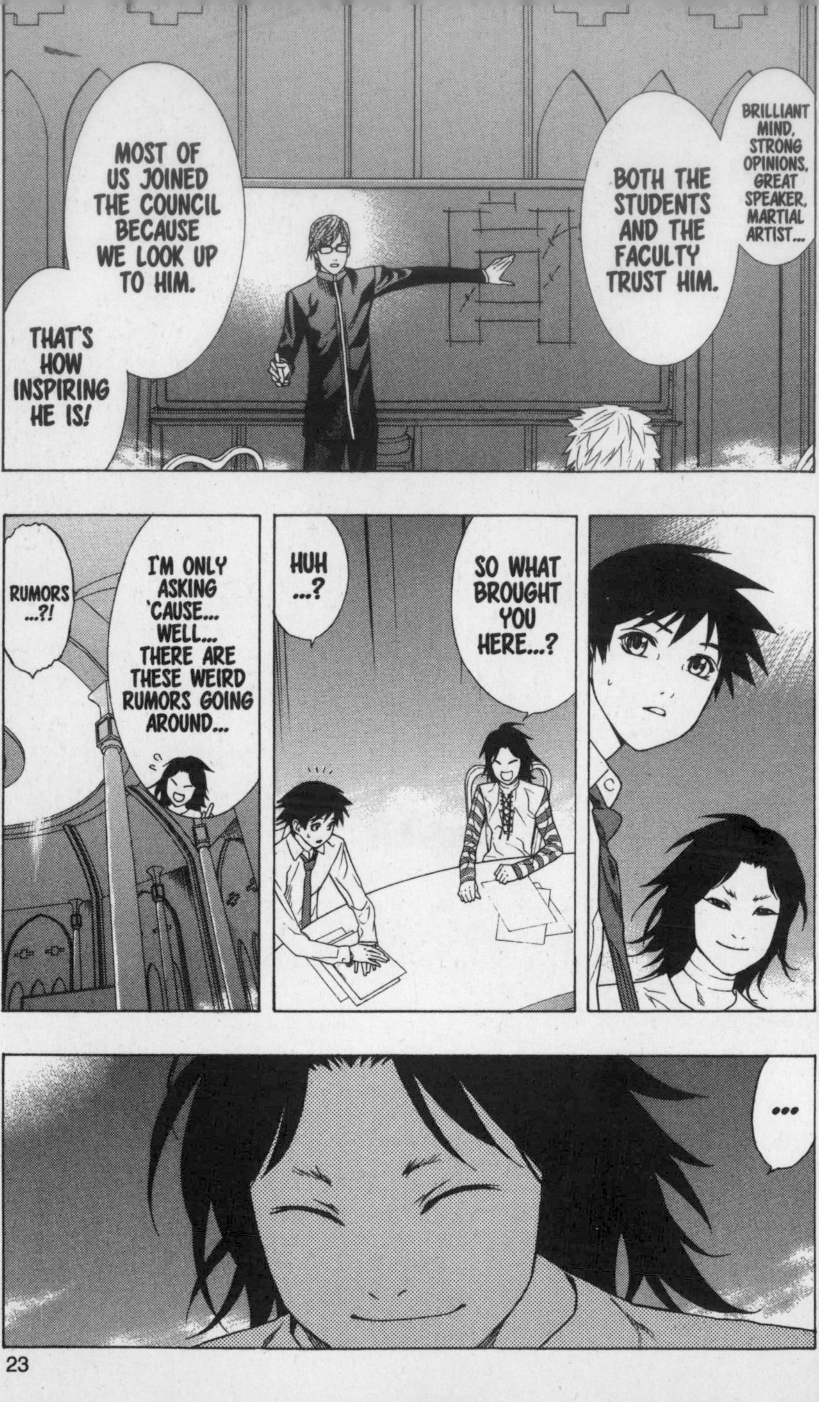
BRILLIANT MIND, STRONG OPINIONS, GREAT SPEAKER, MARTIAL ARTIST...
BOTH THE STUDENTS AND THE FACULTY TRUST HIM.
MOST OF US JOINED THE COUNCIL BECAUSE WE LOOK UP TO HIM.
THAT'S HOW INSPIRING HE IS!
SO WHAT BROUGHT YOU HERE...?
HUH ...?
I'M ONLY ASKING 'CAUSE... WELL... THERE ARE THESE WEIRD RUMORS GOING AROUND...
RUMORS ...?!
...

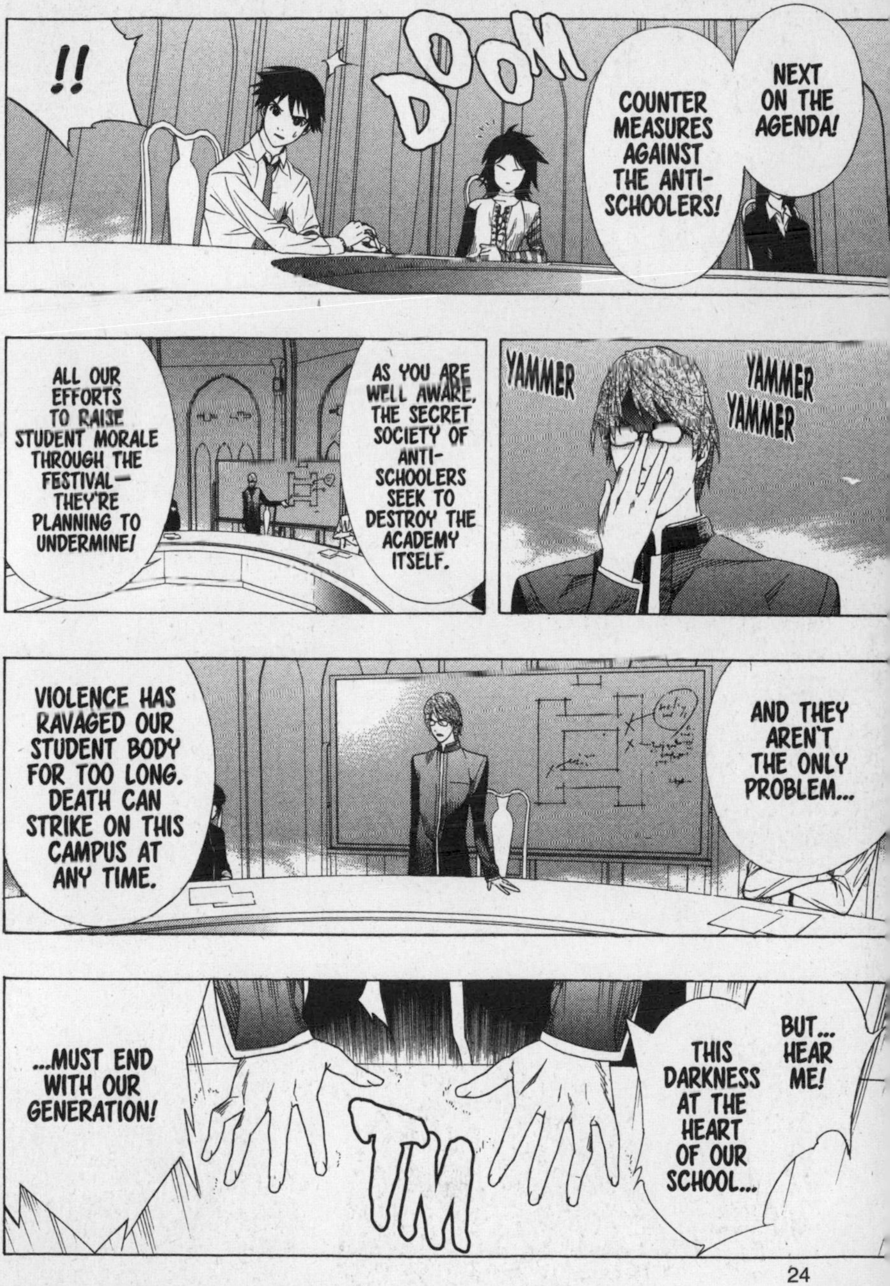
NEXT ON THE AGENDA!
COUNTER MEASURES AGAINST THE ANTI-SCHOOLERS!
DOOM
!!
YAMMER
YAMMER
YAMMER
AS YOU ARE WELL AWARE, THE SECRET SOCIETY OF ANTI-SCHOOLERS SEEK TO DESTROY THE ACADEMY ITSELF.
ALL OUR EFFORTS TO RAISE STUDENT MORALE THROUGH THE FESTIVAL—THEY'RE PLANNING TO UNDERMINE!
AND THEY AREN'T THE ONLY PROBLEM...
VIOLENCE HAS RAVAGED OUR STUDENT BODY FOR TOO LONG. DEATH CAN STRIKE ON THIS CAMPUS AT ANY TIME.
BUT... HEAR ME!
THIS DARKNESS AT THE HEART OF OUR SCHOOL...
TM
...MUST END WITH OUR GENERATION!

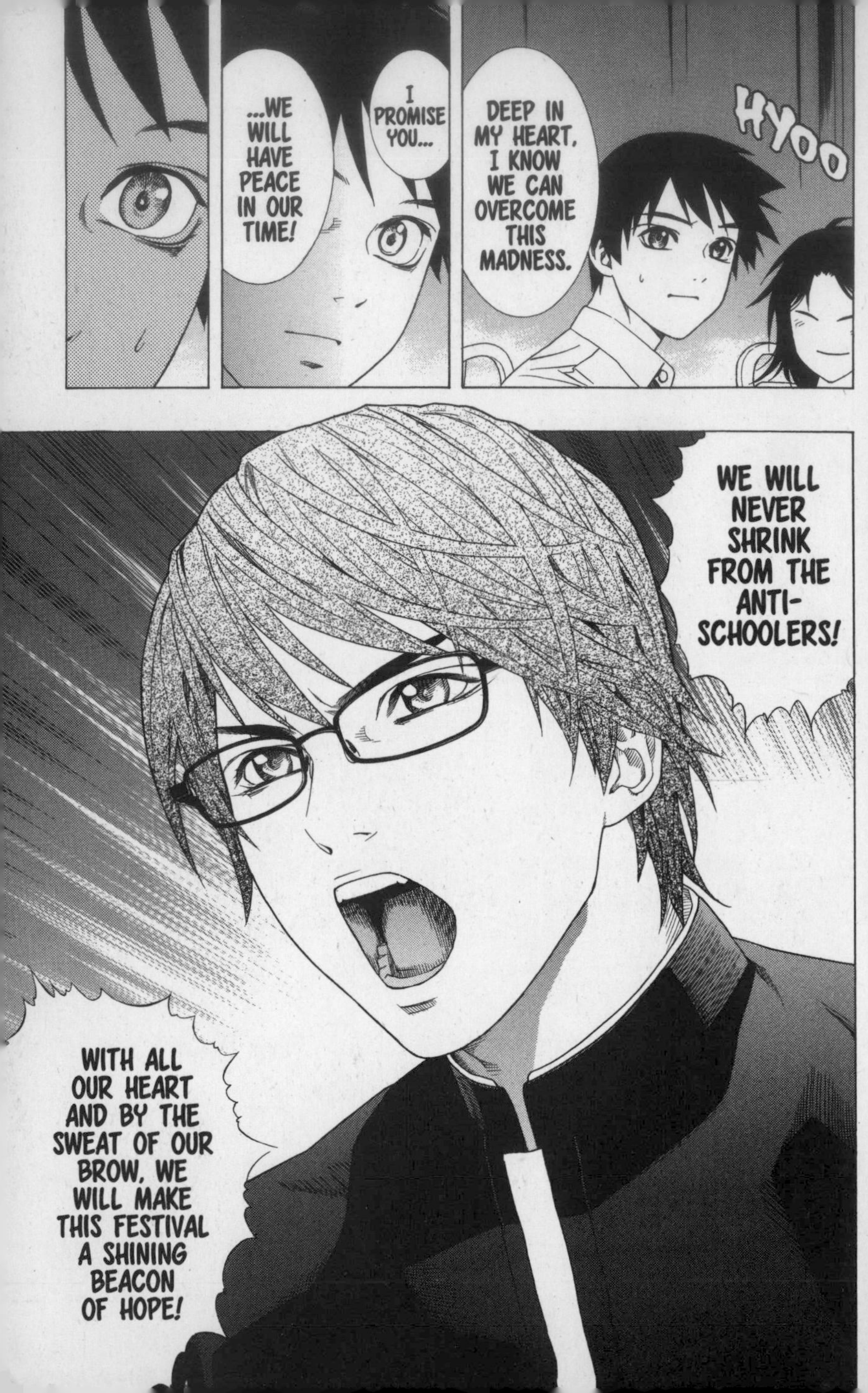
HYOO
DEEP IN MY HEART, I KNOW WE CAN OVERCOME THIS MADNESS.
I PROMISE YOU...
...WE WILL HAVE PEACE IN OUR TIME!
WE WILL NEVER SHRINK FROM THE ANTI-SCHOOLERS!
WITH ALL OUR HEART AND BY THE SWEAT OF OUR BROW, WE WILL MAKE THIS FESTIVAL A SHINING BEACON OF HOPE!

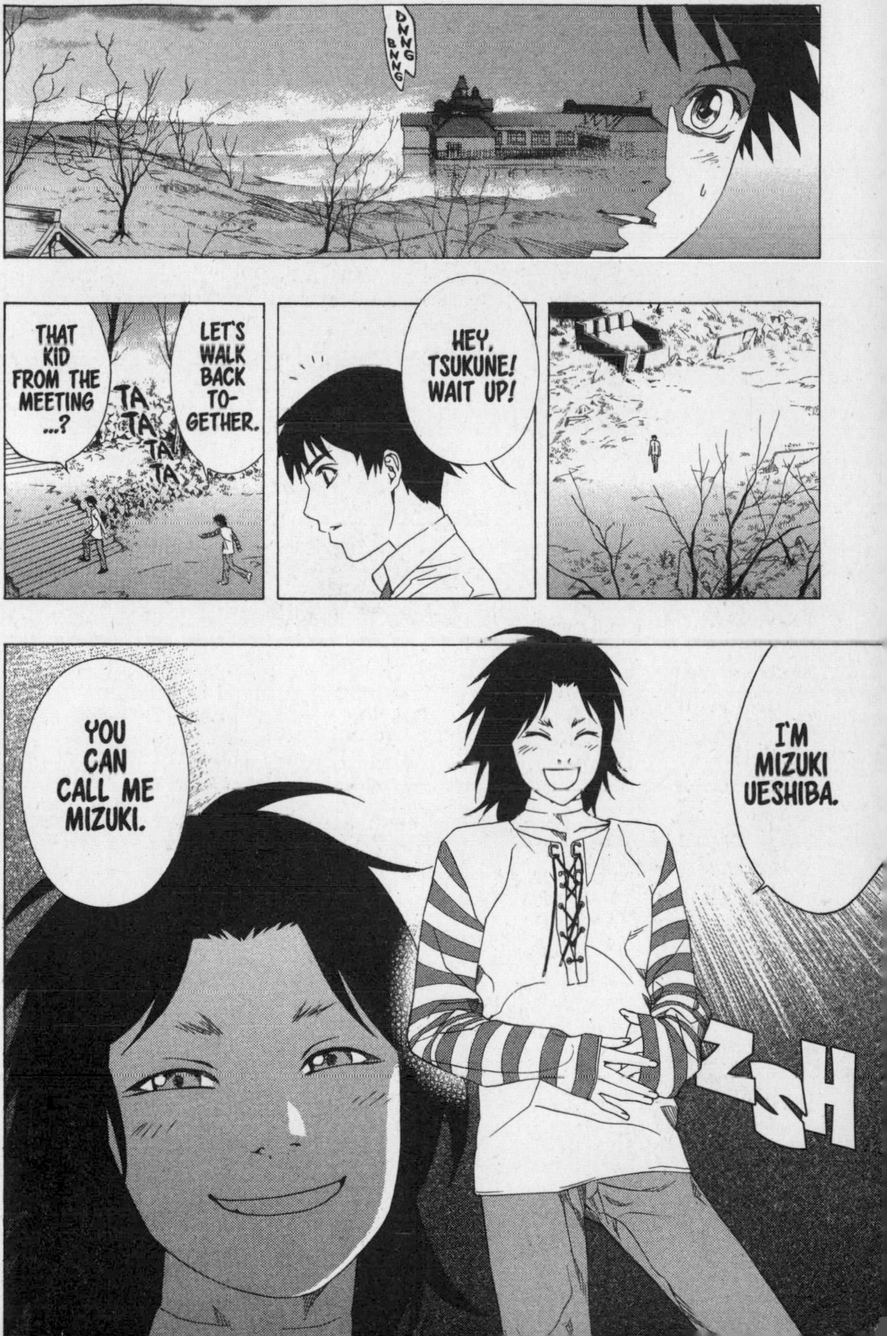
DNNG BNNG
HEY, TSUKUNE! WAIT UP!
LET'S WALK BACK TO-GETHER.
TA TA TA TA
THAT KID FROM THE MEETING ...?
I'M MIZUKI UESHIBA.
ZSH
YOU CAN CALL ME MIZUKI.

READ THIS WAY

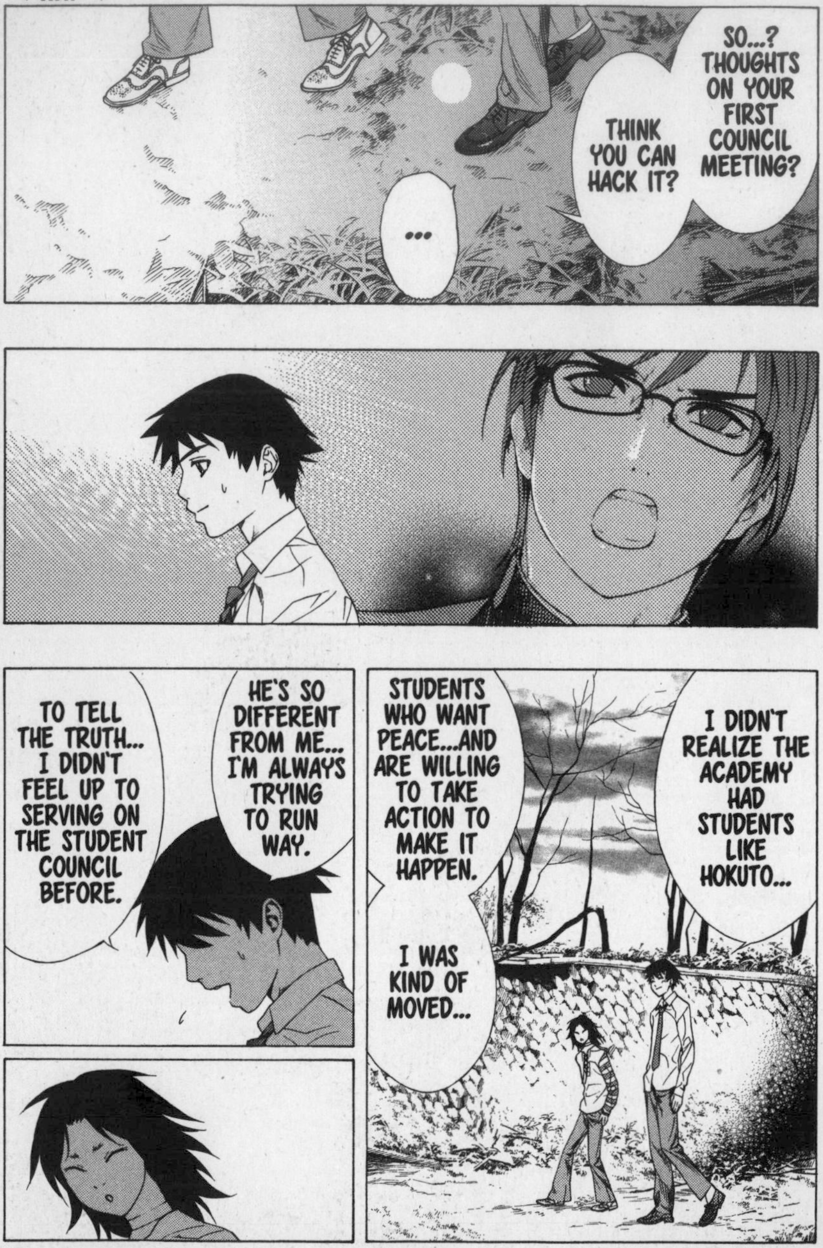
SO...? THOUGHTS ON YOUR FIRST COUNCIL MEETING?
THINK YOU CAN HACK IT?
...
I DIDN'T REALIZE THE ACADEMY HAD STUDENTS LIKE HOKUTO...
STUDENTS WHO WANT PEACE...AND ARE WILLING TO TAKE ACTION TO MAKE IT HAPPEN.
I WAS KIND OF MOVED...
HE'S SO DIFFERENT FROM ME... I'M ALWAYS TRYING TO RUN WAY.
TO TELL THE TRUTH... I DIDN'T FEEL UP TO SERVING ON THE STUDENT COUNCIL BEFORE.

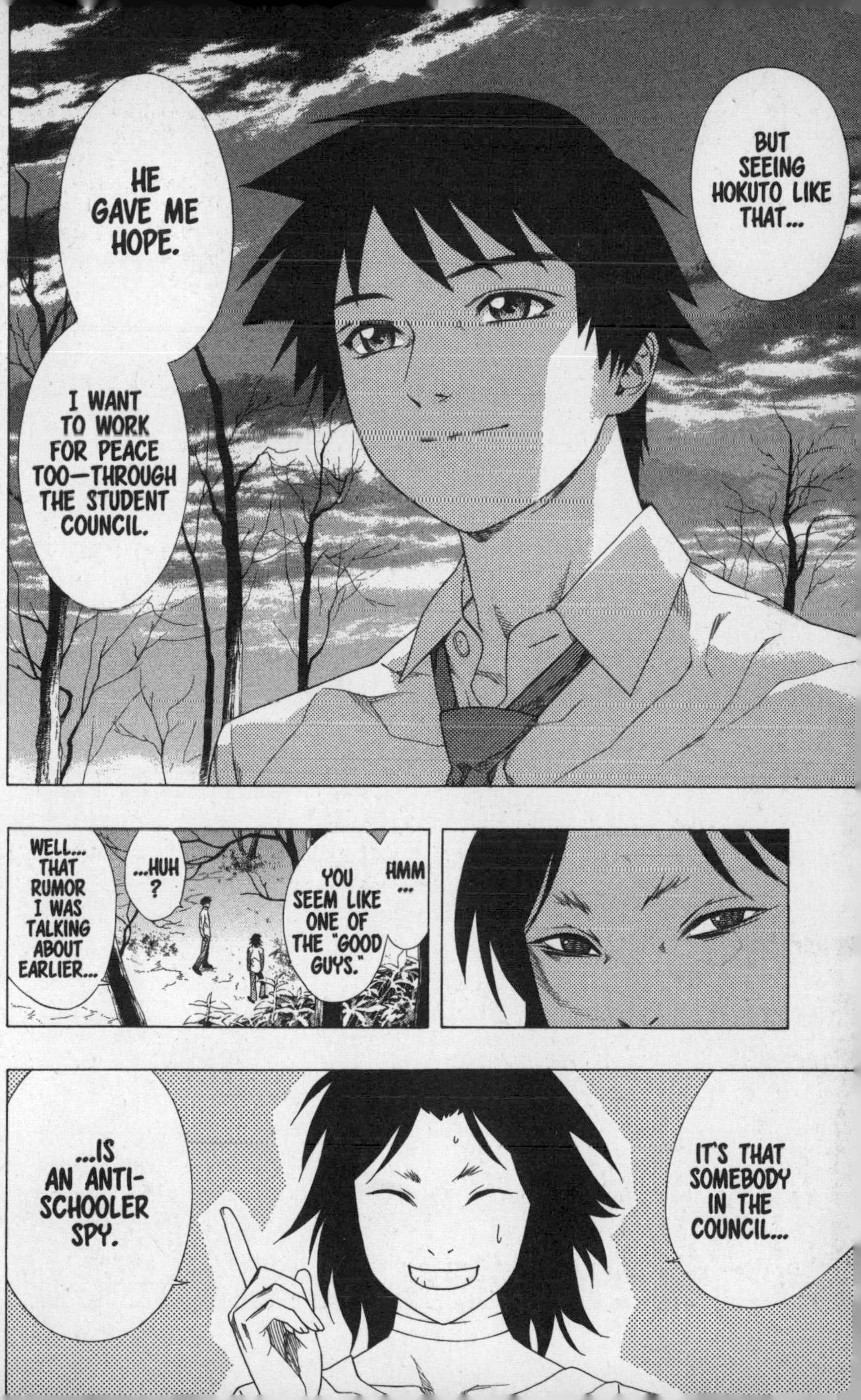
BUT SEEING HOKUTO LIKE THAT...
HE GAVE ME HOPE.
I WANT TO WORK FOR PEACE TOO—THROUGH THE STUDENT COUNCIL.
HMM...
YOU SEEM LIKE ONE OF THE "GOOD GUYS."
...HUH?
WELL... THAT RUMOR I WAS TALKING ABOUT EARLIER...
IT'S THAT SOMEBODY IN THE COUNCIL...
...IS AN ANTI-SCHOOLER SPY.

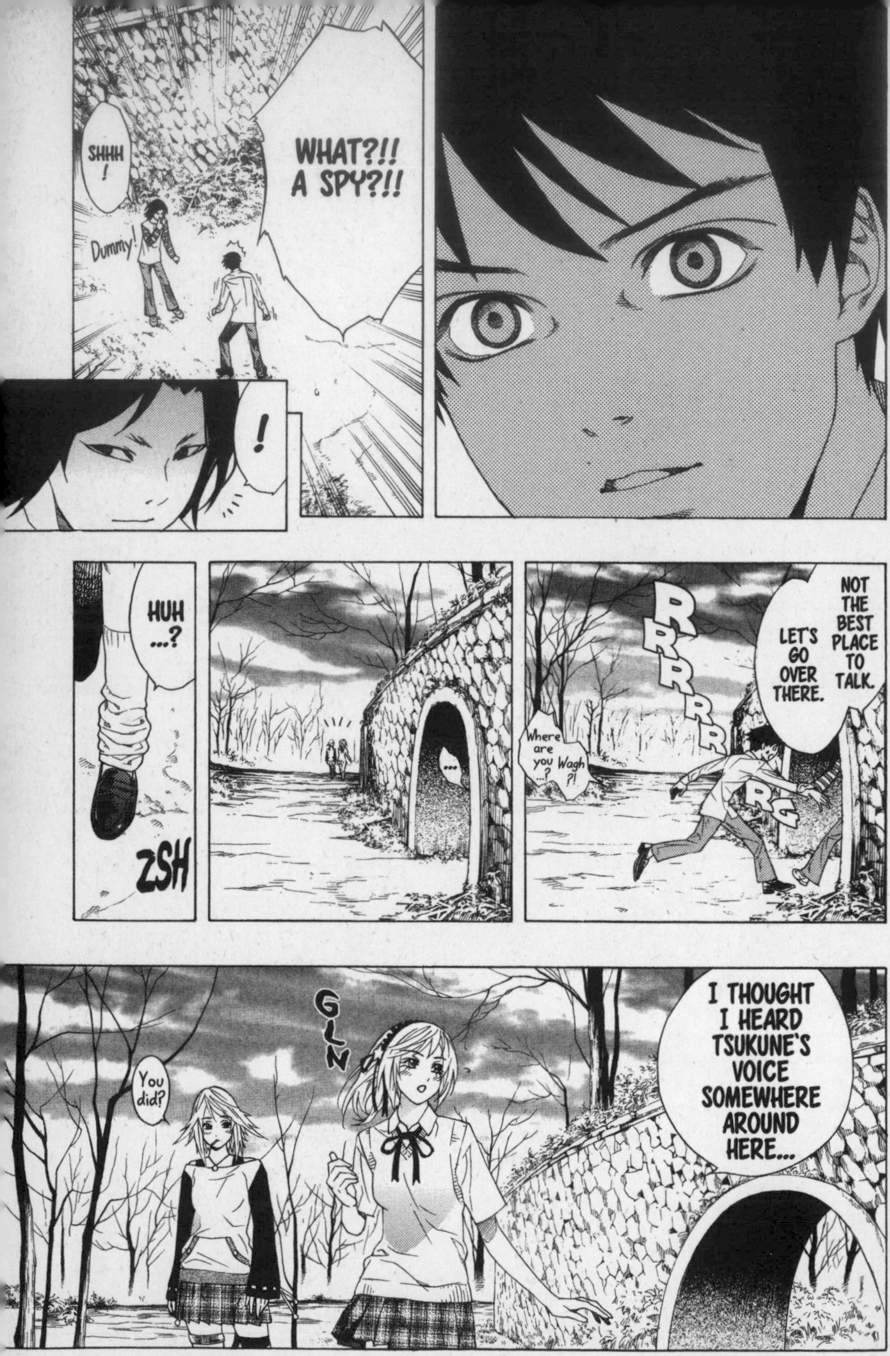
WHAT?!! A SPY?!!
SHHH!
Dummy!
!
NOT THE BEST PLACE TO TALK.
LET'S GO OVER THERE.
RRRRRR
Wagh?!
Where are you...?
RG
...
HUH...?
ZSH
I THOUGHT I HEARD TSUKUNE'S VOICE SOMEWHERE AROUND HERE...
GLN
You did?

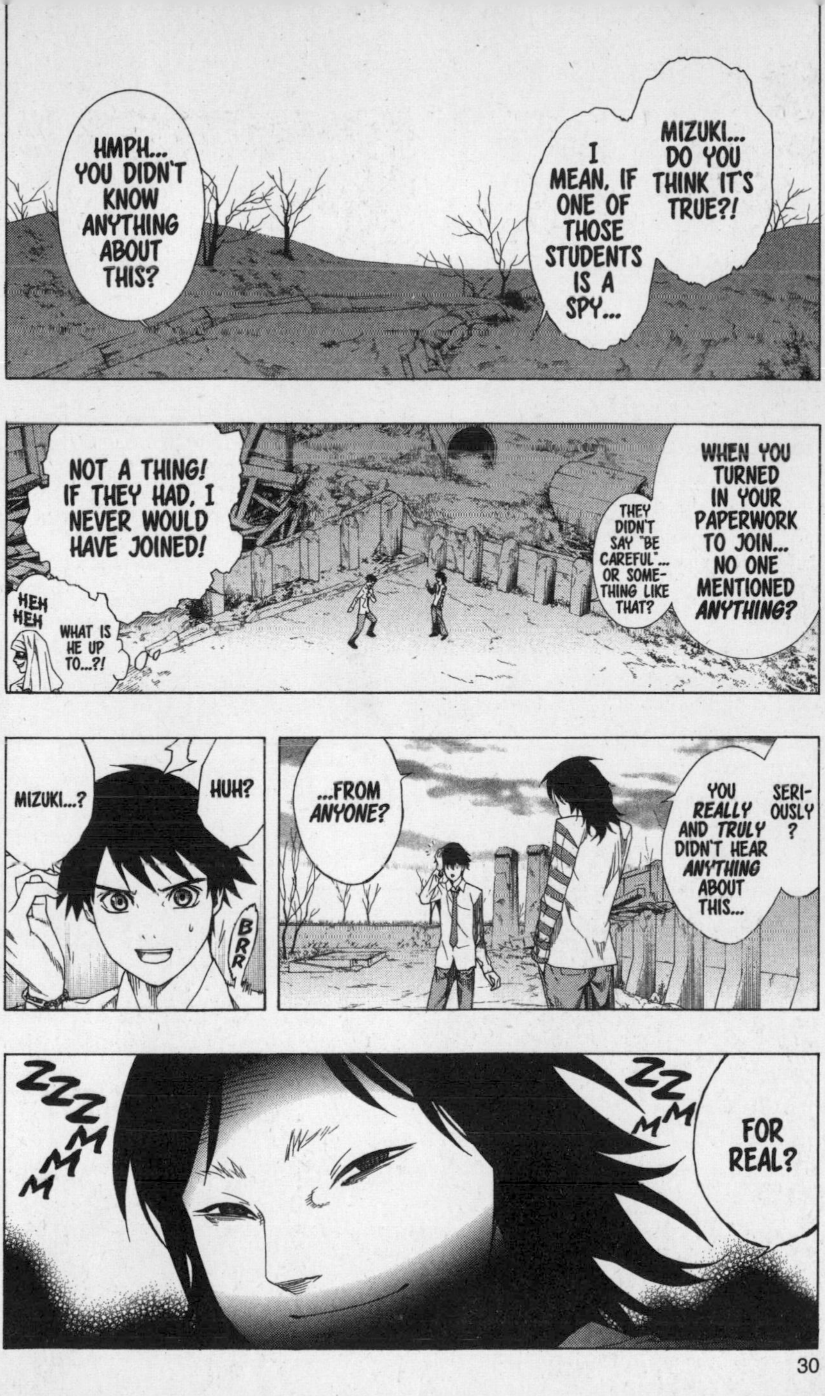
MIZUKI... DO YOU THINK IT'S TRUE?!
I MEAN, IF ONE OF THOSE STUDENTS IS A SPY...
HMPH... YOU DIDN'T KNOW ANYTHING ABOUT THIS?
WHEN YOU TURNED IN YOUR PAPERWORK TO JOIN... NO ONE MENTIONED *ANYTHING?*
THEY DIDN'T SAY "BE CAREFUL"... OR SOMETHING LIKE THAT?
NOT A THING! IF THEY HAD, I NEVER WOULD HAVE JOINED!
HEH HEH
WHAT IS HE UP TO...?!
SERIOUSLY?
YOU *REALLY* AND *TRULY* DIDN'T HEAR *ANYTHING* ABOUT THIS...
...FROM *ANYONE?*
HUH?
MIZUKI...?
BRR
ZZZMMM
FOR REAL?
ZZZZMMMM

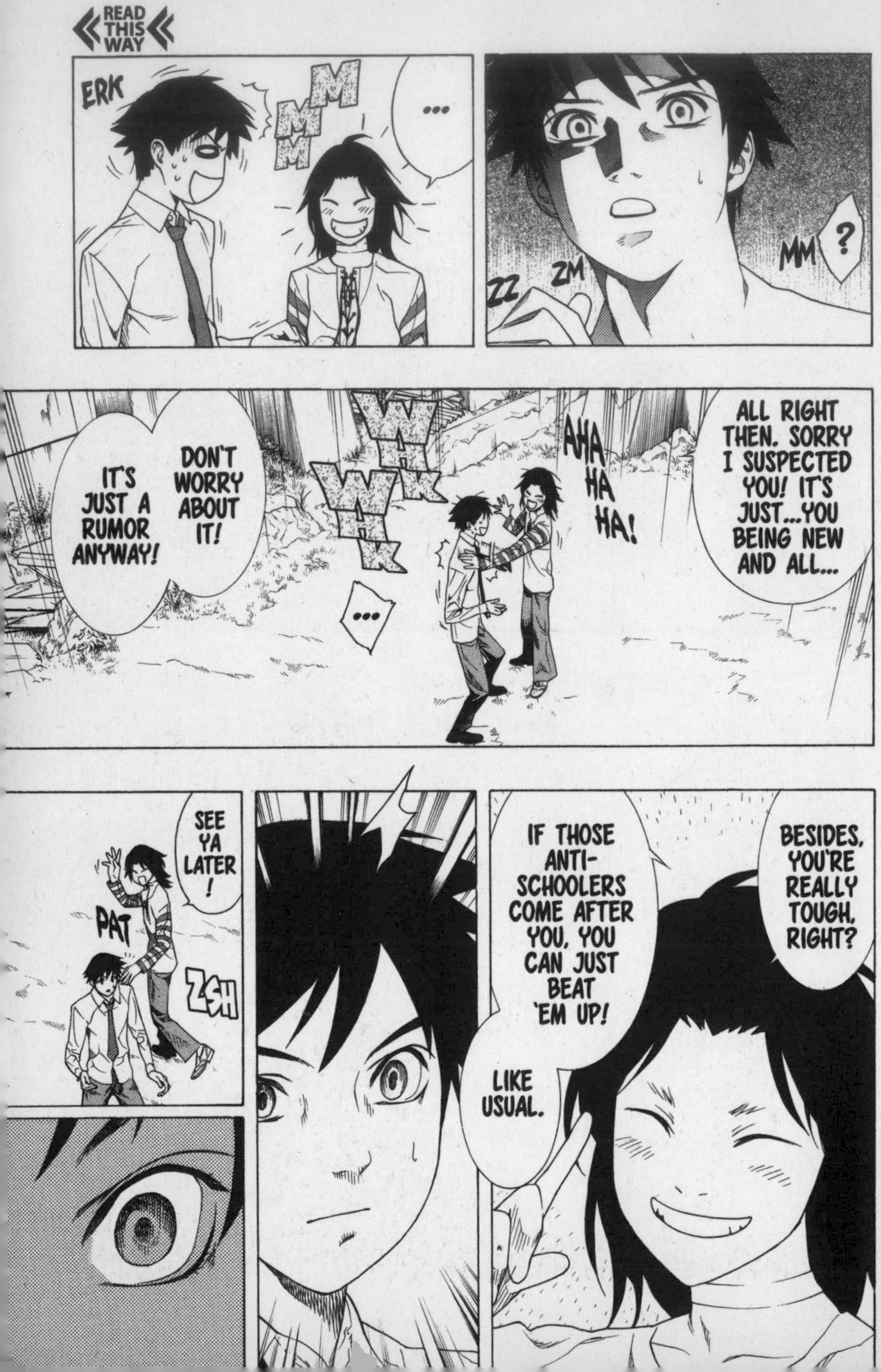
READ THIS WAY
MM
?
ZZ ZM
...
MMMM
ERK
ALL RIGHT THEN. SORRY I SUSPECTED YOU! IT'S JUST...YOU BEING NEW AND ALL...
AHA HA HA!
WHAK WHAK
...
DON'T WORRY ABOUT IT!
IT'S JUST A RUMOR ANYWAY!
BESIDES, YOU'RE REALLY TOUGH, RIGHT?
IF THOSE ANTI-SCHOOLERS COME AFTER YOU, YOU CAN JUST BEAT 'EM UP!
LIKE USUAL.
SEE YA LATER!
PAT
ZSH

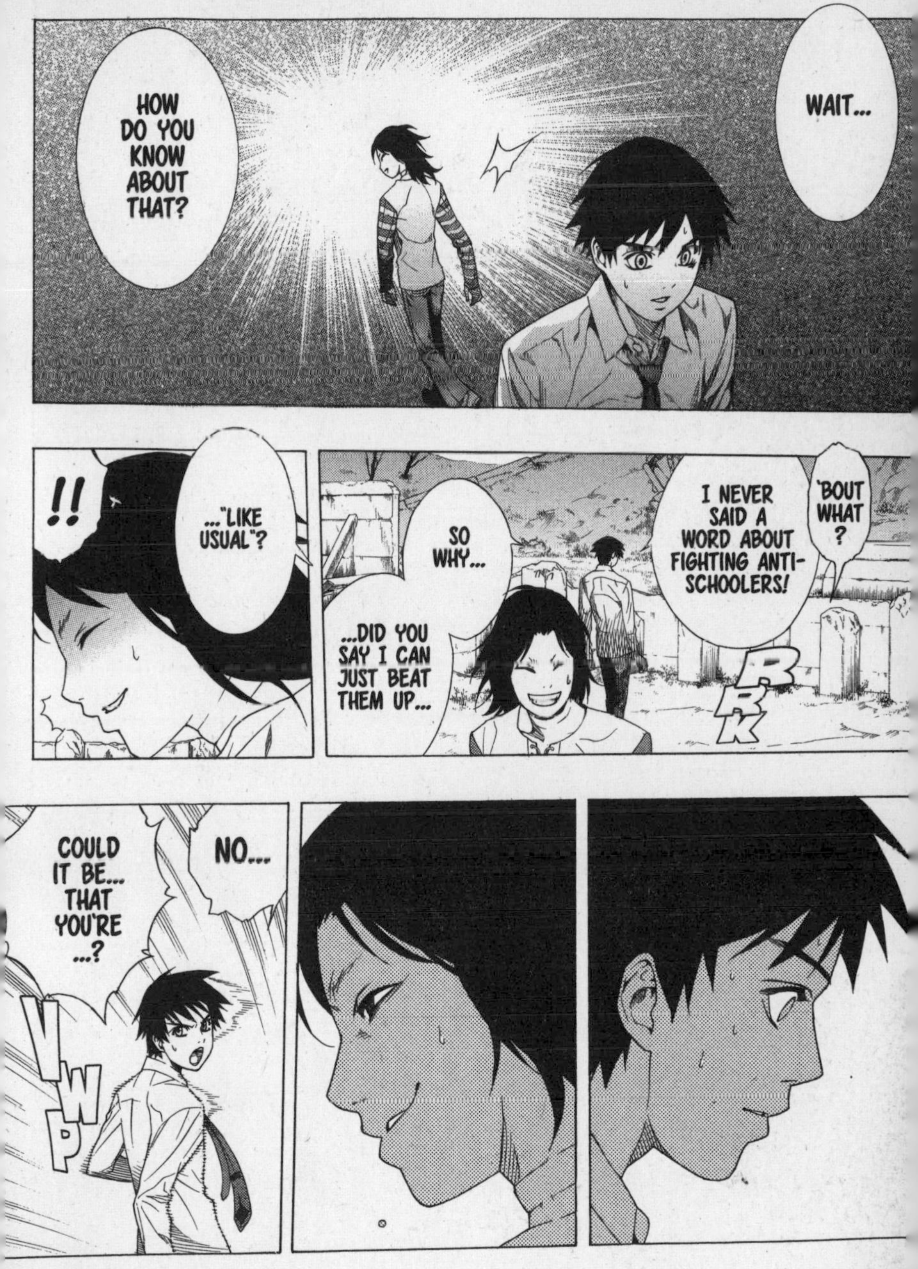
WAIT...
HOW DO YOU KNOW ABOUT THAT?
'BOUT WHAT?
I NEVER SAID A WORD ABOUT FIGHTING ANTI-SCHOOLERS!
SO WHY...
...DID YOU SAY I CAN JUST BEAT THEM UP...
RRRK
...''LIKE USUAL''?
!!
NO...
COULD IT BE... THAT YOU'RE ...?
VWP

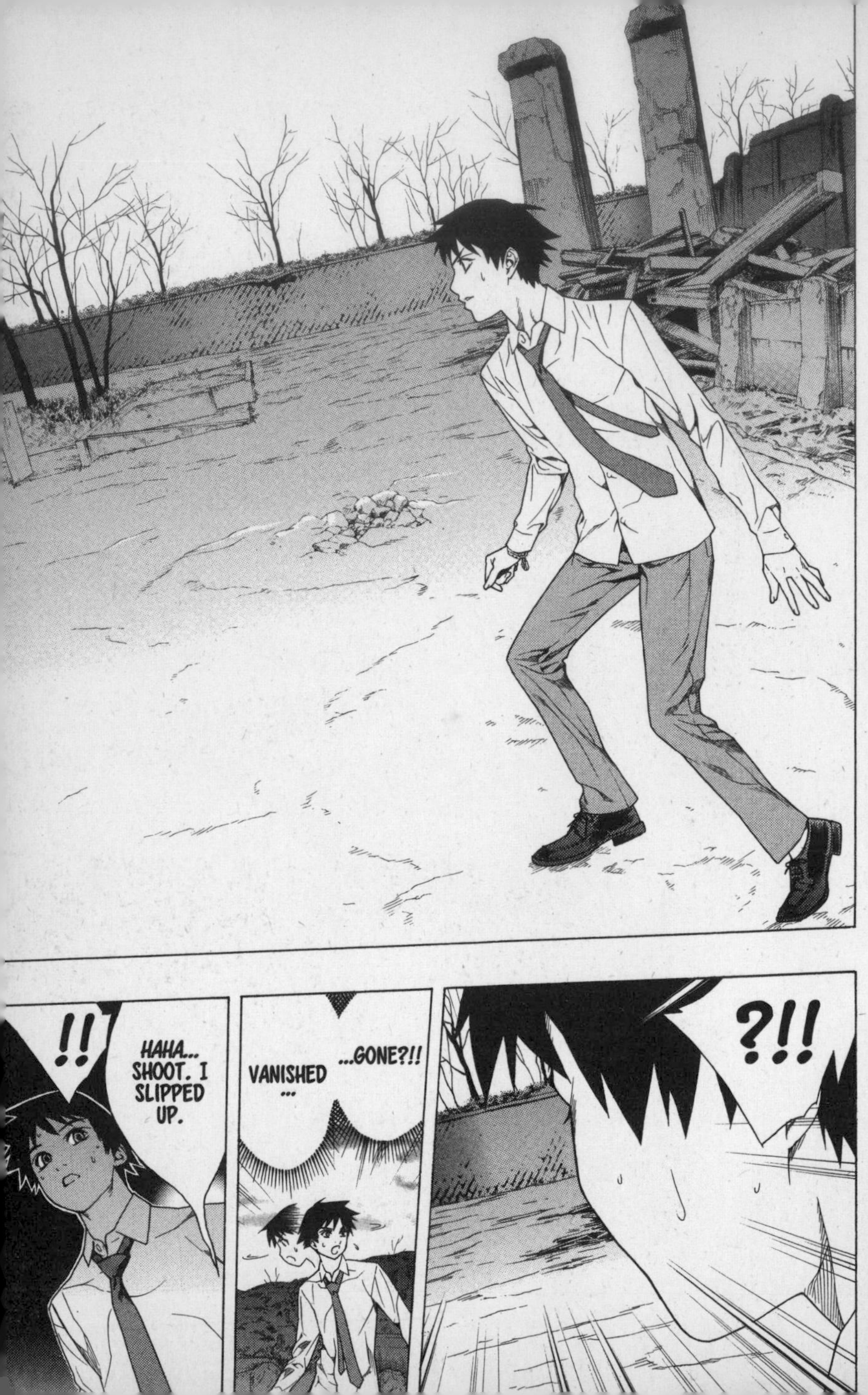
?!!
...GONE?!!
VANISHED ...
HAHA... SHOOT. I SLIPPED UP.
!!

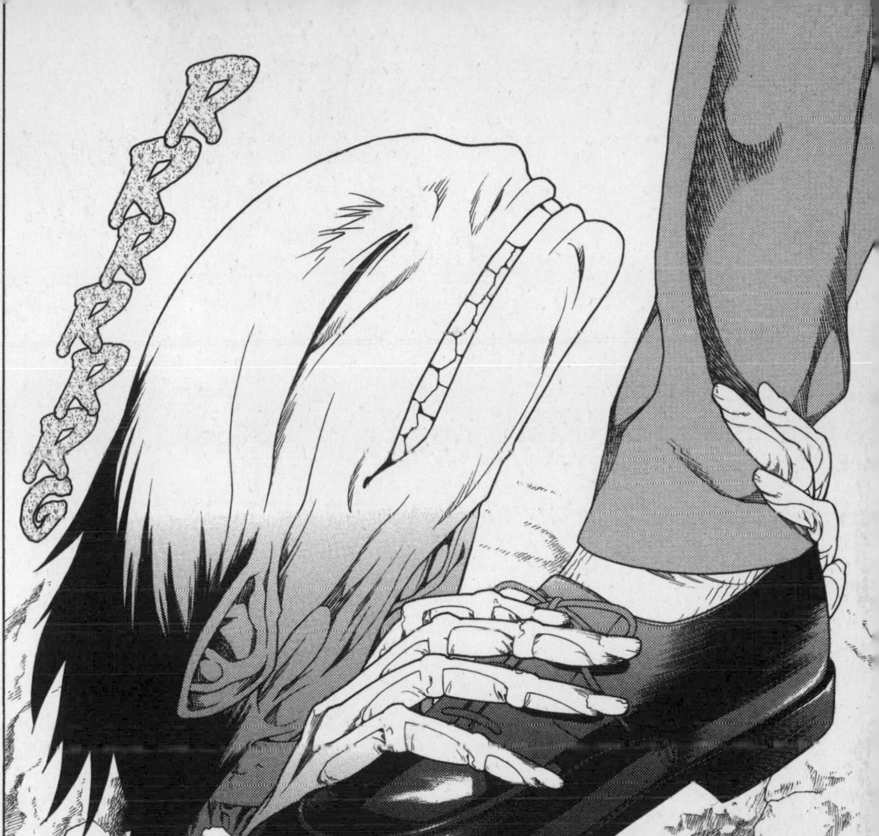
RRRRRRG

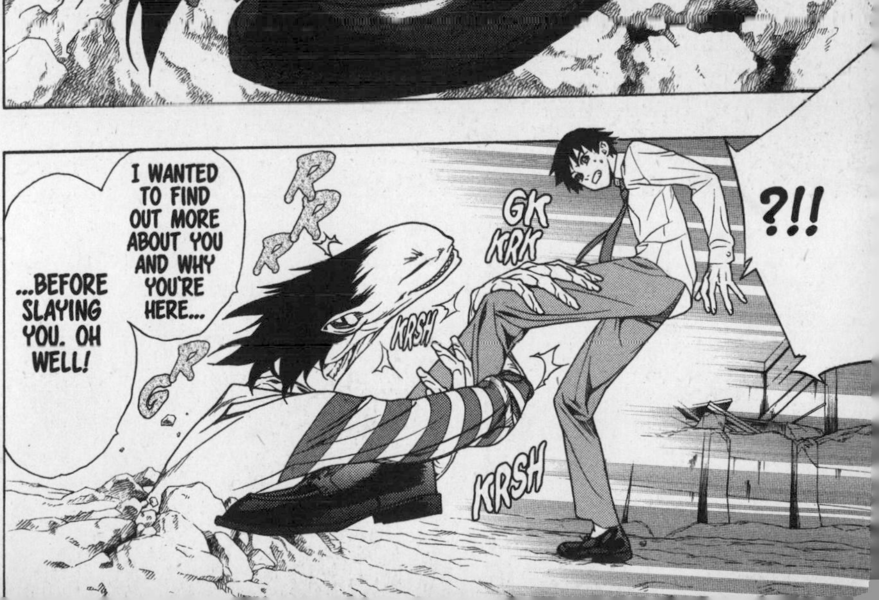
?!!
GK KRK
I WANTED TO FIND OUT MORE ABOUT YOU AND WHY YOU'RE HERE...
...BEFORE SLAYING YOU. OH WELL!
RRRG
KRSH
KRSH

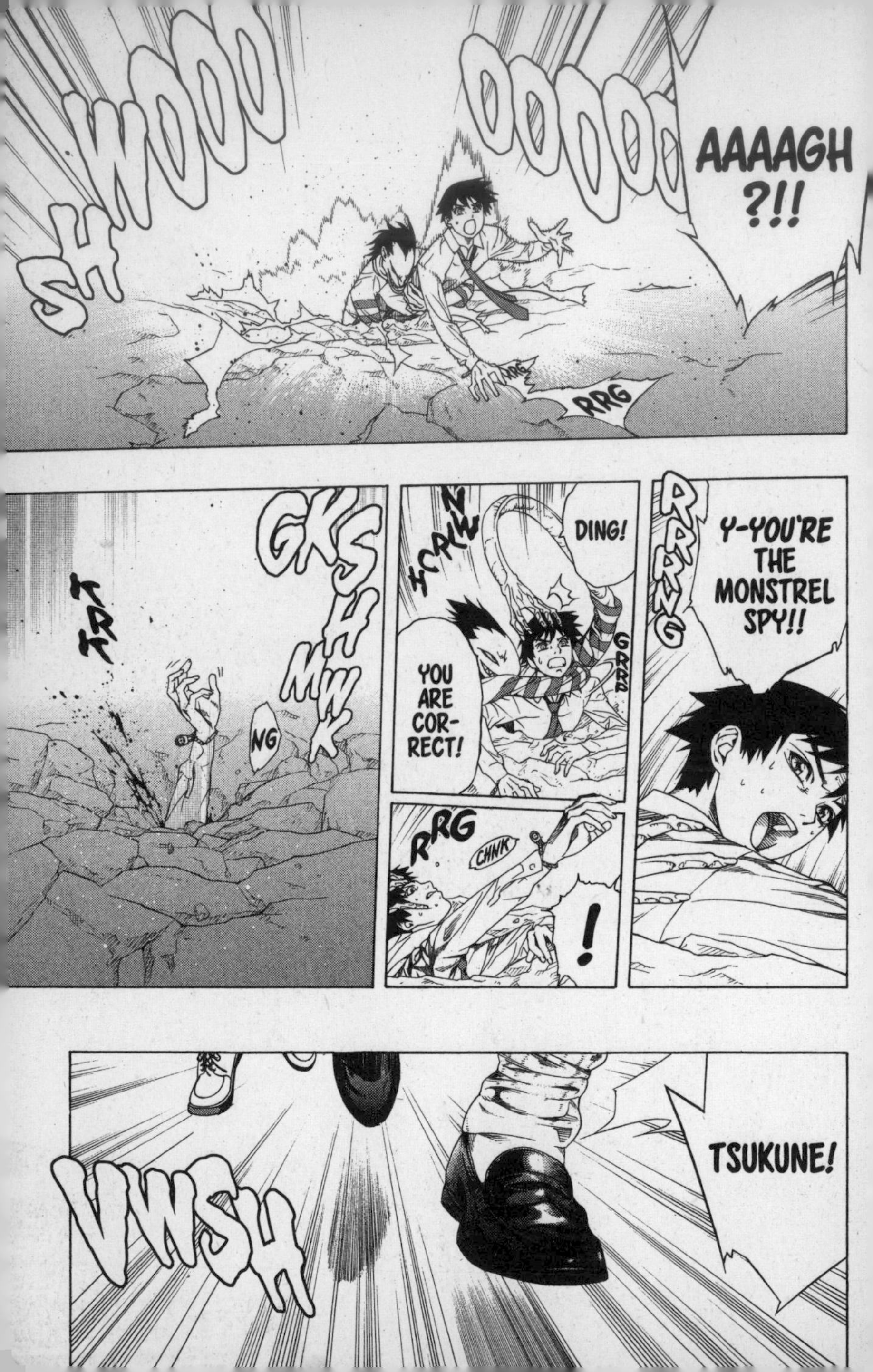

SHWOOOOOOOOO
AAAAGH ?!!
RRG
RRG
RRRNG
Y-YOU'RE THE MONSTREL SPY!!
DING!
YOU ARE COR-RECT!
GRRR
RRG
CHNK
!
GKSHMWK
NG
KRK
TSUKUNE!
VWSH

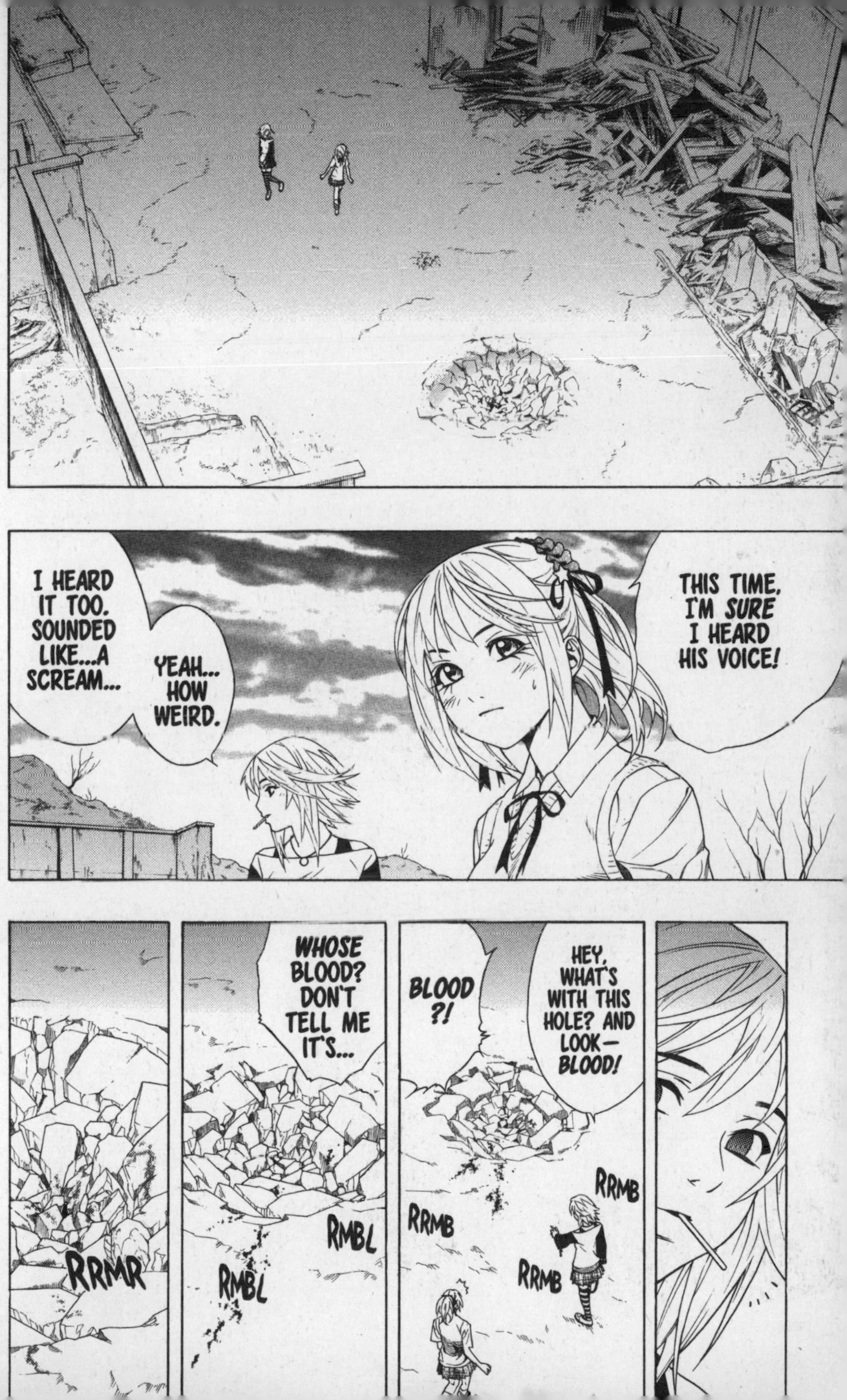
THIS TIME, I'M SURE I HEARD HIS VOICE!
YEAH... HOW WEIRD.
I HEARD IT TOO. SOUNDED LIKE...A SCREAM...
...
HEY, WHAT'S WITH THIS HOLE? AND LOOK—BLOOD!
BLOOD ?!
RRMB
RRMB
RRMB
WHOSE BLOOD? DON'T TELL ME IT'S...
RMBL
RMBL
RRMR

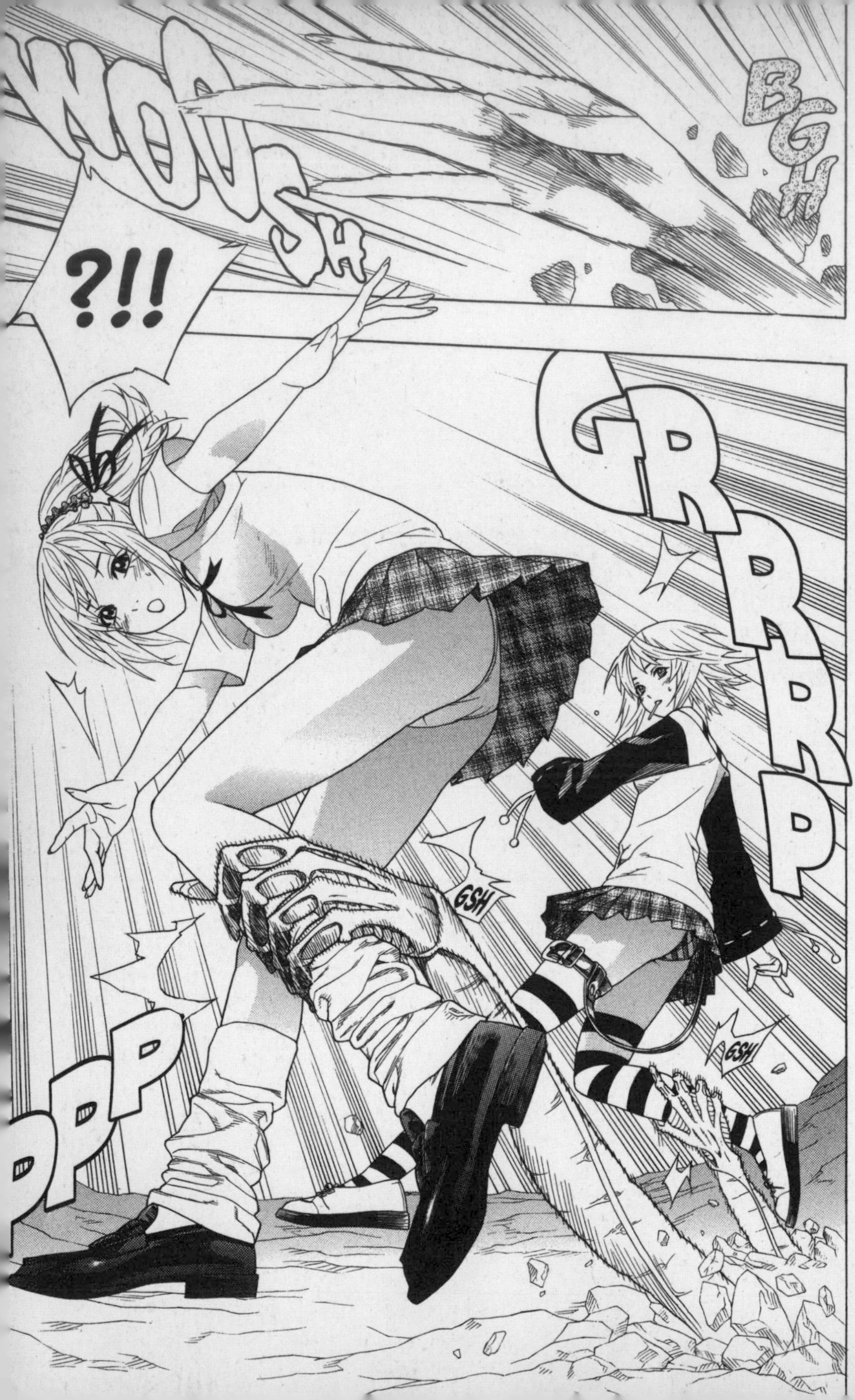
BGH
WOOSH
?!!
GRRRP
GSH
GSH
PPP

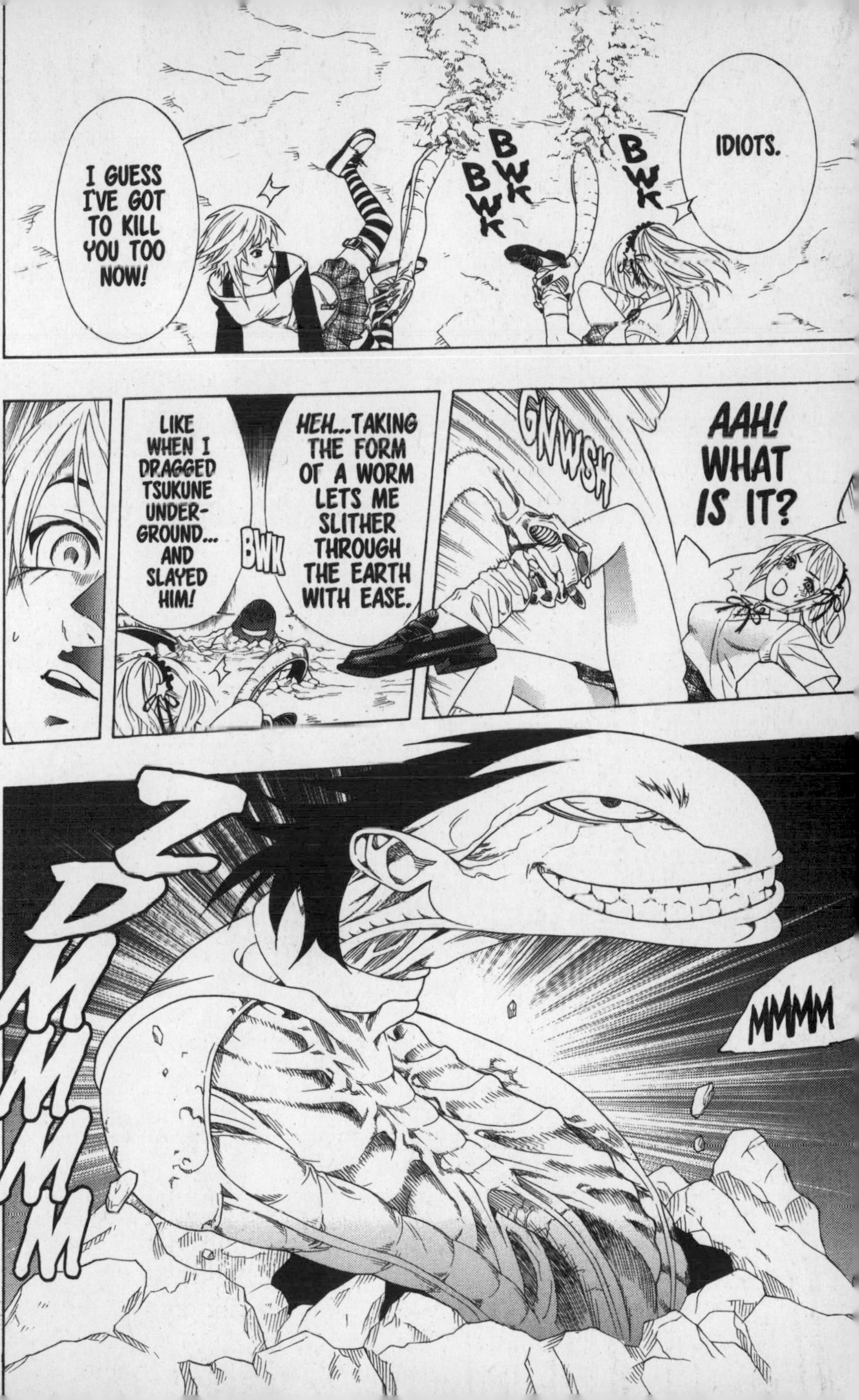
IDIOTS.
BWK BWK
BWK BWK
I GUESS I'VE GOT TO KILL YOU TOO NOW!
AAH! WHAT IS IT?
GNWSH
HEH...TAKING THE FORM OF A WORM LETS ME SLITHER THROUGH THE EARTH WITH EASE.
BWK
LIKE WHEN I DRAGGED TSUKUNE UNDER-GROUND... AND SLAYED HIM!
MMMM
ZDMMMMM

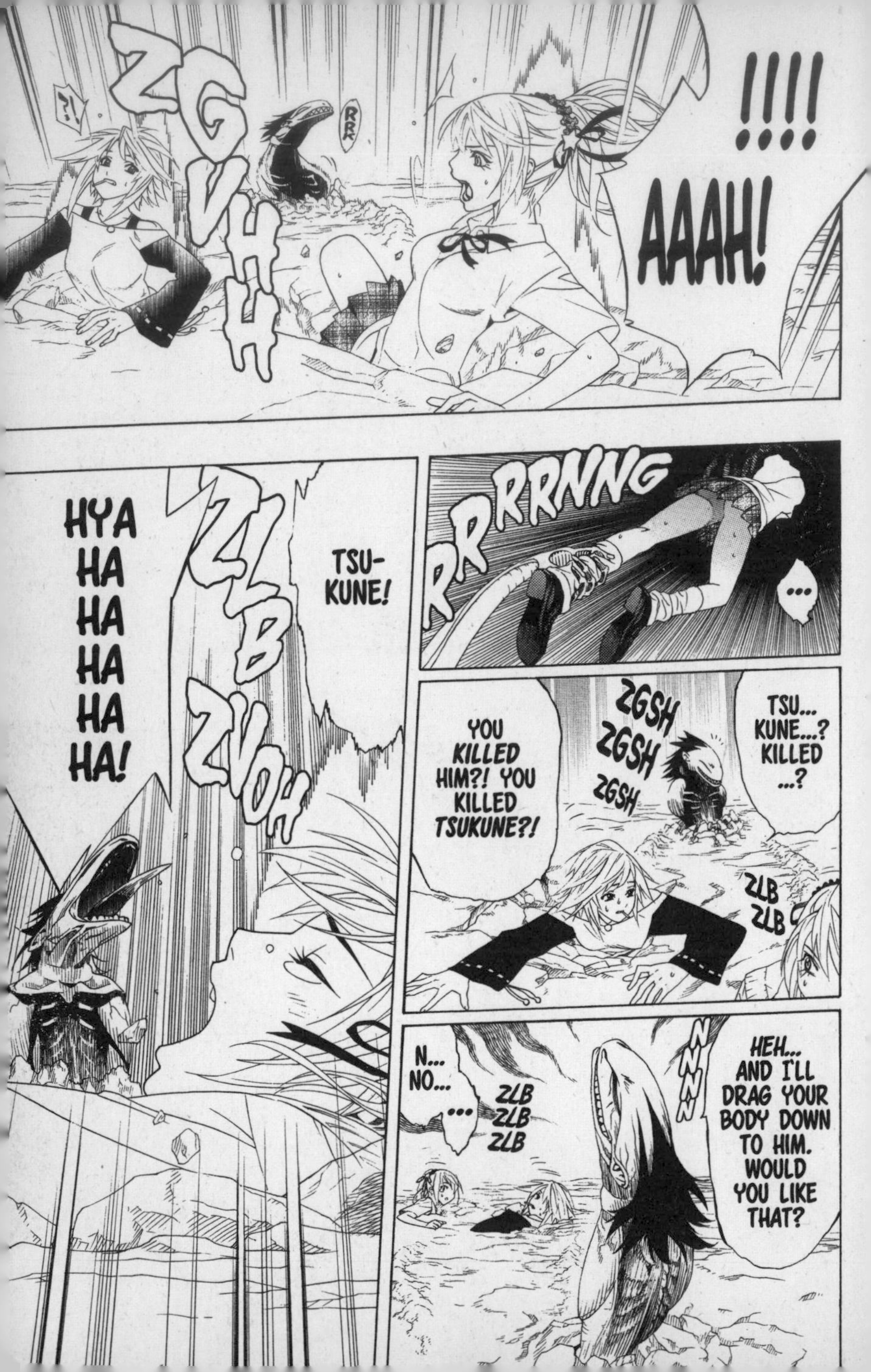
!!!!
AAAH!
RRK
ZGVHH
?!
RRRRRNNG
...
TSU... KUNE...? KILLED ...?
ZGSH ZGSH ZGSH
YOU KILLED HIM?! YOU KILLED TSUKUNE?!
ZLB ZLB
HEH... AND I'LL DRAG YOUR BODY DOWN TO HIM. WOULD YOU LIKE THAT?
NNNN
ZLB ZLB ZLB
N... NO... ...
TSU-KUNE!
ZLB
ZVOH
HYA HA HA HA HA HA!

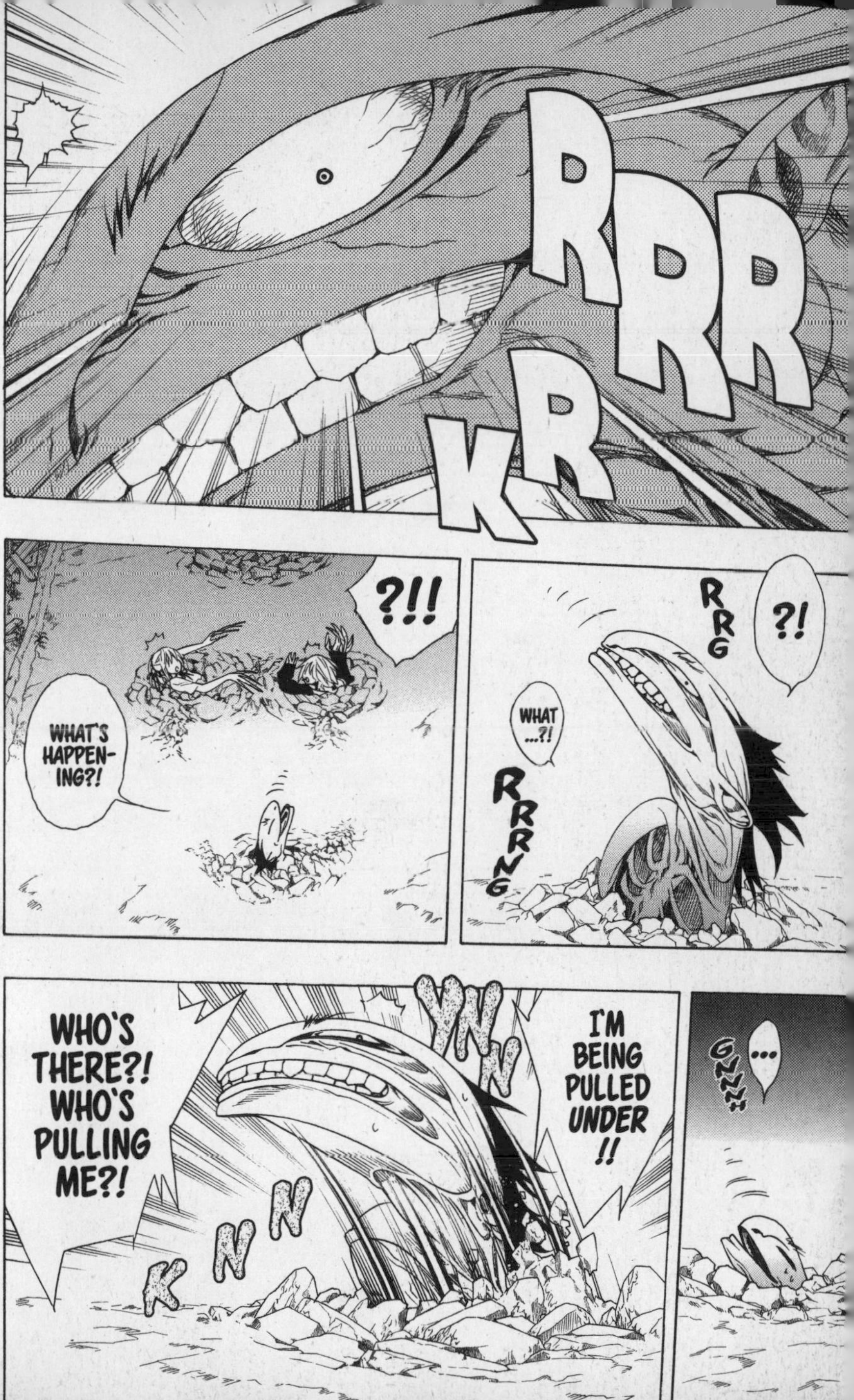
KRRRR
?!
RRG
WHAT ...?!
RRRNG
?!!
WHAT'S HAPPEN-ING?!
...
GNNNH
YNN
I'M BEING PULLED UNDER !!
WHO'S THERE?! WHO'S PULLING ME?!
KNNN

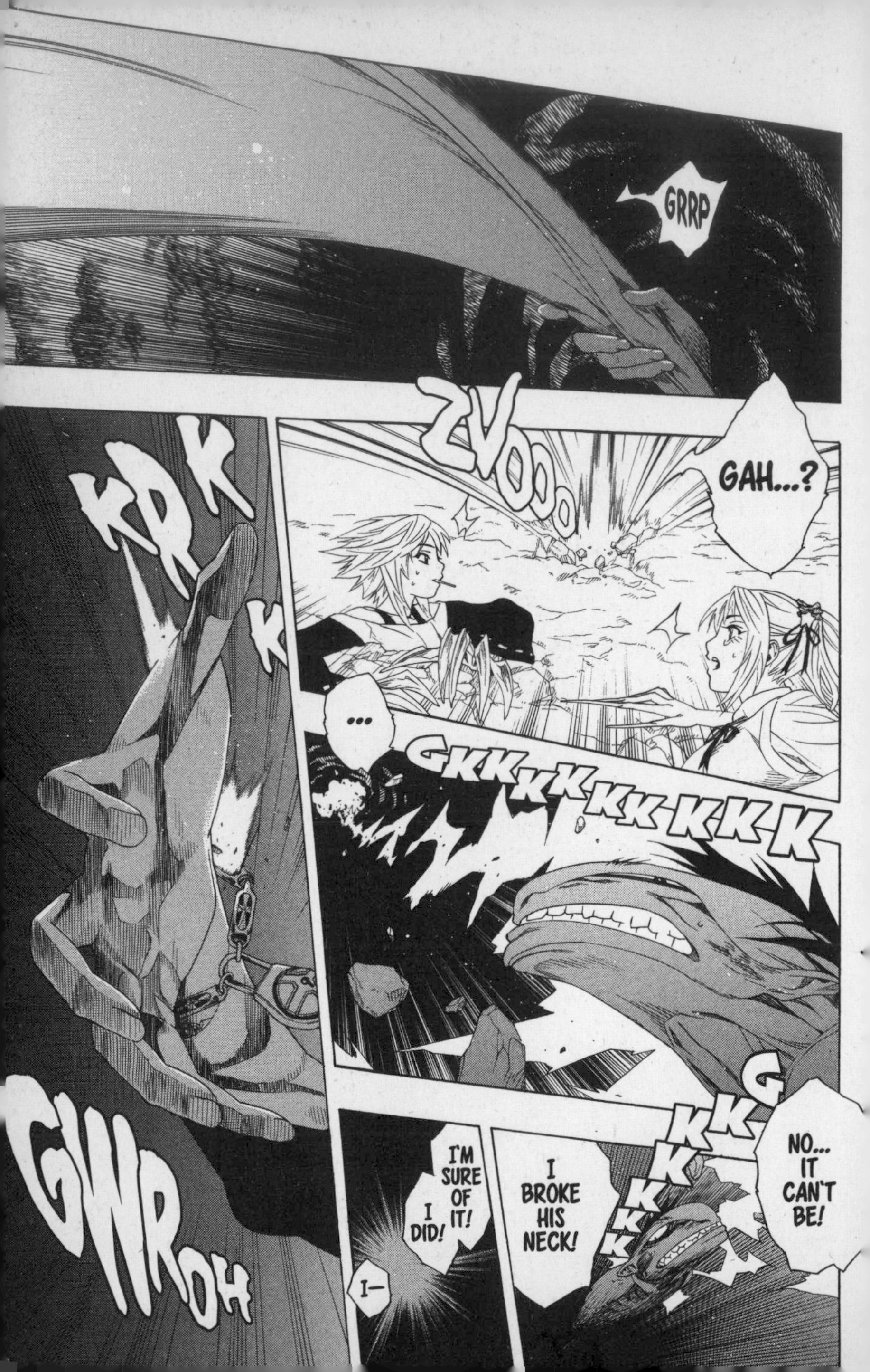
GRRP
ZVOOO
GAH...?
...
GKKKKKKKKKK
GKKKKKKK
NO... IT CAN'T BE!
I BROKE HIS NECK!
I'M SURE OF IT!
I DID!
I—
KRK K
GNROH

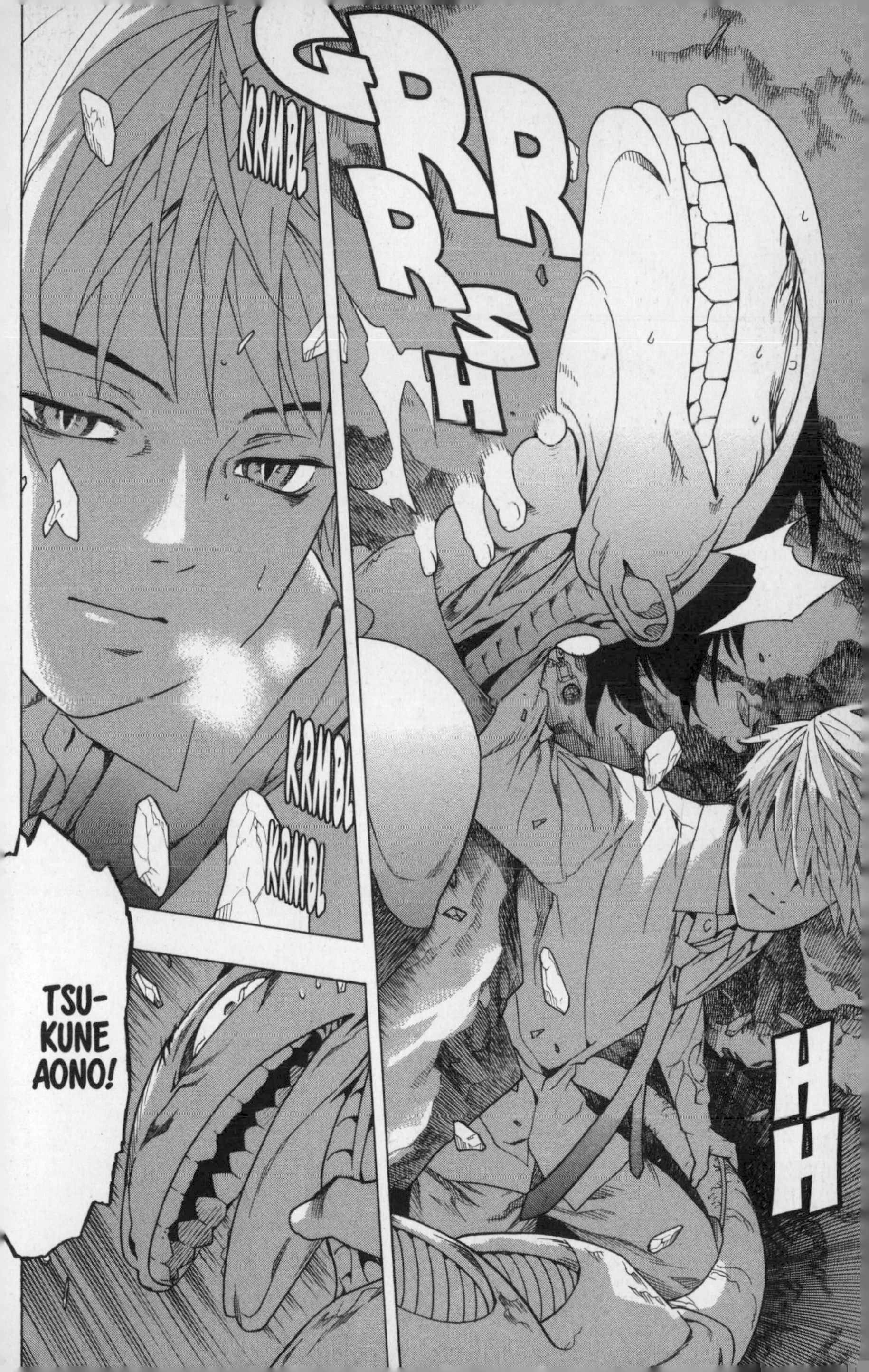
GRRRSH
KRMBL
KRMBL
KRMBL
HHH
TSU-KUNE AONO!

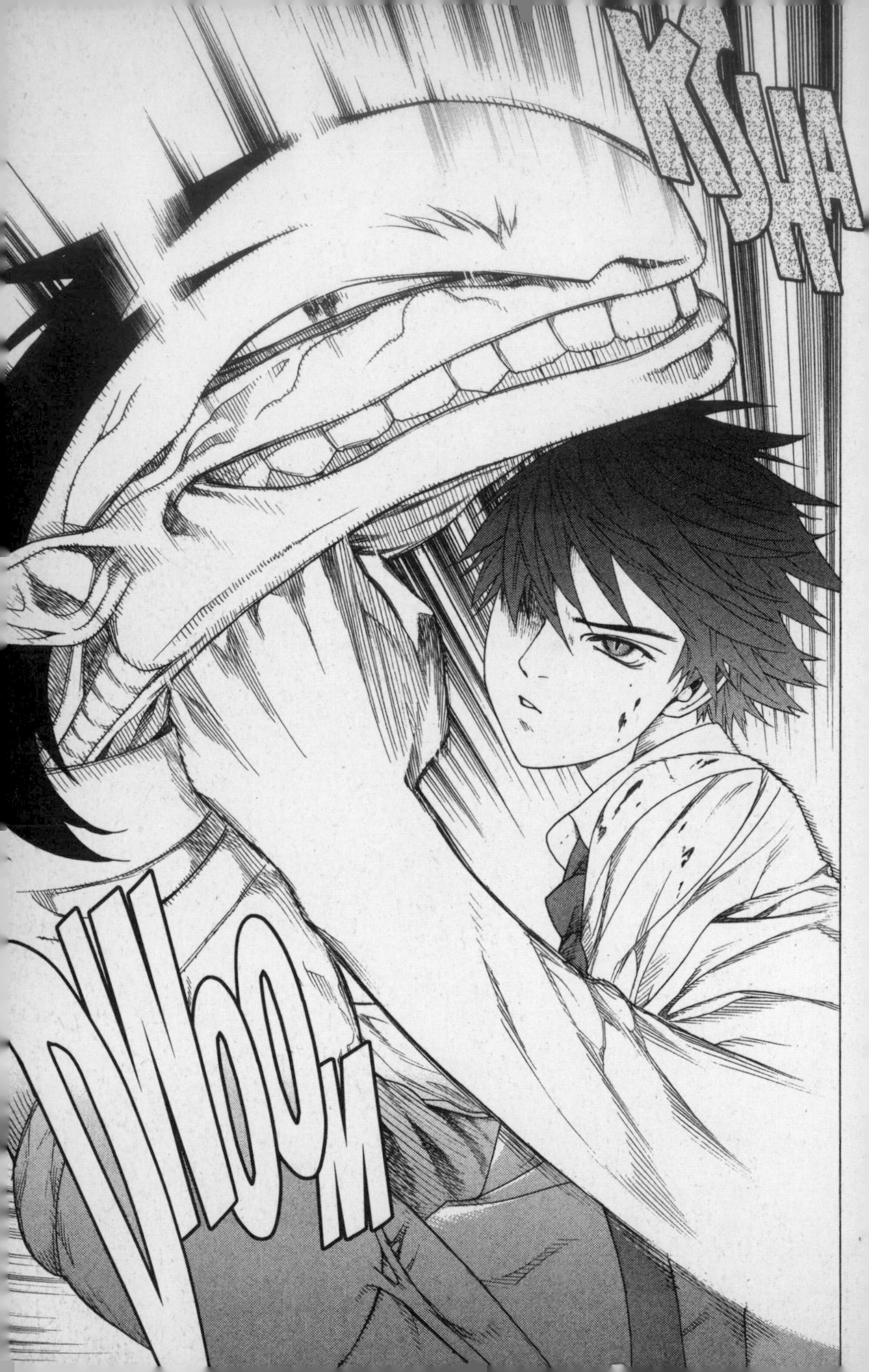
KSHA
WHOOM

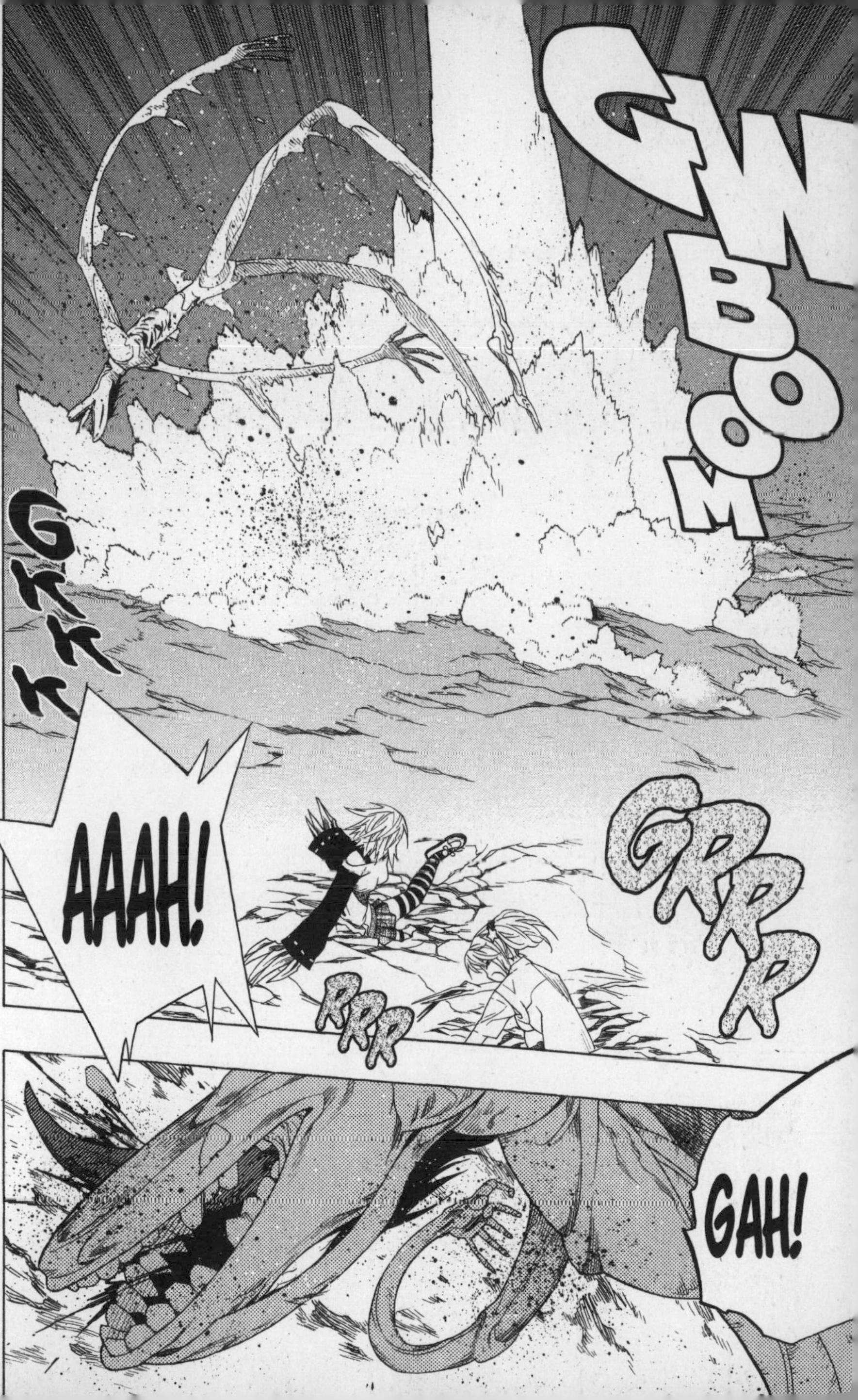

GWBOOM
GKKK
GRRRR
RRR
AAAH!
GAH!

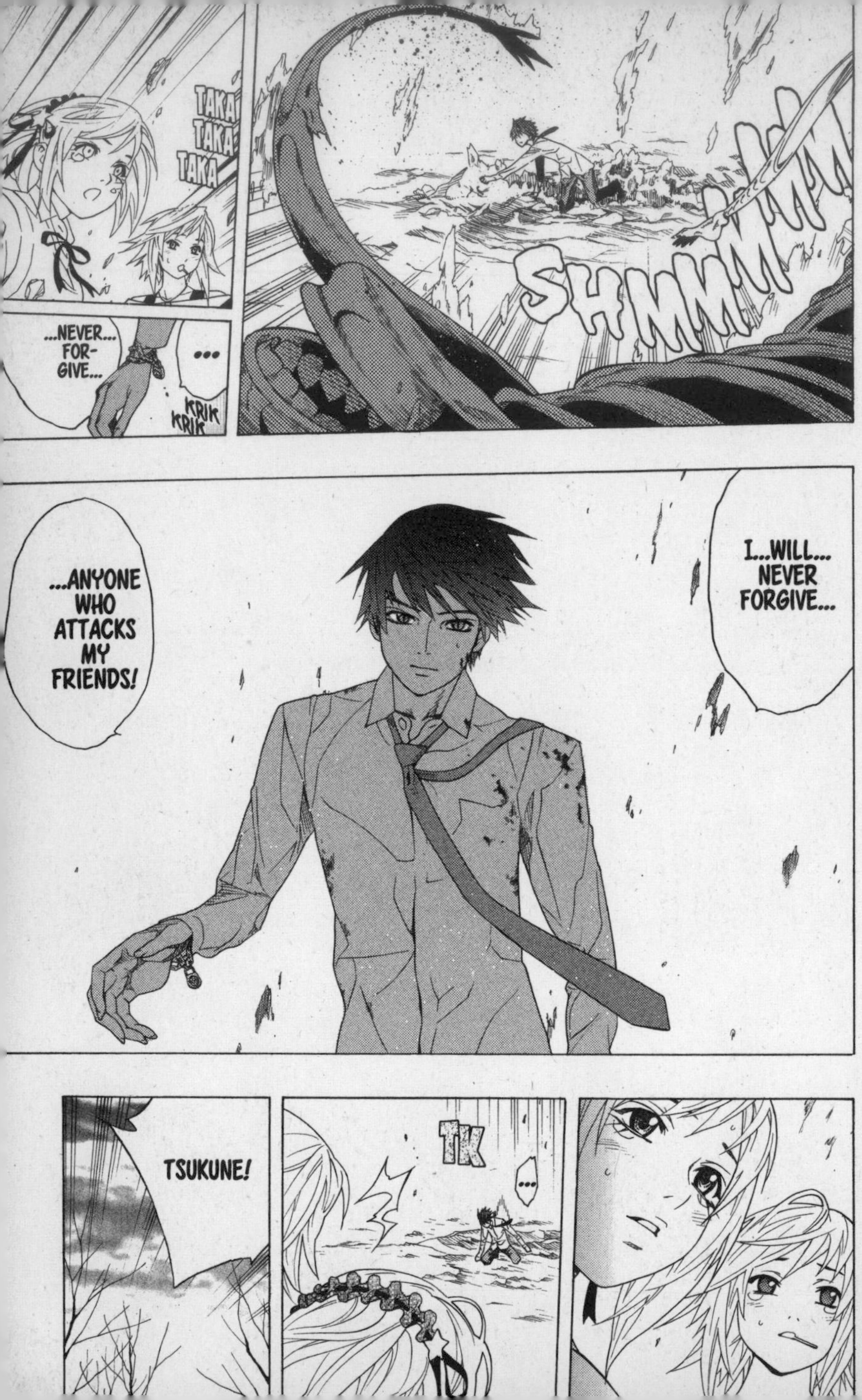
SHMMM
TAKA TAKA TAKA
...
...NEVER... FOR-GIVE...
KRIK KRIK
I...WILL... NEVER FORGIVE...
...ANYONE WHO ATTACKS MY FRIENDS!
TK
...
TSUKUNE!

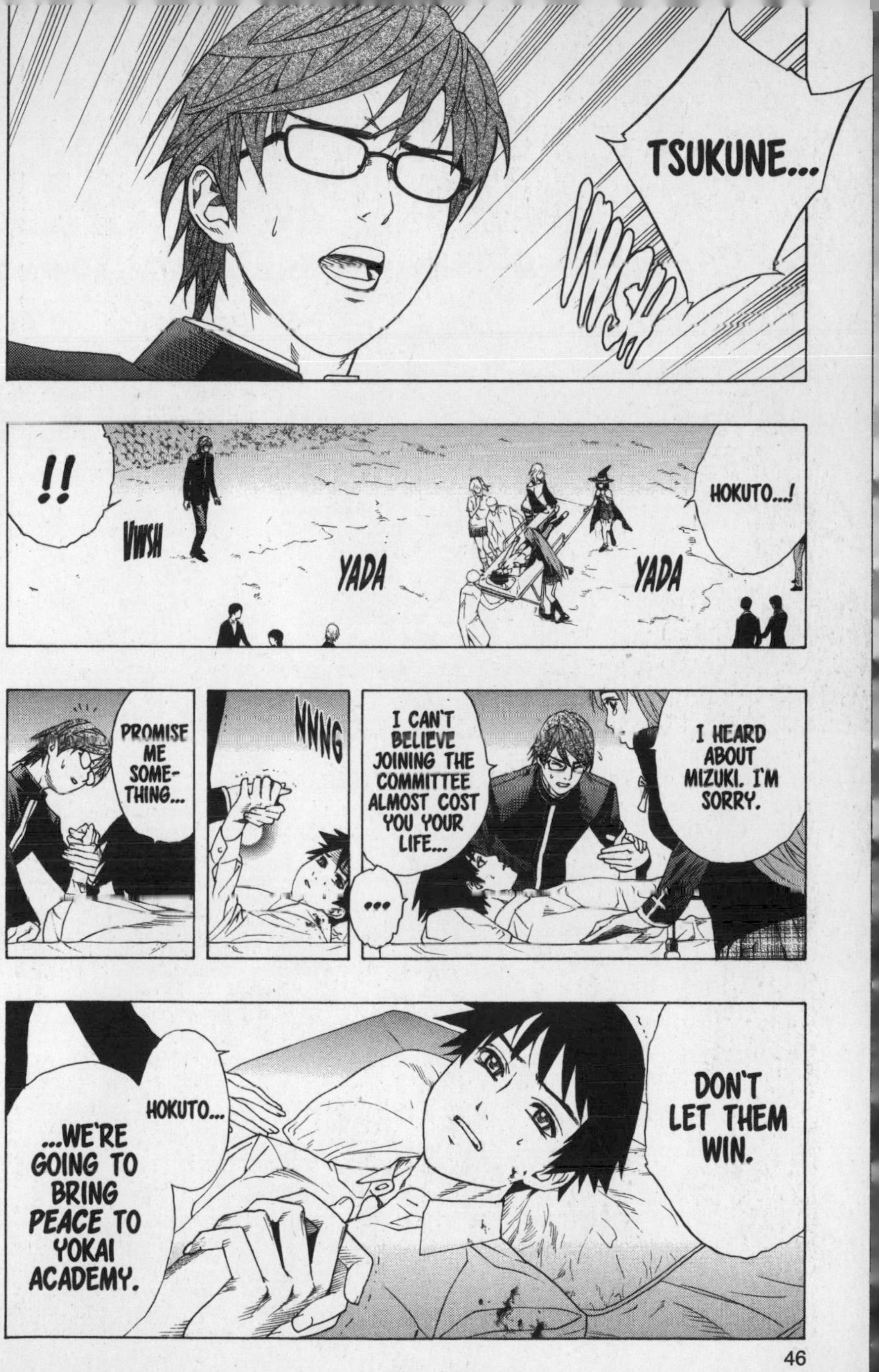
TSUKUNE...
HOKUTO...!
YADA
YADA
VWSH
!!
I HEARD ABOUT MIZUKI. I'M SORRY.
I CAN'T BELIEVE JOINING THE COMMITTEE ALMOST COST YOU YOUR LIFE...
...
NNNG
PROMISE ME SOMETHING...
DON'T LET THEM WIN.
HOKUTO...
...WE'RE GOING TO BRING PEACE TO YOKAI ACADEMY.

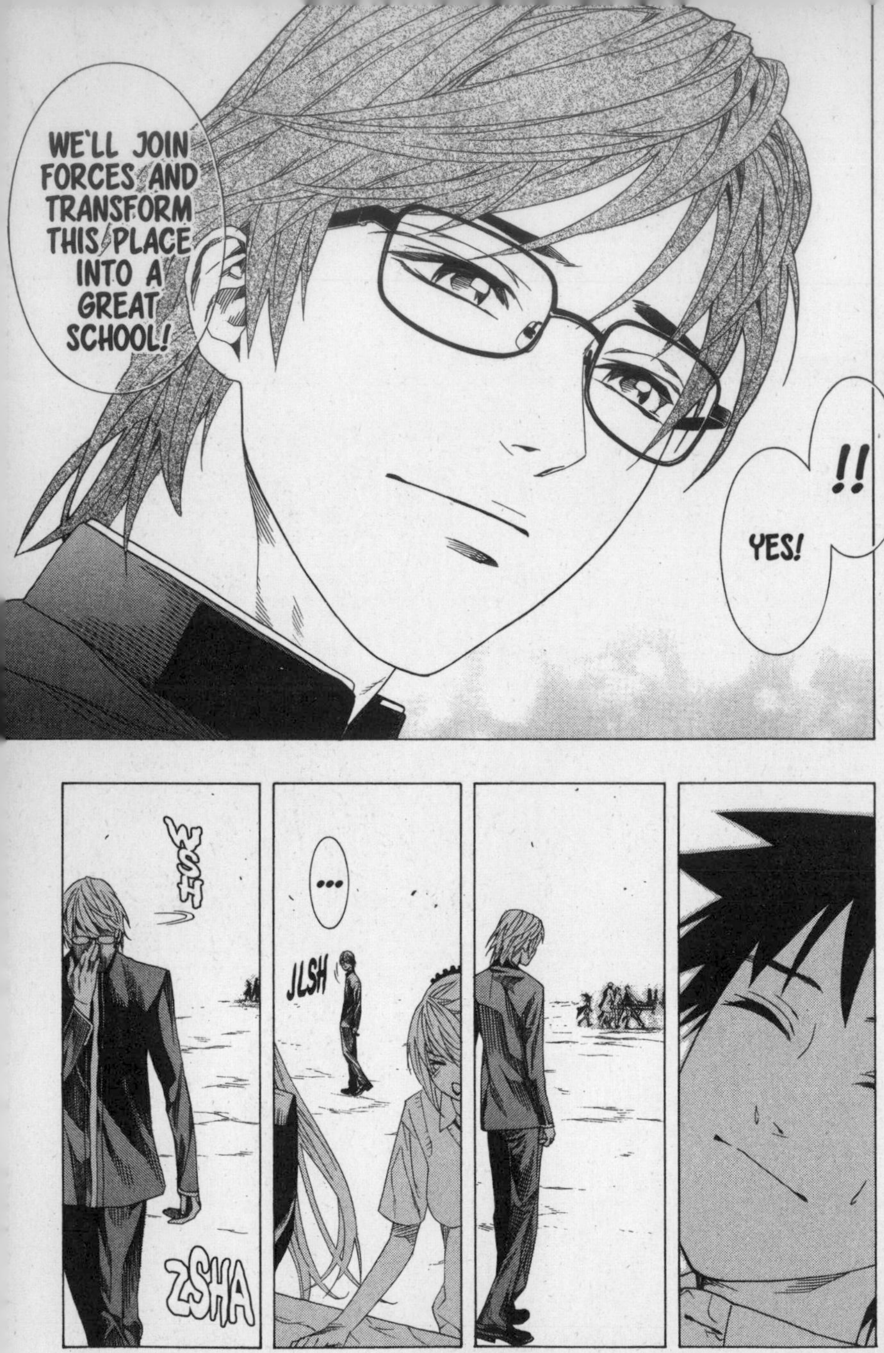
WE'LL JOIN FORCES AND TRANSFORM THIS PLACE INTO A GREAT SCHOOL!
!! YES!
...
JLSH
WSH
ZSHA

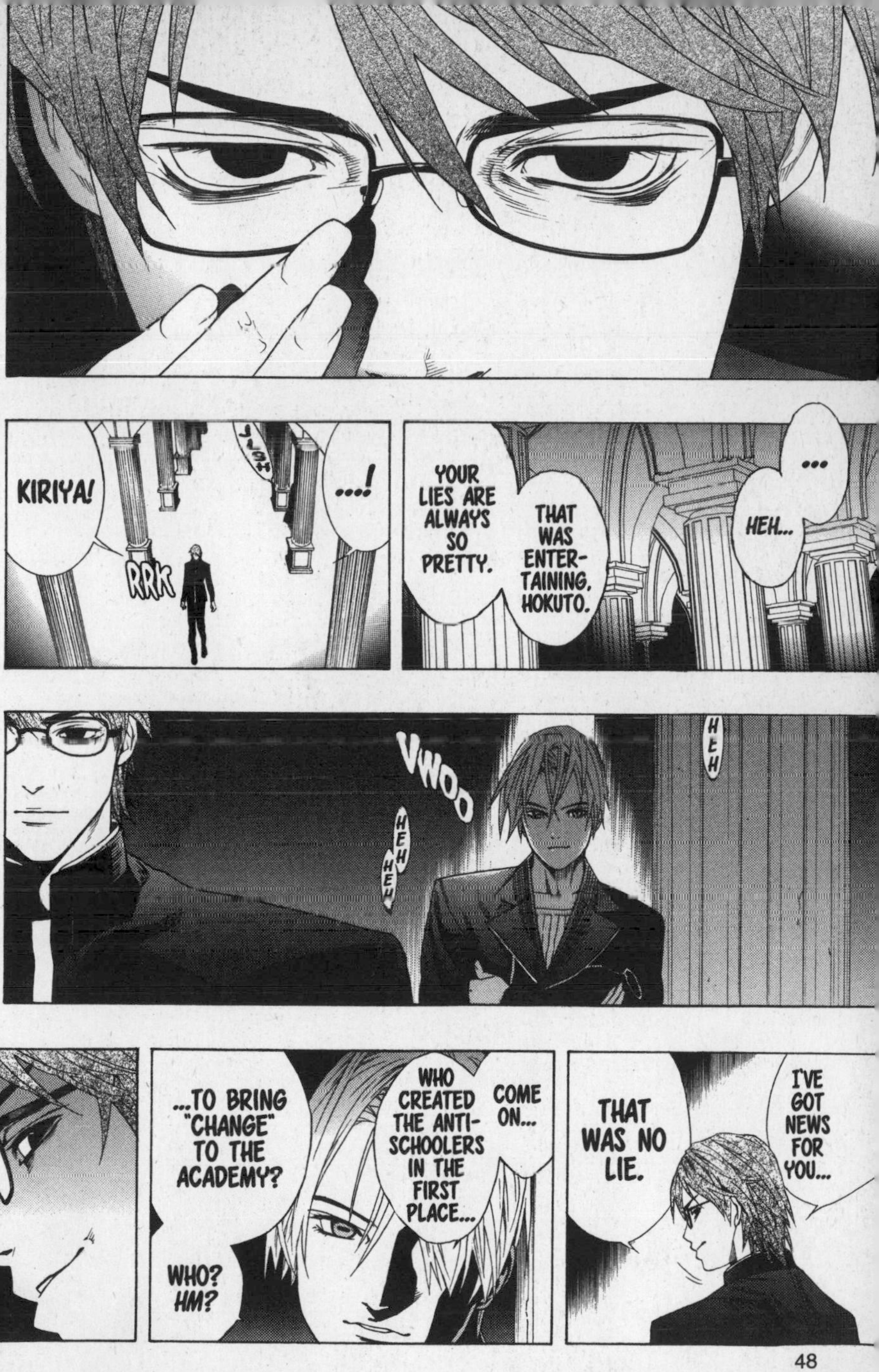
...
HEH...
THAT WAS ENTER-TAINING, HOKUTO.
YOUR LIES ARE ALWAYS SO PRETTY.
...!
RRK
KIRIYA!
HEH
VWOO
HEH HEH
I'VE GOT NEWS FOR YOU...
THAT WAS NO LIE.
COME ON...
WHO CREATED THE ANTI-SCHOOLERS IN THE FIRST PLACE...
...TO BRING "CHANGE" TO THE ACADEMY?
WHO? HM?

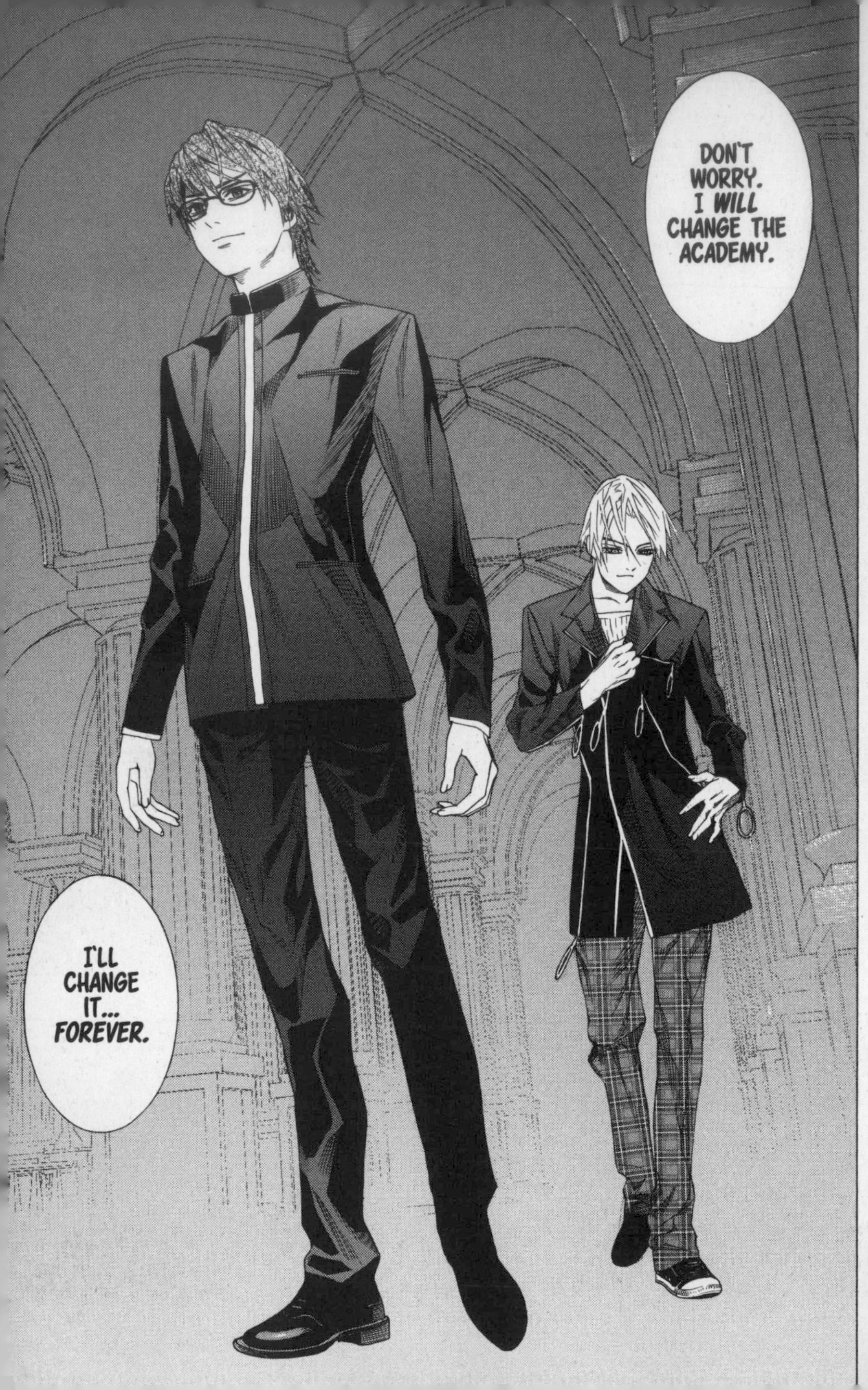
DON'T WORRY. I *WILL* CHANGE THE ACADEMY.
I'LL CHANGE IT... FOREVER.

30 : The Plan

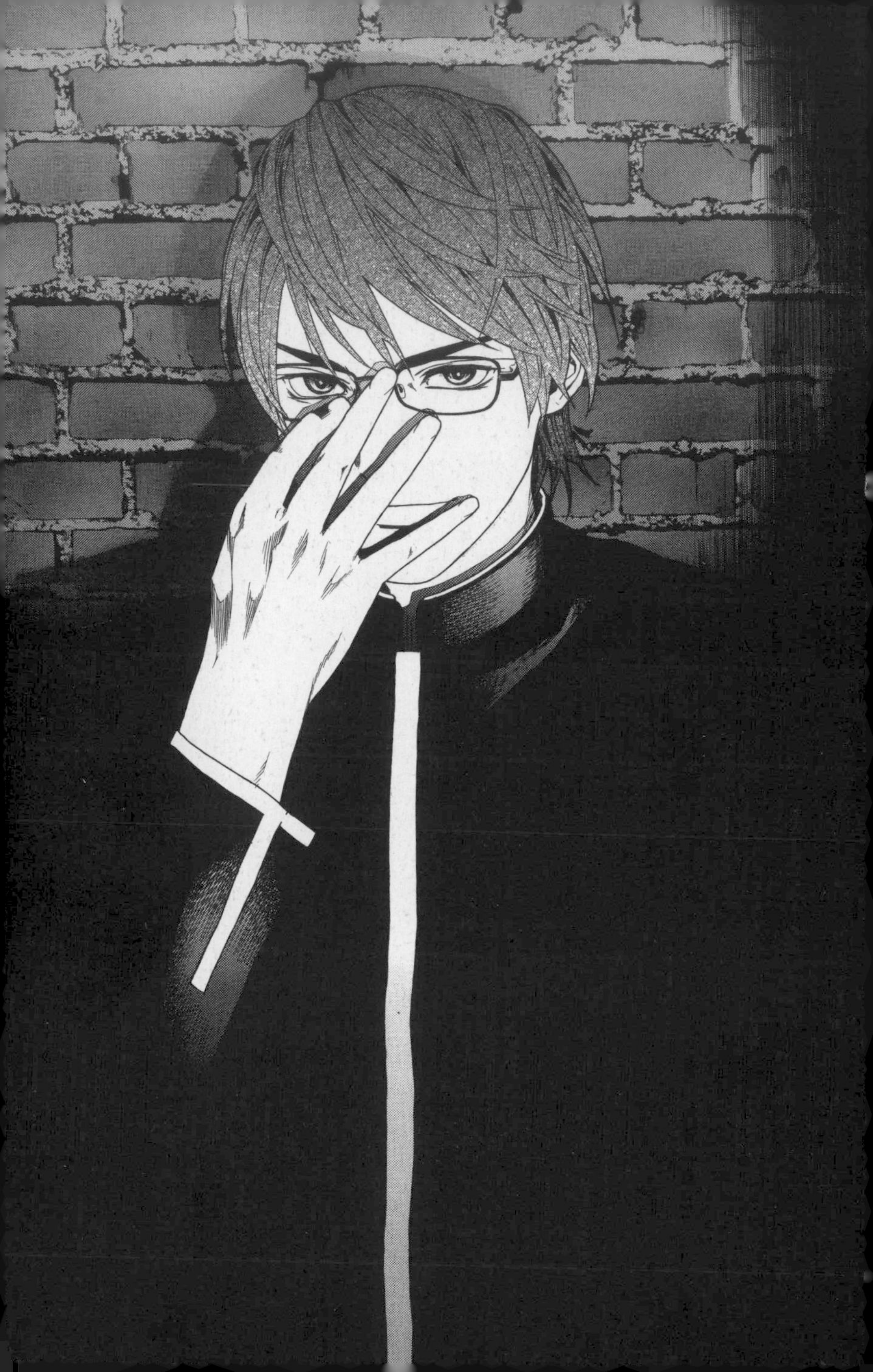

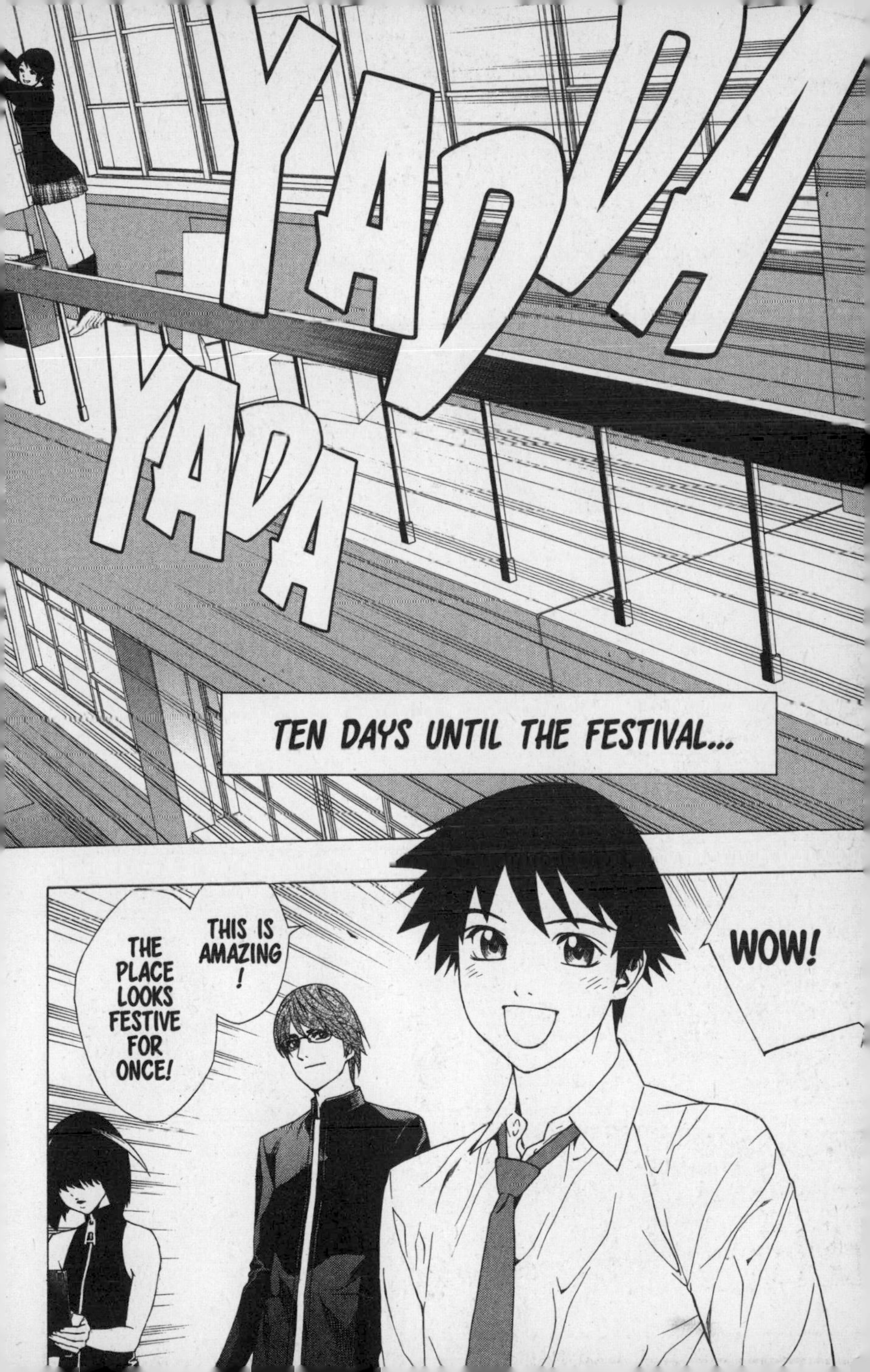
YADA
YADA
TEN DAYS UNTIL THE FESTIVAL...
WOW!
THIS IS AMAZING!
THE PLACE LOOKS FESTIVE FOR ONCE!

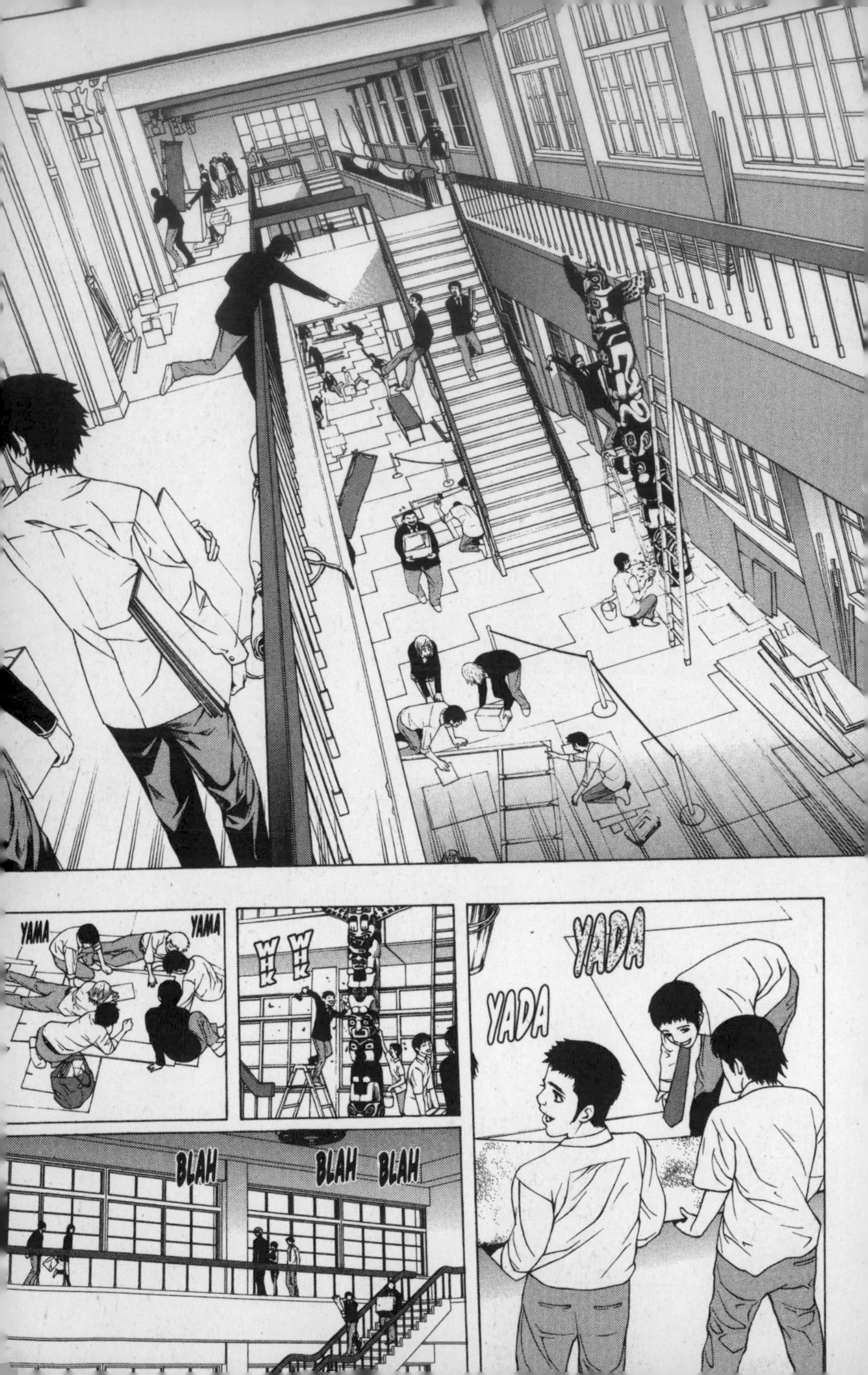
YADA
YADA
WHK
WHK
YAMA
YAMA
BLAH
BLAH
BLAH

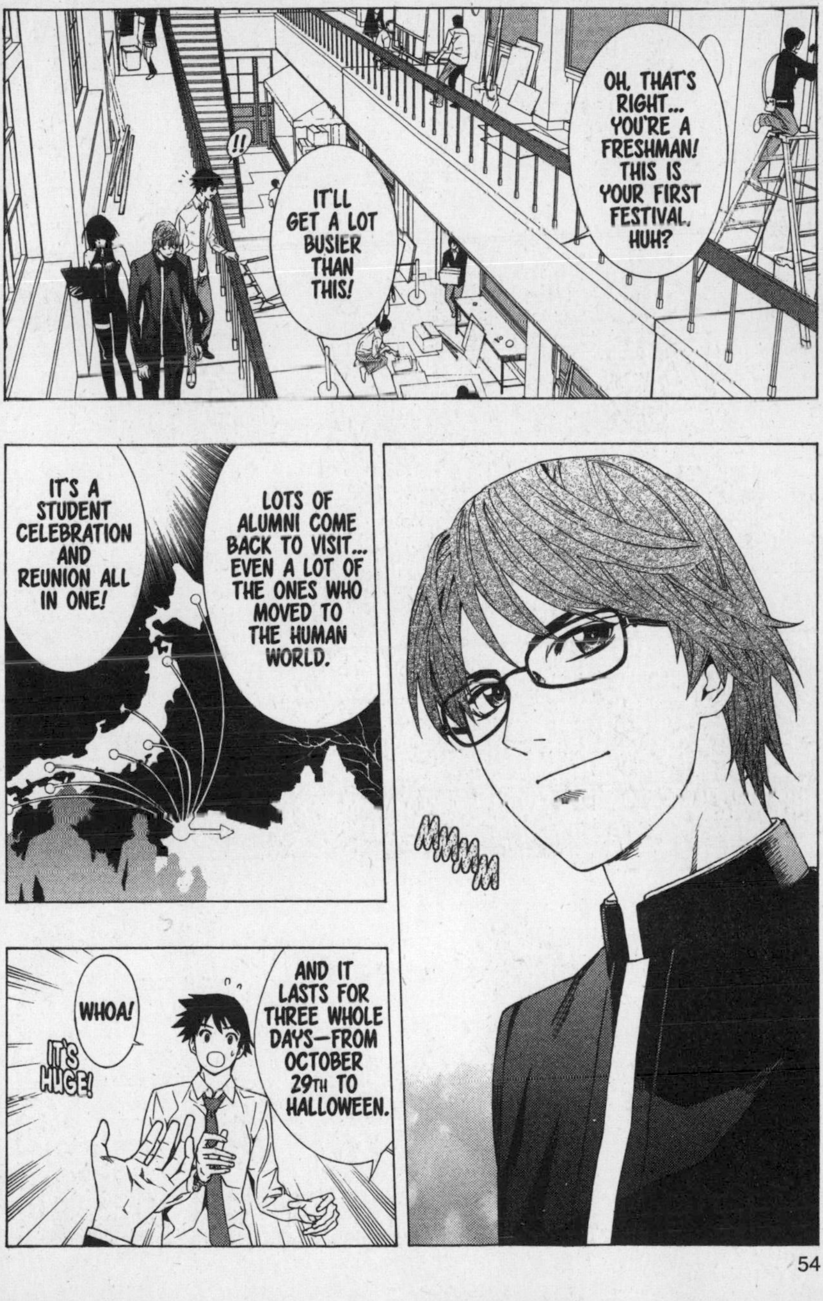
OH, THAT'S RIGHT... YOU'RE A FRESHMAN! THIS IS YOUR FIRST FESTIVAL, HUH?
IT'LL GET A LOT BUSIER THAN THIS!
!!
MMMM
LOTS OF ALUMNI COME BACK TO VISIT... EVEN A LOT OF THE ONES WHO MOVED TO THE HUMAN WORLD.
IT'S A STUDENT CELEBRATION AND REUNION ALL IN ONE!
AND IT LASTS FOR THREE WHOLE DAYS—FROM OCTOBER 29TH TO HALLOWEEN.
WHOA!
IT'S HUGE!

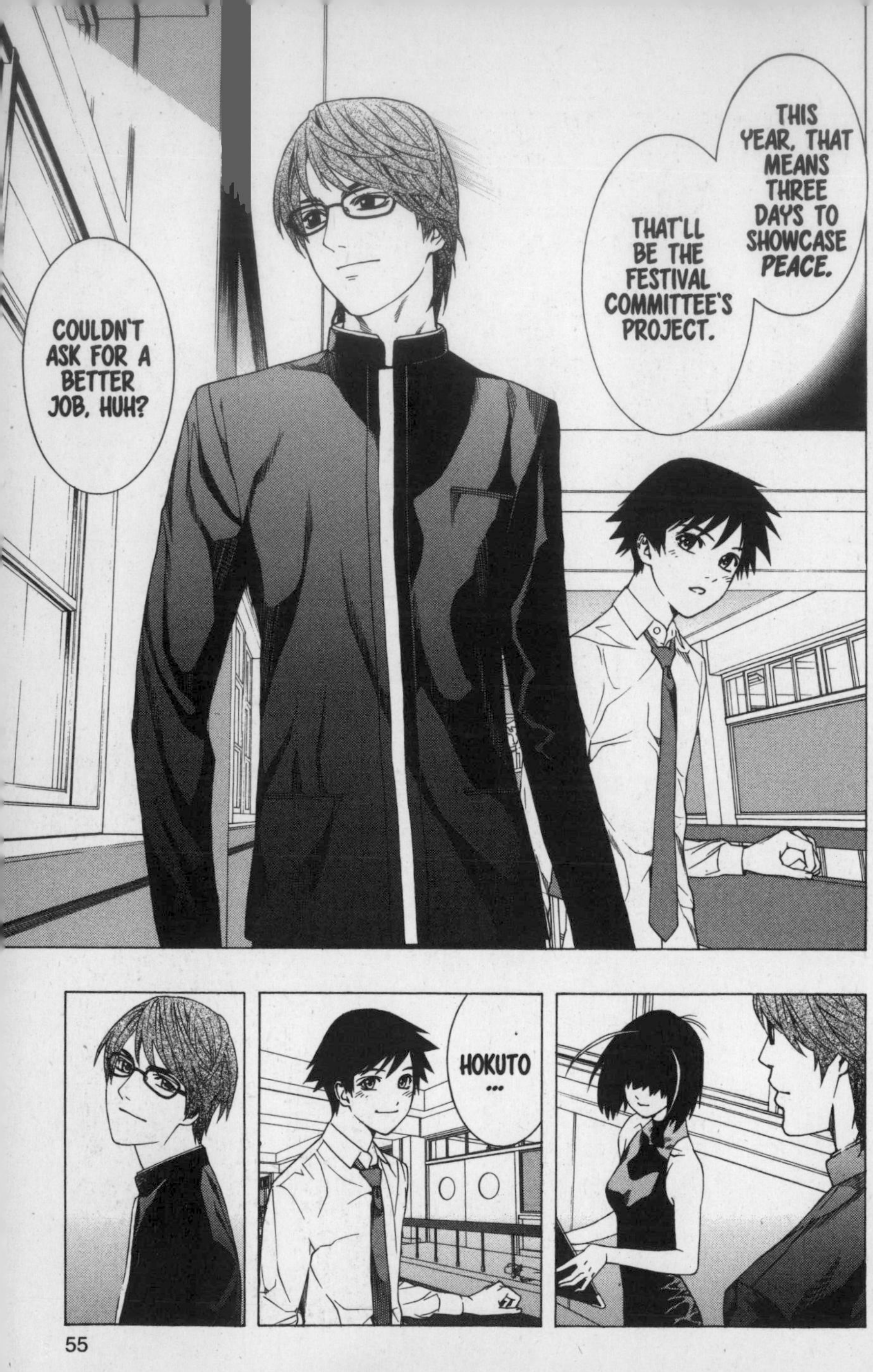
THIS YEAR, THAT MEANS THREE DAYS TO SHOWCASE PEACE.
THAT'LL BE THE FESTIVAL COMMITTEE'S PROJECT.
COULDN'T ASK FOR A BETTER JOB, HUH?
HOKUTO ...

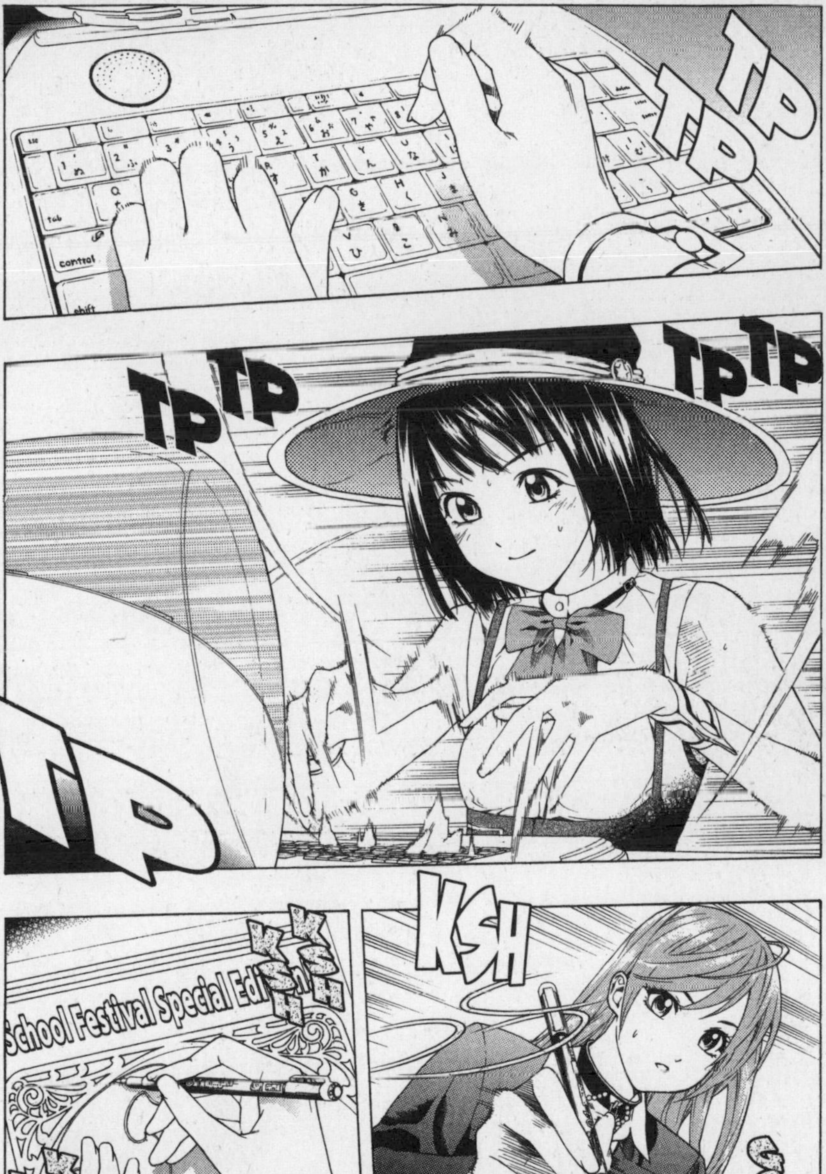
TP TP
TP TP
TP TP
TP
KSH
KSH
School Festival Special Edi
KSH KSH
KSH KSH

READ THIS WAY

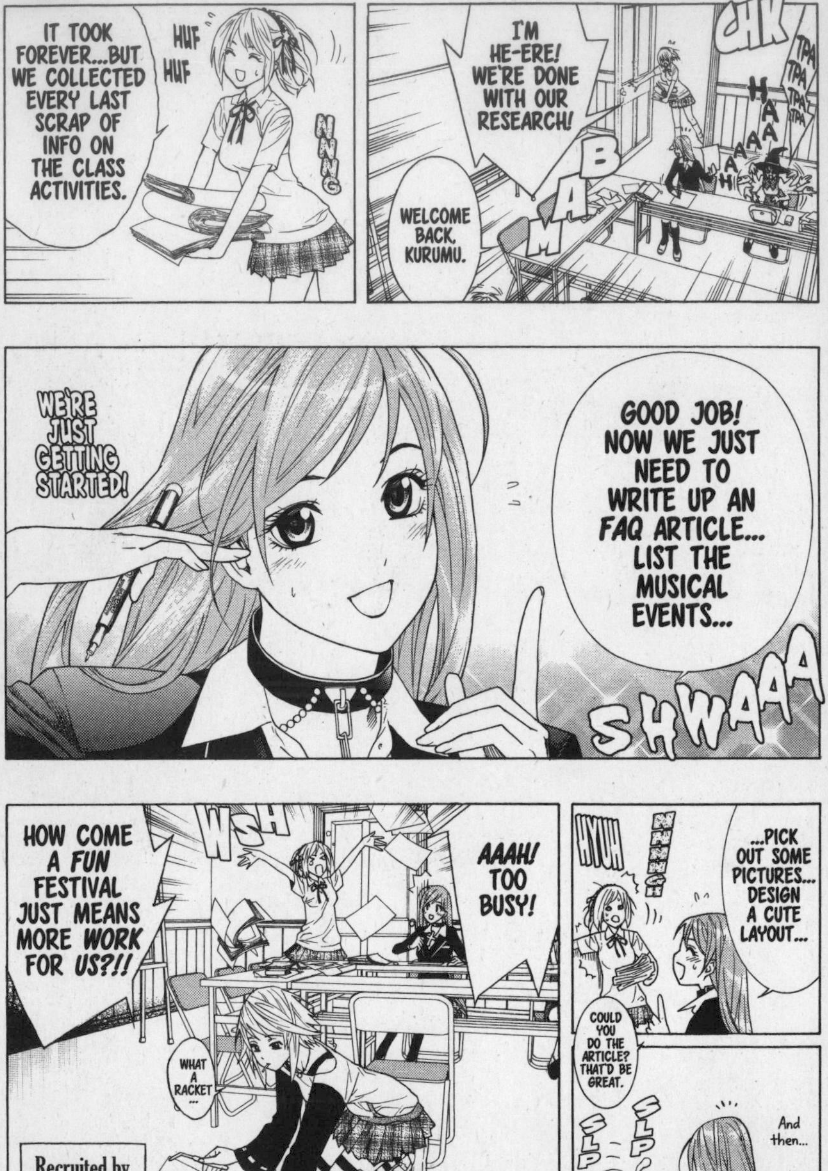
CHK
I'M HE-ERE! WE'RE DONE WITH OUR RESEARCH!
TPA TPA TPA TPA
HAAAAH
BAM
WELCOME BACK, KURUMU.
HUF HUF
IT TOOK FOREVER...BUT WE COLLECTED EVERY LAST SCRAP OF INFO ON THE CLASS ACTIVITIES.
NNNG
GOOD JOB! NOW WE JUST NEED TO WRITE UP AN FAQ ARTICLE... LIST THE MUSICAL EVENTS...
WE'RE JUST GETTING STARTED!
SHWAAA
...PICK OUT SOME PICTURES... DESIGN A CUTE LAYOUT...
HYUH
NNNGH
COULD YOU DO THE ARTICLE? THAT'D BE GREAT.
SLP SLP
...
And then...
WSH
AAAH! TOO BUSY!
HOW COME A FUN FESTIVAL JUST MEANS MORE WORK FOR US?!!
WHAT A RACKET...
Recruited by Tsukune.

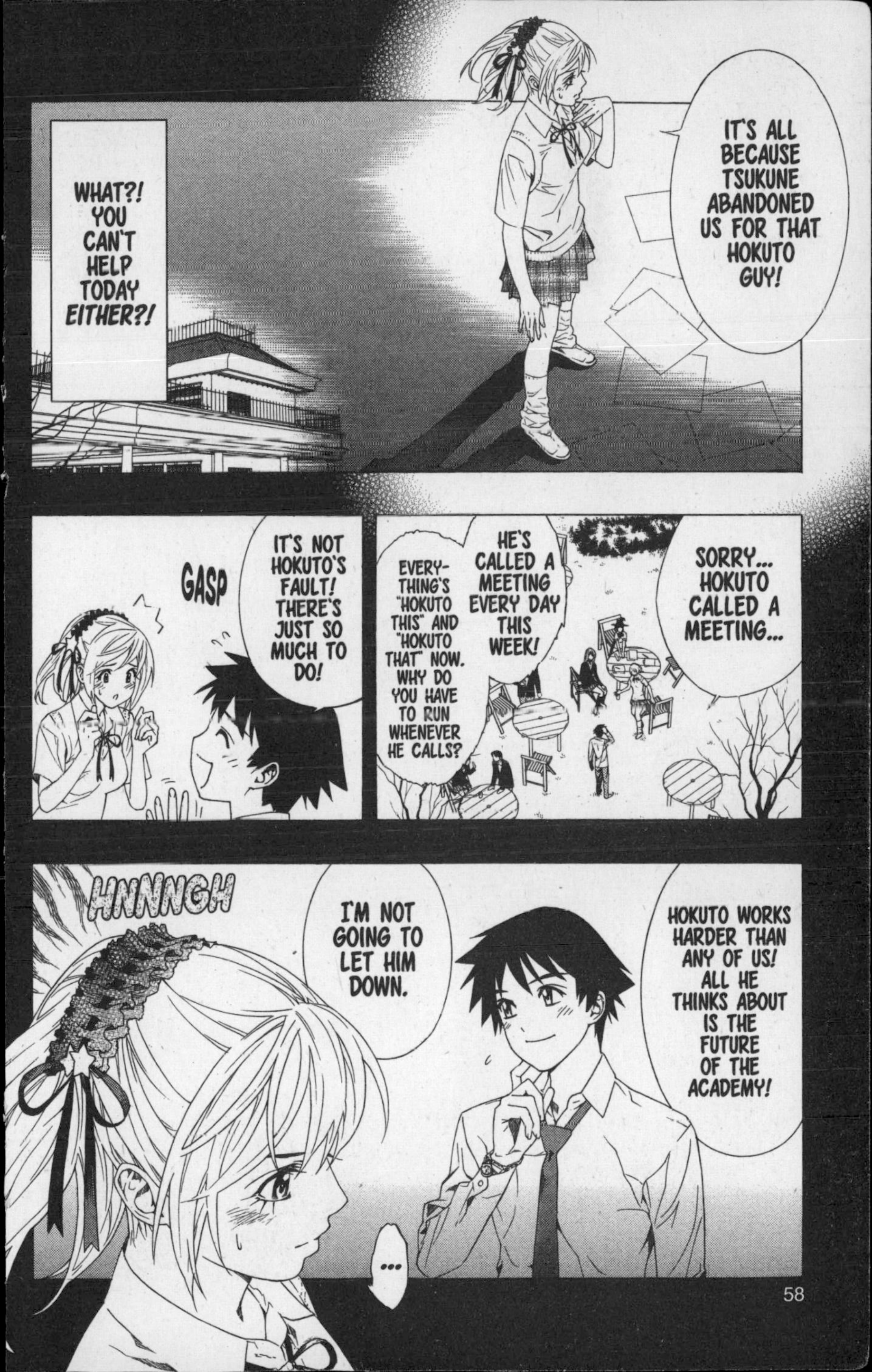
IT'S ALL BECAUSE TSUKUNE ABANDONED US FOR THAT HOKUTO GUY!
WHAT?! YOU CAN'T HELP TODAY EITHER?!
SORRY... HOKUTO CALLED A MEETING...
HE'S CALLED A MEETING EVERY DAY THIS WEEK!
EVERY-THING'S "HOKUTO THIS" AND "HOKUTO THAT" NOW. WHY DO YOU HAVE TO RUN WHENEVER HE CALLS?
IT'S NOT HOKUTO'S FAULT! THERE'S JUST SO MUCH TO DO!
GASP
HOKUTO WORKS HARDER THAN ANY OF US! ALL HE THINKS ABOUT IS THE FUTURE OF THE ACADEMY!
I'M NOT GOING TO LET HIM DOWN.
HNNNGH
...

READ THIS WAY

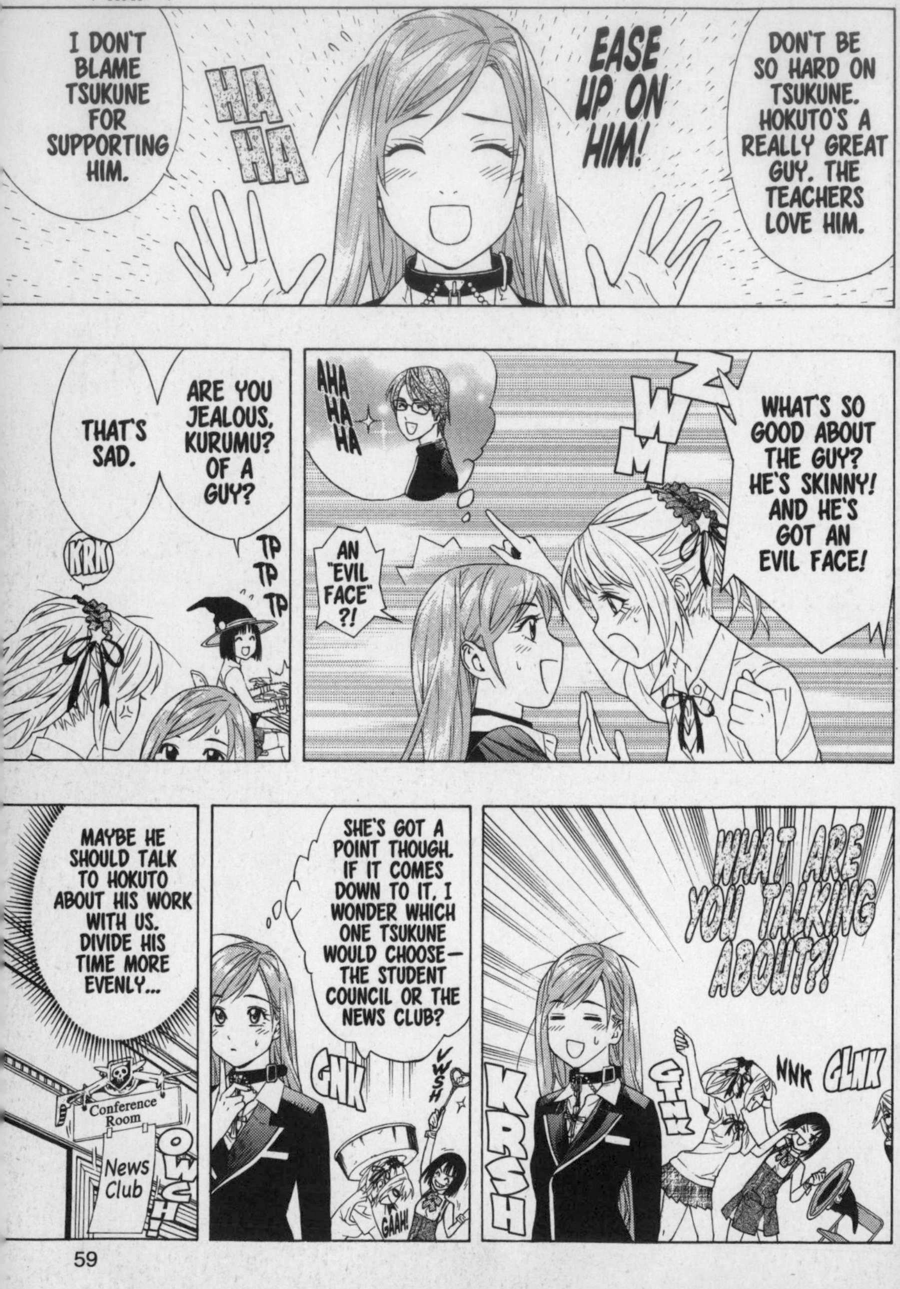
DON'T BE SO HARD ON TSUKUNE. HOKUTO'S A REALLY GREAT GUY. THE TEACHERS LOVE HIM.
EASE UP ON HIM!
HA HA
I DON'T BLAME TSUKUNE FOR SUPPORTING HIM.
WHAT'S SO GOOD ABOUT THE GUY? HE'S SKINNY! AND HE'S GOT AN EVIL FACE!
ZWM
AHA HA HA
AN "EVIL FACE"?!
ARE YOU JEALOUS, KURUMU? OF A GUY?
THAT'S SAD.
TP TP TP
KRK
WHAT ARE YOU TALKING ABOUT?!
GLNK
NNK
GTNK
KRSH
SHE'S GOT A POINT THOUGH. IF IT COMES DOWN TO IT, I WONDER WHICH ONE TSUKUNE WOULD CHOOSE—THE STUDENT COUNCIL OR THE NEWS CLUB?
GNK
VWSH
GAAH!
MAYBE HE SHOULD TALK TO HOKUTO ABOUT HIS WORK WITH US. DIVIDE HIS TIME MORE EVENLY...
Conference Room
News Club
OWCH!!

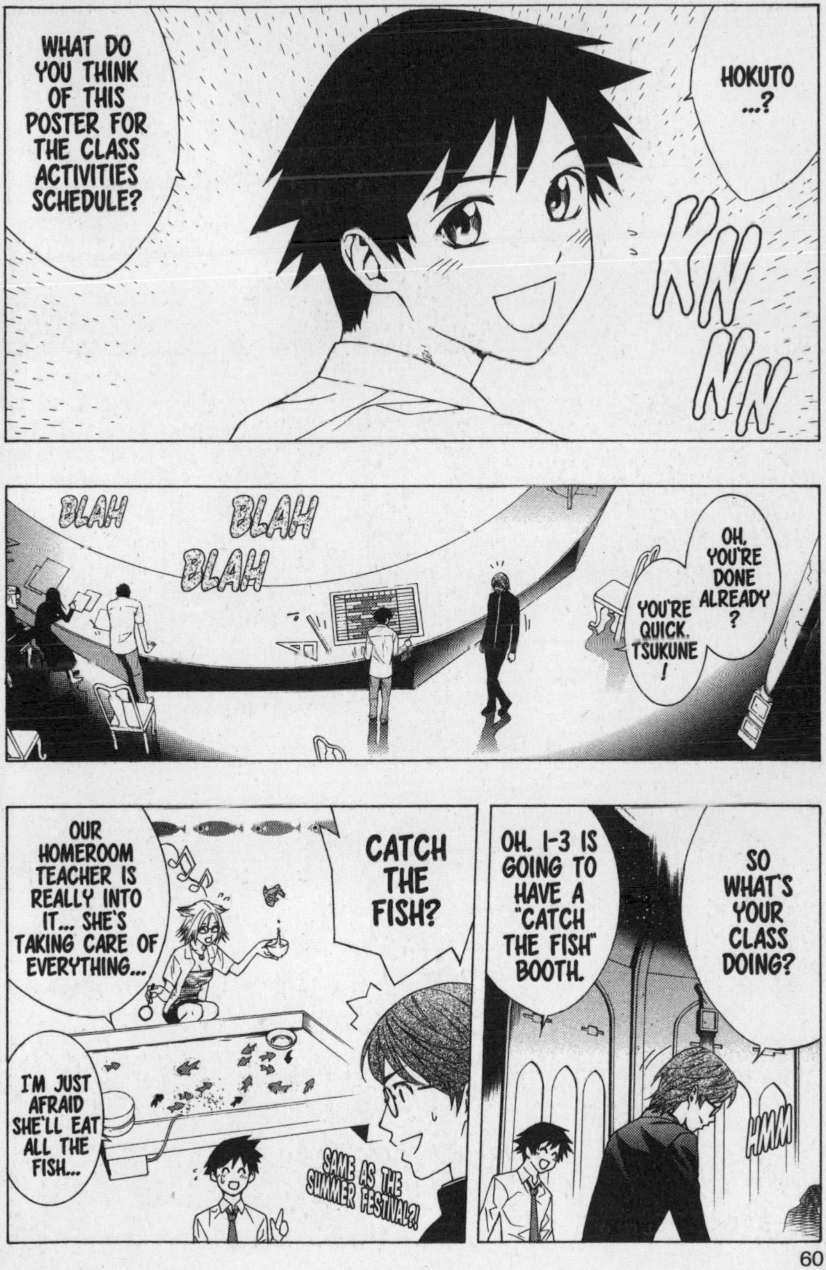
HOKUTO ...?
KNNN
WHAT DO YOU THINK OF THIS POSTER FOR THE CLASS ACTIVITIES SCHEDULE?
OH, YOU'RE DONE ALREADY?
YOU'RE QUICK, TSUKUNE!
BLAH
BLAH
BLAH
SO WHAT'S YOUR CLASS DOING?
HMM
OH. 1-3 IS GOING TO HAVE A "CATCH THE FISH" BOOTH.
CATCH THE FISH?
OUR HOMEROOM TEACHER IS REALLY INTO IT... SHE'S TAKING CARE OF EVERYTHING...
SAME AS THE SUMMER FESTIVAL?!
I'M JUST AFRAID SHE'LL EAT ALL THE FISH...

READ THIS WAY

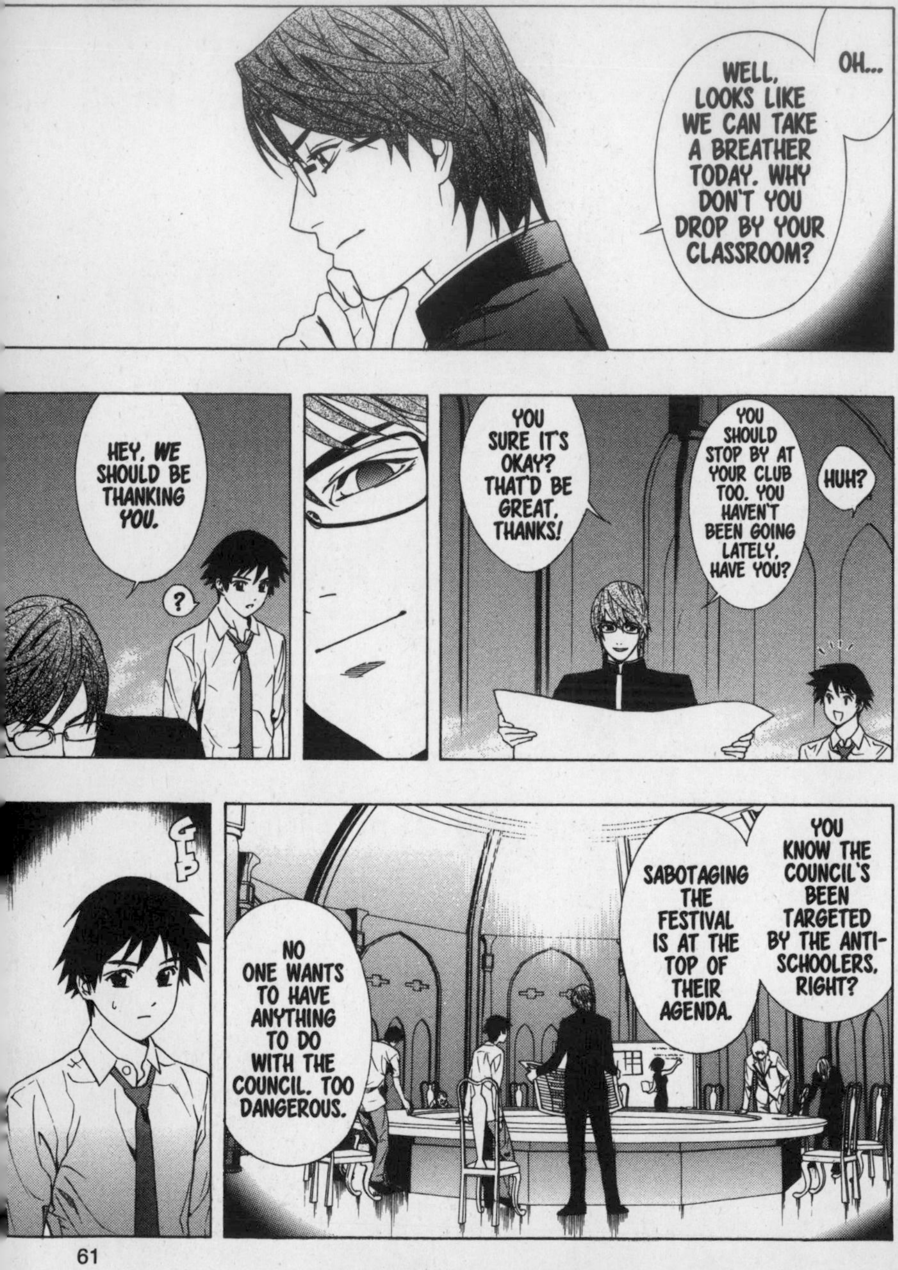

OH...
WELL, LOOKS LIKE WE CAN TAKE A BREATHER TODAY. WHY DON'T YOU DROP BY YOUR CLASSROOM?
YOU SURE IT'S OKAY? THAT'D BE GREAT, THANKS!
YOU SHOULD STOP BY AT YOUR CLUB TOO. YOU HAVEN'T BEEN GOING LATELY, HAVE YOU?
HUH?
HEY, WE SHOULD BE THANKING YOU.
?
YOU KNOW THE COUNCIL'S BEEN TARGETED BY THE ANTI-SCHOOLERS, RIGHT?
SABOTAGING THE FESTIVAL IS AT THE TOP OF THEIR AGENDA.
NO ONE WANTS TO HAVE ANYTHING TO DO WITH THE COUNCIL. TOO DANGEROUS.
GLP

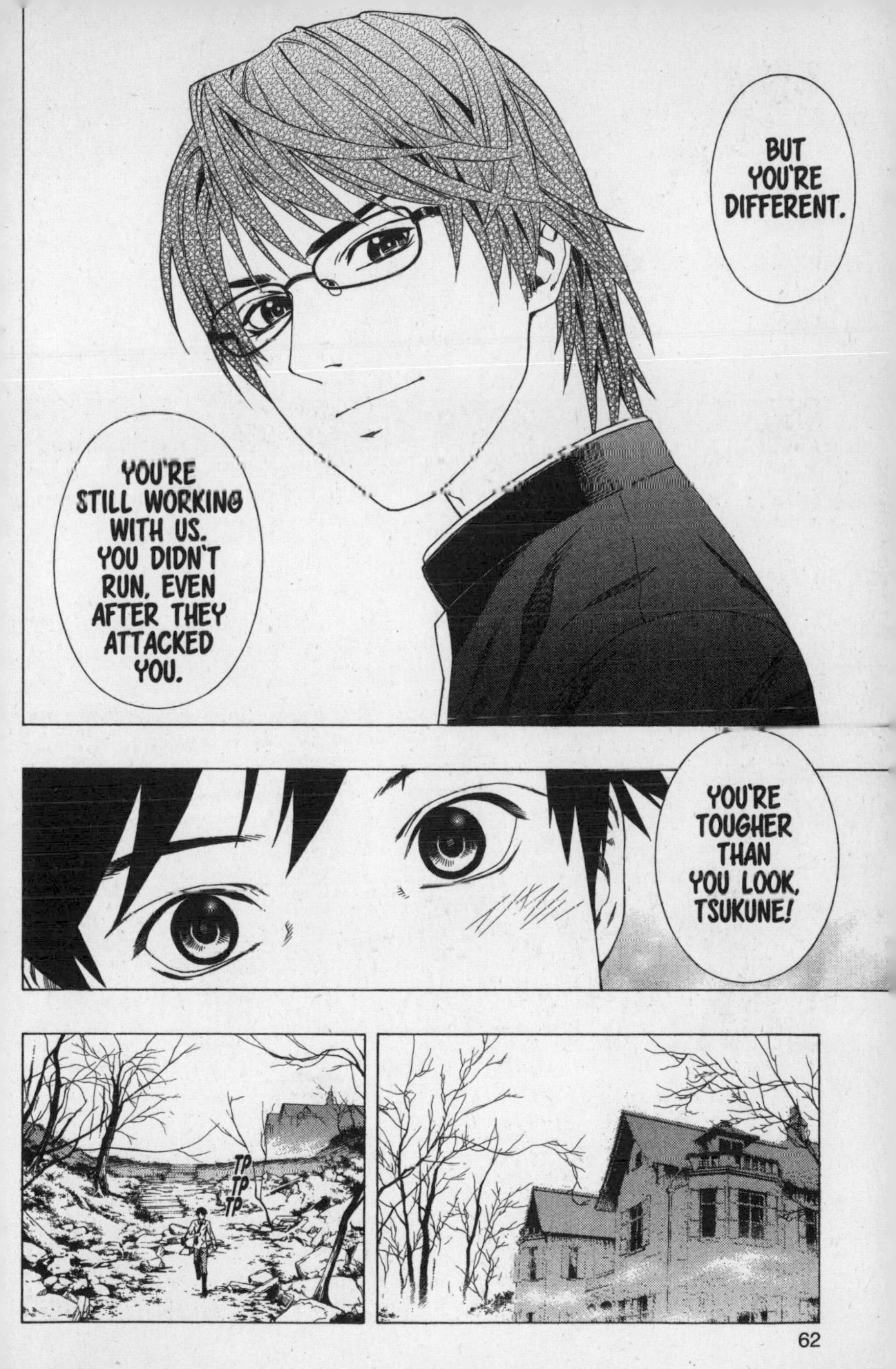
BUT YOU'RE DIFFERENT.
YOU'RE STILL WORKING WITH US. YOU DIDN'T RUN, EVEN AFTER THEY ATTACKED YOU.
YOU'RE TOUGHER THAN YOU LOOK, TSUKUNE!
TP TP TP

READ THIS WAY

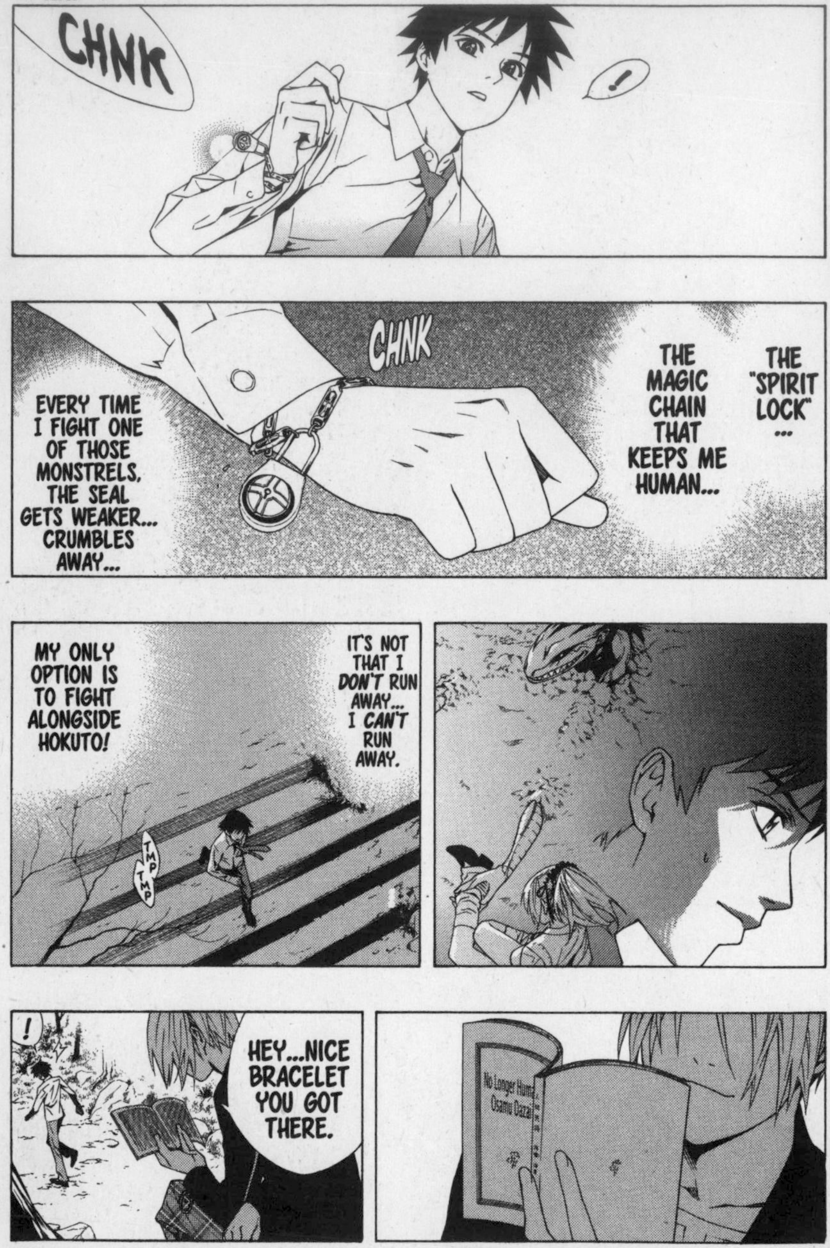

CHNK
!
THE "SPIRIT LOCK"...
THE MAGIC CHAIN THAT KEEPS ME HUMAN...
CHNK
EVERY TIME I FIGHT ONE OF THOSE MONSTRELS, THE SEAL GETS WEAKER... CRUMBLES AWAY...
IT'S NOT THAT I *DON'T* RUN AWAY... I *CAN'T* RUN AWAY.
MY ONLY OPTION IS TO FIGHT ALONGSIDE HOKUTO!
TMP TMP
No Longer Huma
Osamu Dazai
HEY...NICE BRACELET YOU GOT THERE.
!

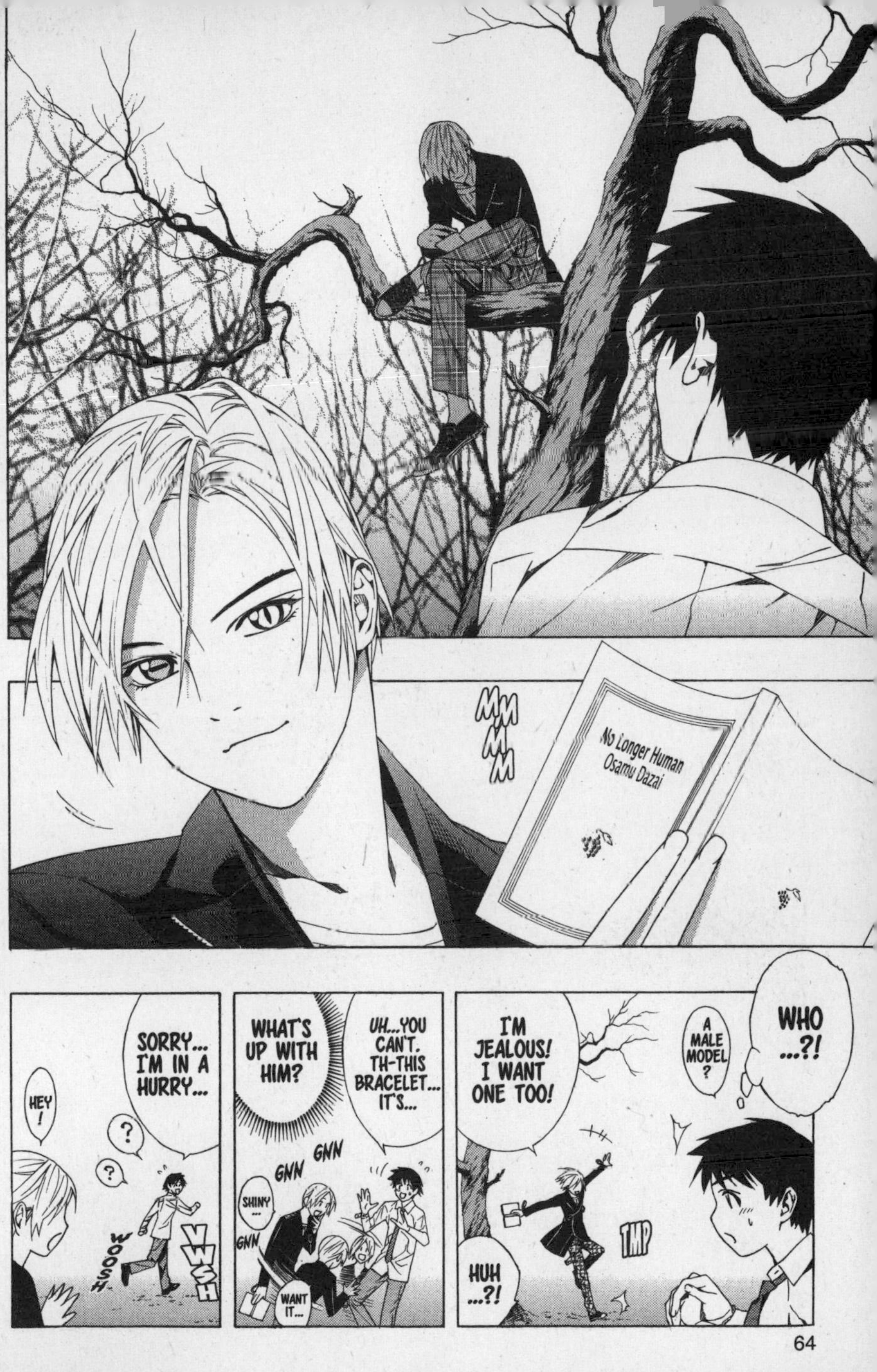
MMMM
No Longer Human
Osamu Dazai
WHO ...?!
A MALE MODEL ?
I'M JEALOUS! I WANT ONE TOO!
TMP
HUH ...?!
UH...YOU CAN'T. TH-THIS BRACELET... IT'S...
WHAT'S UP WITH HIM?
GNN
GNN
SHINY ...
GNN
WANT IT...
SORRY... I'M IN A HURRY...
HEY !
?
?
WOOSH
VWSH

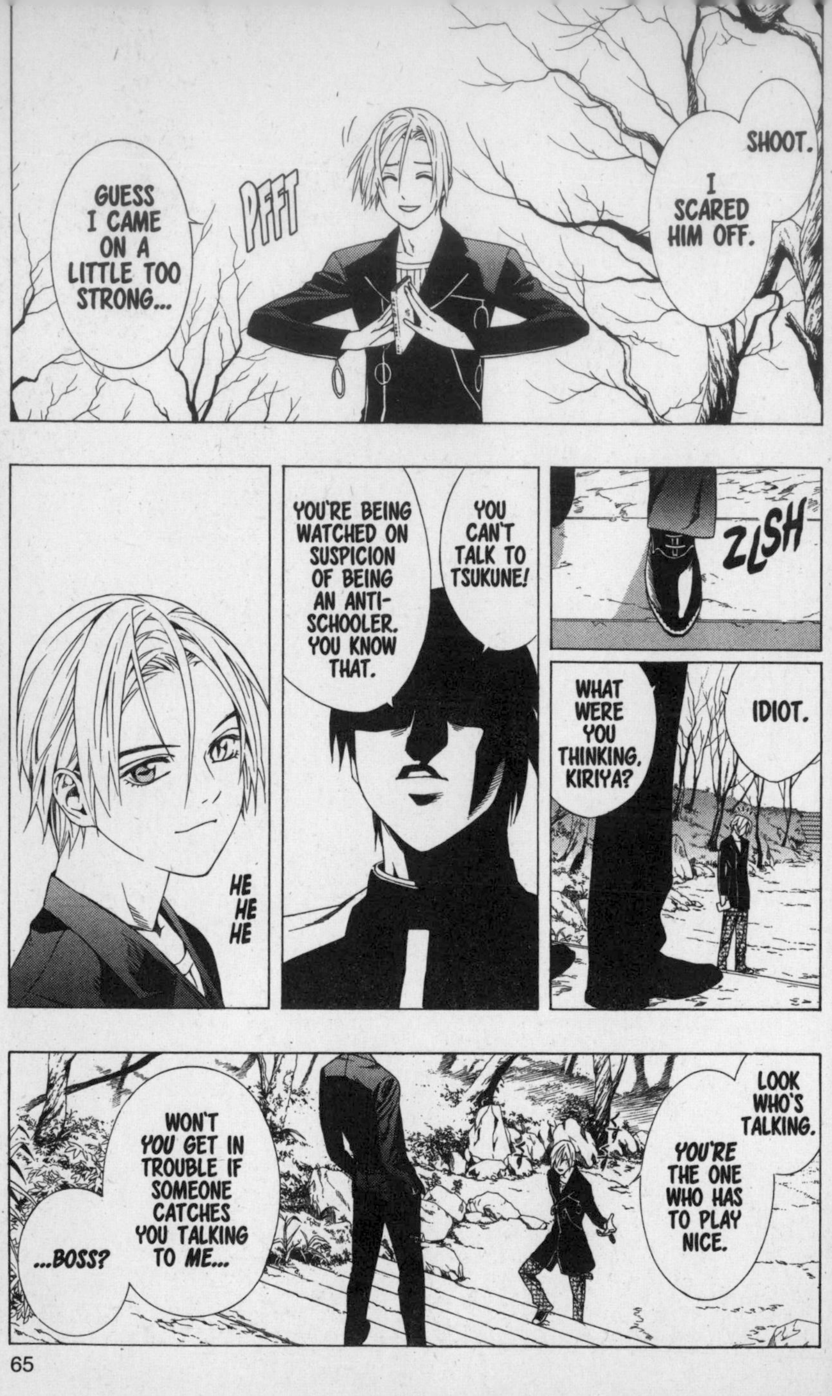
SHOOT.
I SCARED HIM OFF.
PFFT
GUESS I CAME ON A LITTLE TOO STRONG...
ZLSH
IDIOT.
WHAT WERE YOU THINKING, KIRIYA?
YOU CAN'T TALK TO TSUKUNE!
YOU'RE BEING WATCHED ON SUSPICION OF BEING AN ANTI-SCHOOLER. YOU KNOW THAT.
HE HE HE
LOOK WHO'S TALKING.
YOU'RE THE ONE WHO HAS TO PLAY NICE.
WON'T YOU GET IN TROUBLE IF SOMEONE CATCHES YOU TALKING TO ME...
...BOSS?

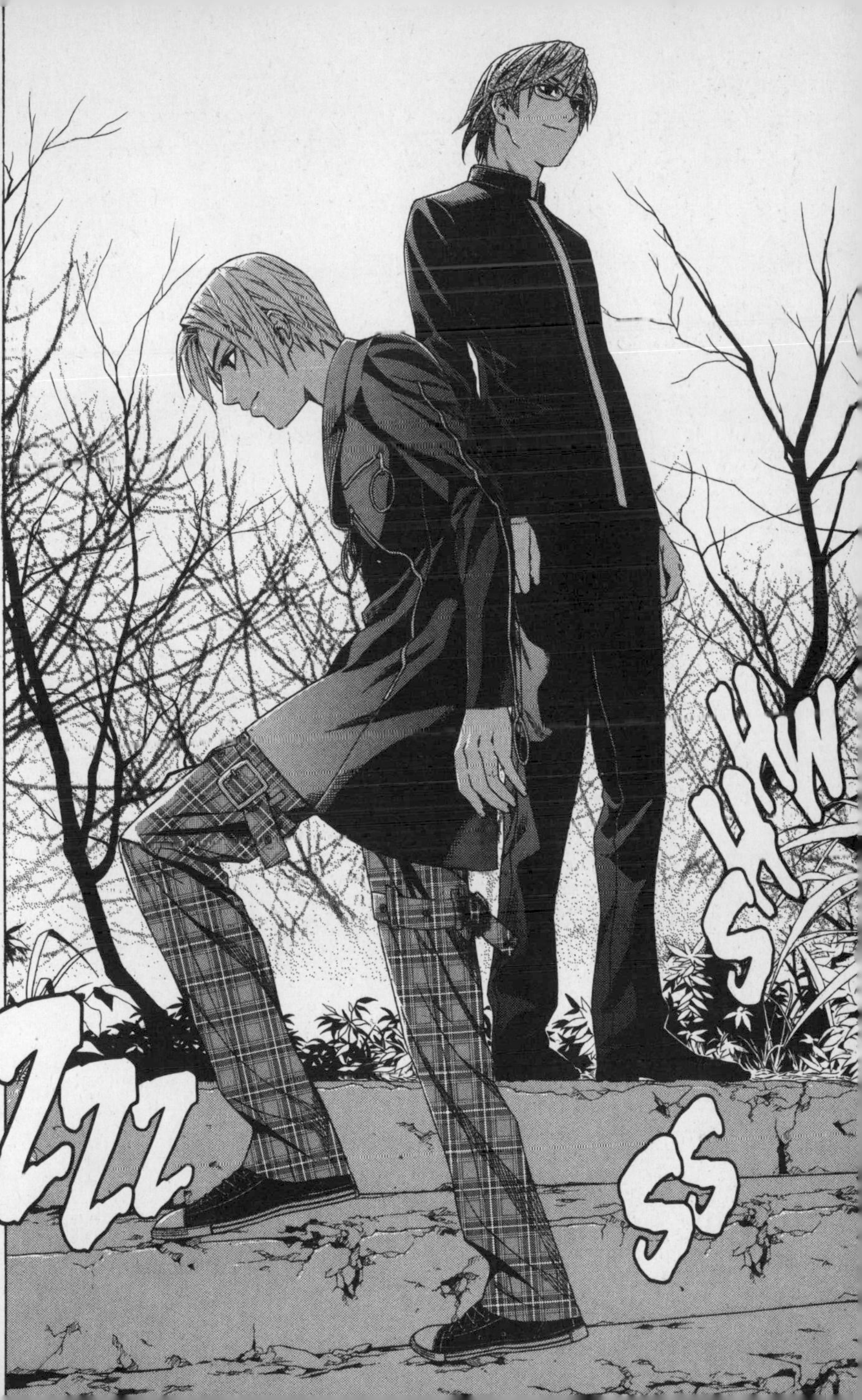
SHHW
SS
ZZZ

READ THIS WAY

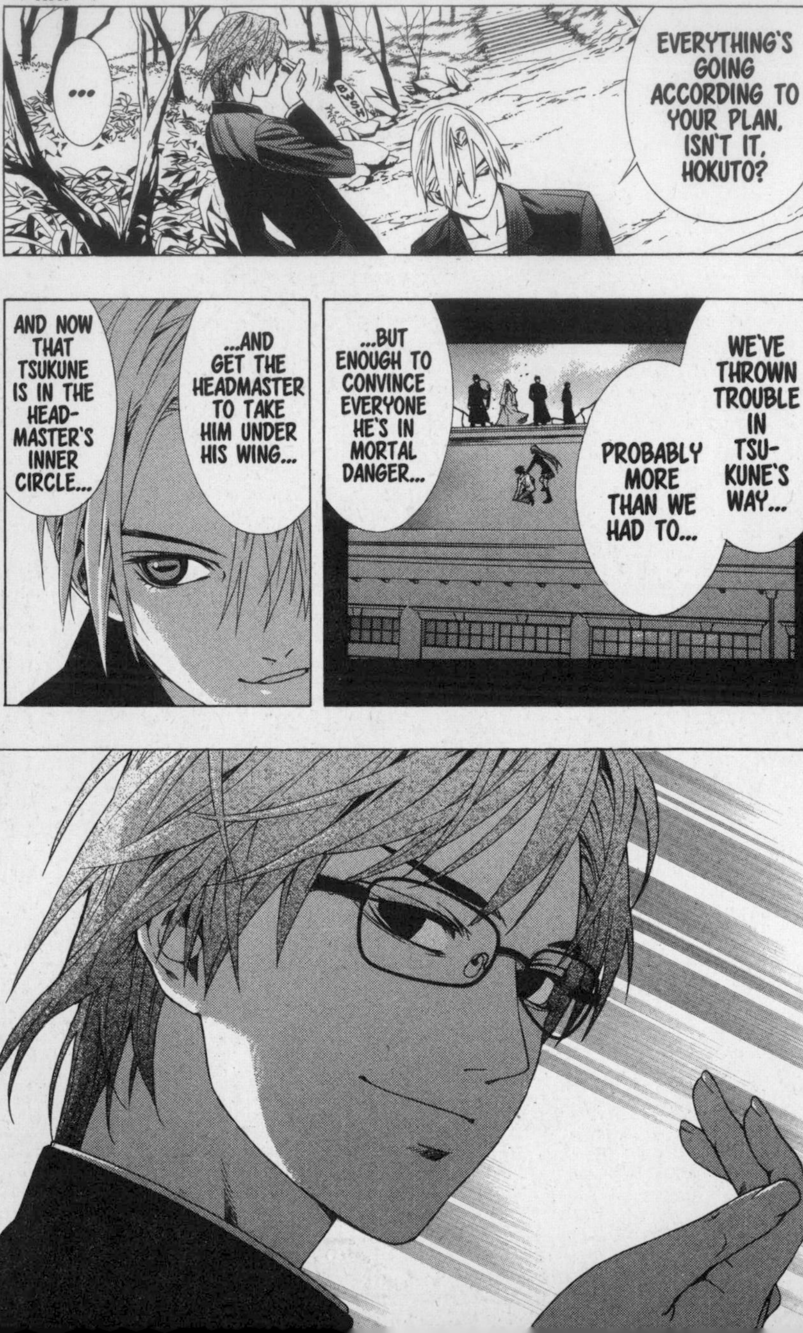
EVERYTHING'S GOING ACCORDING TO YOUR PLAN, ISN'T IT, HOKUTO?
BWSH
...
WE'VE THROWN TROUBLE IN TSU-KUNE'S WAY...
PROBABLY MORE THAN WE HAD TO...
...BUT ENOUGH TO CONVINCE EVERYONE HE'S IN MORTAL DANGER...
...AND GET THE HEADMASTER TO TAKE HIM UNDER HIS WING...
AND NOW THAT TSUKUNE IS IN THE HEAD-MASTER'S INNER CIRCLE...

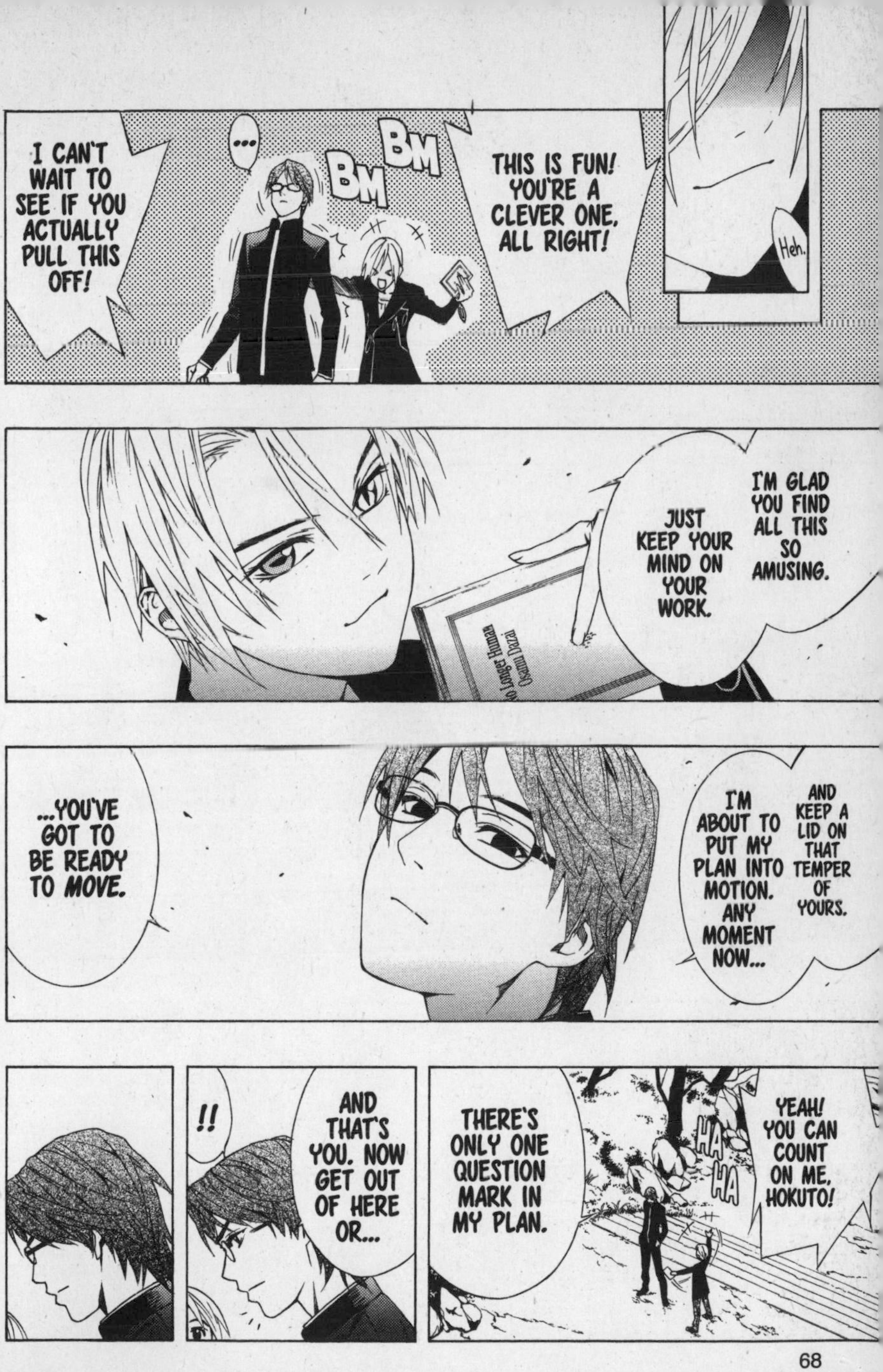
Heh.
THIS IS FUN! YOU'RE A CLEVER ONE, ALL RIGHT!
BM
BM
...
I CAN'T WAIT TO SEE IF YOU ACTUALLY PULL THIS OFF!
I'M GLAD YOU FIND ALL THIS SO AMUSING.
JUST KEEP YOUR MIND ON YOUR WORK.
No Longer Human
Osamu Dazai
AND KEEP A LID ON THAT TEMPER OF YOURS.
I'M ABOUT TO PUT MY PLAN INTO MOTION. ANY MOMENT NOW...
...YOU'VE GOT TO BE READY TO *MOVE.*
YEAH! YOU CAN COUNT ON ME, HOKUTO!
HA
HA
THERE'S ONLY ONE QUESTION MARK IN MY PLAN.
AND THAT'S YOU. NOW GET OUT OF HERE OR...
!!

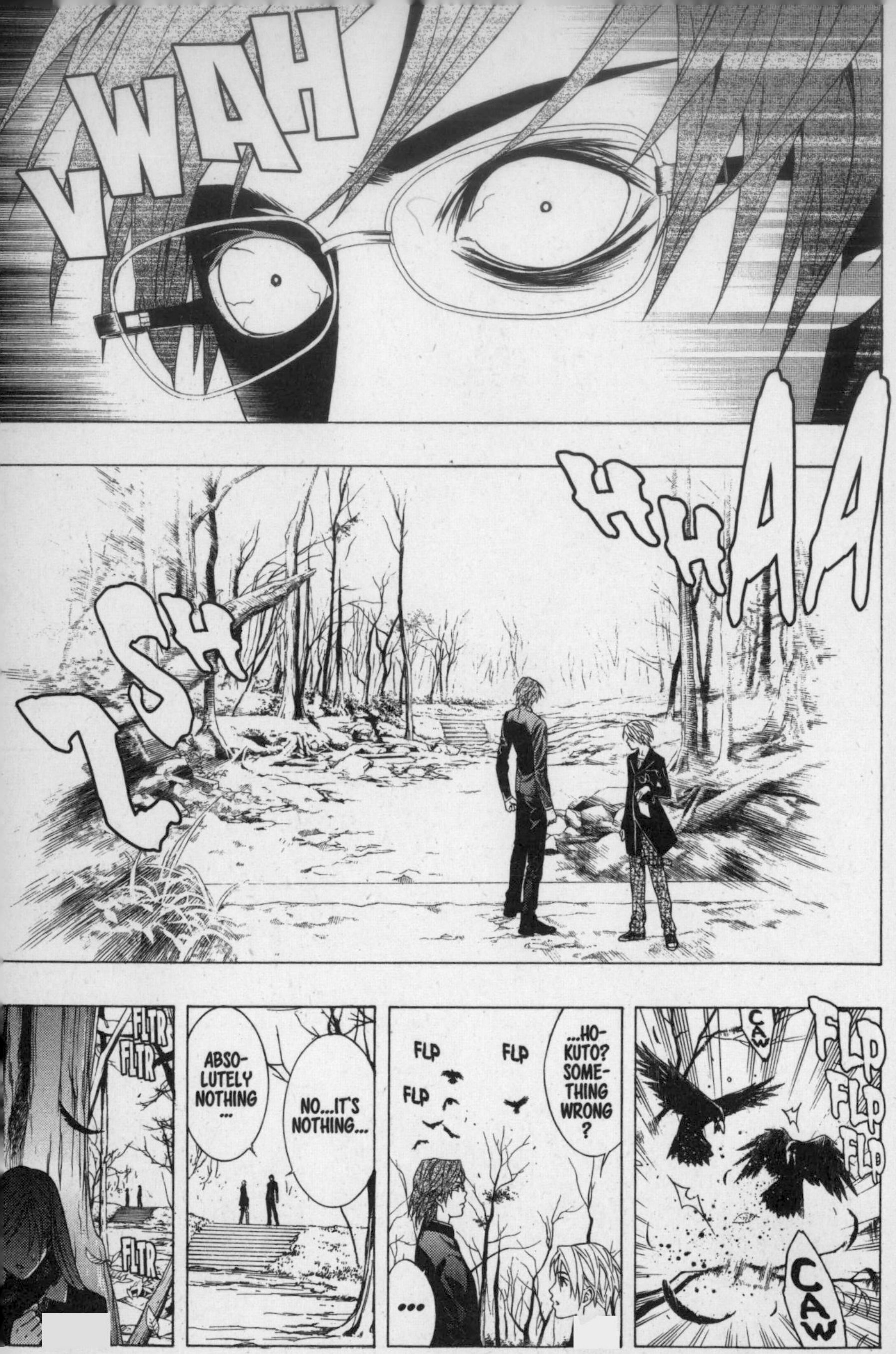
VWAH
HHAA
ZSH
CAW
FLP
FLP
FLP
CAW
...HO-KUTO? SOME-THING WRONG?
FLP
FLP
FLP
...
NO...IT'S NOTHING...
ABSO-LUTELY NOTHING ...
FLTR
FLTR
FLTR

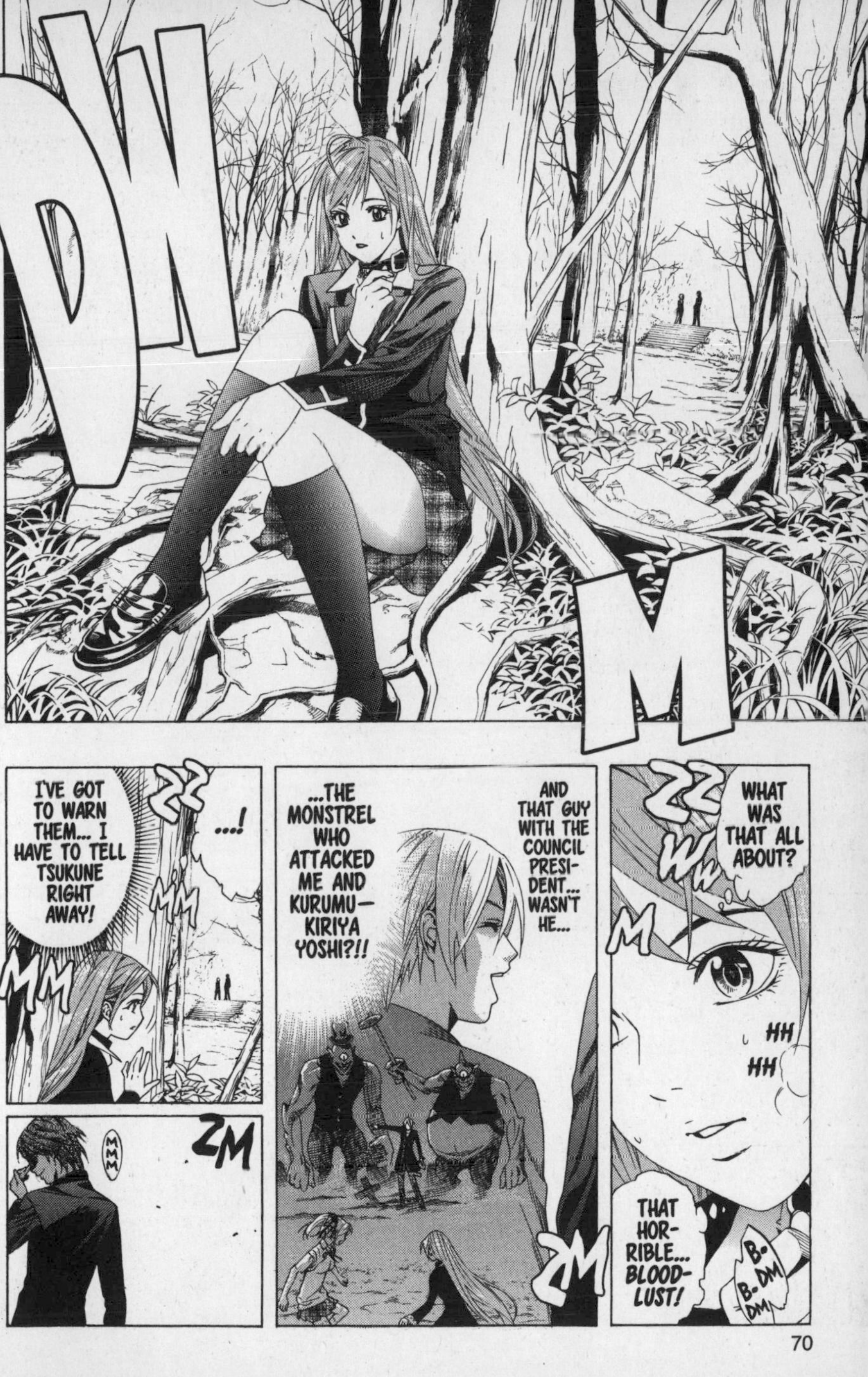
DWM
ZZWM
WHAT WAS THAT ALL ABOUT?
HH HH
THAT HORRIBLE... BLOODLUST!
B-DM B-DM
AND THAT GUY WITH THE COUNCIL PRESIDENT... WASN'T HE...
...THE MONSTREL WHO ATTACKED ME AND KURUMU-KIRIYA YOSHI?!!
ZM
ZZMMMM
...!
I'VE GOT TO WARN THEM... I HAVE TO TELL TSUKUNE RIGHT AWAY!
MMM
ZM

READ THIS WAY

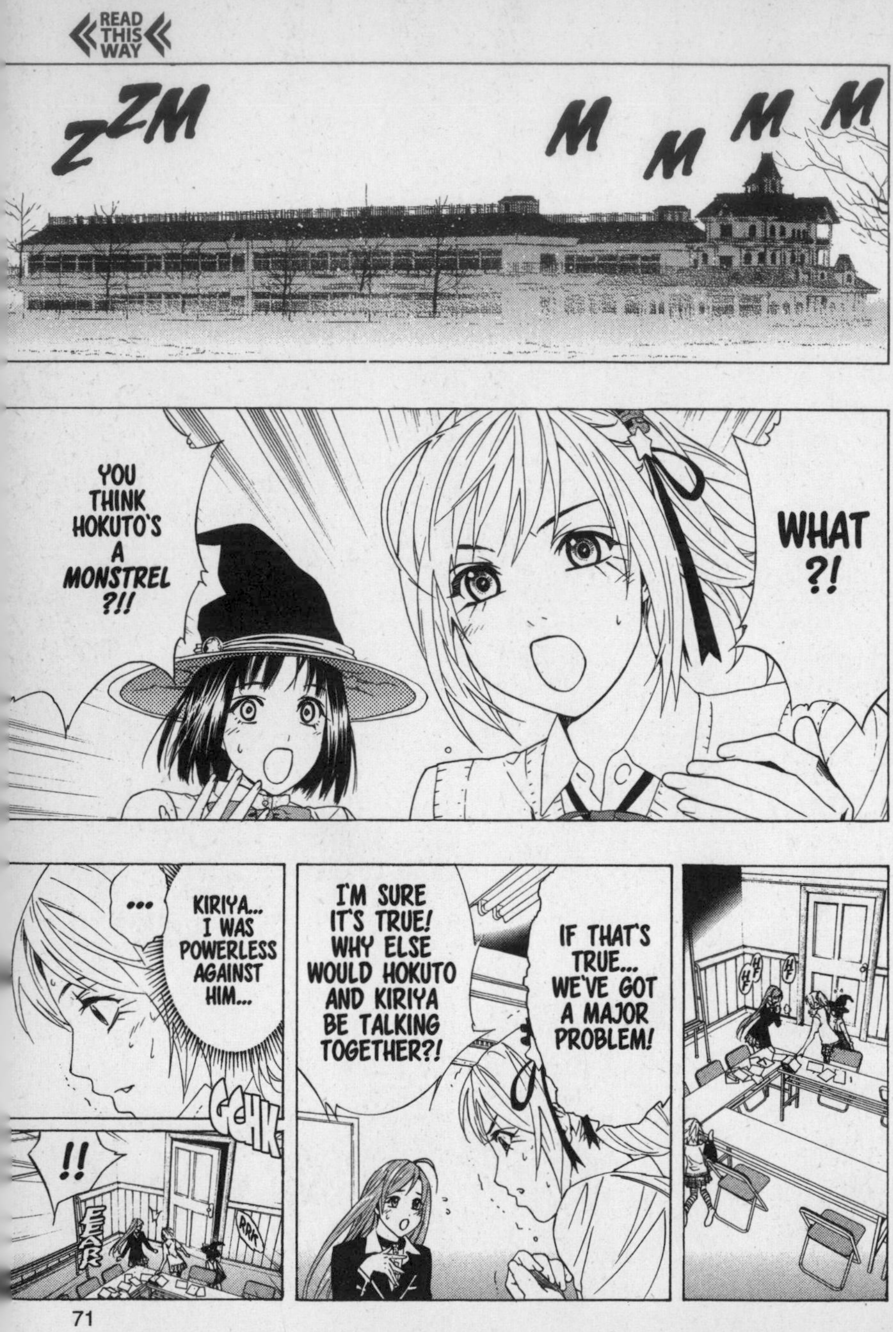
ZZM
MMMM
WHAT ?!
YOU THINK HOKUTO'S A MONSTREL ?!!
HF HF
IF THAT'S TRUE... WE'VE GOT A MAJOR PROBLEM!
I'M SURE IT'S TRUE! WHY ELSE WOULD HOKUTO AND KIRIYA BE TALKING TOGETHER?!
KIRIYA... I WAS POWERLESS AGAINST HIM...
...
GCHK
!!
RRK
EEAR

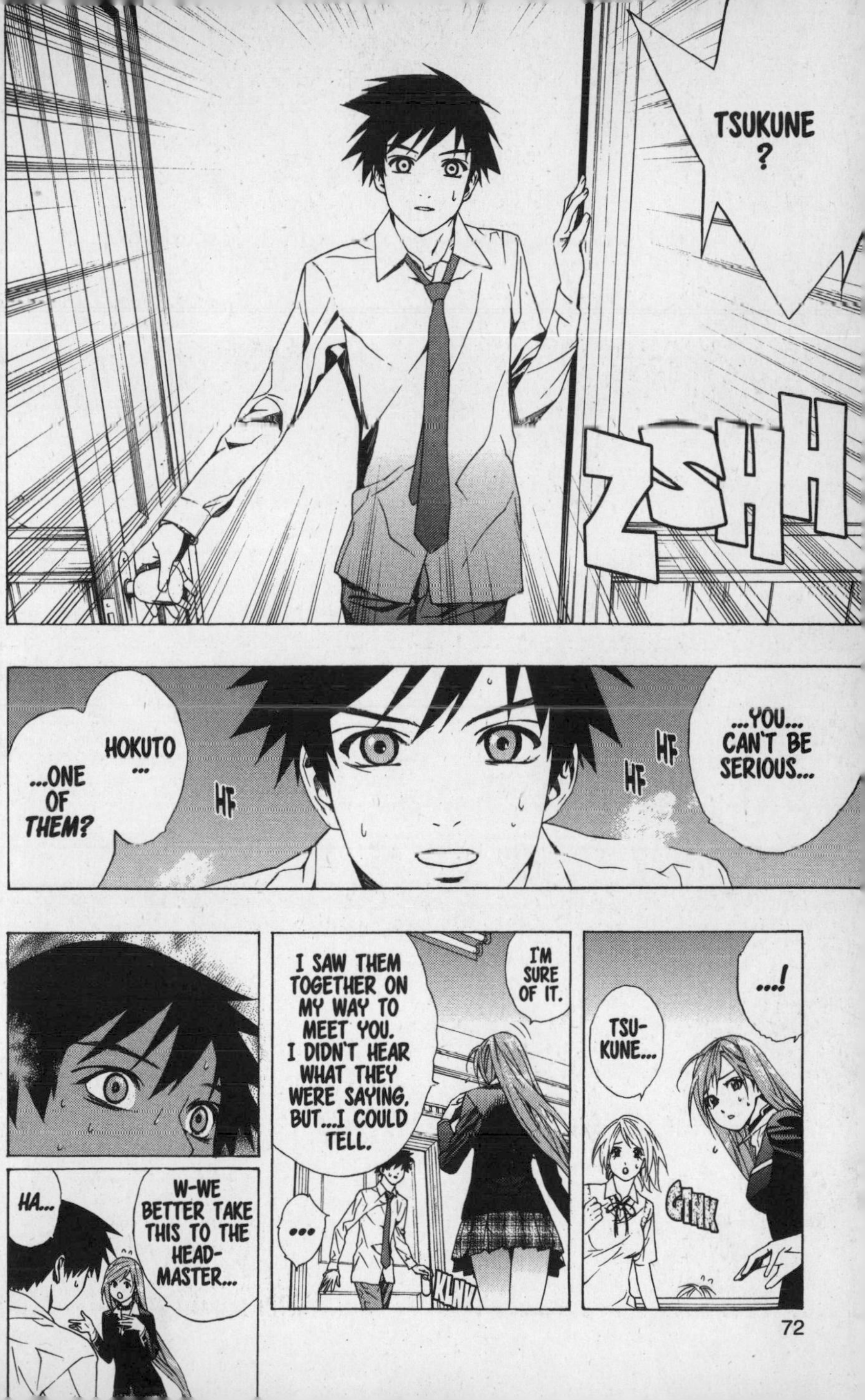
TSUKUNE ?
ZSH
...YOU... CAN'T BE SERIOUS...
HF
HF
HOKUTO ...
...ONE OF THEM?
HF
...!
TSU-KUNE...
GTHK
I'M SURE OF IT.
I SAW THEM TOGETHER ON MY WAY TO MEET YOU. I DIDN'T HEAR WHAT THEY WERE SAYING, BUT...I COULD TELL.
...
KLNK
W-WE BETTER TAKE THIS TO THE HEAD-MASTER...
HA...

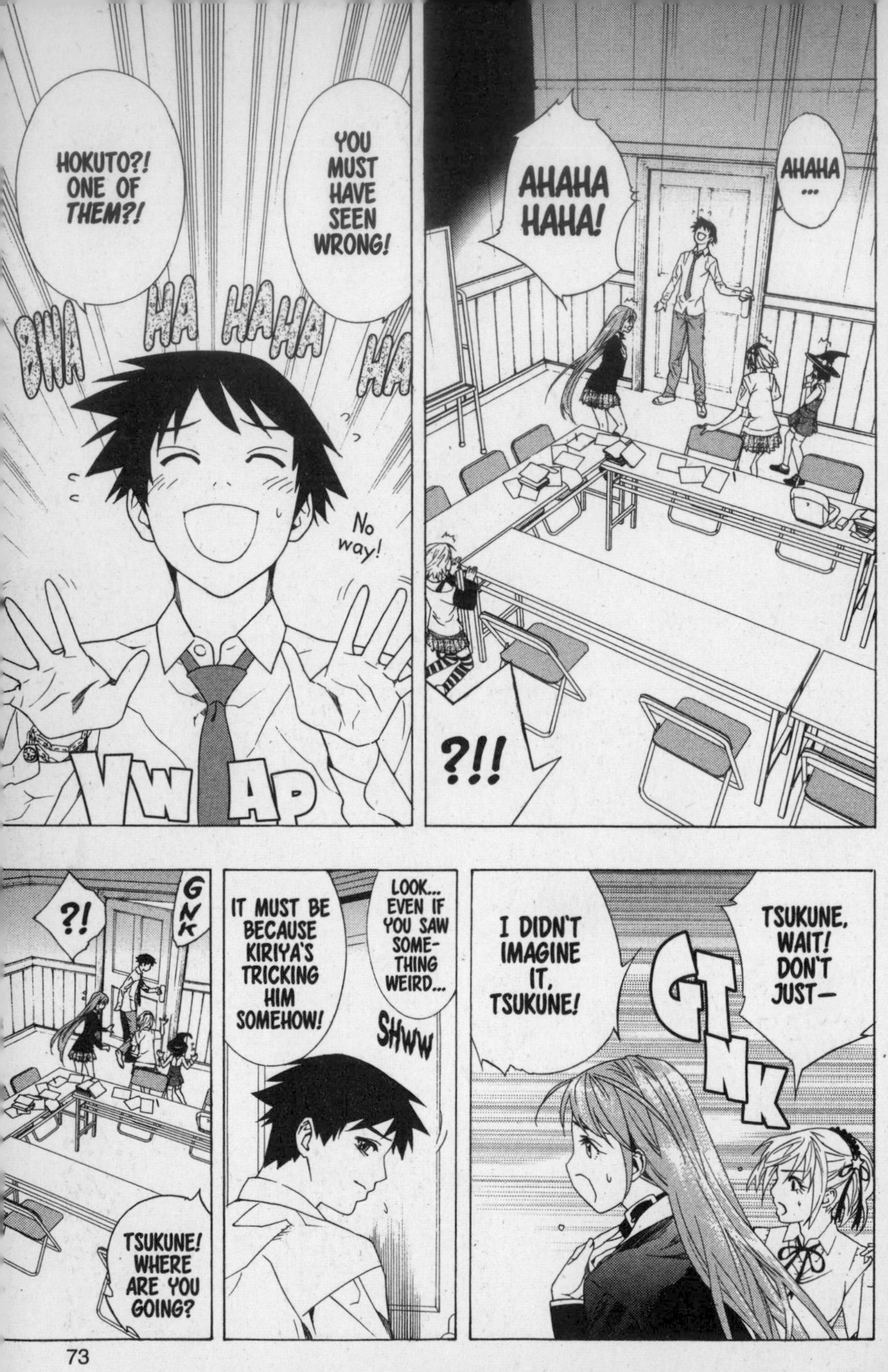
AHAHA...
AHAHA HAHA!
?!!
HOKUTO?! ONE OF THEM?!
YOU MUST HAVE SEEN WRONG!
BHA HA HAHA HA
No way!
VWAP
TSUKUNE, WAIT! DON'T JUST—
GTNK
I DIDN'T IMAGINE IT, TSUKUNE!
LOOK... EVEN IF YOU SAW SOMETHING WEIRD...
IT MUST BE BECAUSE KIRIYA'S TRICKING HIM SOMEHOW!
SHWW
GNK
?!
TSUKUNE! WHERE ARE YOU GOING?

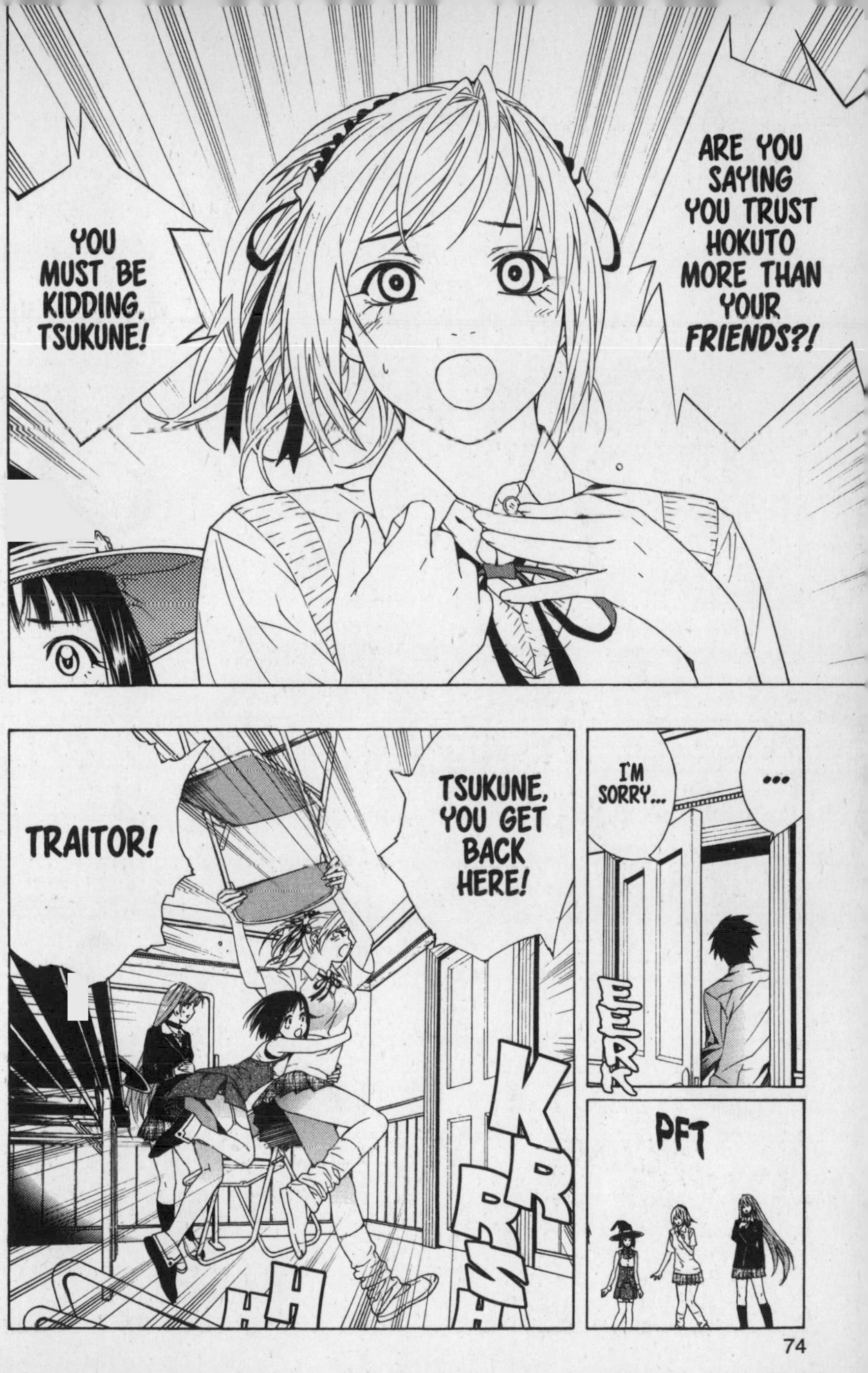
ARE YOU SAYING YOU TRUST HOKUTO MORE THAN YOUR FRIENDS?!
YOU MUST BE KIDDING, TSUKUNE!
...
I'M SORRY...
EERK
PFT
TSUKUNE, YOU GET BACK HERE!
TRAITOR!
KRRSSHH

READ THIS WAY

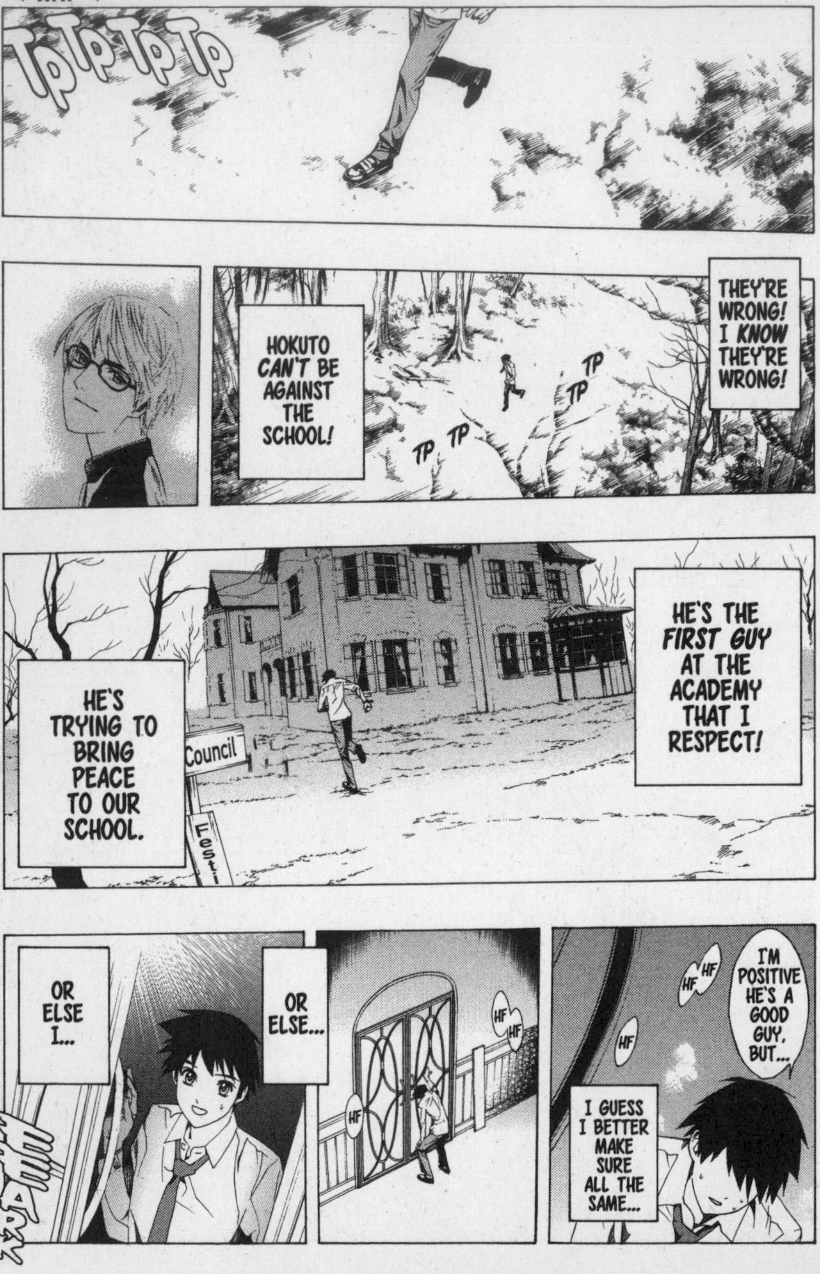
TpTpTpTp
THEY'RE WRONG! I KNOW THEY'RE WRONG!
TP TP
HOKUTO CAN'T BE AGAINST THE SCHOOL!
TP TP
HE'S THE FIRST GUY AT THE ACADEMY THAT I RESPECT!
HE'S TRYING TO BRING PEACE TO OUR SCHOOL.
Council
Festi
I'M POSITIVE HE'S A GOOD GUY, BUT...
HF HF
HF
I GUESS I BETTER MAKE SURE ALL THE SAME...
OR ELSE...
HF HF
HF
OR ELSE I...

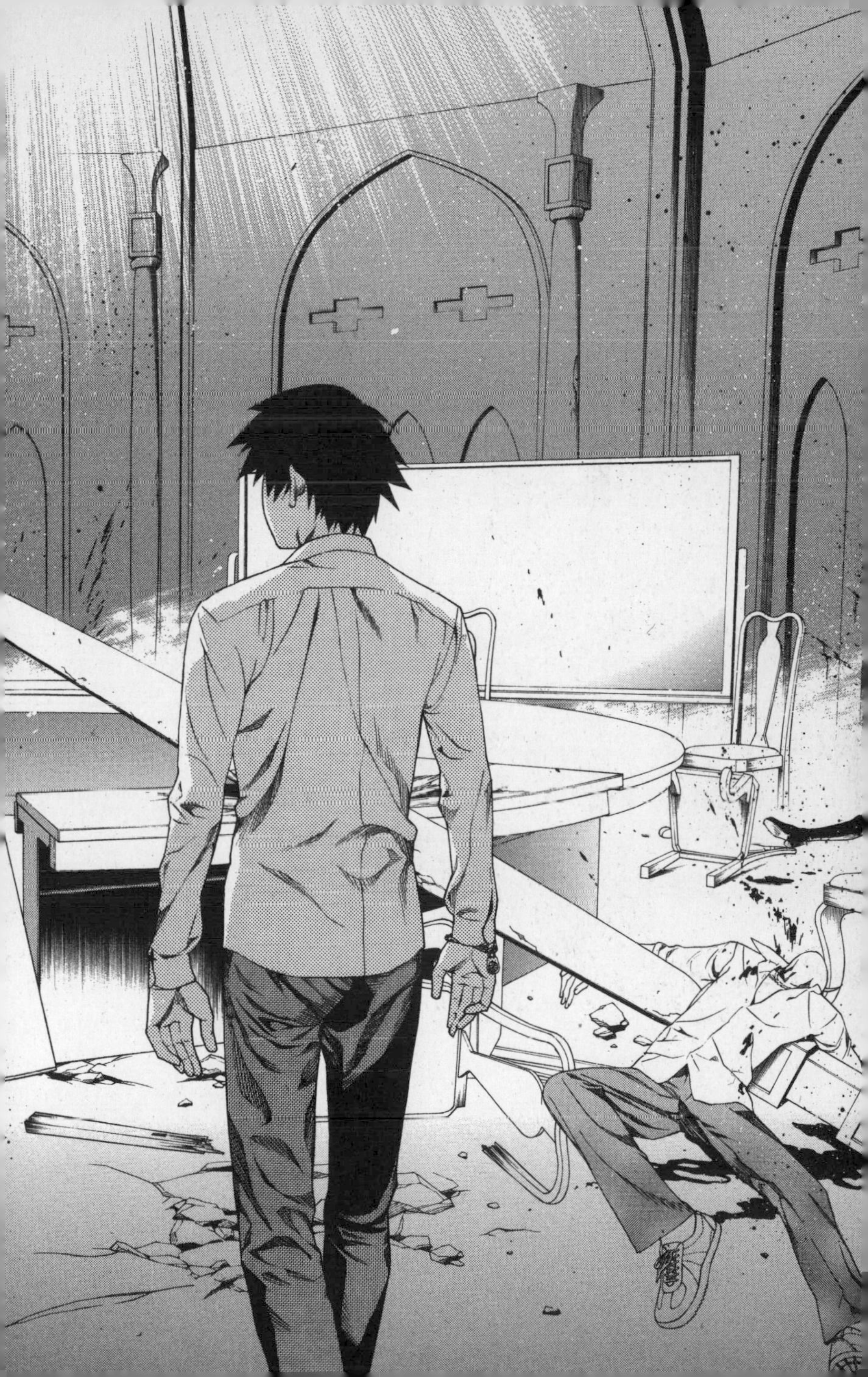

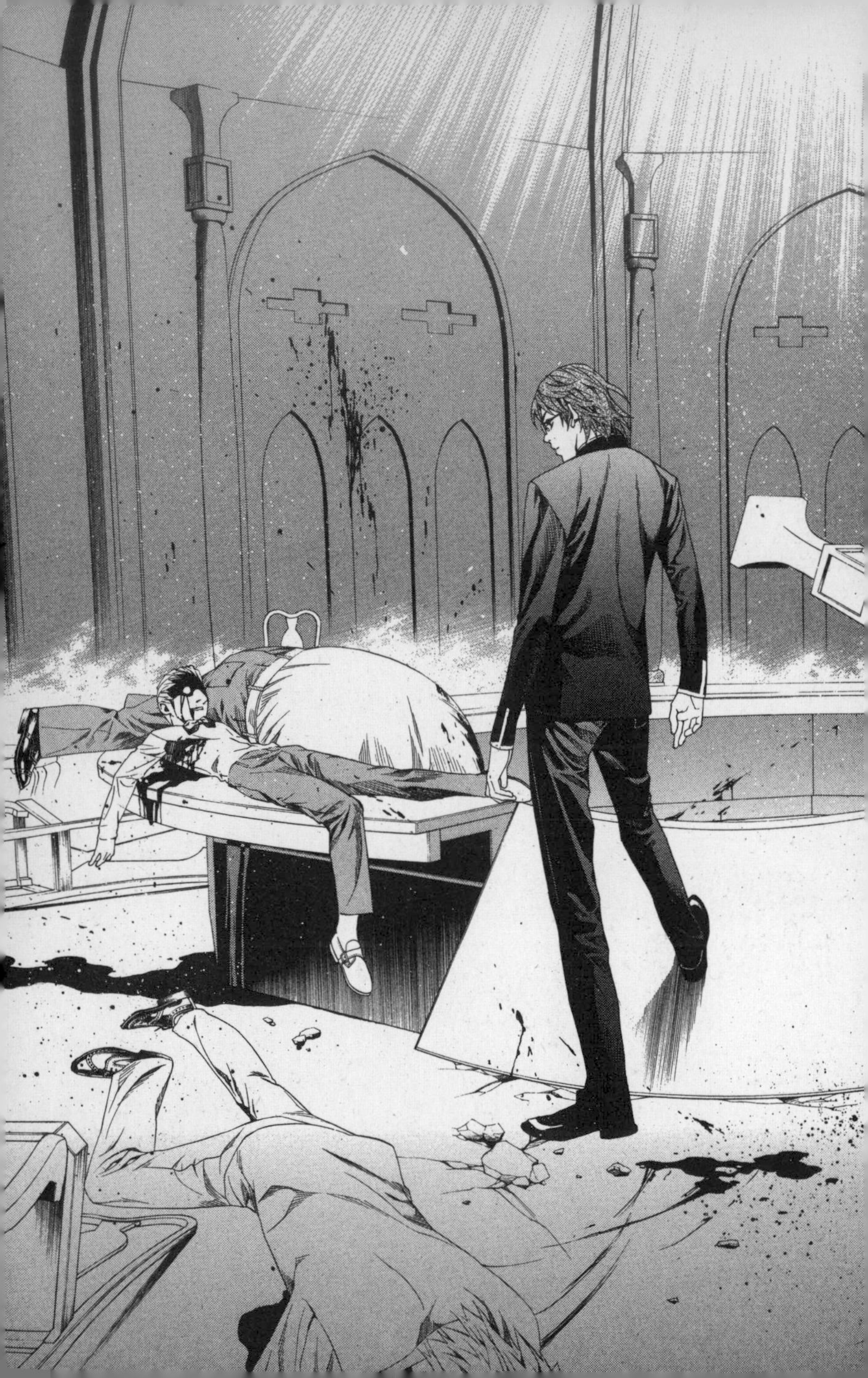

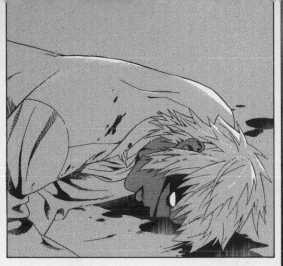

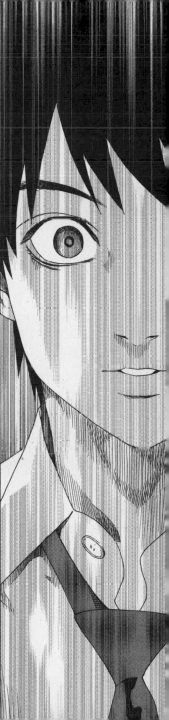

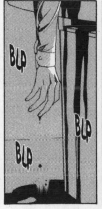

BLP

BLP

BLP

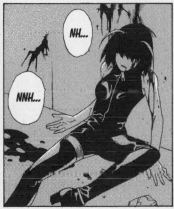

NH...

NNH...

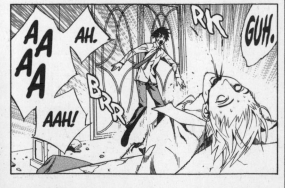

AAAA

AH.

RK

GUH.

BRR

AAH!

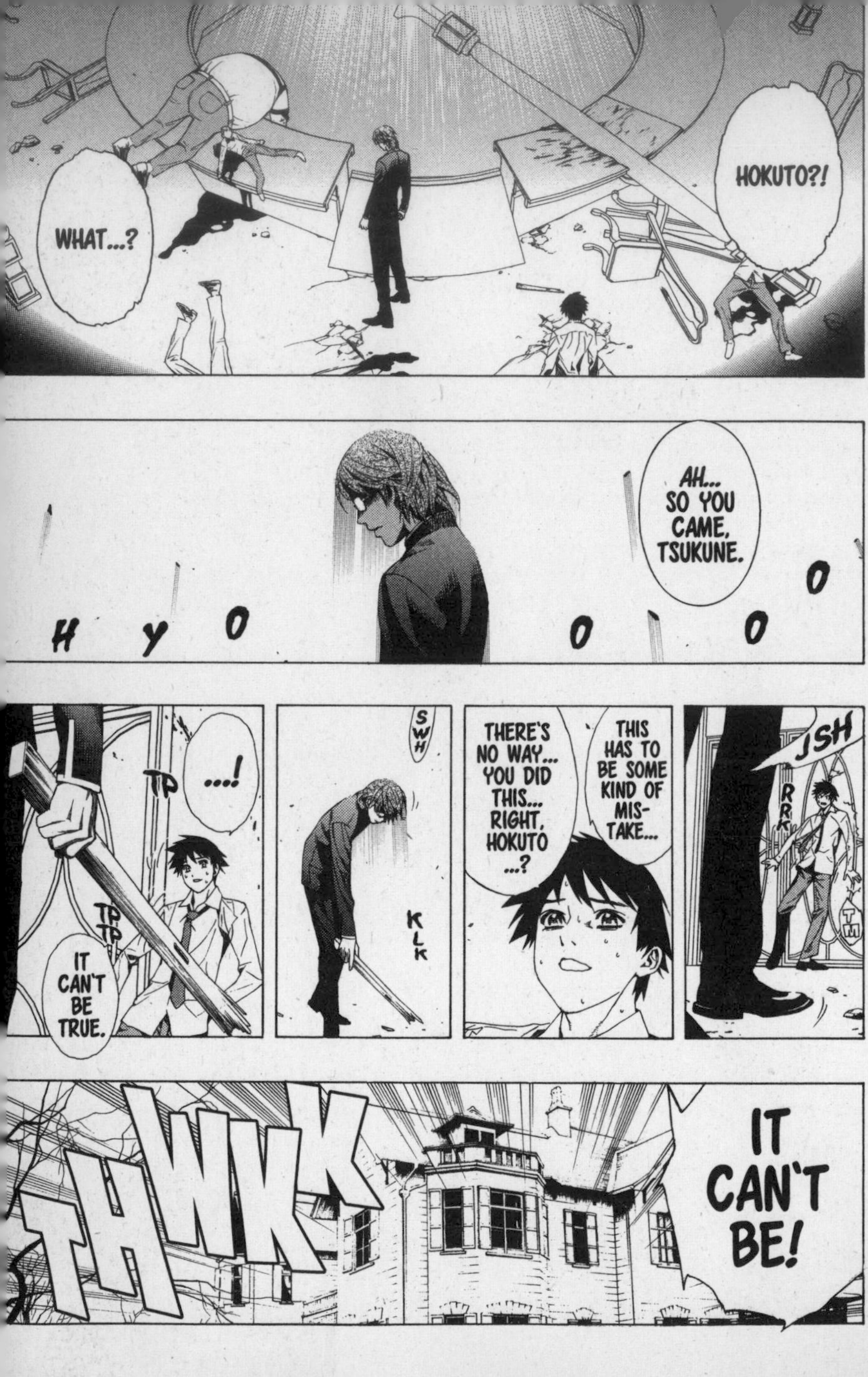
HOKUTO?!
WHAT...?
AH... SO YOU CAME, TSUKUNE.
HYOOOO
JSH
RRK
THIS HAS TO BE SOME KIND OF MIS-TAKE...
THERE'S NO WAY... YOU DID THIS... RIGHT, HOKUTO ...?
SWH
KLK
...!
TP
TP TP
IT CAN'T BE TRUE.
IT CAN'T BE!
THWKK

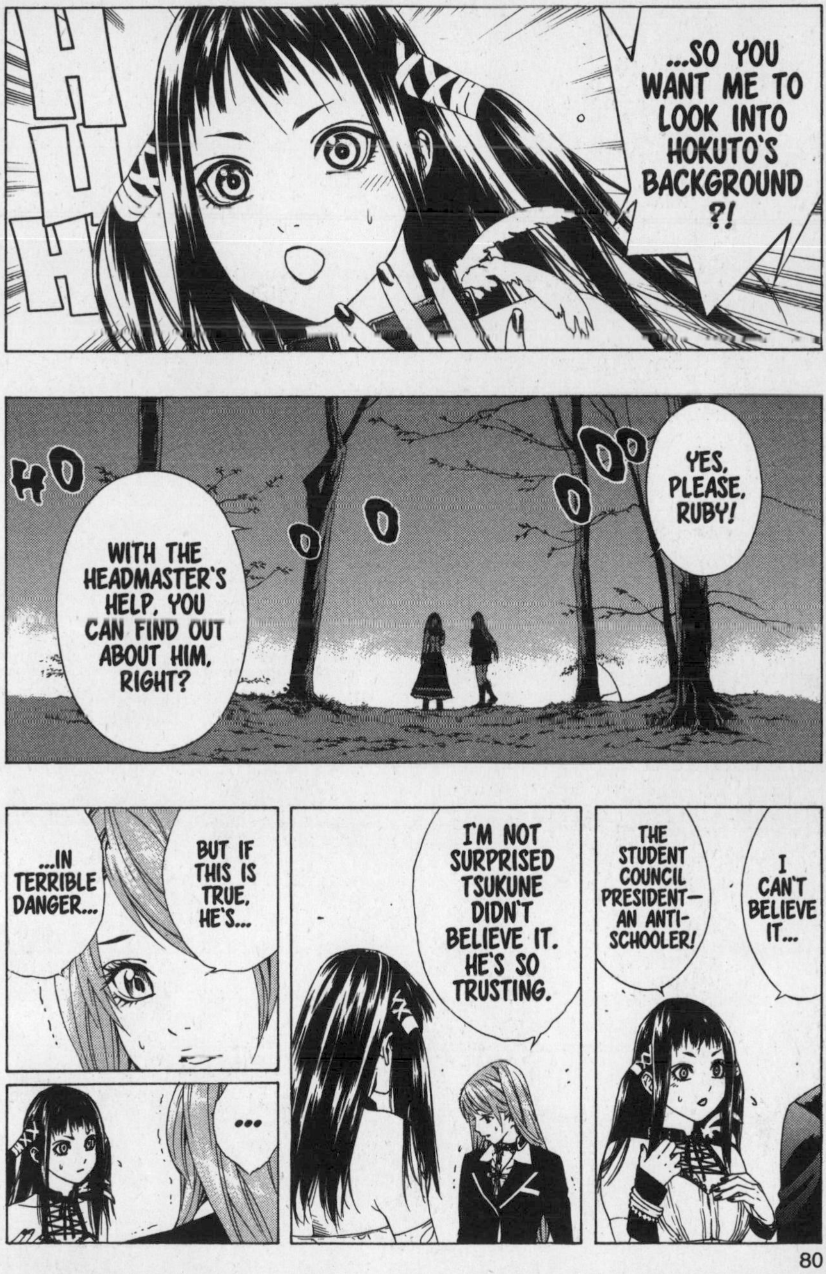
...SO YOU WANT ME TO LOOK INTO HOKUTO'S BACKGROUND?!
HUHH
YES, PLEASE, RUBY!
HOOOOOO
WITH THE HEADMASTER'S HELP, YOU CAN FIND OUT ABOUT HIM, RIGHT?
I CAN'T BELIEVE IT...
THE STUDENT COUNCIL PRESIDENT—AN ANTI-SCHOOLER!
I'M NOT SURPRISED TSUKUNE DIDN'T BELIEVE IT. HE'S SO TRUSTING.
BUT IF THIS IS TRUE, HE'S...
...IN TERRIBLE DANGER...
...

READ THIS WAY

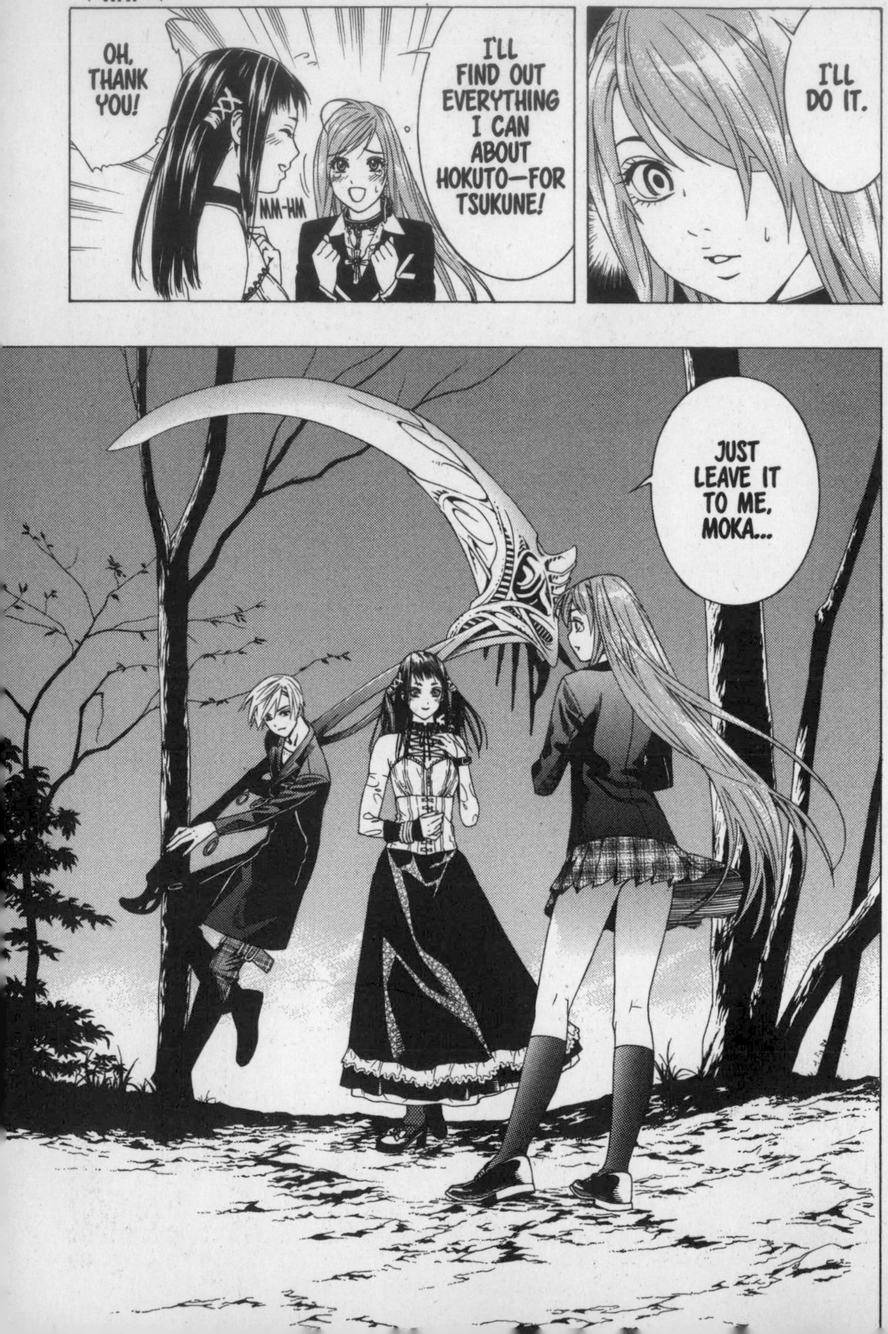
I'LL DO IT.
I'LL FIND OUT EVERYTHING I CAN ABOUT HOKUTO—FOR TSUKUNE!
OH, THANK YOU!
MM-HM
JUST LEAVE IT TO ME, MOKA...

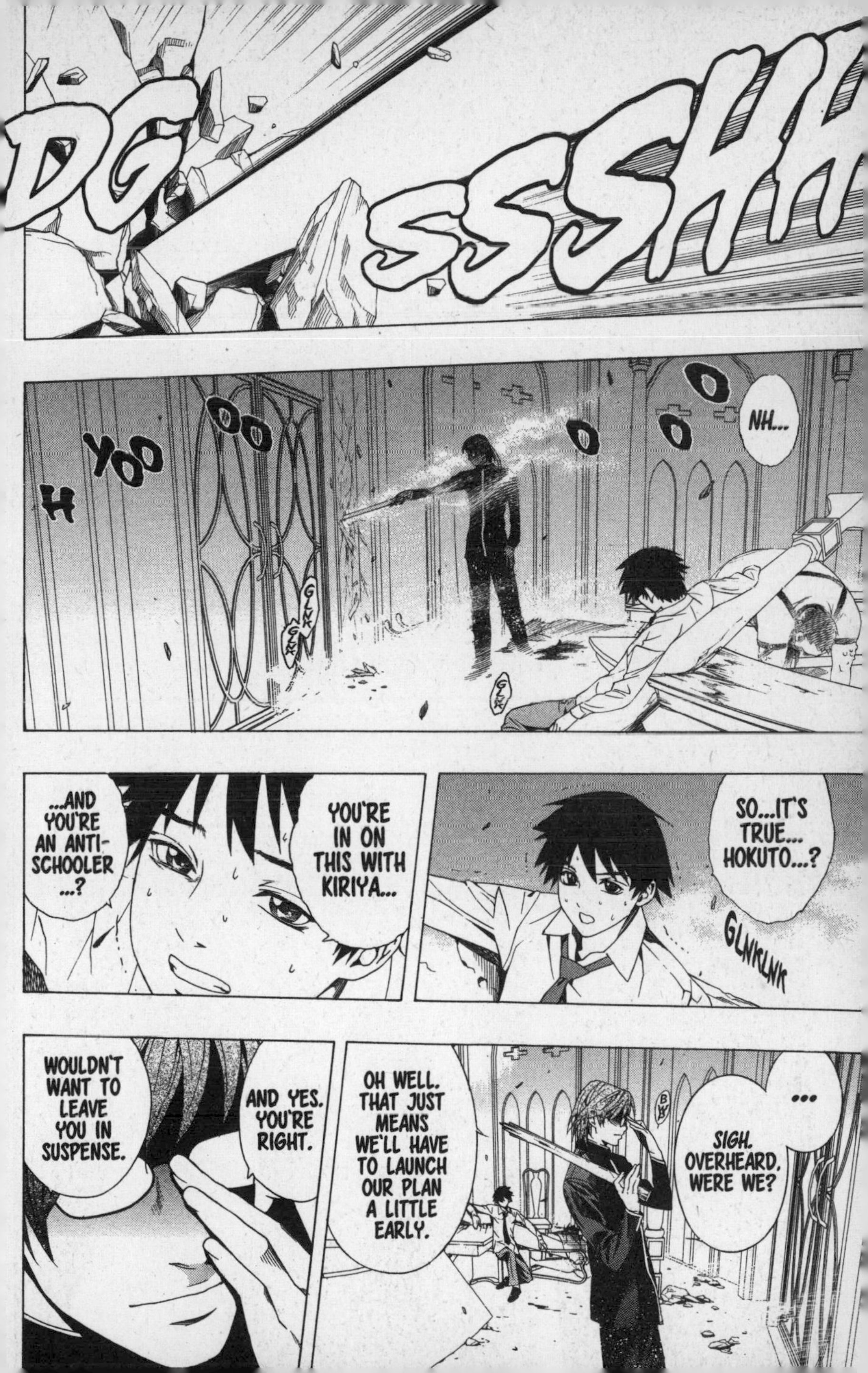
DG
SSSHH
NH...
HYOOOOOOO
GLNK
GLNK
GLNK
SO...IT'S TRUE... HOKUTO...?
GLNKLNK
YOU'RE IN ON THIS WITH KIRIYA...
...AND YOU'RE AN ANTI-SCHOOLER ...?
...
SIGH. OVERHEARD, WERE WE?
BW
OH WELL. THAT JUST MEANS WE'LL HAVE TO LAUNCH OUR PLAN A LITTLE EARLY.
AND YES. YOU'RE RIGHT.
WOULDN'T WANT TO LEAVE YOU IN SUSPENSE.

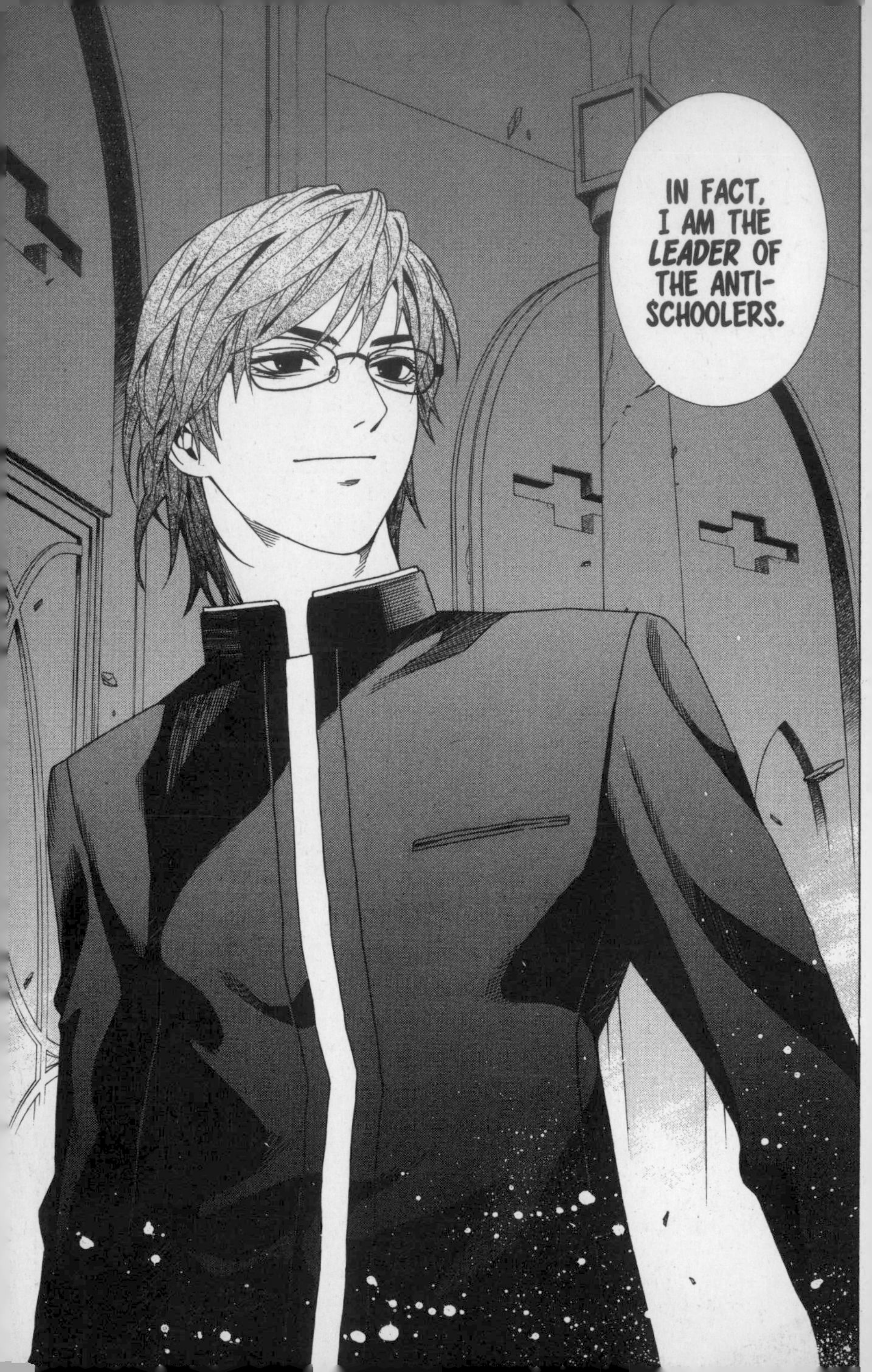
IN FACT, I AM THE *LEADER* OF THE ANTI-SCHOOLERS.

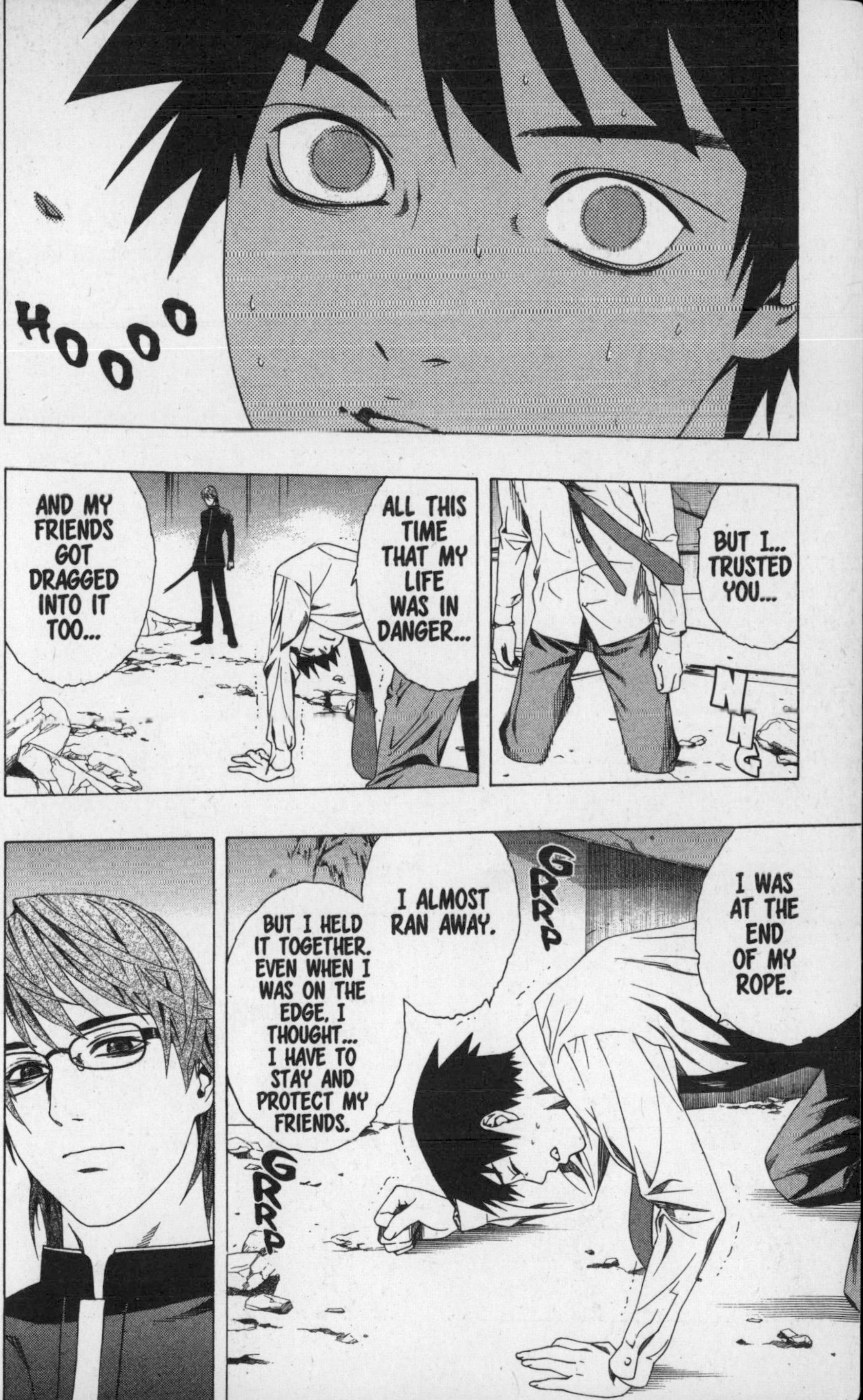
HOOOO
BUT I... TRUSTED YOU...
NNG
ALL THIS TIME THAT MY LIFE WAS IN DANGER...
AND MY FRIENDS GOT DRAGGED INTO IT TOO...
I WAS AT THE END OF MY ROPE.
GRRP
I ALMOST RAN AWAY.
BUT I HELD IT TOGETHER. EVEN WHEN I WAS ON THE EDGE, I THOUGHT... I HAVE TO STAY AND PROTECT MY FRIENDS.
GRRP

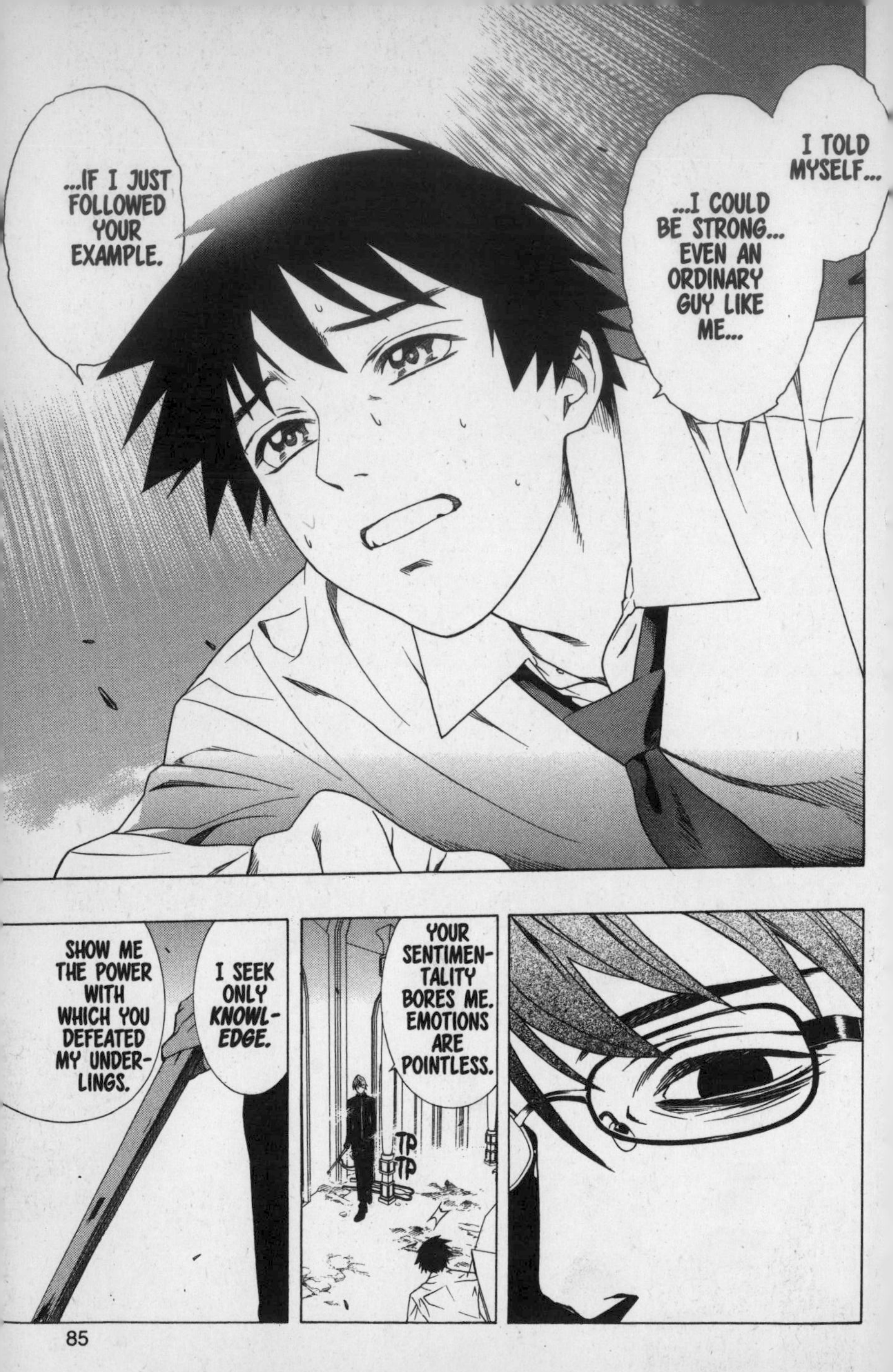
I TOLD MYSELF...
...I COULD BE STRONG... EVEN AN ORDINARY GUY LIKE ME...
...IF I JUST FOLLOWED YOUR EXAMPLE.
YOUR SENTIMENTALITY BORES ME. EMOTIONS ARE POINTLESS.
TP TP
I SEEK ONLY KNOWLEDGE.
SHOW ME THE POWER WITH WHICH YOU DEFEATED MY UNDERLINGS.

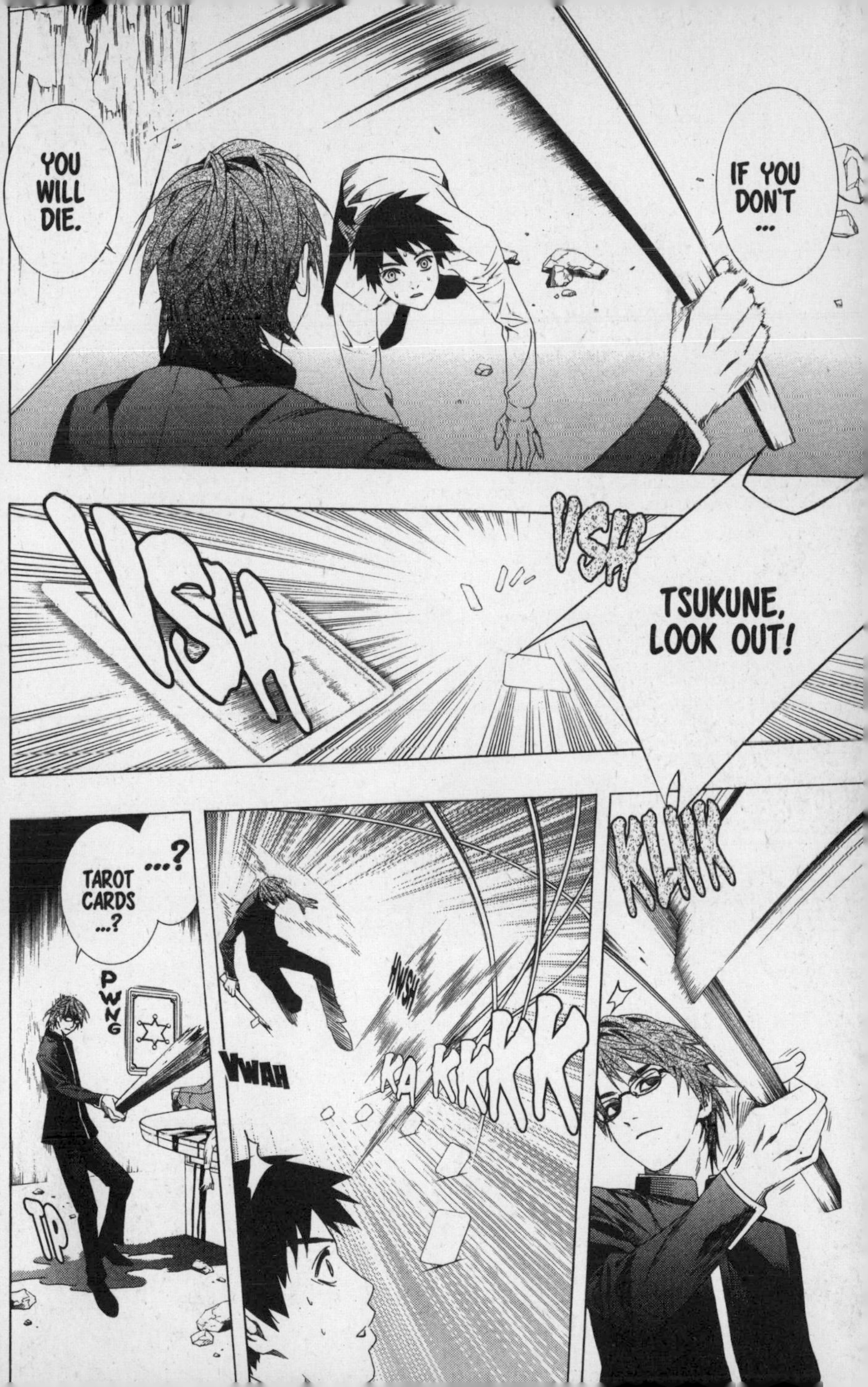
IF YOU DON'T ...
YOU WILL DIE.
VSH
TSUKUNE, LOOK OUT!
VSH
KLINK
HWSH
KA KKKKK
VWAH
...?
TAROT CARDS ...?
PWNG
TIP

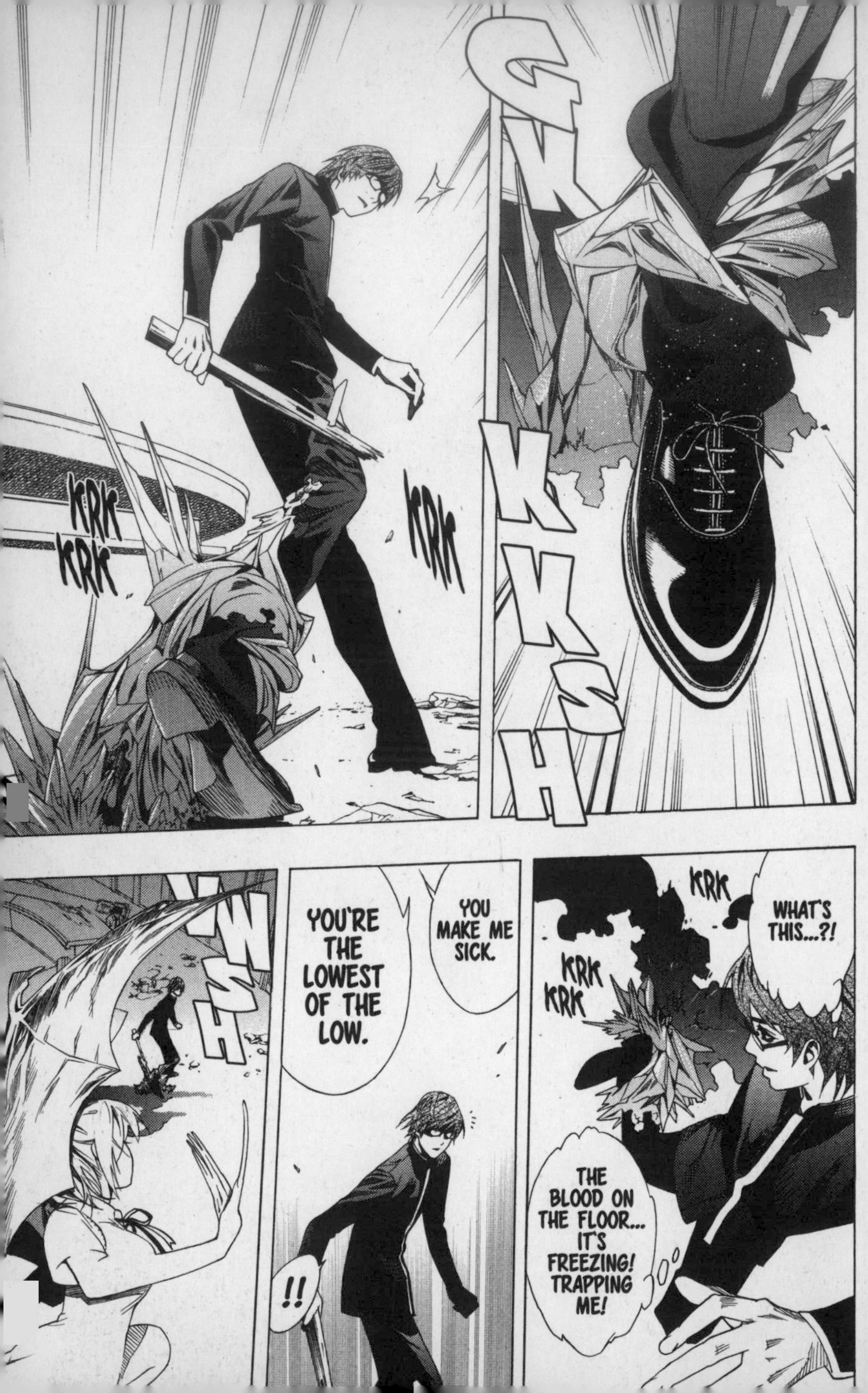
GNKKSH
KRK KRK
KRK
KRK
WHAT'S THIS...?!
KRK KRK
THE BLOOD ON THE FLOOR... IT'S FREEZING! TRAPPING ME!
YOU MAKE ME SICK.
YOU'RE THE LOWEST OF THE LOW.
!!
VWSH

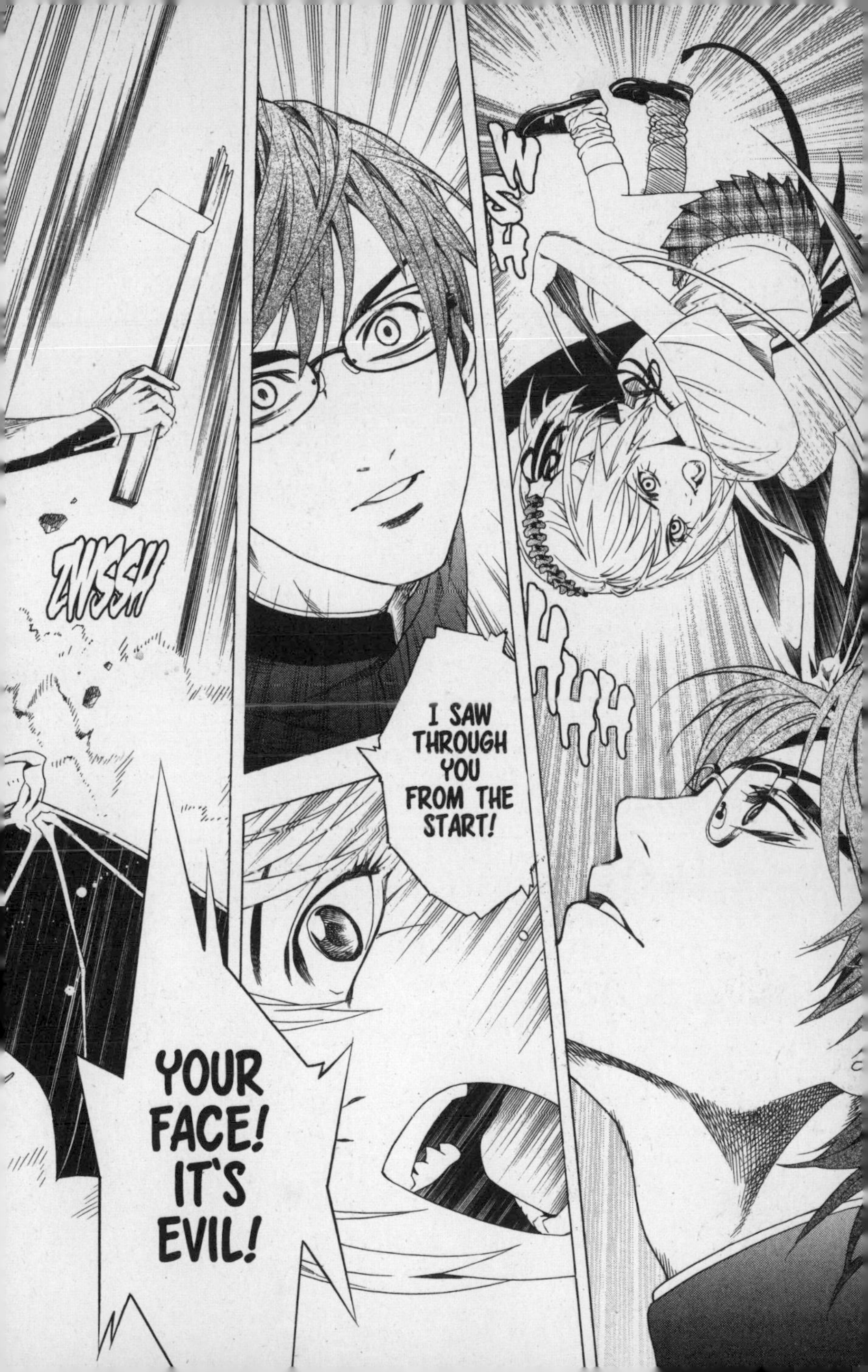
WSH
HHHH
I SAW THROUGH YOU FROM THE START!
YOUR FACE! IT'S EVIL!
ZWSSH

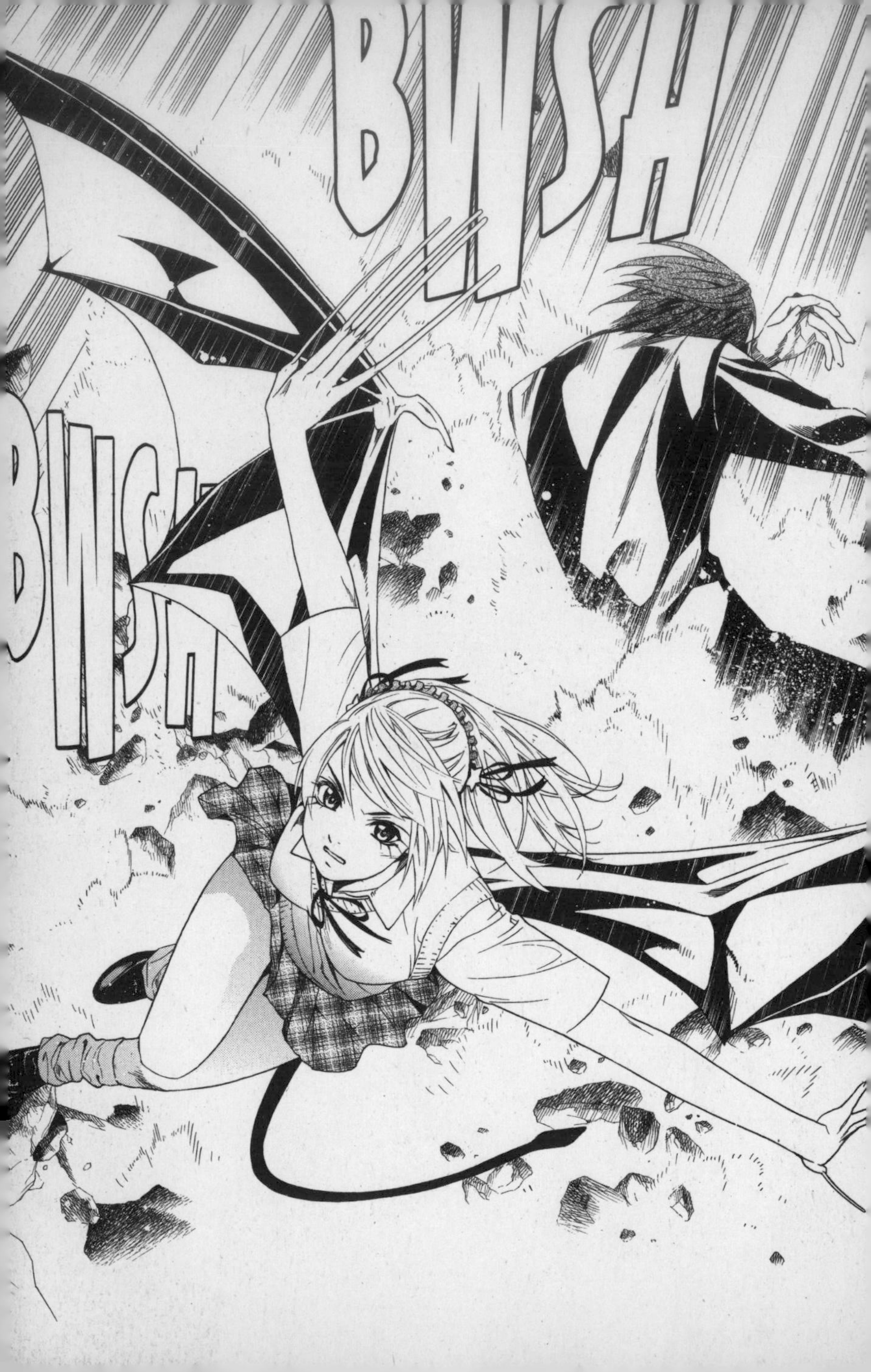
BWSH
BWSH

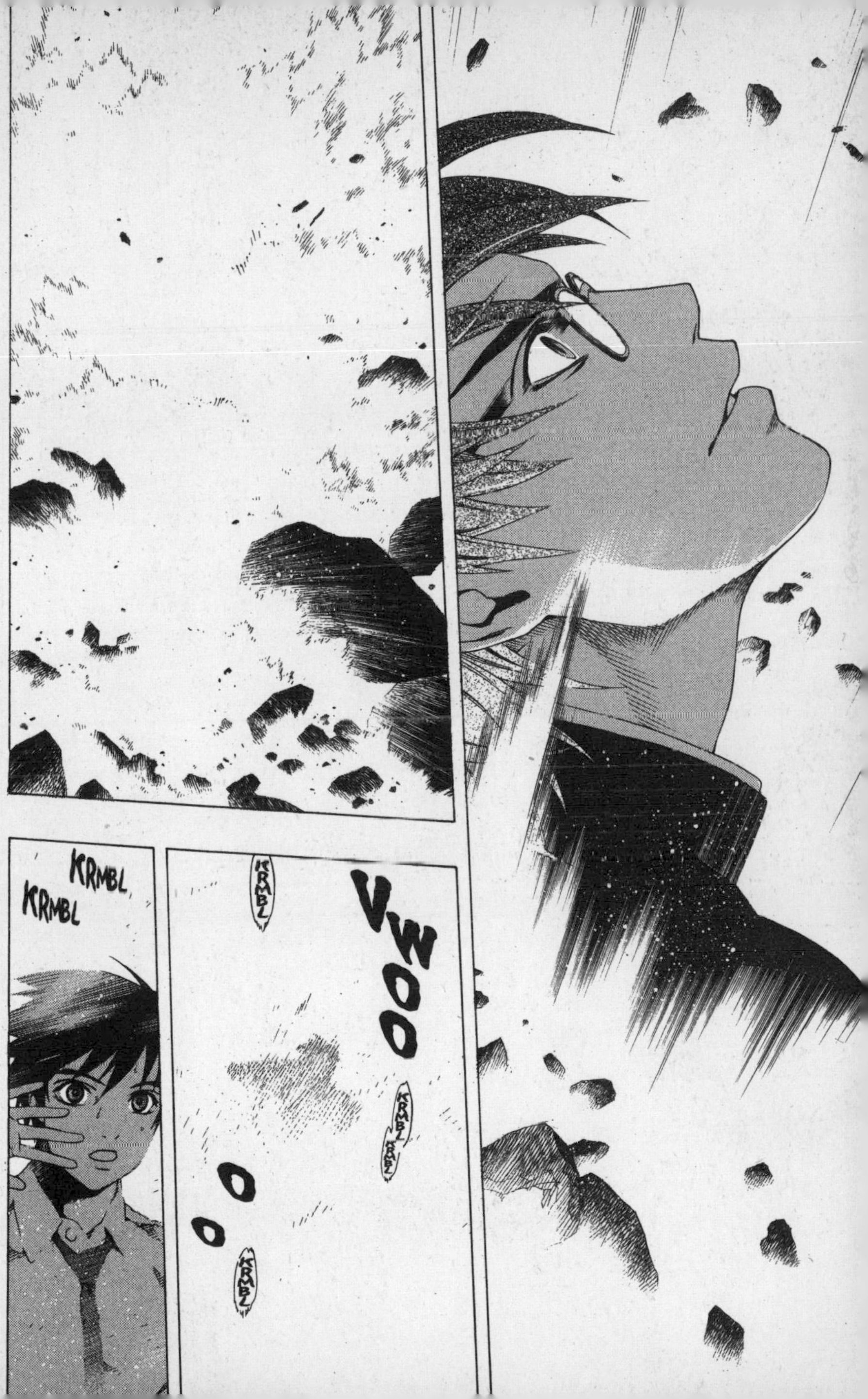
KRMBL
VWOOOO
KRMBL
KRMBL
KRMBL
KRMBL
KRMBL

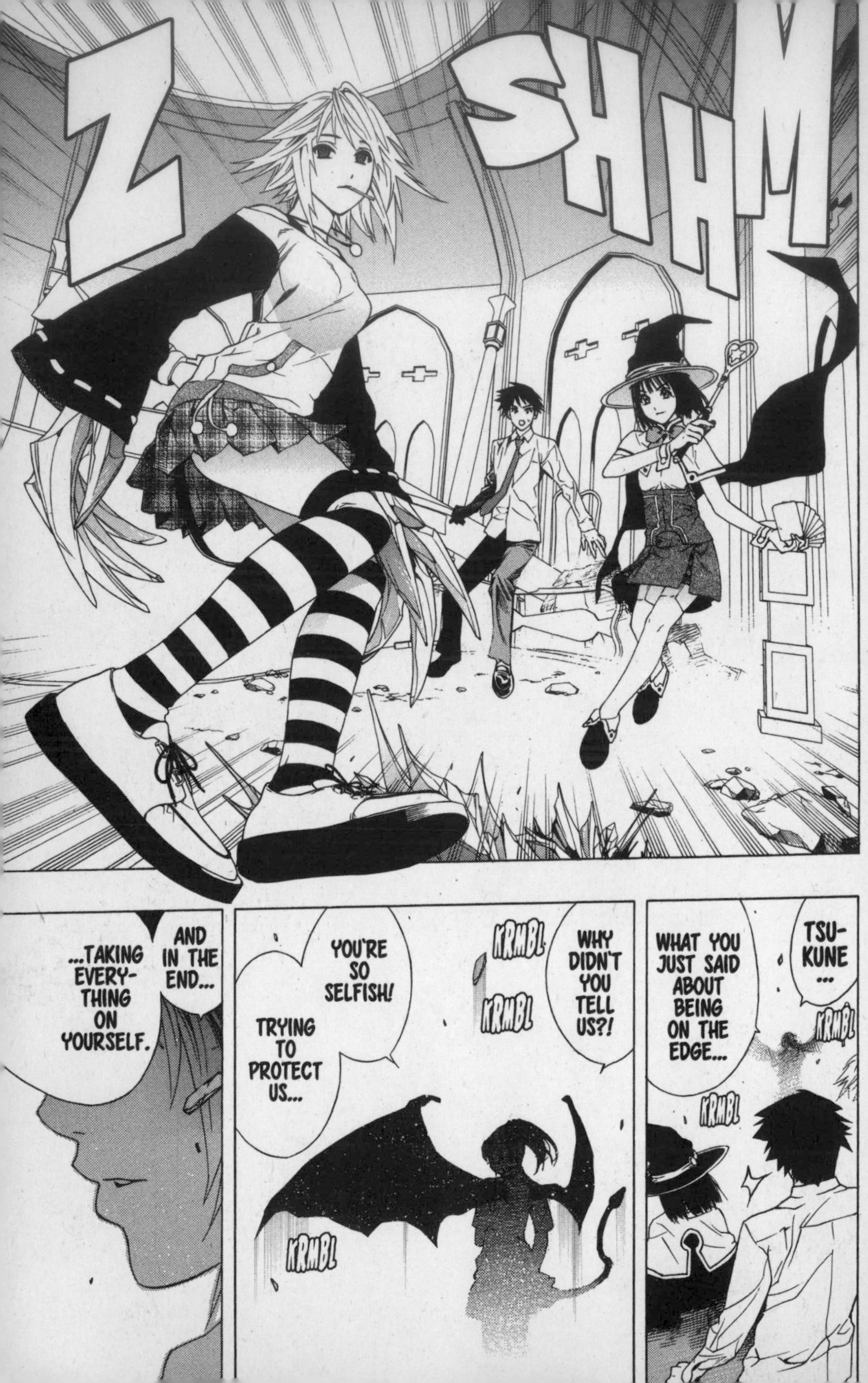
ZSHM
TSU-KUNE...
KRMBL
WHAT YOU JUST SAID ABOUT BEING ON THE EDGE...
KRMBL
KRMBL
WHY DIDN'T YOU TELL US?!
KRMBL
YOU'RE SO SELFISH!
TRYING TO PROTECT US...
KRMBL
AND IN THE END...
...TAKING EVERY-THING ON YOURSELF.

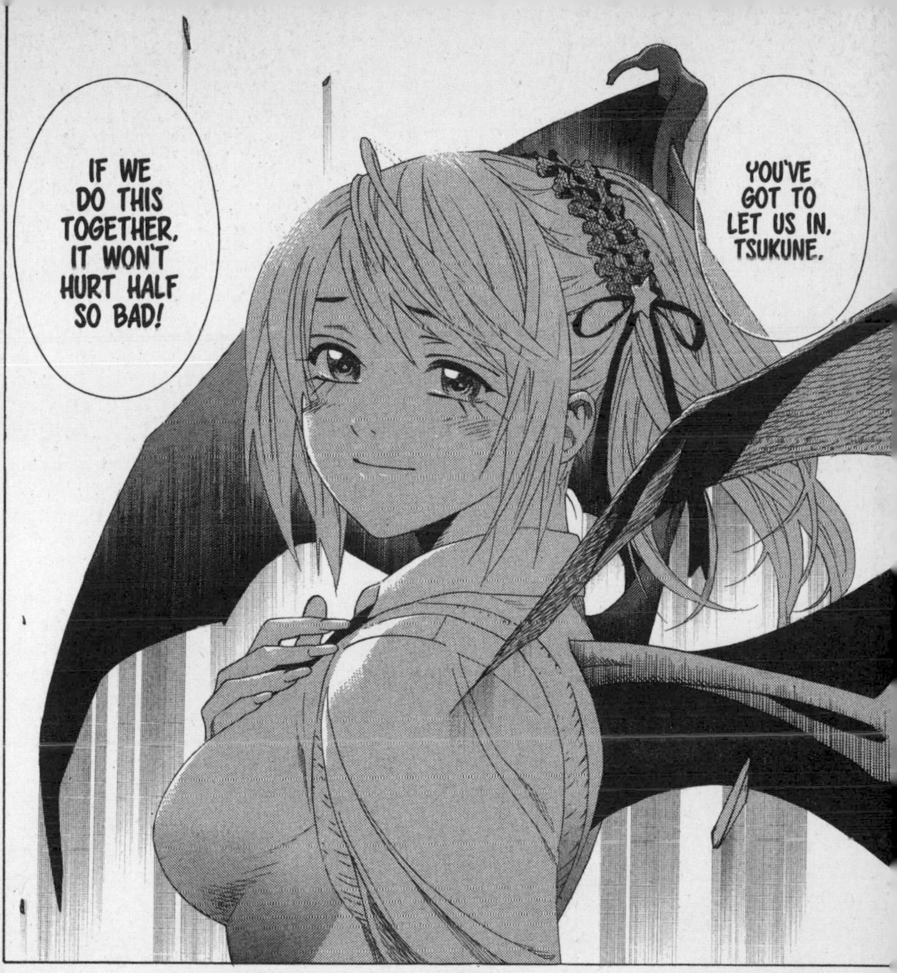
YOU'VE GOT TO LET US IN, TSUKUNE.
IF WE DO THIS TOGETHER, IT WON'T HURT HALF SO BAD!

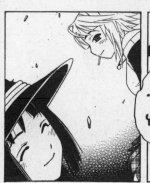

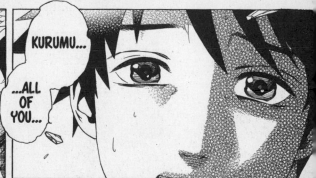

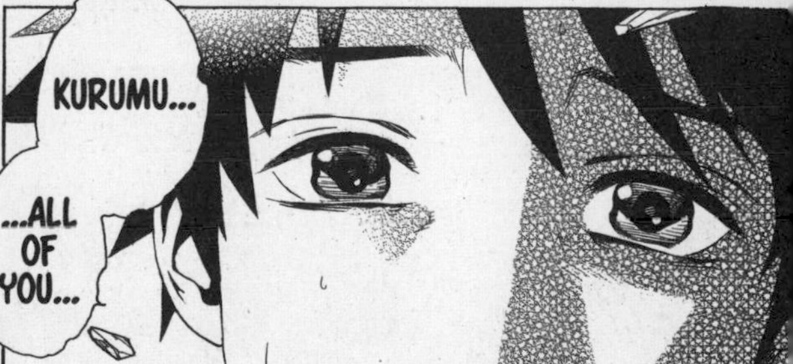
KURUMU...
...ALL OF YOU...

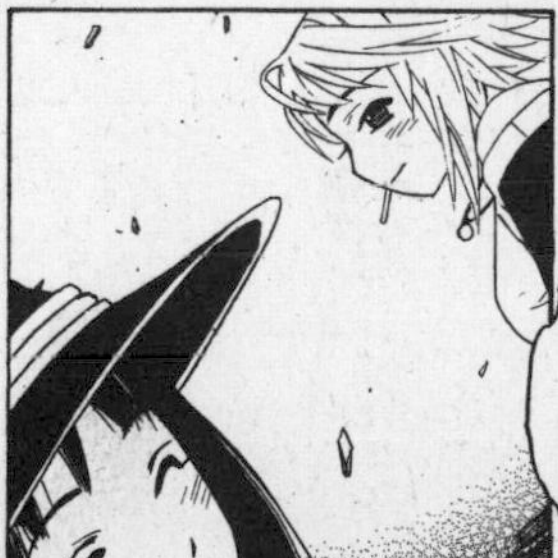

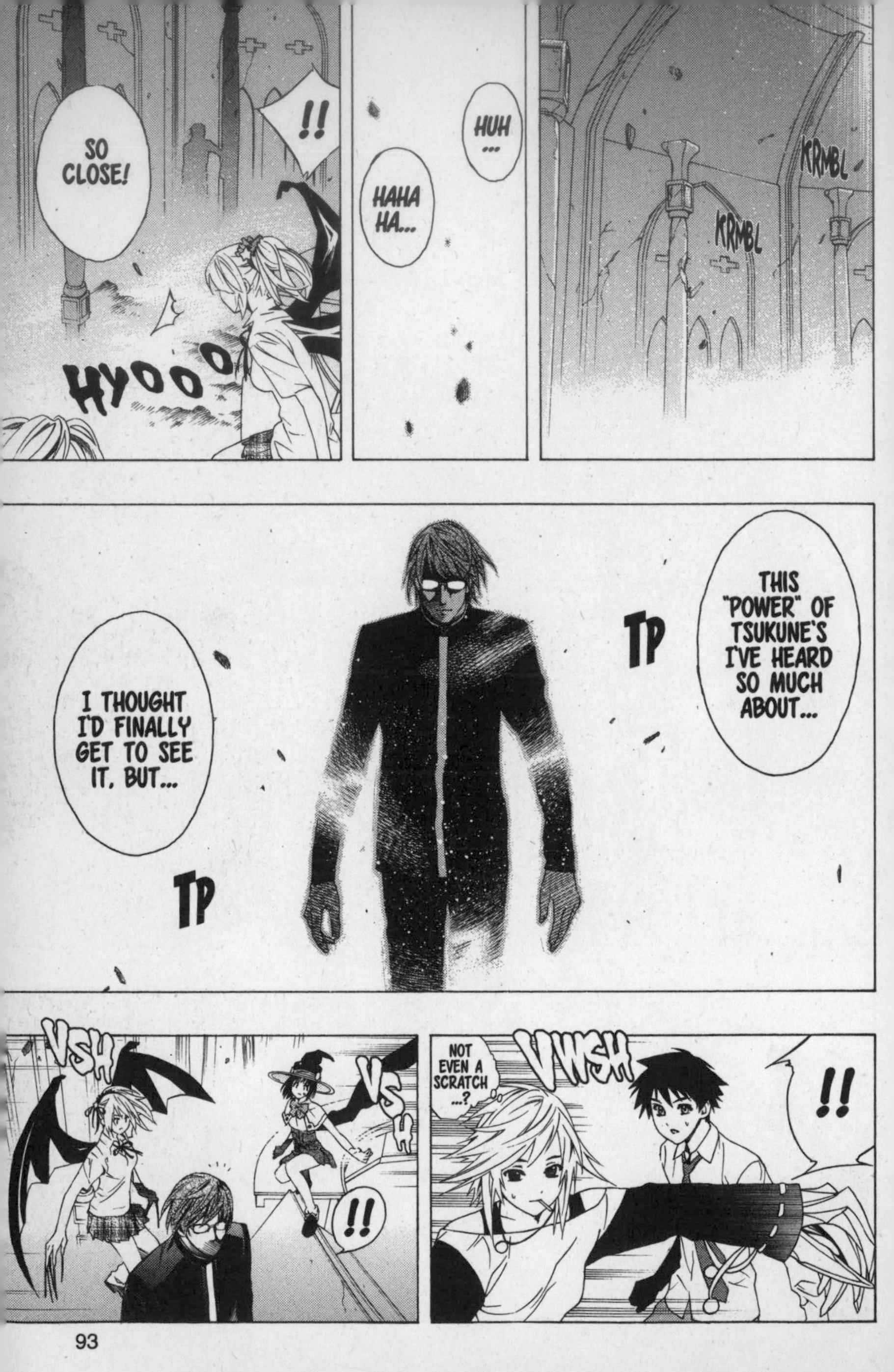
KRMBL
KRMBL
HUH ...
HAHA HA...
!!
SO CLOSE!
HYOOO
THIS "POWER" OF TSUKUNE'S I'VE HEARD SO MUCH ABOUT...
TP
I THOUGHT I'D FINALLY GET TO SEE IT, BUT...
TP
!!
VWSH
NOT EVEN A SCRATCH ...?
VSH
!!
VSH

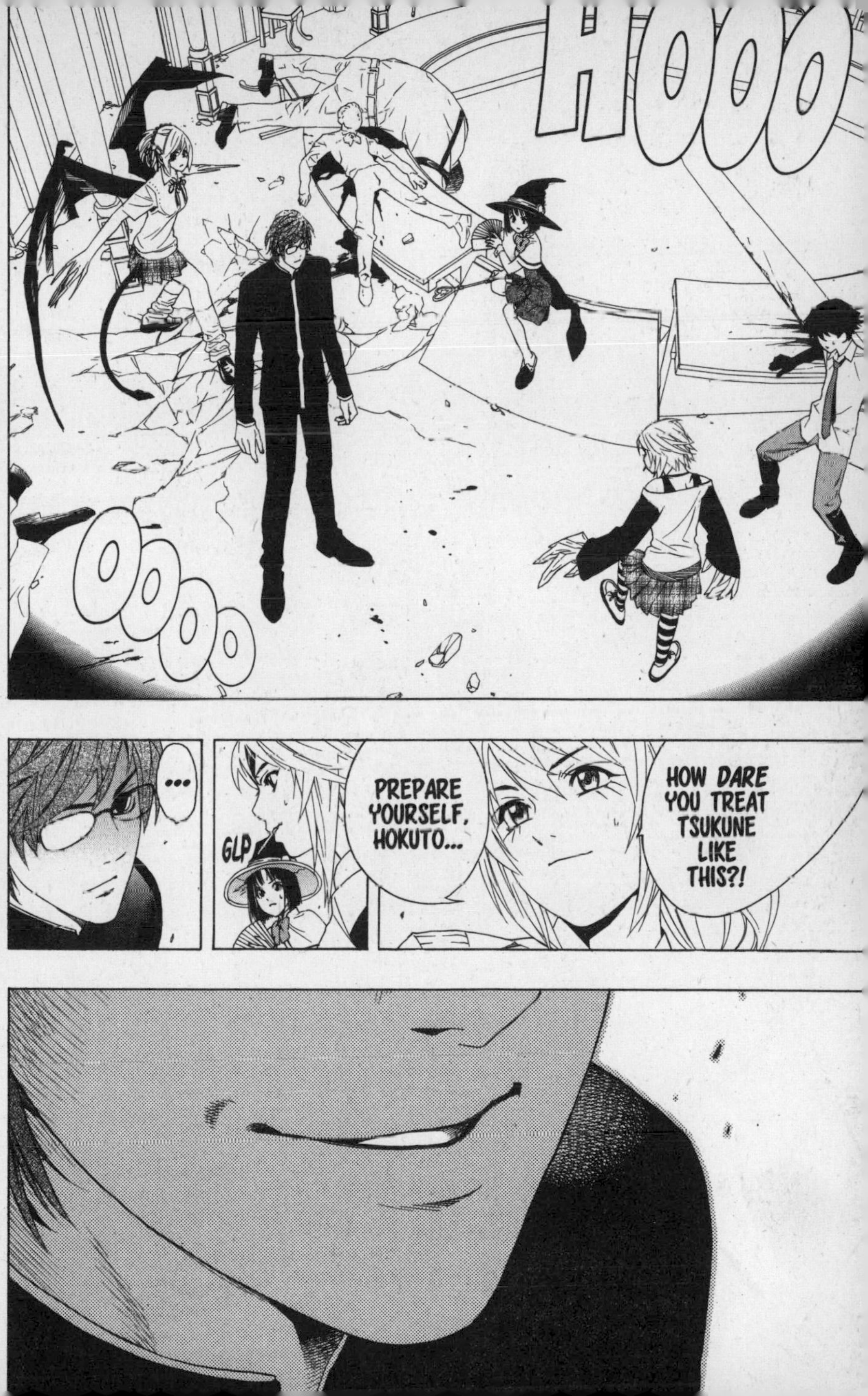
HOOO
OOOO
HOW DARE YOU TREAT TSUKUNE LIKE THIS?!
PREPARE YOURSELF, HOKUTO...
GLP
...

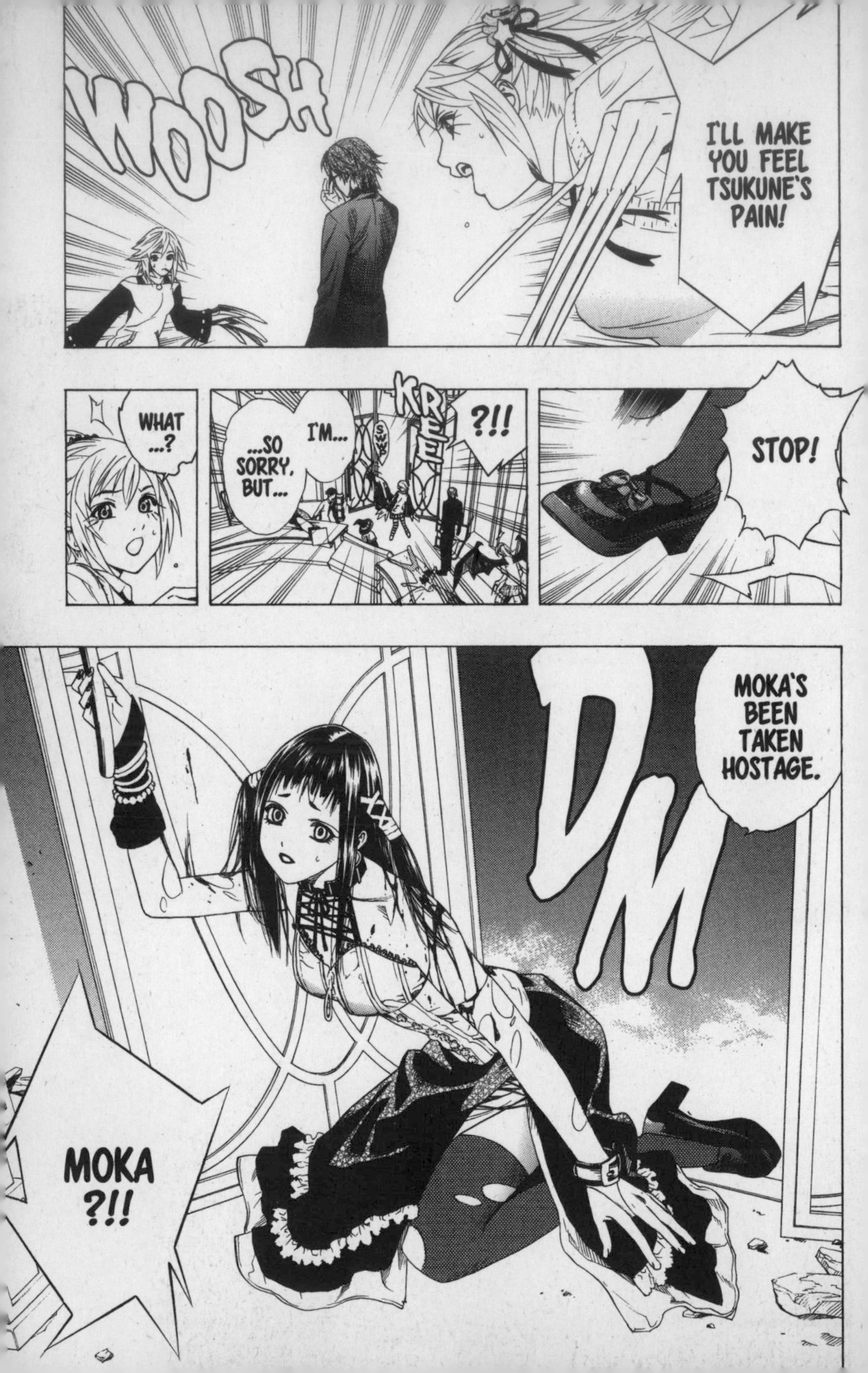
WOOSH
I'LL MAKE YOU FEEL TSUKUNE'S PAIN!
STOP!
?!!
KREE
I'M...
...SO SORRY, BUT...
WHAT ...?
MOKA'S BEEN TAKEN HOSTAGE.
DM
MOKA ?!!

31: True Colors

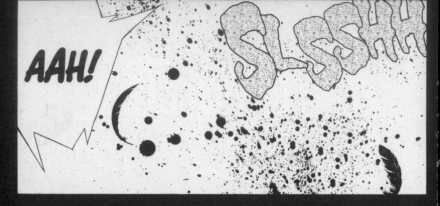

AAH!

SLSSHH

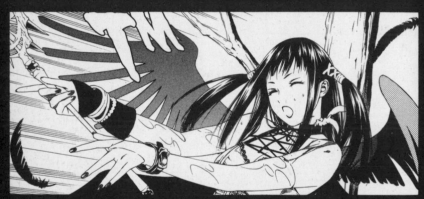

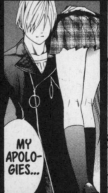

MY APOLO-GIES...

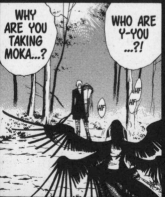

WHY ARE YOU TAKING MOKA...?

WHO ARE Y-YOU ...?!

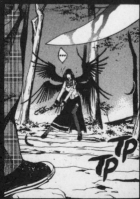

97

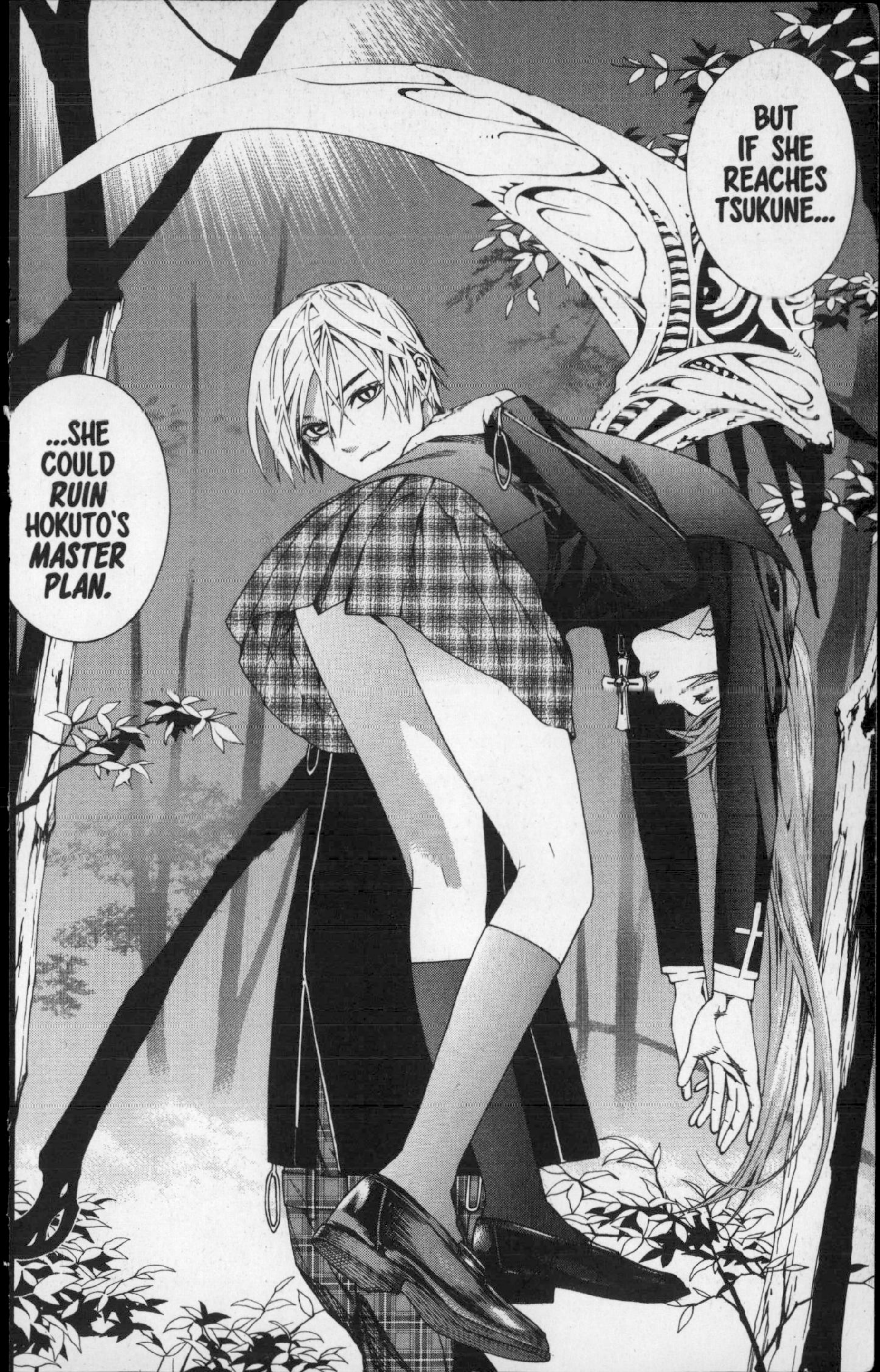
BUT IF SHE REACHES TSUKUNE...
...SHE COULD RUIN HOKUTO'S MASTER PLAN.

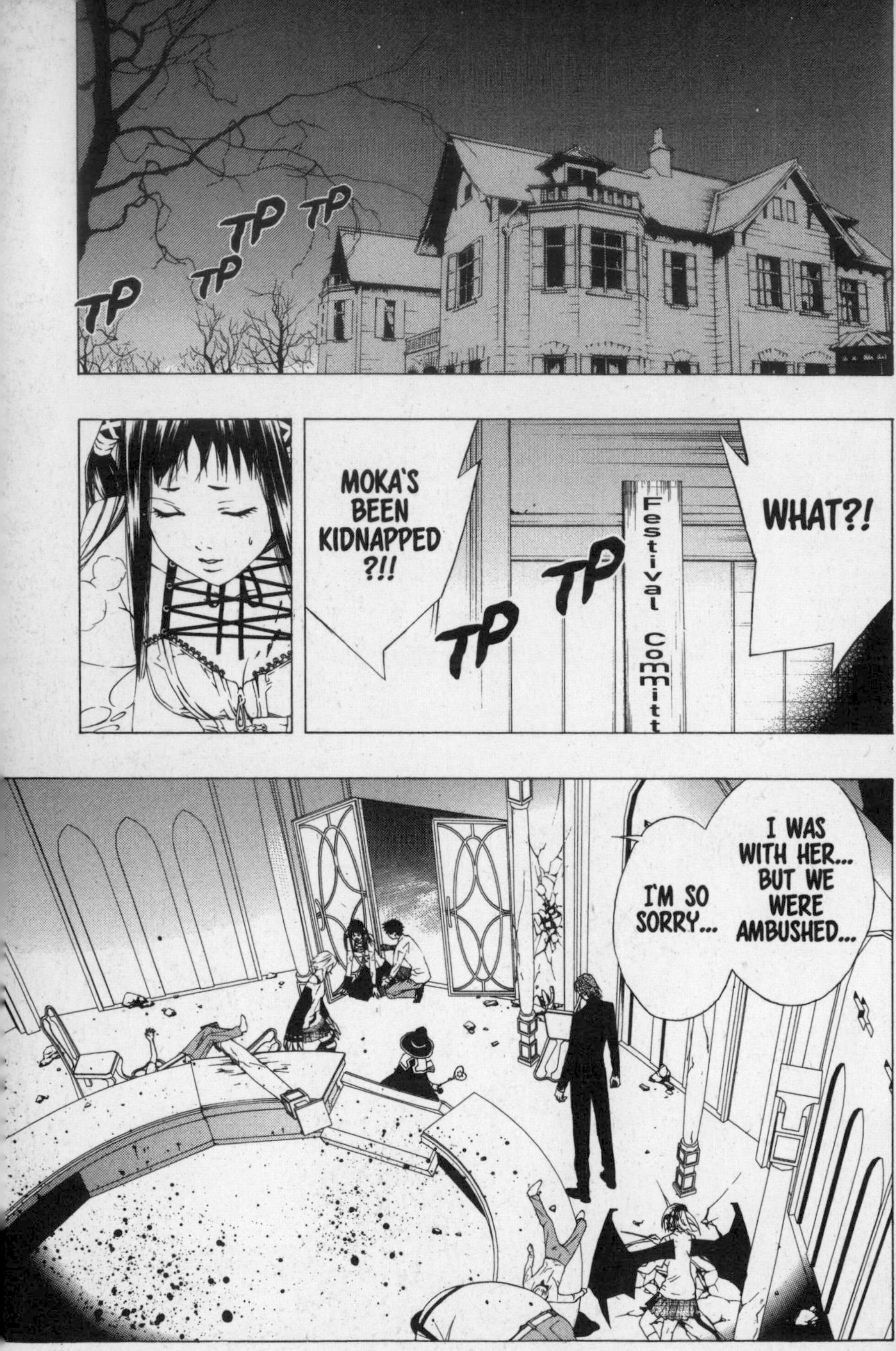
TP TP TP TP TP
WHAT?!
Festival Committ
TP TP
MOKA'S BEEN KIDNAPPED?!!
I WAS WITH HER... BUT WE WERE AMBUSHED...
I'M SO SORRY...

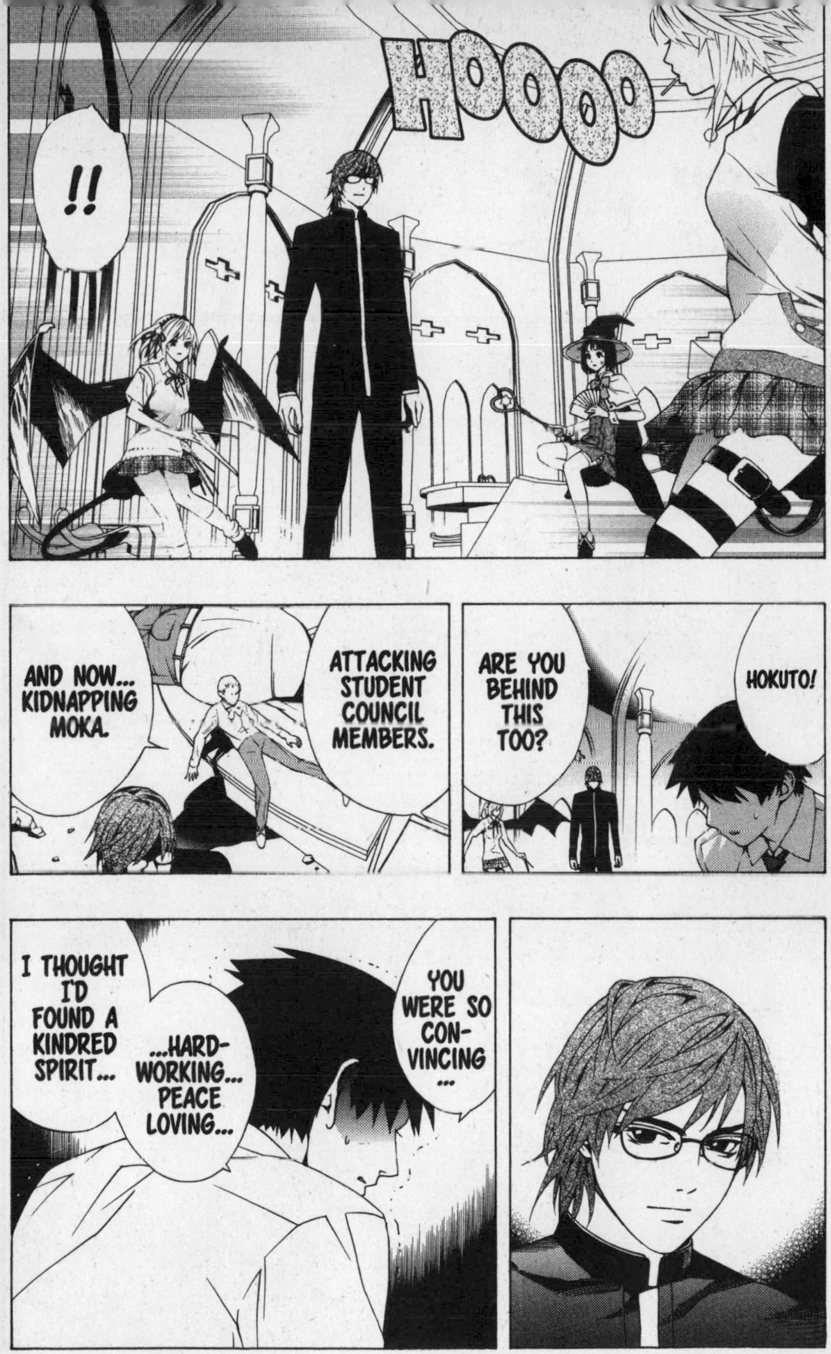
HOOOO
!!
HOKUTO!
ARE YOU BEHIND THIS TOO?
ATTACKING STUDENT COUNCIL MEMBERS.
AND NOW... KIDNAPPING MOKA.
YOU WERE SO CON-VINCING ...
...HARD-WORKING... PEACE LOVING...
I THOUGHT I'D FOUND A KINDRED SPIRIT...

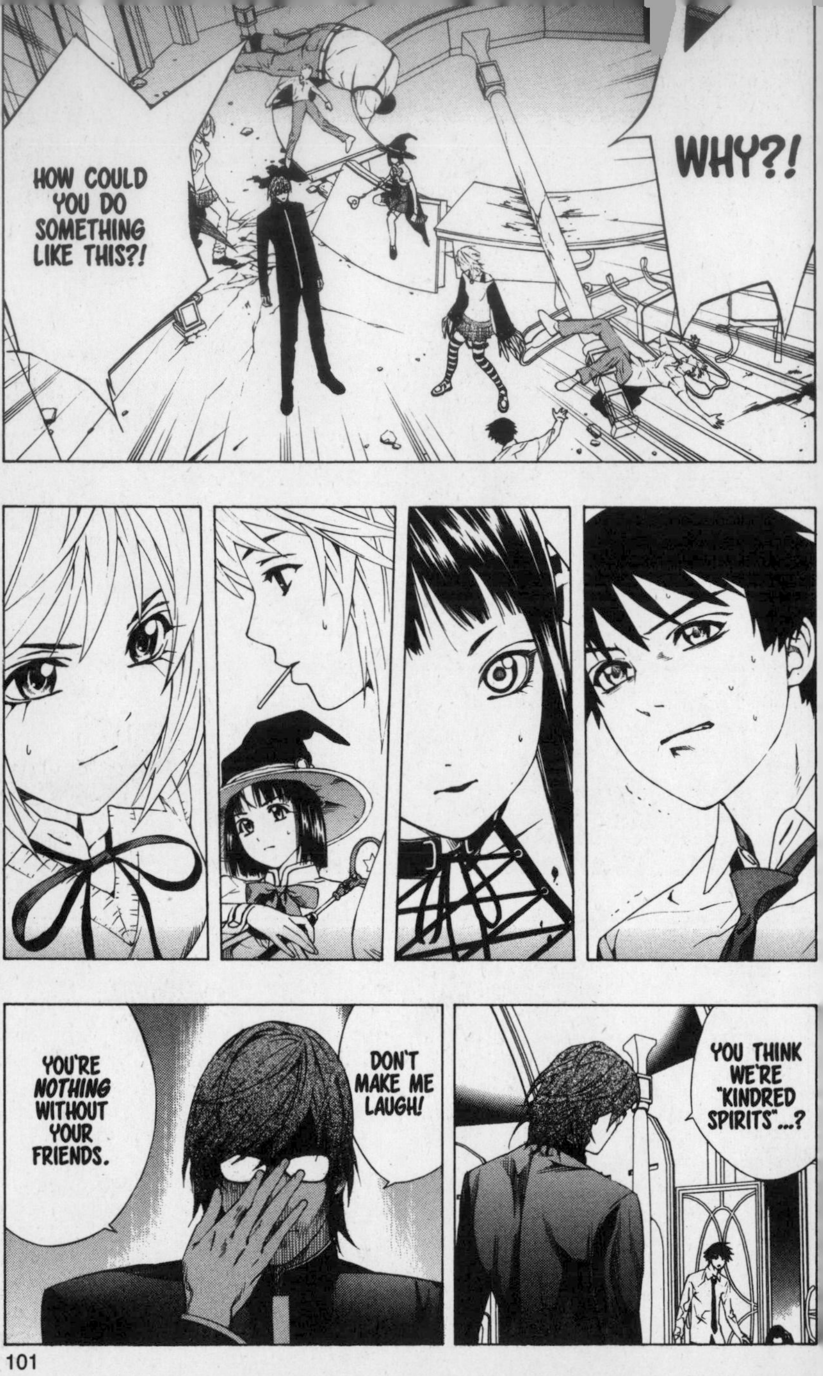
WHY?!
HOW COULD YOU DO SOMETHING LIKE THIS?!
YOU THINK WE'RE "KINDRED SPIRITS"...?
DON'T MAKE ME LAUGH!
YOU'RE *NOTHING* WITHOUT YOUR FRIENDS.

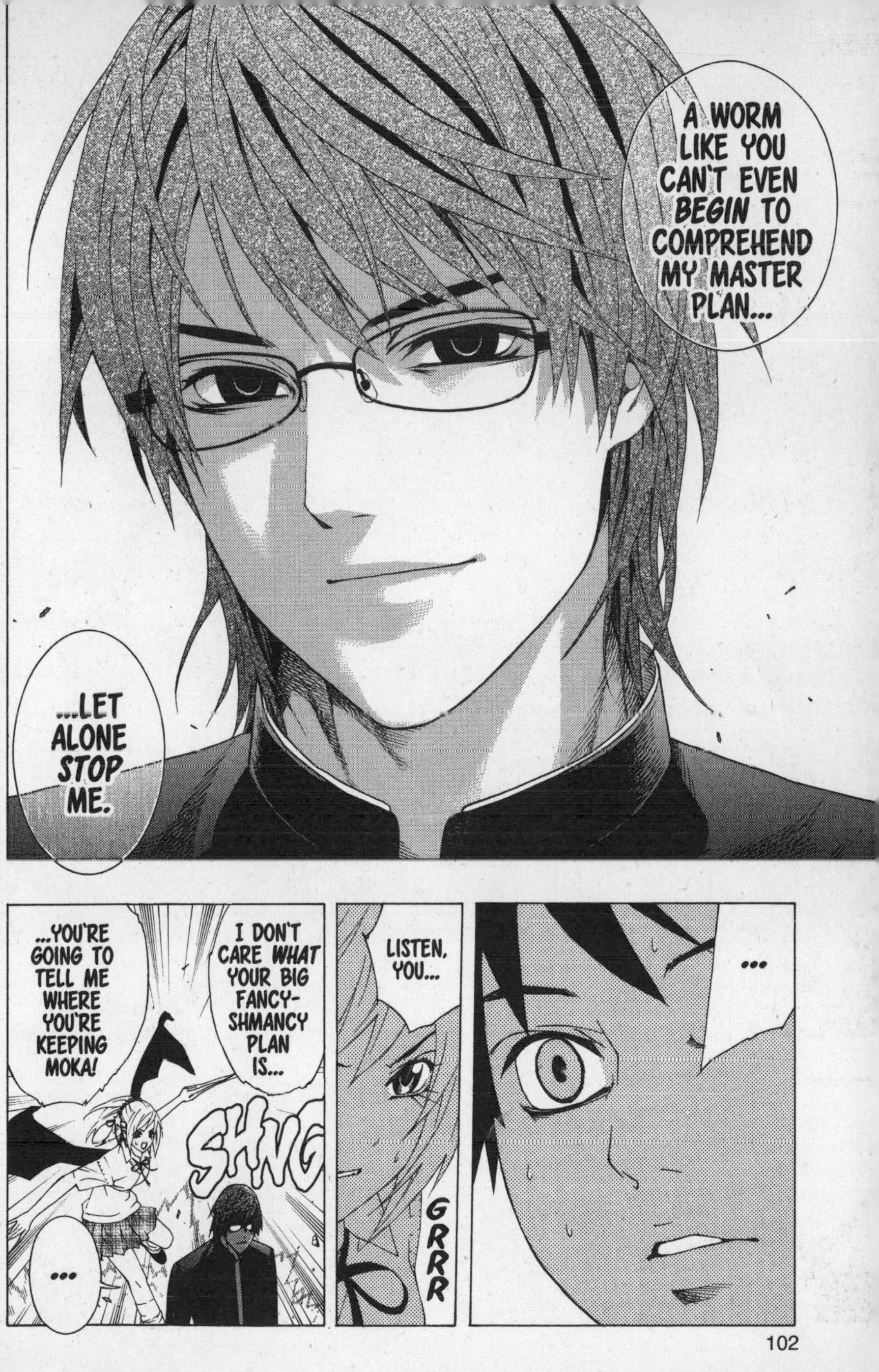
A WORM LIKE YOU CAN'T EVEN BEGIN TO COMPREHEND MY MASTER PLAN...
...LET ALONE STOP ME.
...
LISTEN, YOU...
GRRR
I DON'T CARE WHAT YOUR BIG FANCY-SHMANCY PLAN IS...
...YOU'RE GOING TO TELL ME WHERE YOU'RE KEEPING MOKA!
SHNG
...

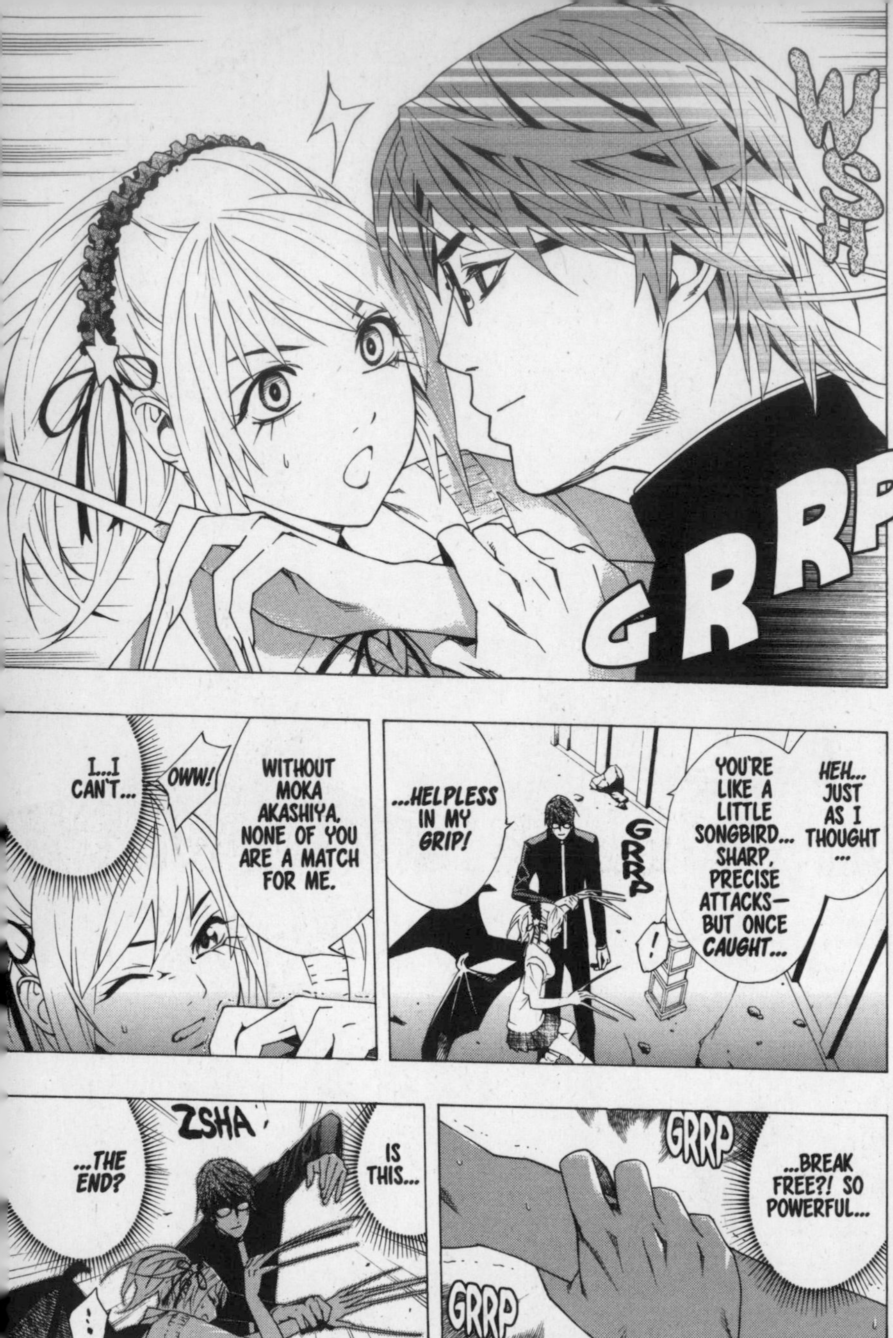
WSH
GRRP
HEH... JUST AS I THOUGHT ...
YOU'RE LIKE A LITTLE SONGBIRD... SHARP, PRECISE ATTACKS— BUT ONCE CAUGHT...
GRRP
...HELPLESS IN MY GRIP!
!
WITHOUT MOKA AKASHIYA, NONE OF YOU ARE A MATCH FOR ME.
OWW!
I...I CAN'T...
GRRP
...BREAK FREE?! SO POWERFUL...
GRRP
ZSHA
IS THIS...
...THE END?
!...

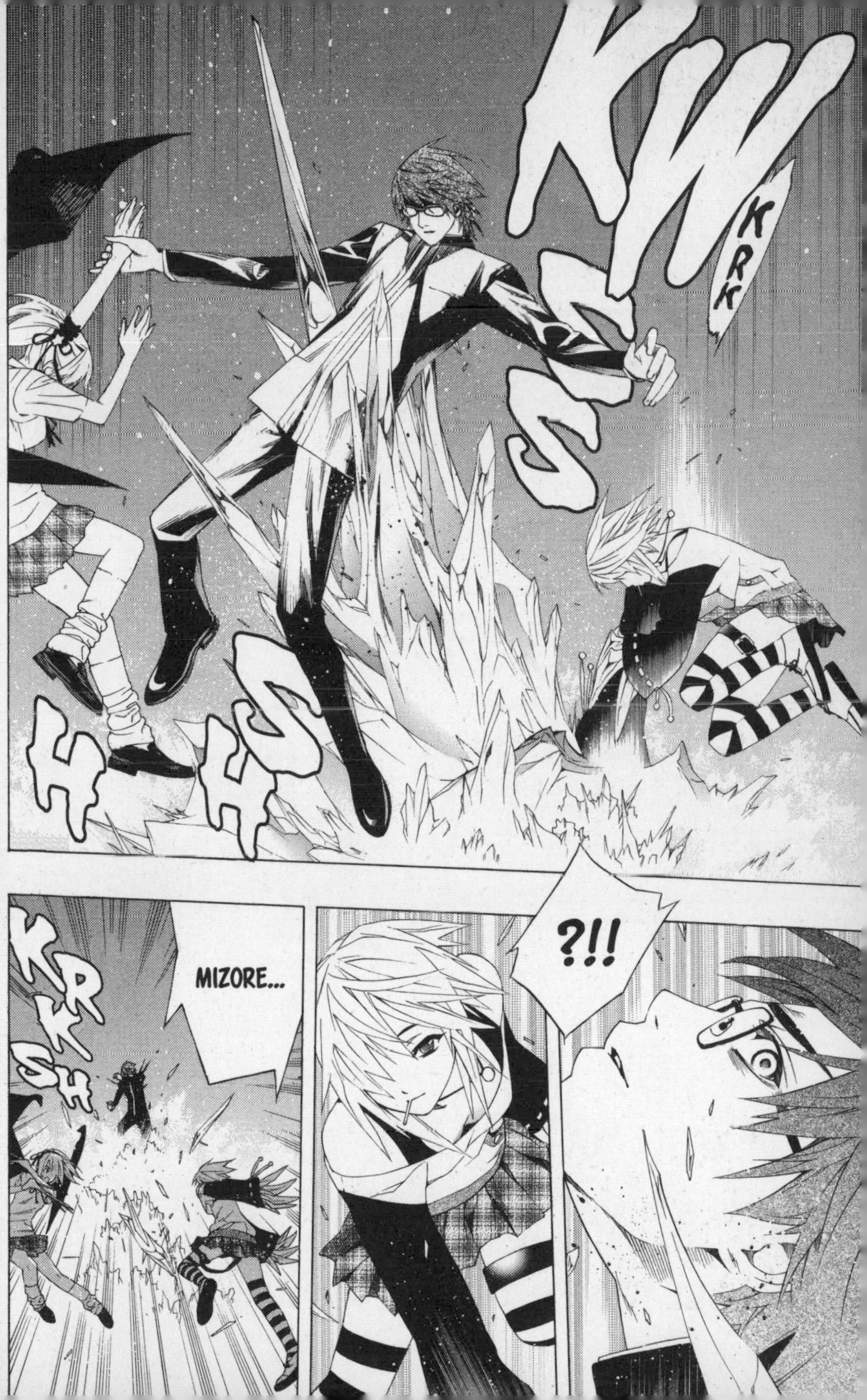
KRK
?!!
MIZORE...
KRKSH

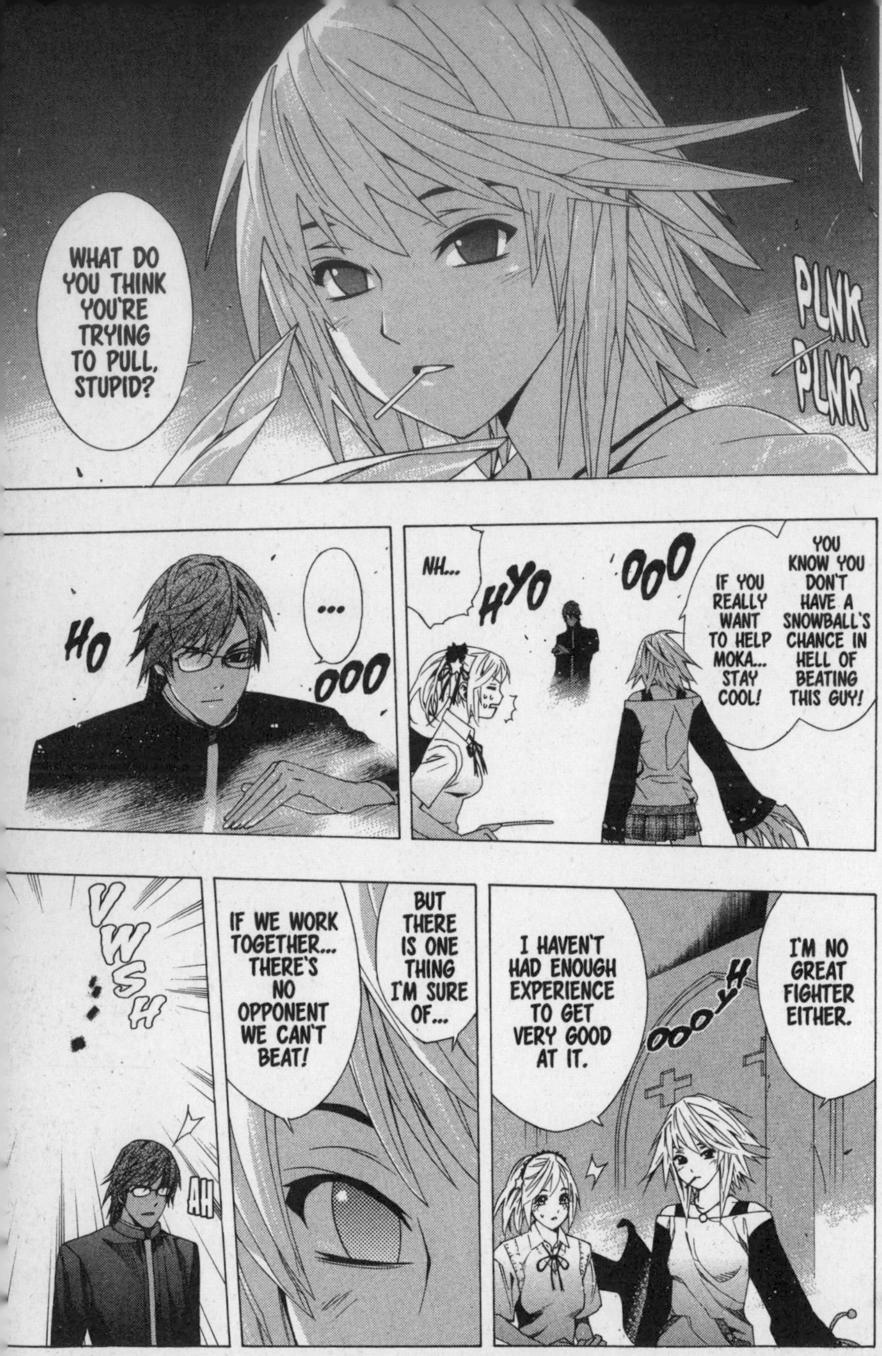

WHAT DO YOU THINK YOU'RE TRYING TO PULL, STUPID?
PLNK PLNK
YOU KNOW YOU DON'T HAVE A SNOWBALL'S CHANCE IN HELL OF BEATING THIS GUY!
IF YOU REALLY WANT TO HELP MOKA... STAY COOL!
HYOOOO
NH...
...
HOOOO
I'M NO GREAT FIGHTER EITHER.
OOOYH
I HAVEN'T HAD ENOUGH EXPERIENCE TO GET VERY GOOD AT IT.
BUT THERE IS ONE THING I'M SURE OF...
IF WE WORK TOGETHER... THERE'S NO OPPONENT WE CAN'T BEAT!
VWSH
AH

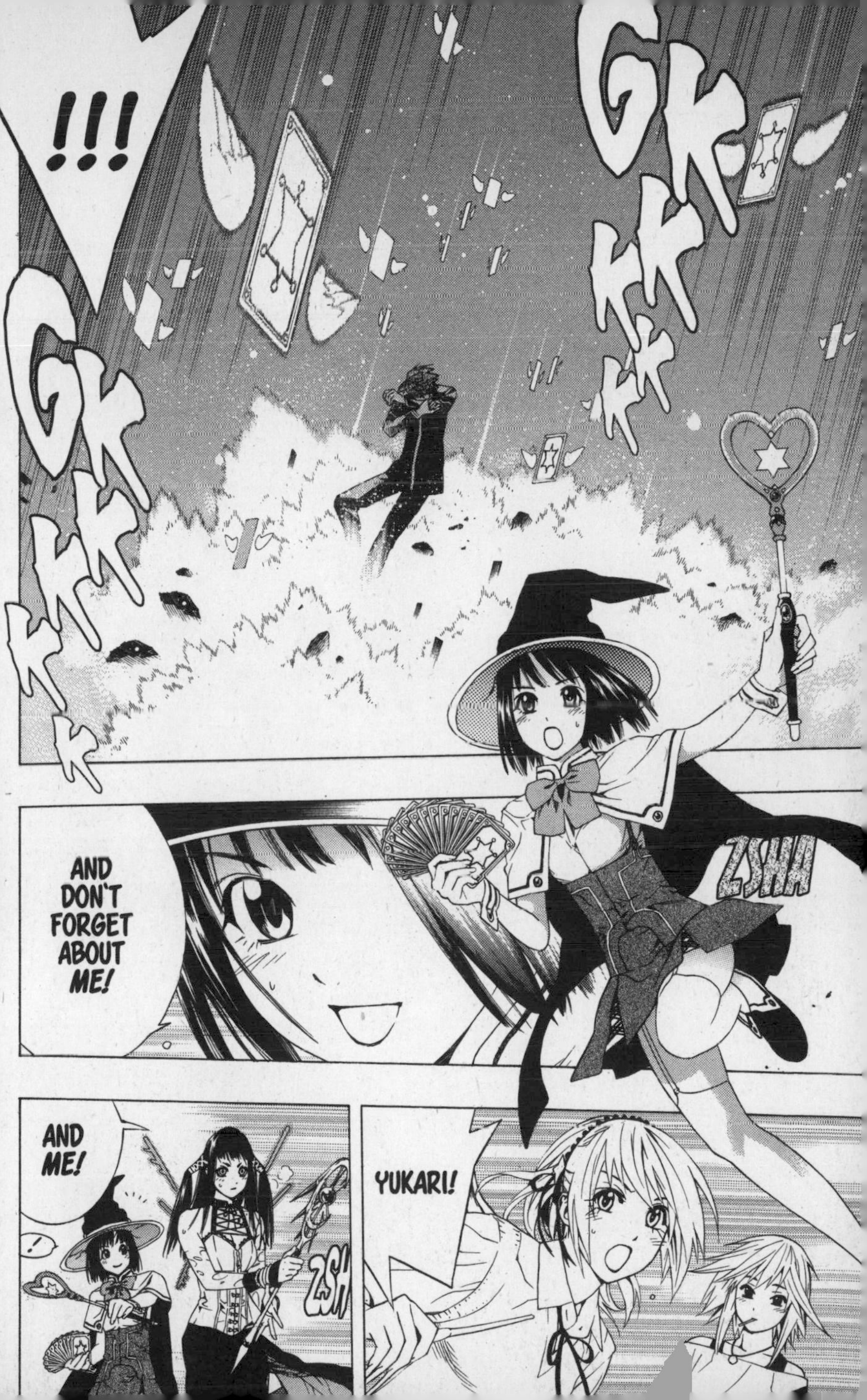
GK-KK-KK
!!!
GKKKKKK
ZSHA
AND DON'T FORGET ABOUT ME!
YUKARI!
AND ME!
ZSH
!

READ THIS WAY

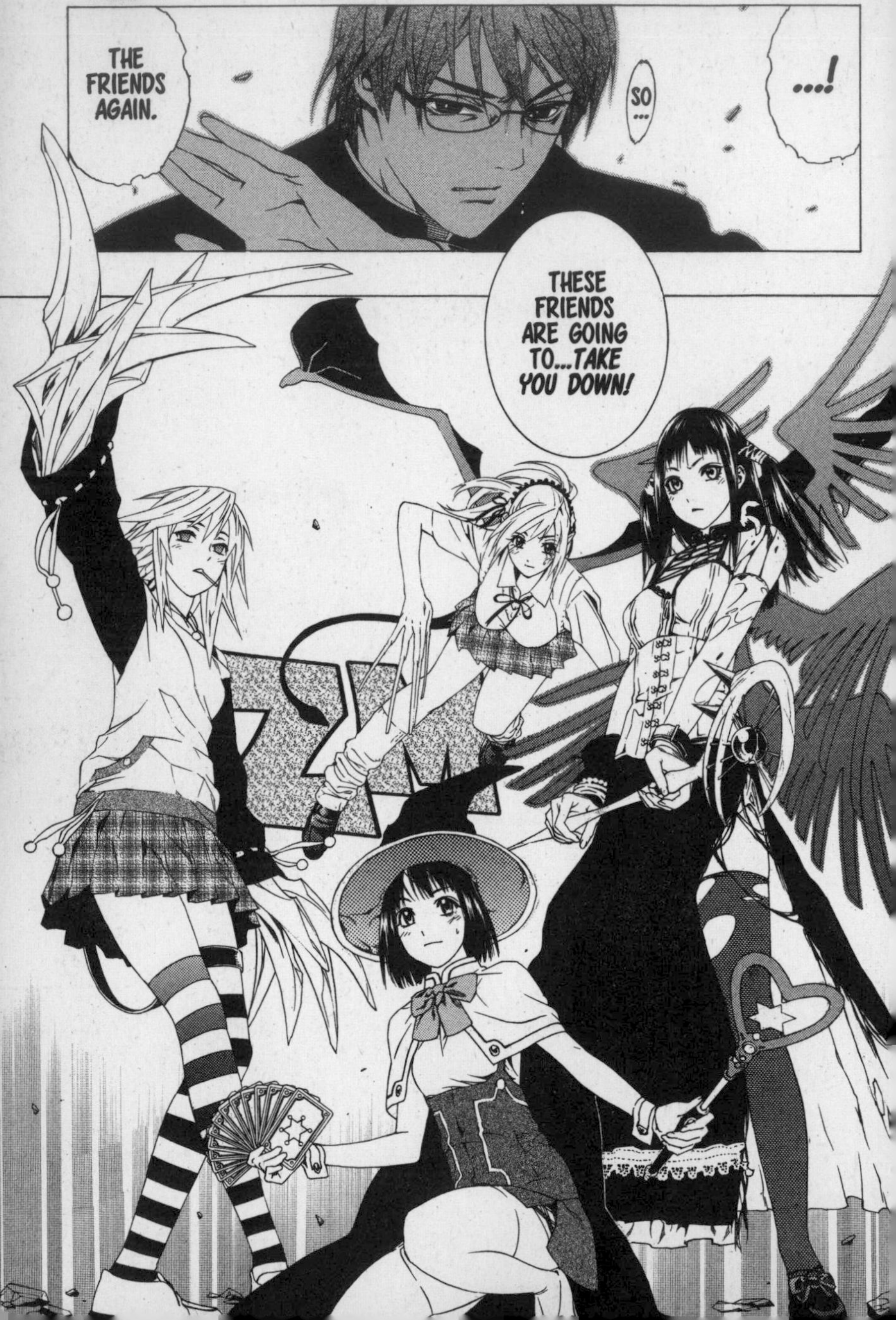
...!
SO...
THE FRIENDS AGAIN.
THESE FRIENDS ARE GOING TO...TAKE YOU DOWN!

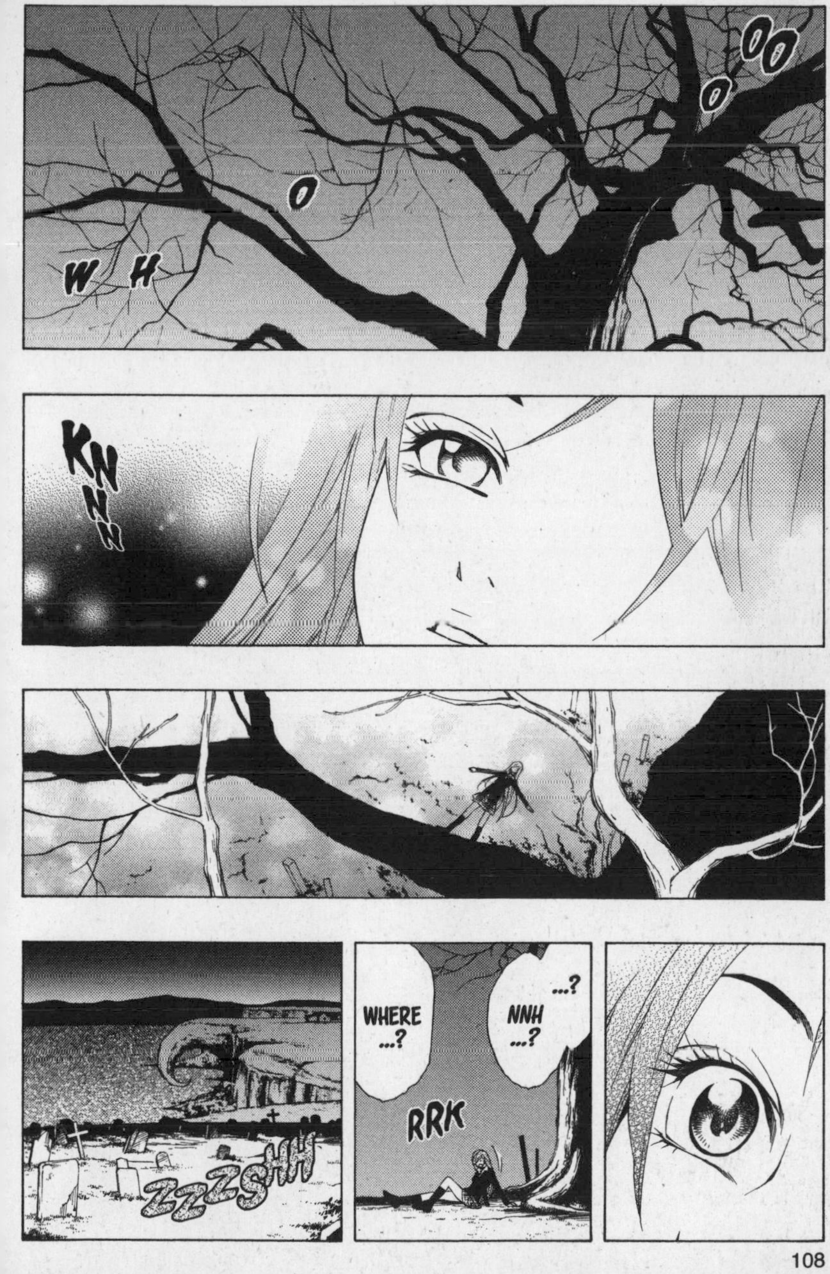
WHOOOO
KNNNN
...? NNH ...?
WHERE ...?
RRK
ZZZSHH

READ THIS WAY

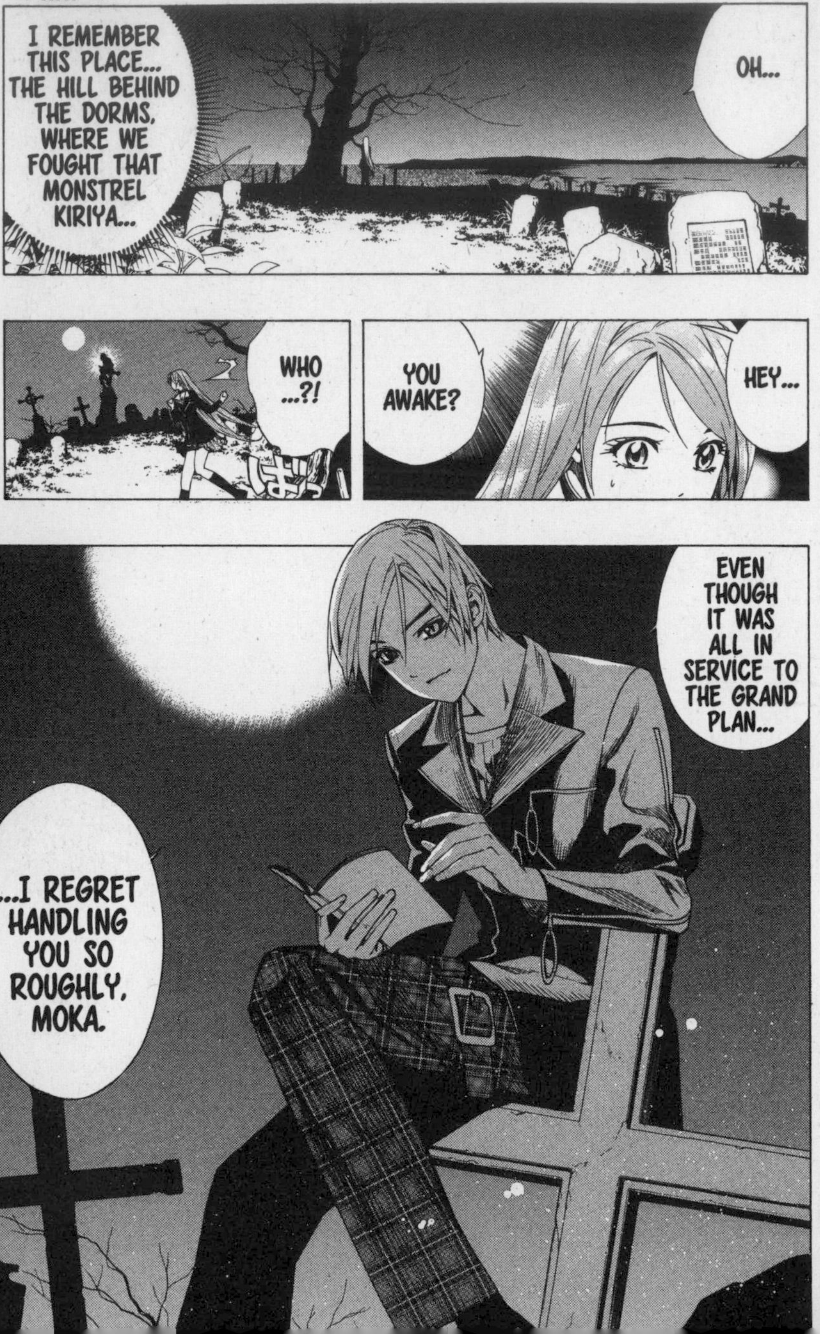
OH...
I REMEMBER THIS PLACE... THE HILL BEHIND THE DORMS, WHERE WE FOUGHT THAT MONSTREL KIRIYA...
HEY...
YOU AWAKE?
WHO ...?!
EVEN THOUGH IT WAS ALL IN SERVICE TO THE GRAND PLAN...
...I REGRET HANDLING YOU SO ROUGHLY, MOKA.

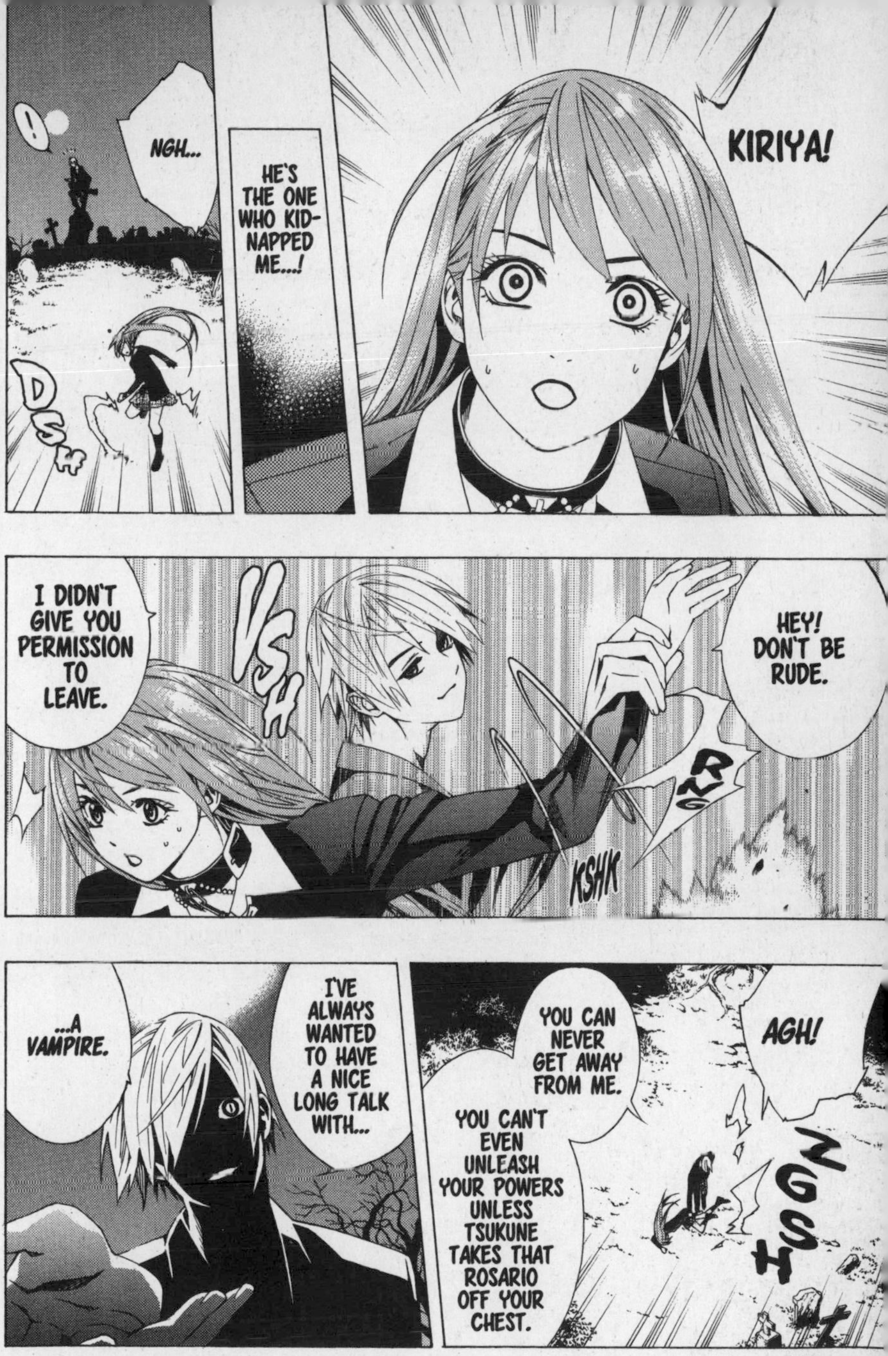
KIRIYA!
HE'S THE ONE WHO KID-NAPPED ME...!
!
NGH...
DSH
HEY! DON'T BE RUDE.
RNG
VSH
I DIDN'T GIVE YOU PERMISSION TO LEAVE.
KSHK
AGH!
ZGSH
YOU CAN NEVER GET AWAY FROM ME.
YOU CAN'T EVEN UNLEASH YOUR POWERS UNLESS TSUKUNE TAKES THAT ROSARIO OFF YOUR CHEST.
I'VE ALWAYS WANTED TO HAVE A NICE LONG TALK WITH...
...A VAMPIRE.

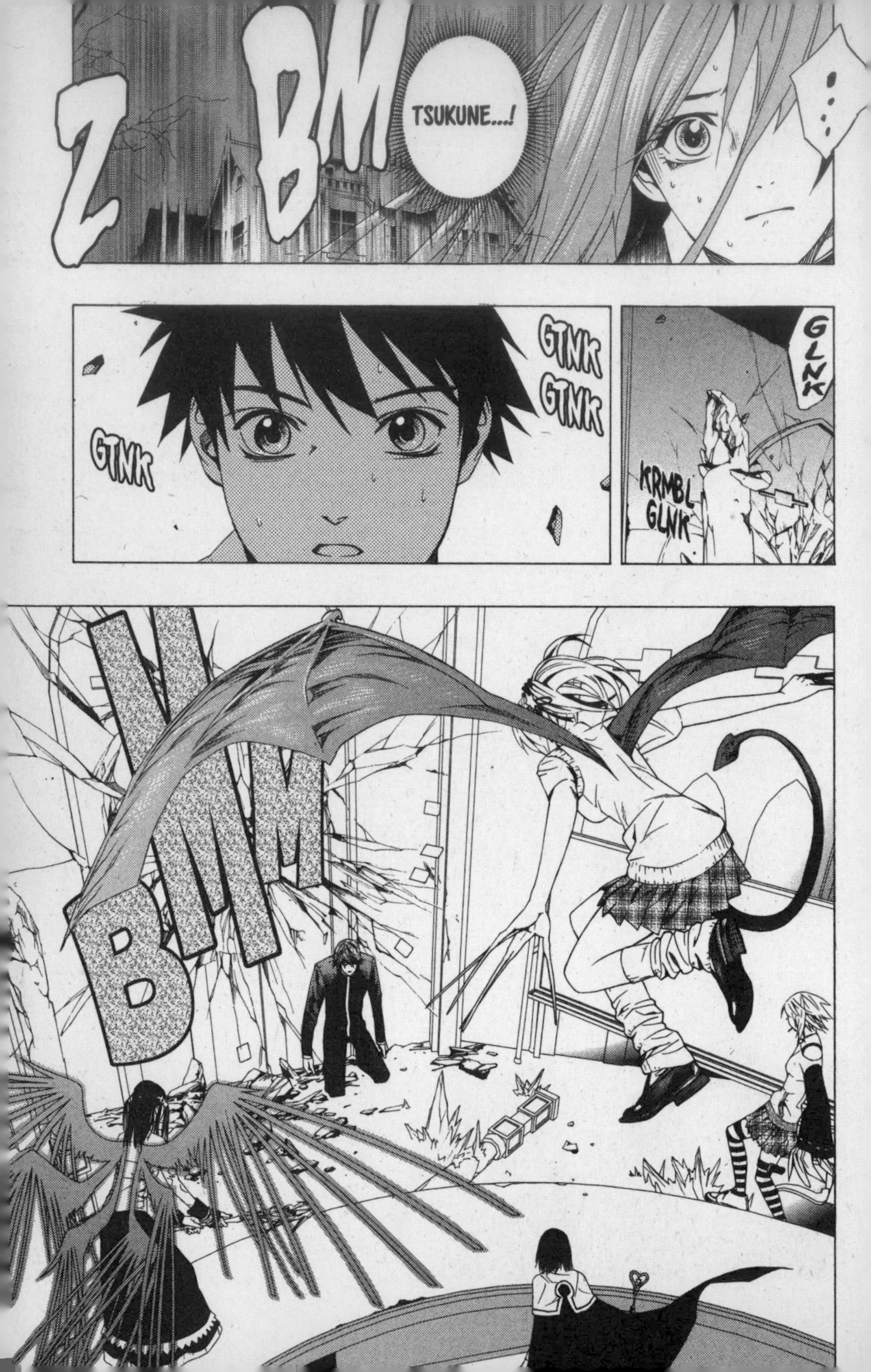
...
TSUKUNE...!
ZBM
GLNK
KRMBL GLNK
GTNK GTNK
GTNK

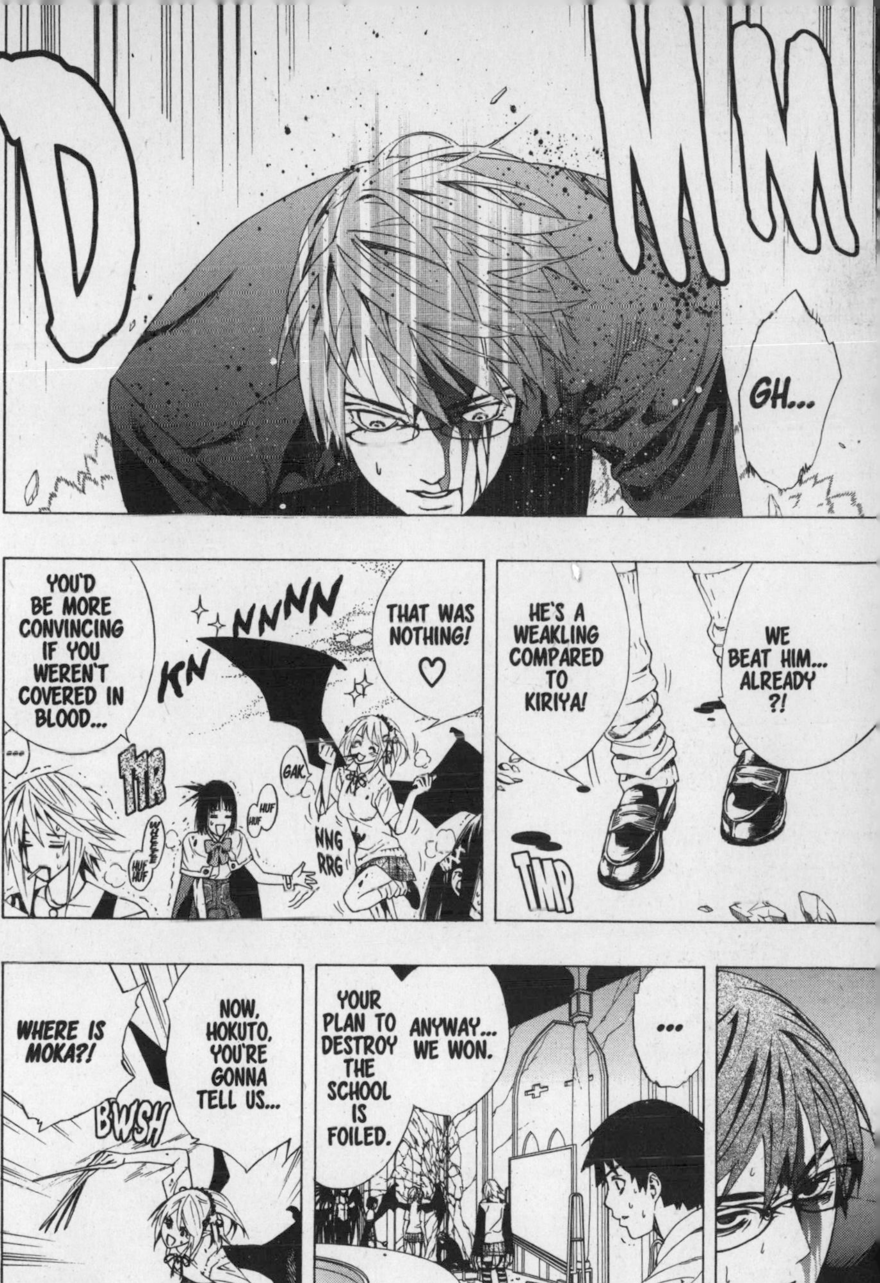
DMM
GH...
WE BEAT HIM... ALREADY?!
HE'S A WEAKLING COMPARED TO KIRIYA!
TMP
THAT WAS NOTHING! ♡
KNNNNN
YOU'D BE MORE CONVINCING IF YOU WEREN'T COVERED IN BLOOD...
GAK
HUF HUF
NNG RRG
HUF HUF
...
ANYWAY... WE WON.
YOUR PLAN TO DESTROY THE SCHOOL IS FOILED.
NOW, HOKUTO, YOU'RE GONNA TELL US...
WHERE IS MOKA?!
BWSH

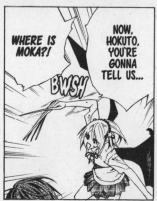

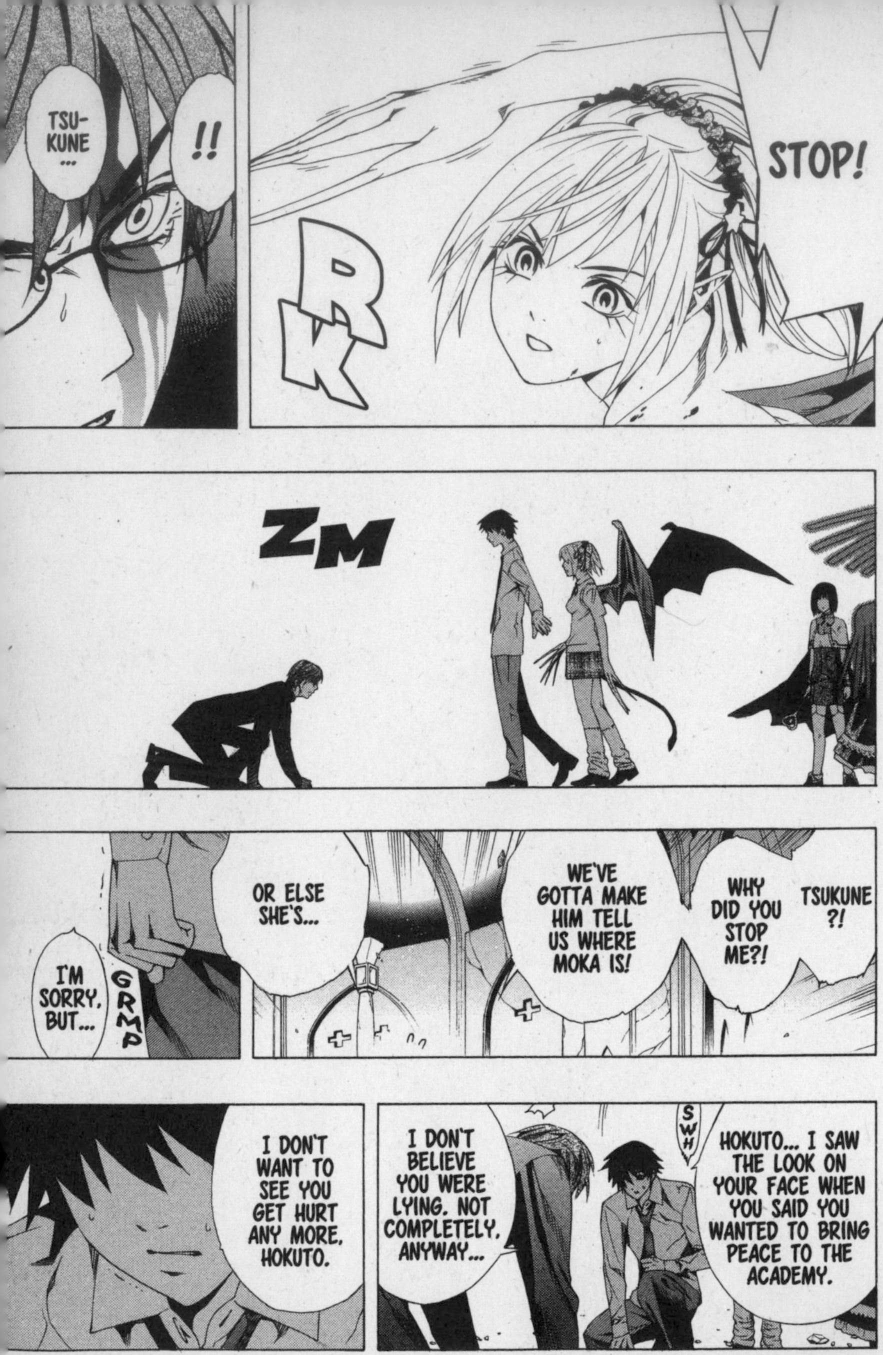
STOP!
RK
!!
TSU-KUNE...
ZM
TSUKUNE?!
WHY DID YOU STOP ME?!
WE'VE GOTTA MAKE HIM TELL US WHERE MOKA IS!
OR ELSE SHE'S...
GRMP
I'M SORRY, BUT...
SWH
HOKUTO... I SAW THE LOOK ON YOUR FACE WHEN YOU SAID YOU WANTED TO BRING PEACE TO THE ACADEMY.
I DON'T BELIEVE YOU WERE LYING. NOT COMPLETELY, ANYWAY...
I DON'T WANT TO SEE YOU GET HURT ANY MORE, HOKUTO.

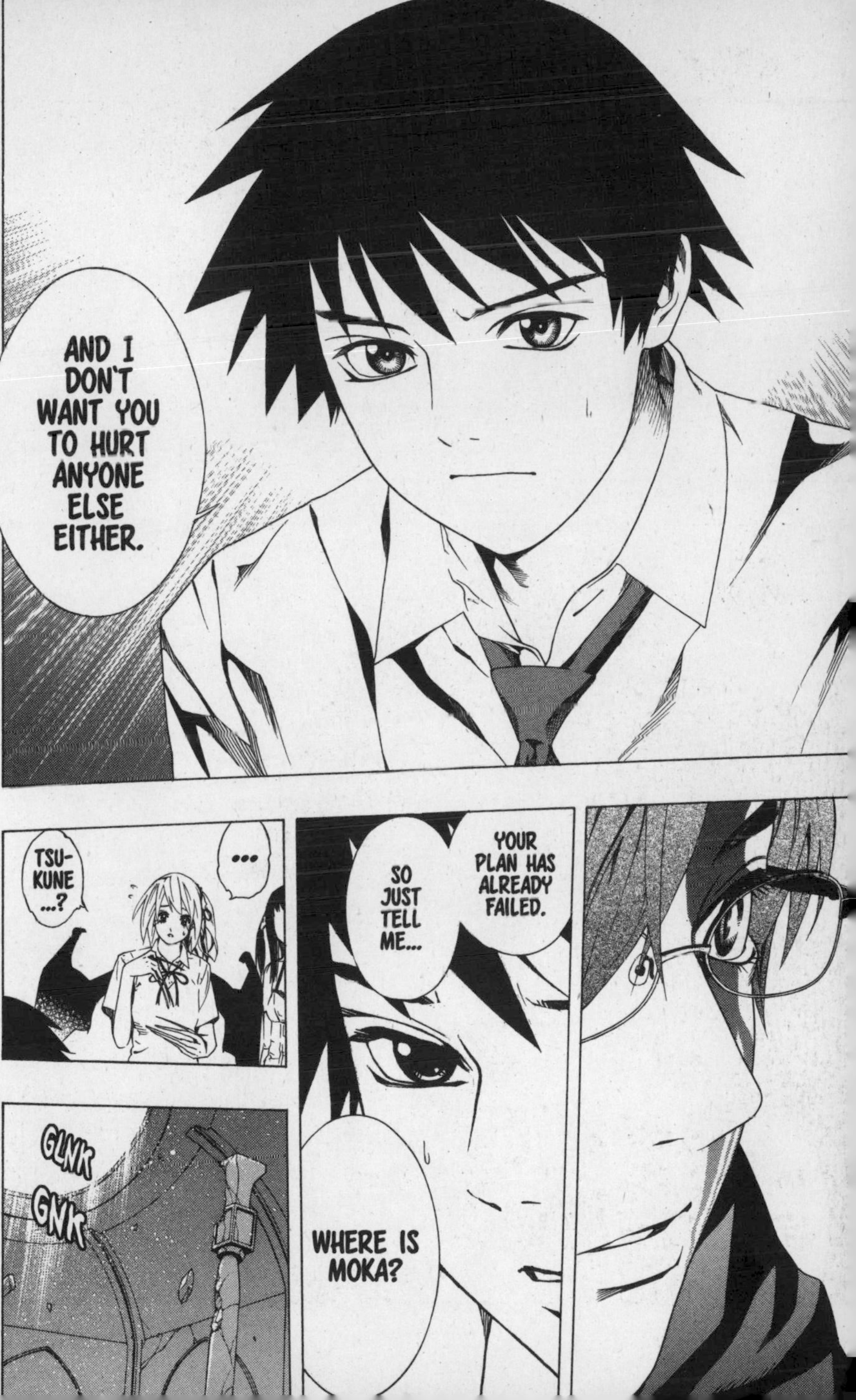
AND I DON'T WANT YOU TO HURT ANYONE ELSE EITHER.
YOUR PLAN HAS ALREADY FAILED.
SO JUST TELL ME...
WHERE IS MOKA?
...
TSU-KUNE ...?
GLNK
GNK

READ THIS WAY

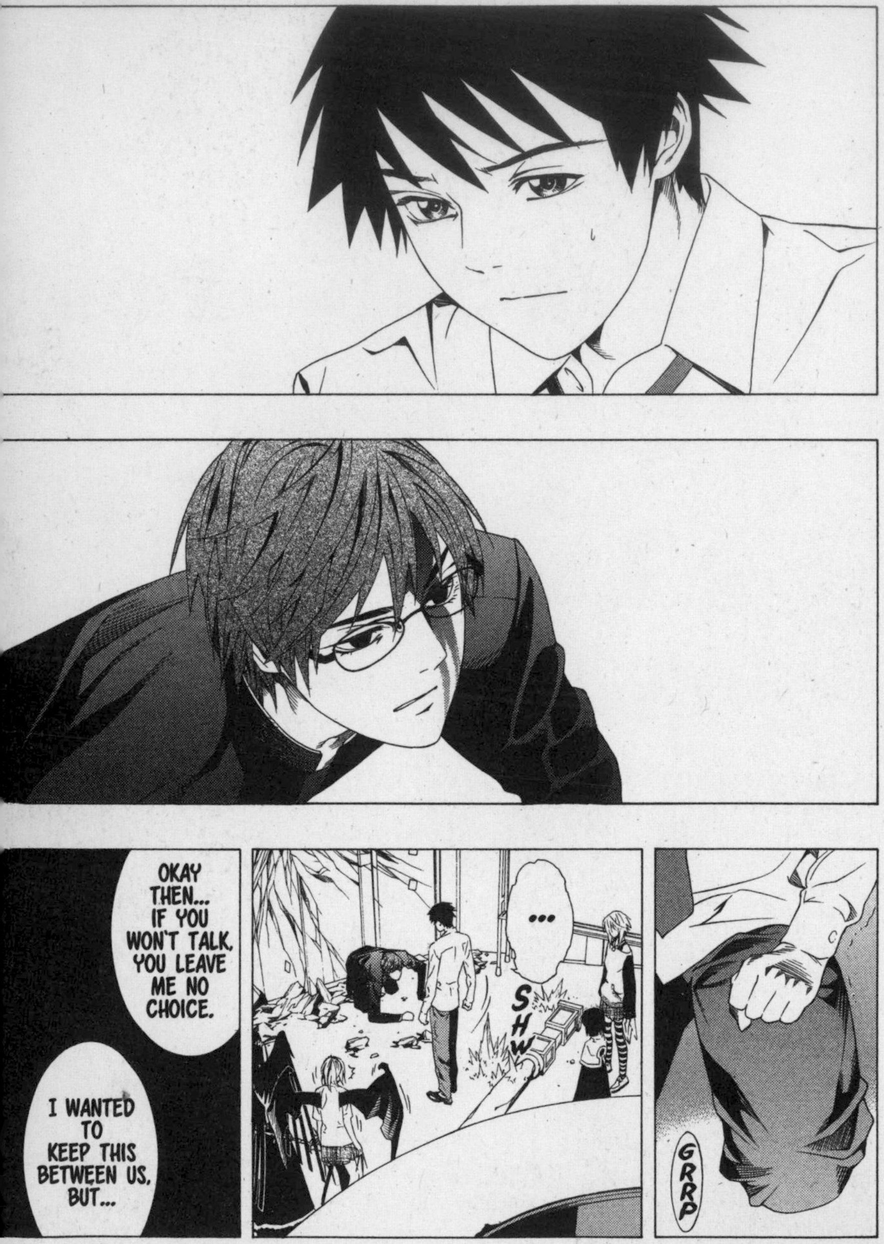
GRRP
...
SHW
OKAY THEN... IF YOU WON'T TALK, YOU LEAVE ME NO CHOICE.
I WANTED TO KEEP THIS BETWEEN US, BUT...

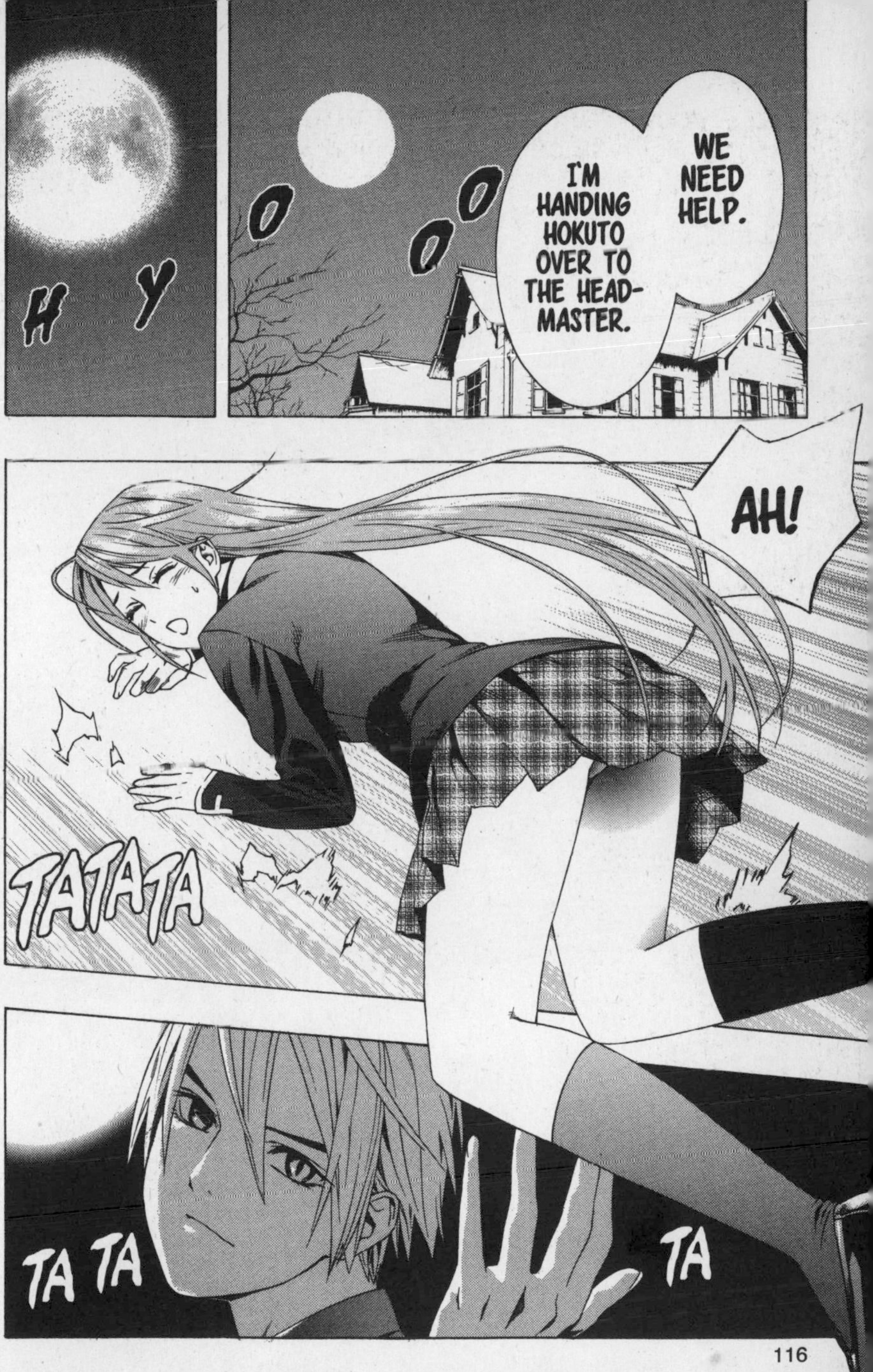
WE NEED HELP.
I'M HANDING HOKUTO OVER TO THE HEAD-MASTER.
H Y O O O O
AH!
TATATA
TA TA
TA

READ THIS WAY

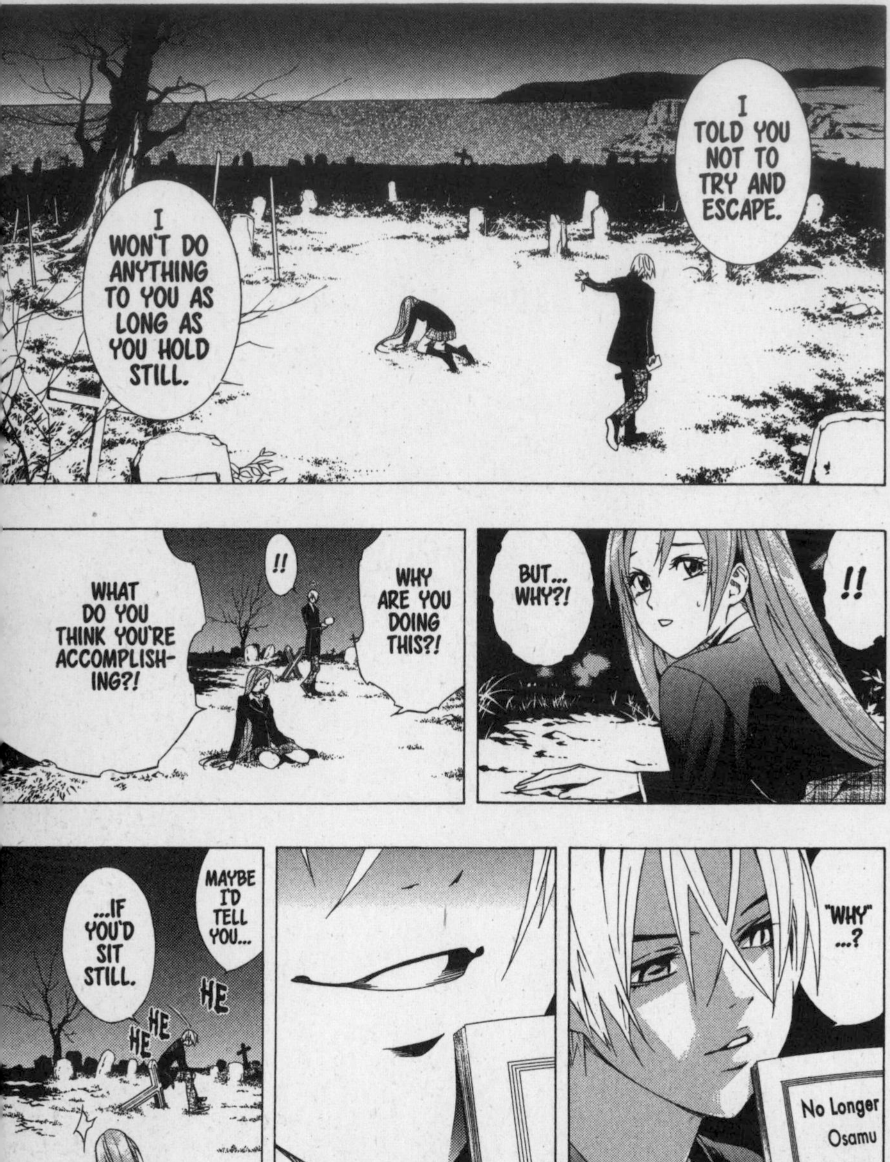
I TOLD YOU NOT TO TRY AND ESCAPE.
I WON'T DO ANYTHING TO YOU AS LONG AS YOU HOLD STILL.
!!
BUT... WHY?!
WHY ARE YOU DOING THIS?!
!!
WHAT DO YOU THINK YOU'RE ACCOMPLISHING?!
"WHY" ...?
No Longer
Osamu
MAYBE I'D TELL YOU...
...IF YOU'D SIT STILL.
HE
HE
HE

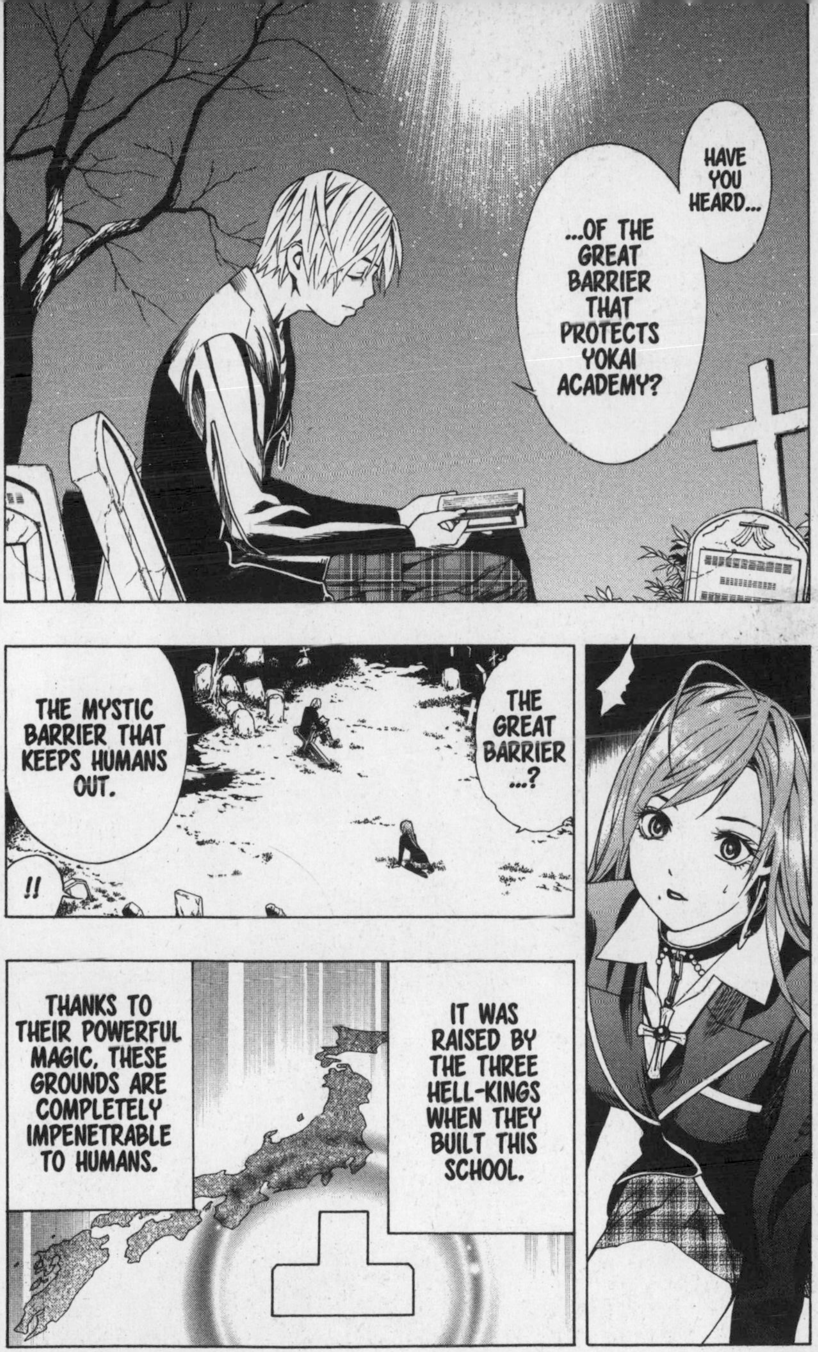
HAVE YOU HEARD...
...OF THE GREAT BARRIER THAT PROTECTS YOKAI ACADEMY?
THE GREAT BARRIER ...?
THE MYSTIC BARRIER THAT KEEPS HUMANS OUT.
!!
IT WAS RAISED BY THE THREE HELL-KINGS WHEN THEY BUILT THIS SCHOOL.
THANKS TO THEIR POWERFUL MAGIC, THESE GROUNDS ARE COMPLETELY IMPENETRABLE TO HUMANS.

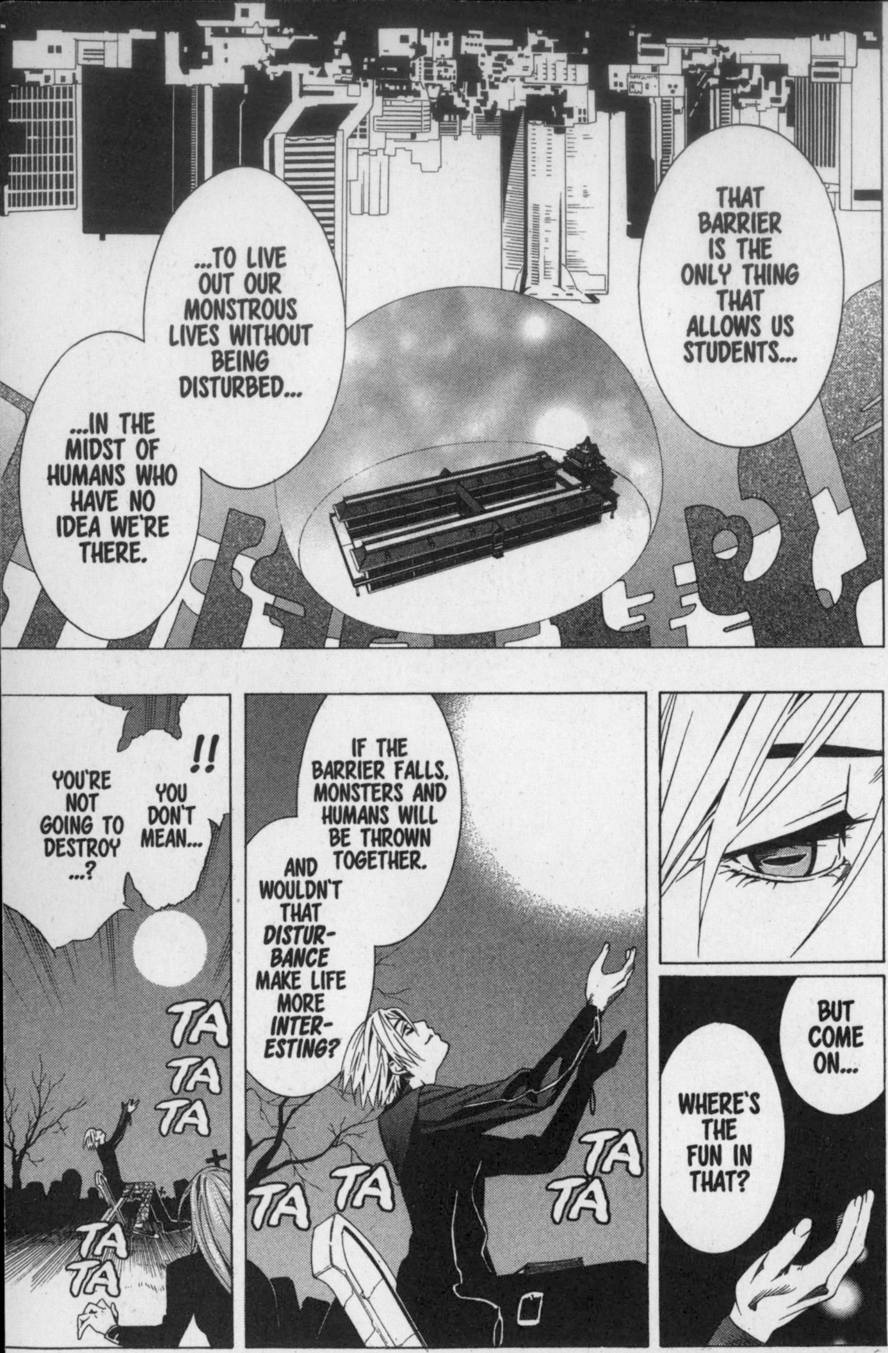
THAT BARRIER IS THE ONLY THING THAT ALLOWS US STUDENTS...
...TO LIVE OUT OUR MONSTROUS LIVES WITHOUT BEING DISTURBED...
...IN THE MIDST OF HUMANS WHO HAVE NO IDEA WE'RE THERE.
BUT COME ON...
WHERE'S THE FUN IN THAT?
IF THE BARRIER FALLS, MONSTERS AND HUMANS WILL BE THROWN TOGETHER.
AND WOULDN'T THAT DISTURBANCE MAKE LIFE MORE INTERESTING?
TA TA
TA
TA
!!
YOU DON'T MEAN...
YOU'RE NOT GOING TO DESTROY ...?
TA TA TA
TA TA

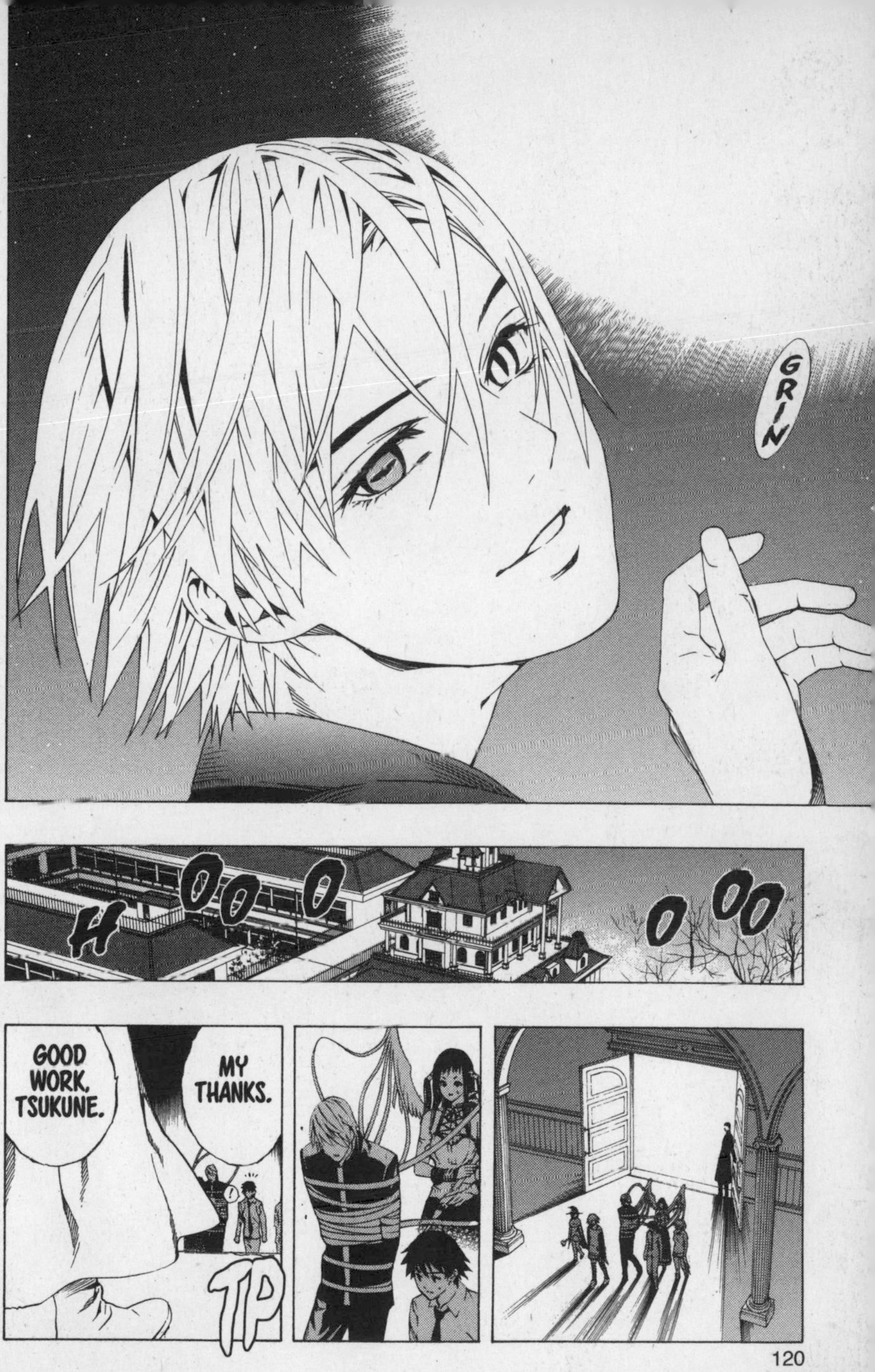
GRIN
HOOOOOO
MY THANKS.
GOOD WORK, TSUKUNE.
TP

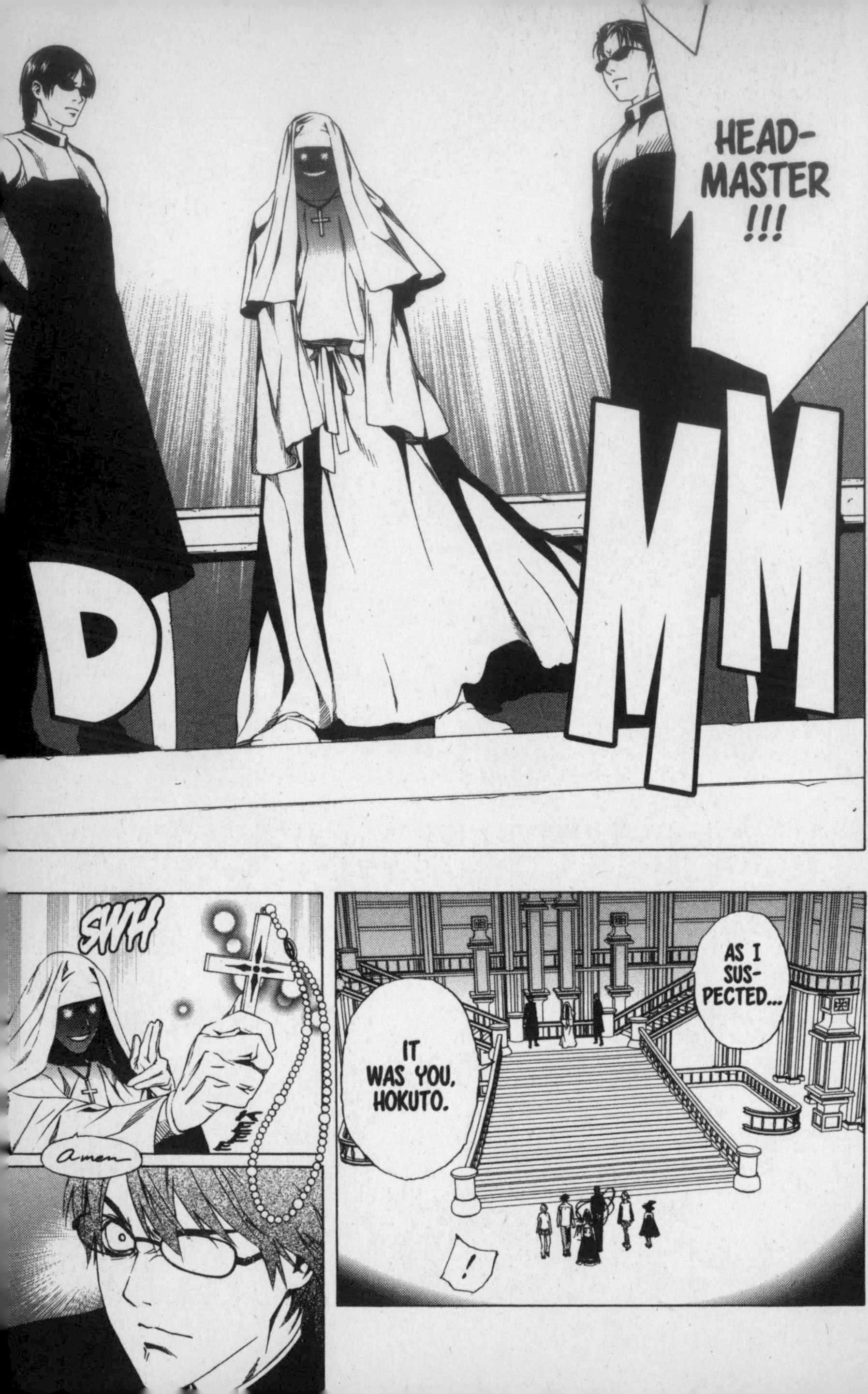
HEAD-MASTER!!!
DMM
AS I SUS-PECTED...
IT WAS YOU, HOKUTO.
!
SWH
amen

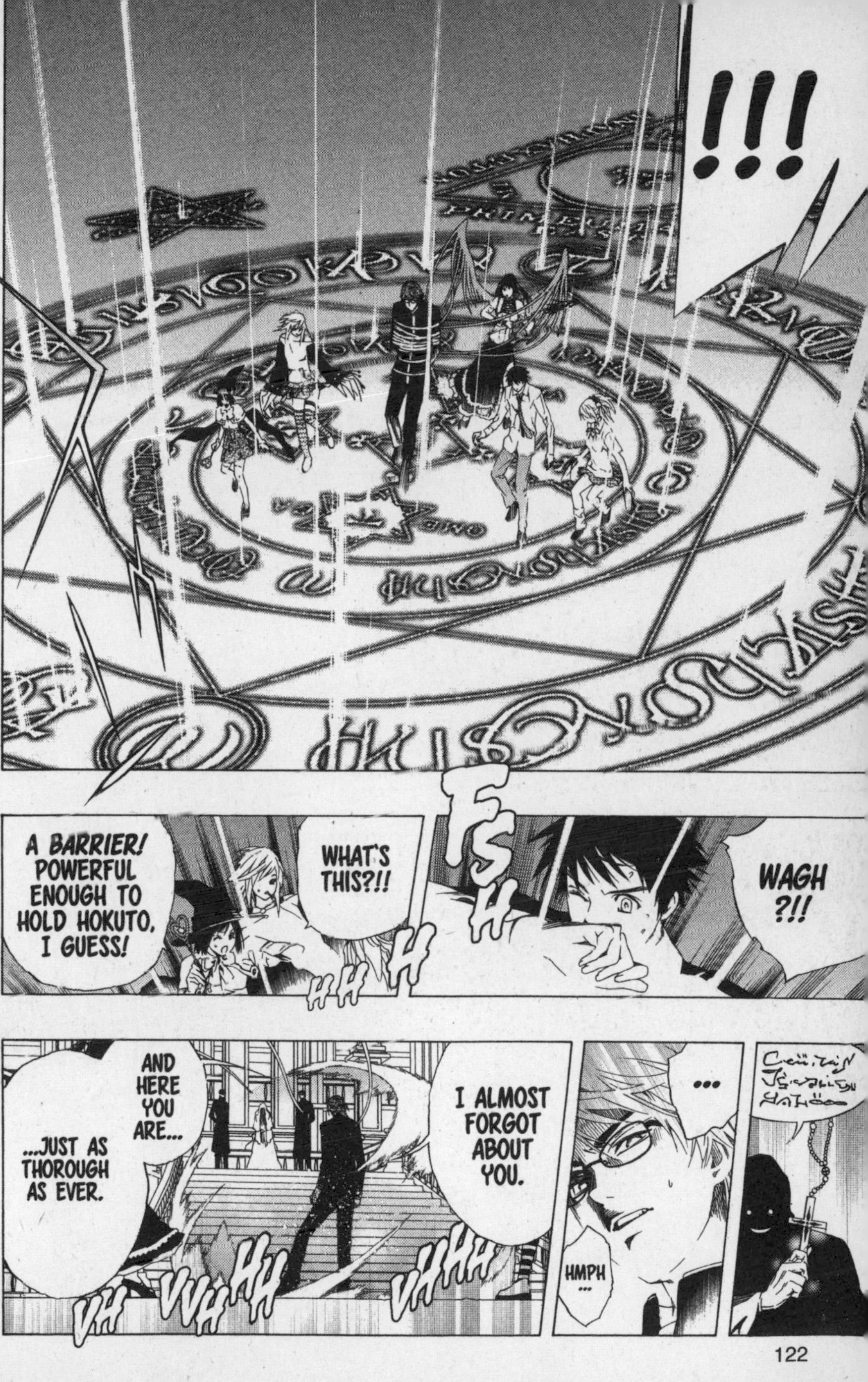
!!!
WAGH ?!!
FSHHH
WHAT'S THIS?!!
A BARRIER! POWERFUL ENOUGH TO HOLD HOKUTO, I GUESS!
HHH
...
HMPH ...
I ALMOST FORGOT ABOUT YOU.
VHHH
AND HERE YOU ARE...
...JUST AS THOROUGH AS EVER.
VVHHH
VH

READ THIS WAY

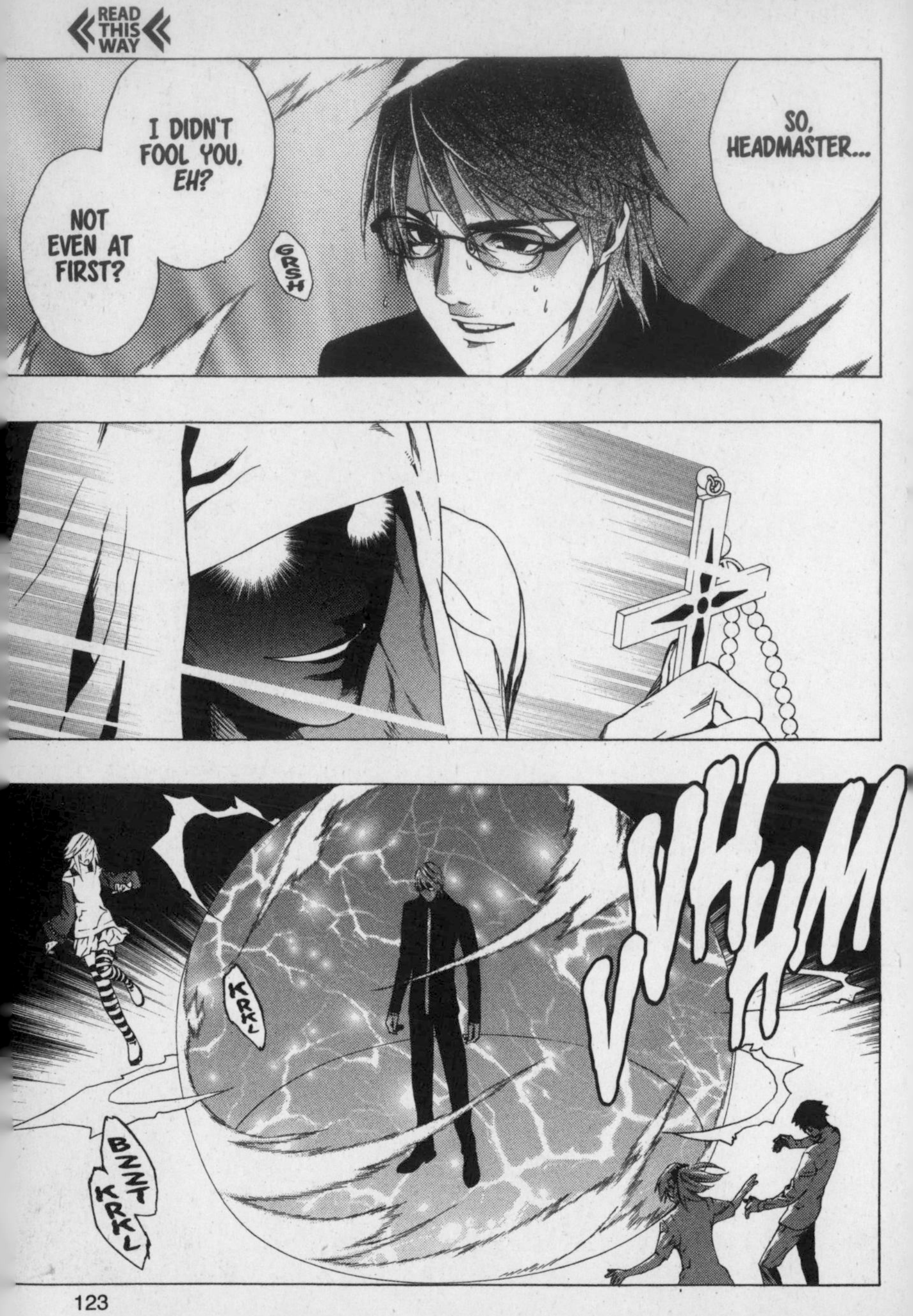

SO, HEADMASTER...
I DIDN'T FOOL YOU, EH?
NOT EVEN AT FIRST?
GRSH
VHUM
KRKL
BZZT KRKL

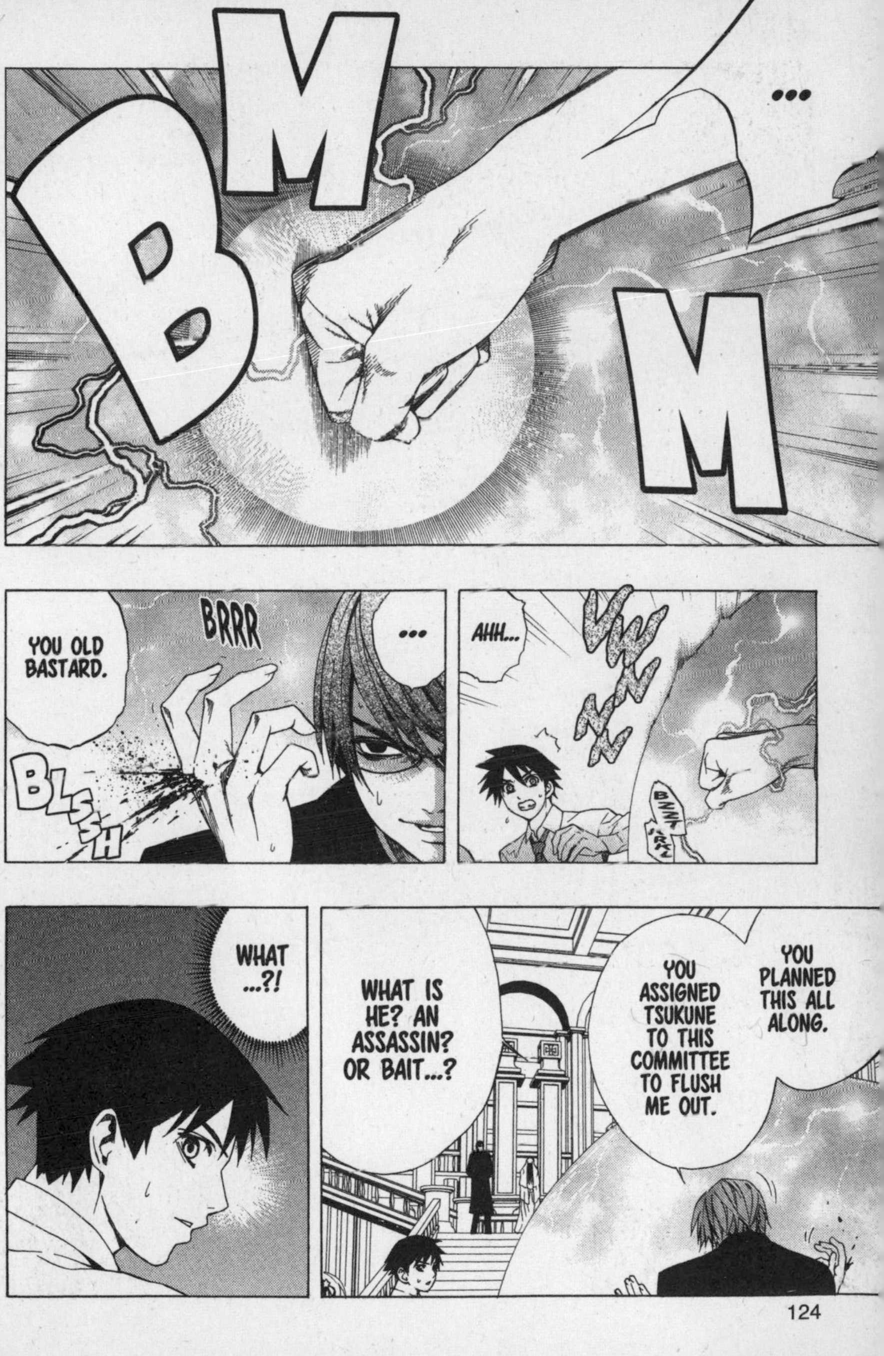
...
BMM
AHH...
VWNNN
BZZT
...
BRRR
YOU OLD BASTARD.
BLSSH
YOU PLANNED THIS ALL ALONG.
YOU ASSIGNED TSUKUNE TO THIS COMMITTEE TO FLUSH ME OUT.
WHAT IS HE? AN ASSASSIN? OR BAIT...?
WHAT ...?!

READ THIS WAY

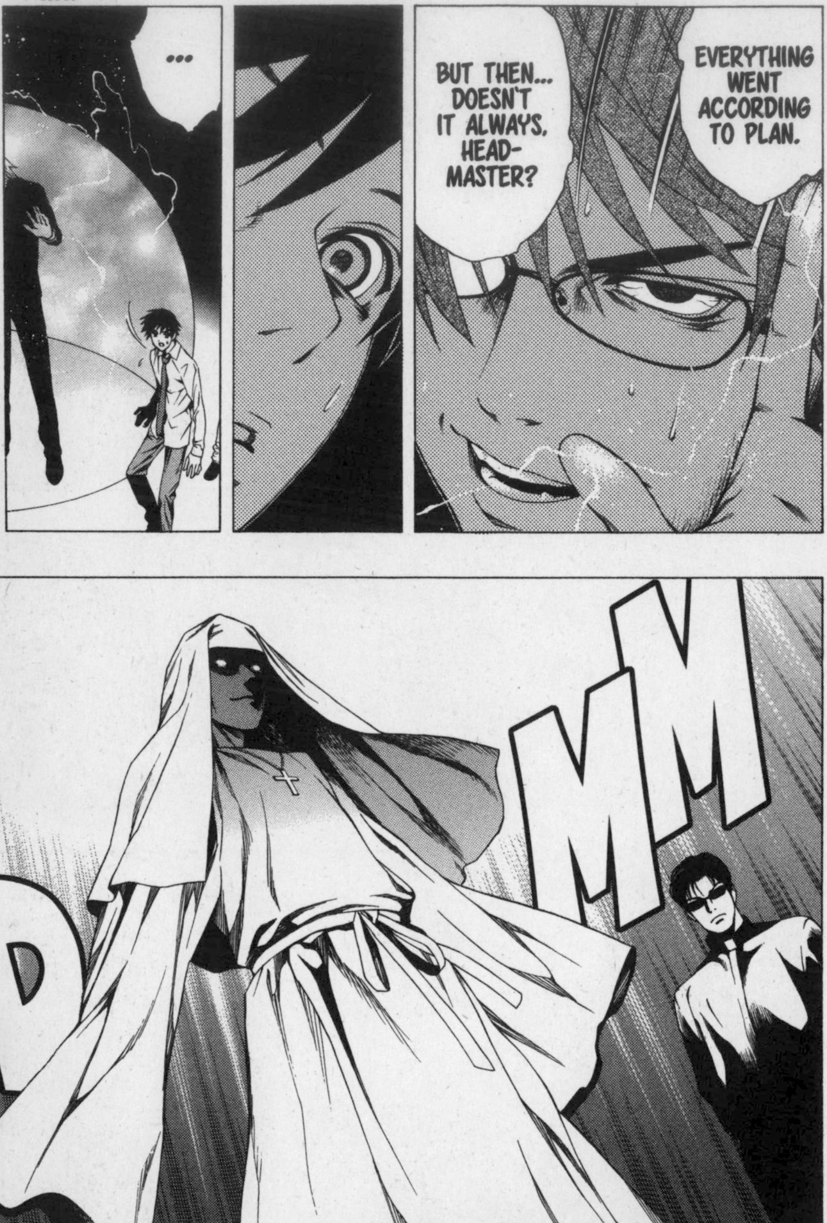
EVERYTHING WENT ACCORDING TO PLAN.
BUT THEN... DOESN'T IT ALWAYS, HEAD-MASTER?
...
DMMM

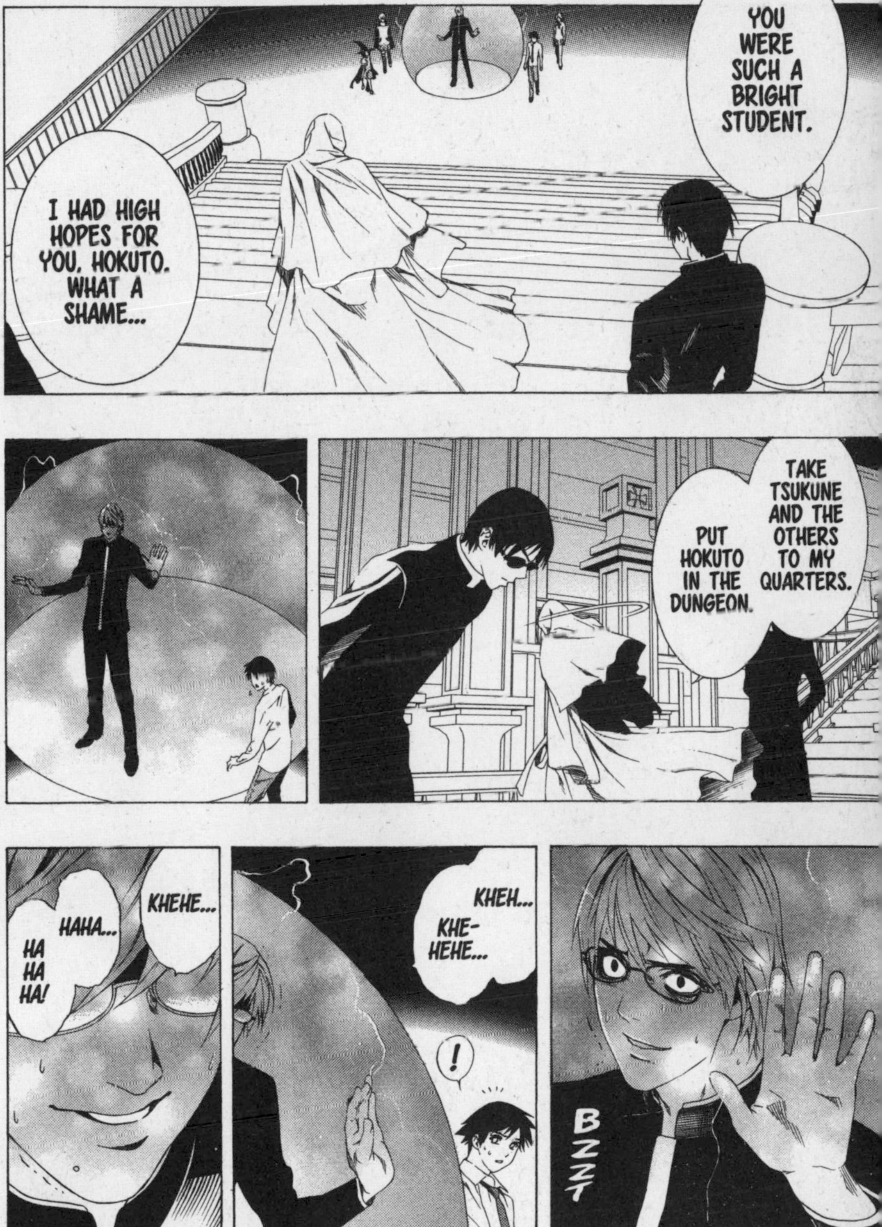
YOU WERE SUCH A BRIGHT STUDENT.
I HAD HIGH HOPES FOR YOU, HOKUTO. WHAT A SHAME...
TAKE TSUKUNE AND THE OTHERS TO MY QUARTERS.
PUT HOKUTO IN THE DUNGEON.
BZZT
KHEH...
KHE-HEHE...
!
KHEHE...
HAHA...
HA HA HA!

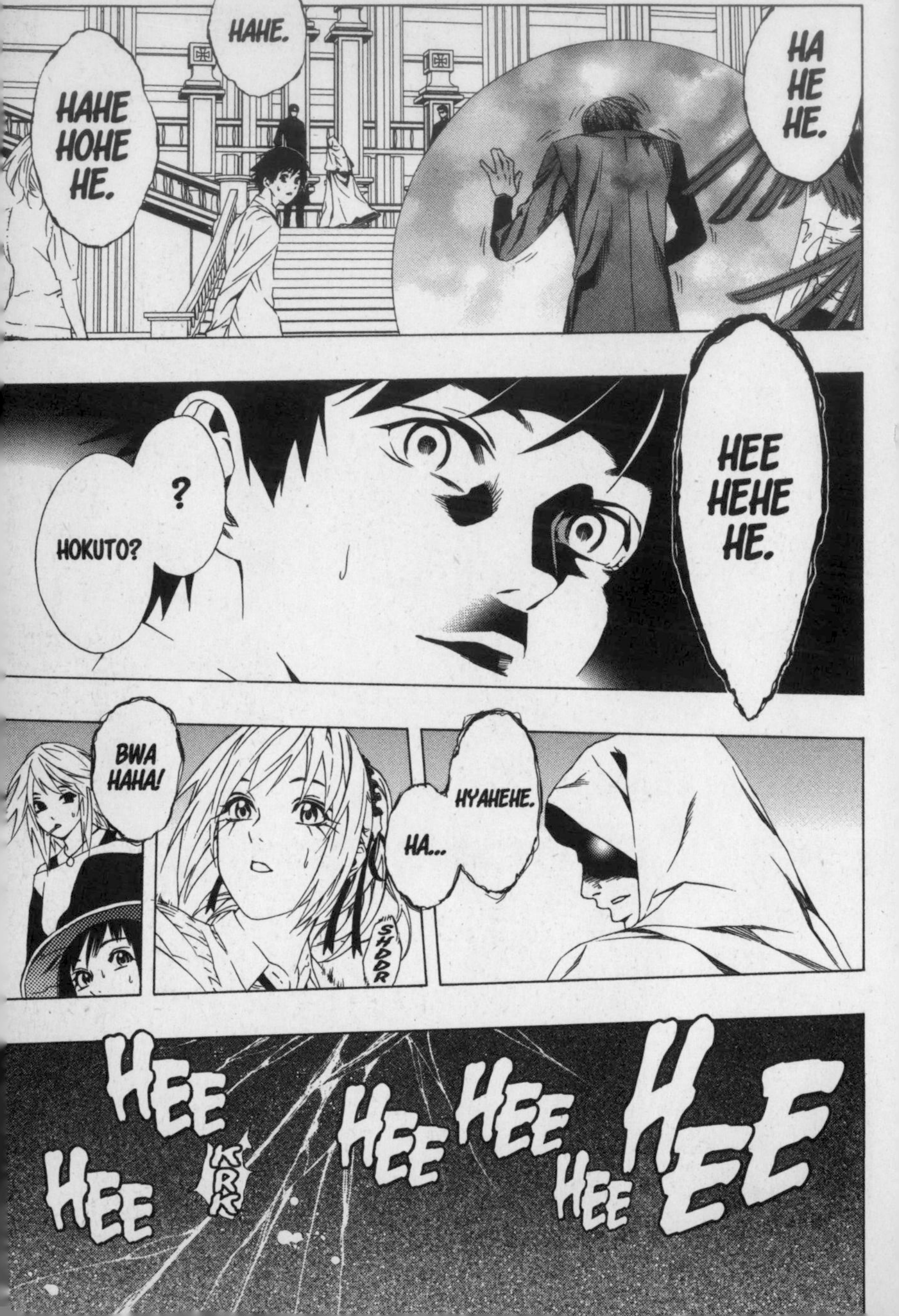
HA HE HE.
HAHE.
HAHE HOHE HE.
HEE HEHE HE.
?
HOKUTO?
HYAHEHE.
HA...
SHDDR
BWA HAHA!
HEE
HEE
HEE
HEE
KRK
HEE
HEE

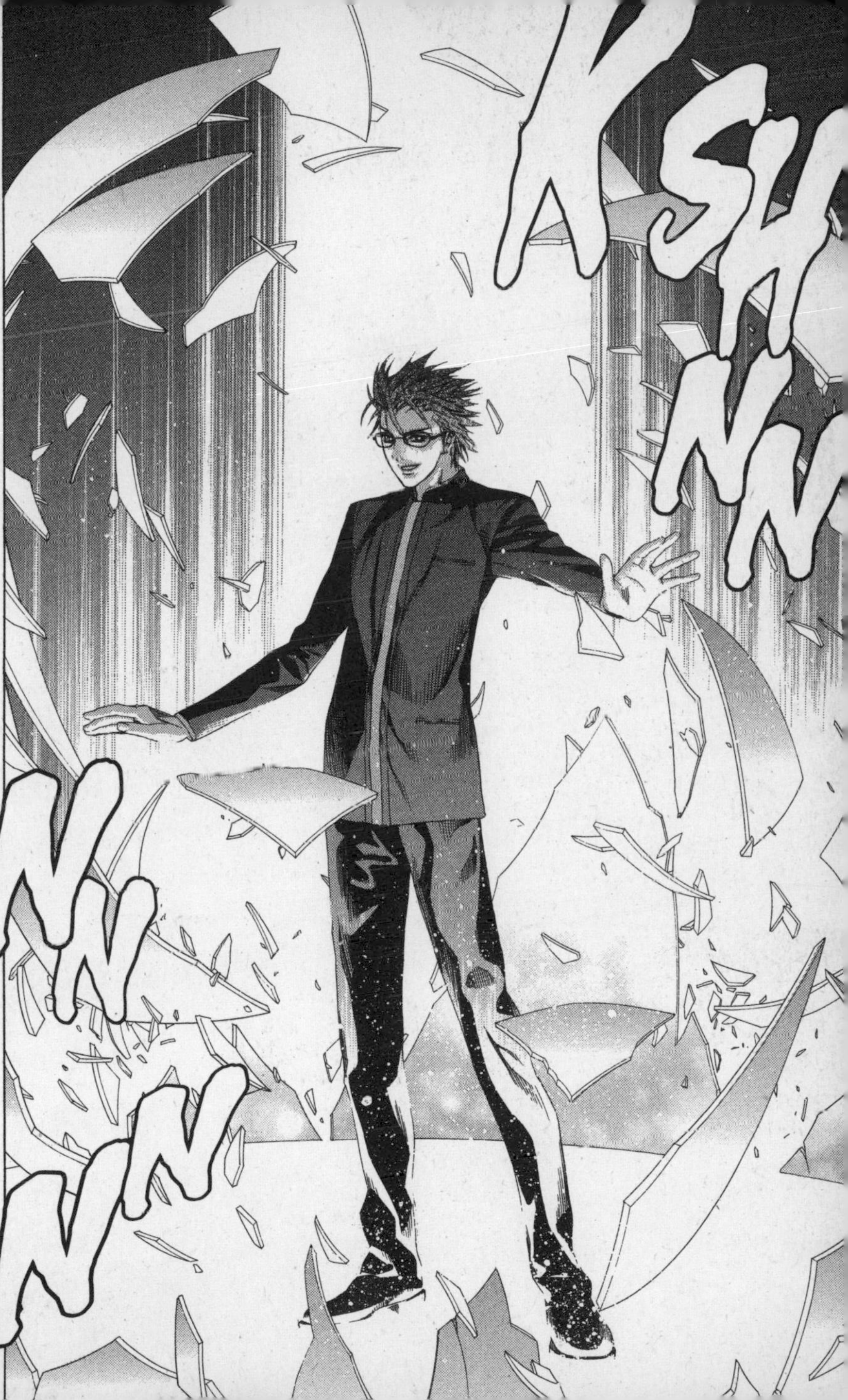
K'SHNN
NNNN

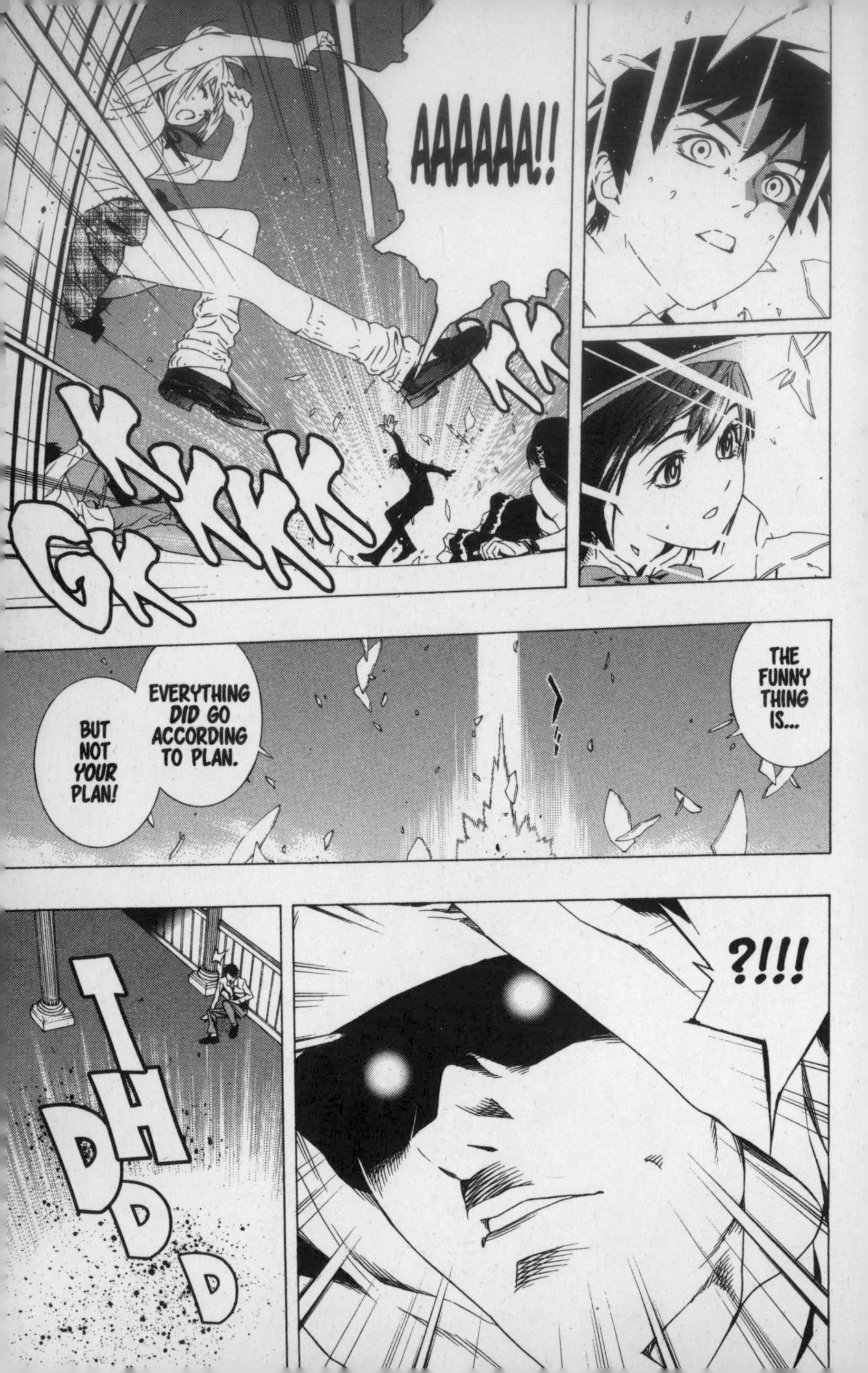
AAAAAA!!
GKKKK
THE FUNNY THING IS...
EVERYTHING *DID* GO ACCORDING TO PLAN.
BUT NOT *YOUR* PLAN!
?!!!
THDDD

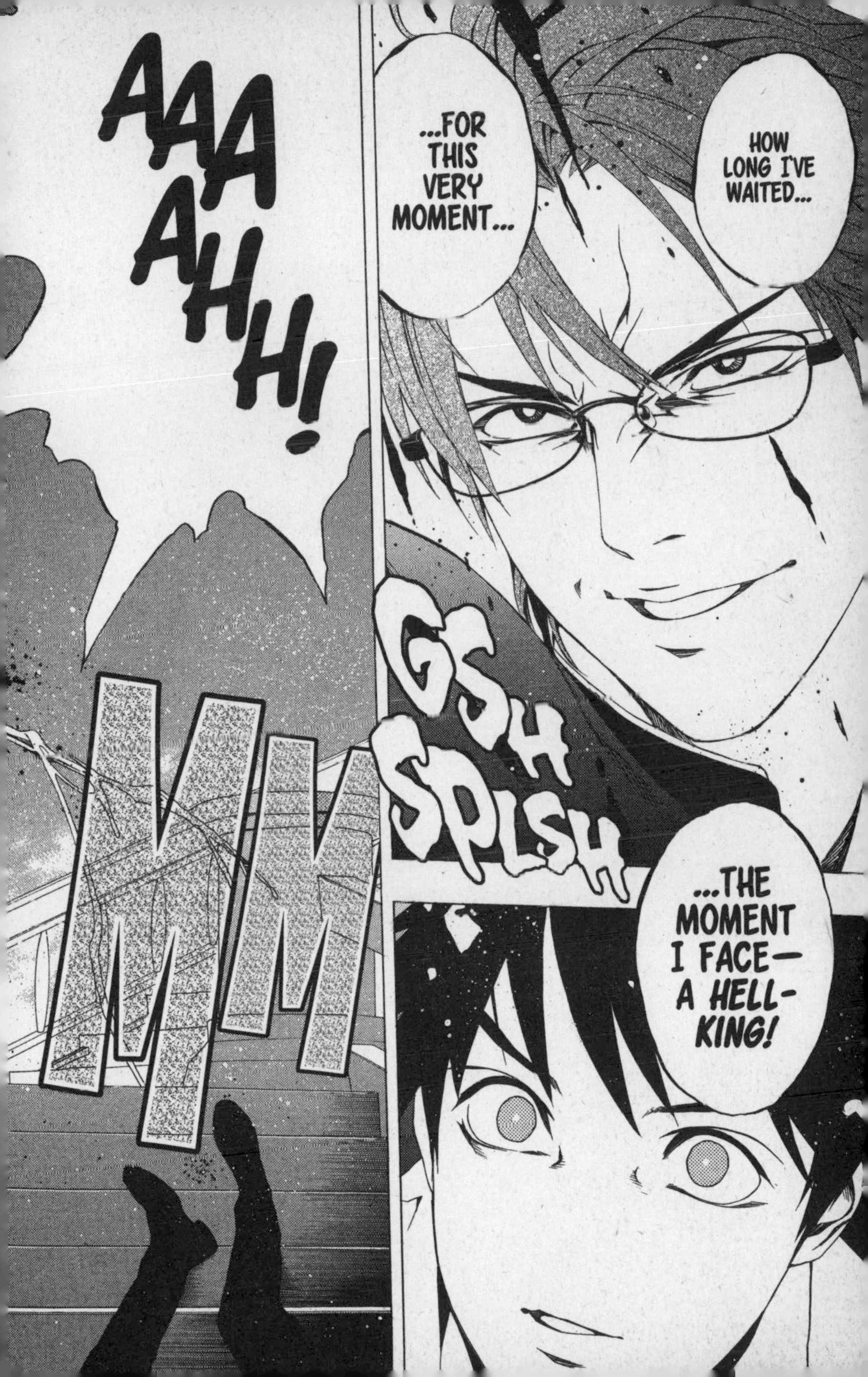
HOW LONG I'VE WAITED...
...FOR THIS VERY MOMENT...
GSH SPLSH
...THE MOMENT I FACE— A HELL-KING!
AAAAHHH!
MMM

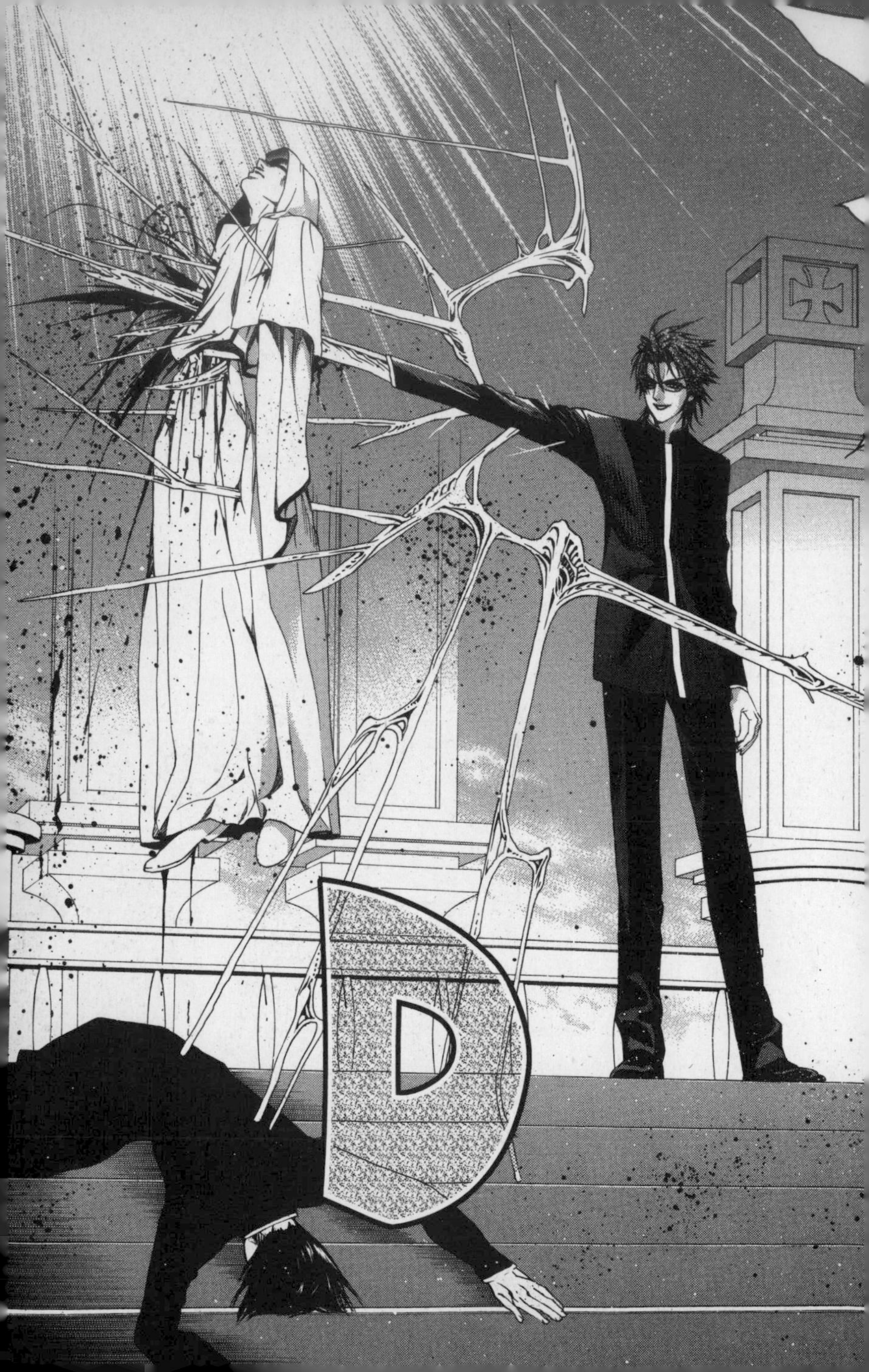
D

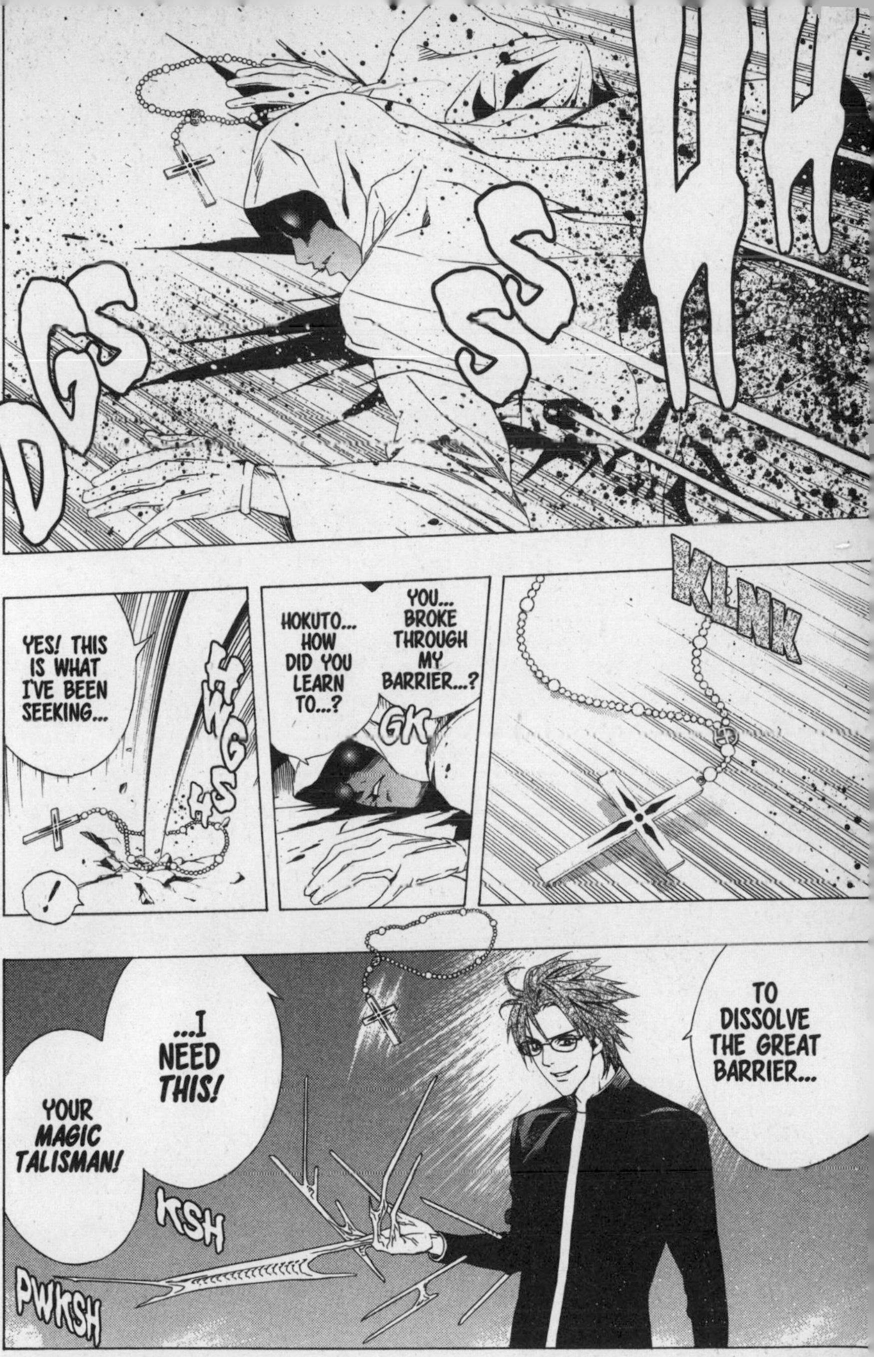
DGS
SS
KLINK
YOU... BROKE THROUGH MY BARRIER...?
HOKUTO... HOW DID YOU LEARN TO...?
GK
HWGSH
YES! THIS IS WHAT I'VE BEEN SEEKING...
!
TO DISSOLVE THE GREAT BARRIER...
...I NEED THIS!
YOUR MAGIC TALISMAN!
KSH
PWKSH

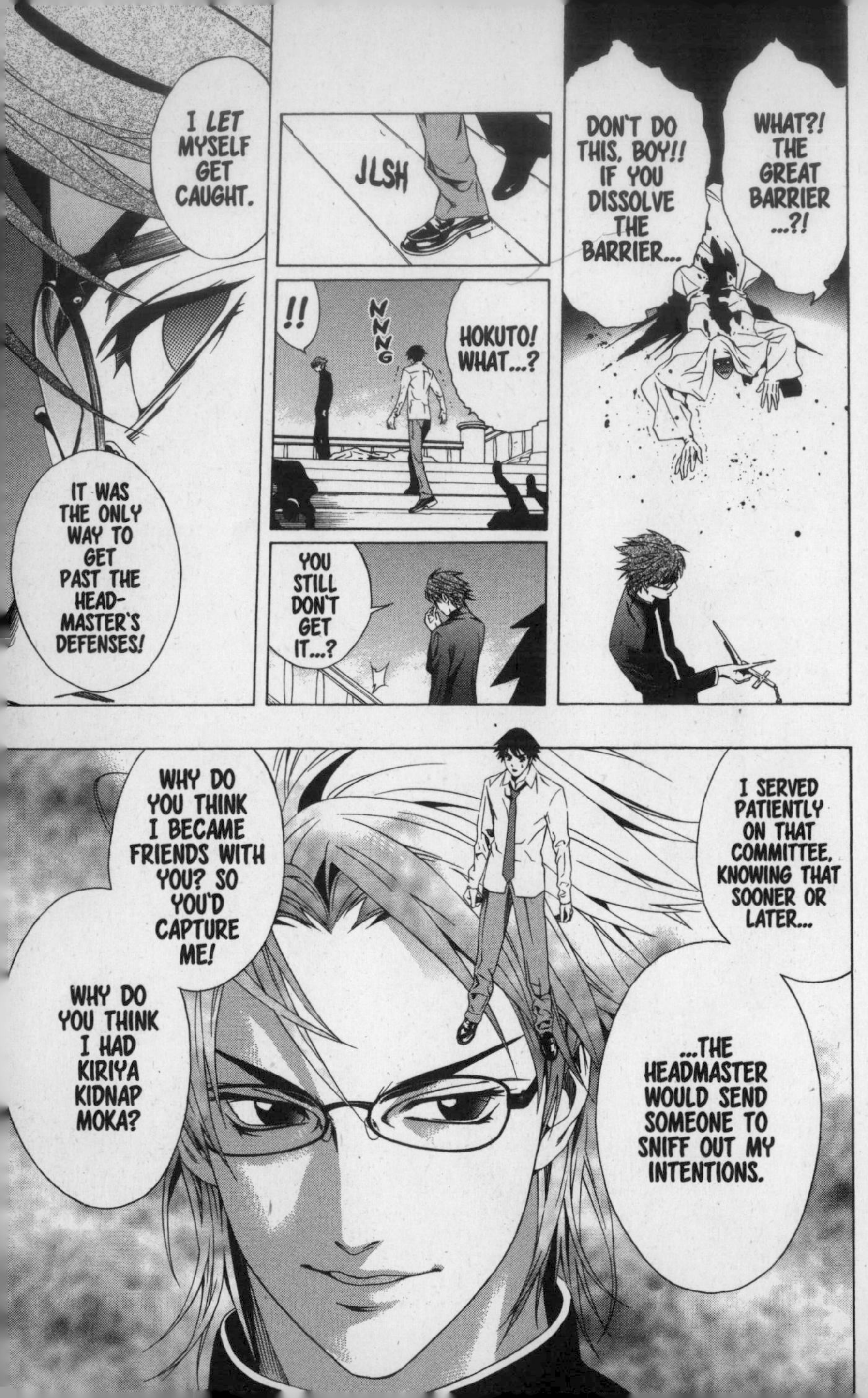
WHAT?! THE GREAT BARRIER ...?!
DON'T DO THIS, BOY!! IF YOU DISSOLVE THE BARRIER...
JLSH
HOKUTO! WHAT...?
NNNG
!!
YOU STILL DON'T GET IT...?
I LET MYSELF GET CAUGHT.
IT WAS THE ONLY WAY TO GET PAST THE HEAD-MASTER'S DEFENSES!
I SERVED PATIENTLY ON THAT COMMITTEE, KNOWING THAT SOONER OR LATER...
...THE HEADMASTER WOULD SEND SOMEONE TO SNIFF OUT MY INTENTIONS.
WHY DO YOU THINK I BECAME FRIENDS WITH YOU? SO YOU'D CAPTURE ME!
WHY DO YOU THINK I HAD KIRIYA KIDNAP MOKA?

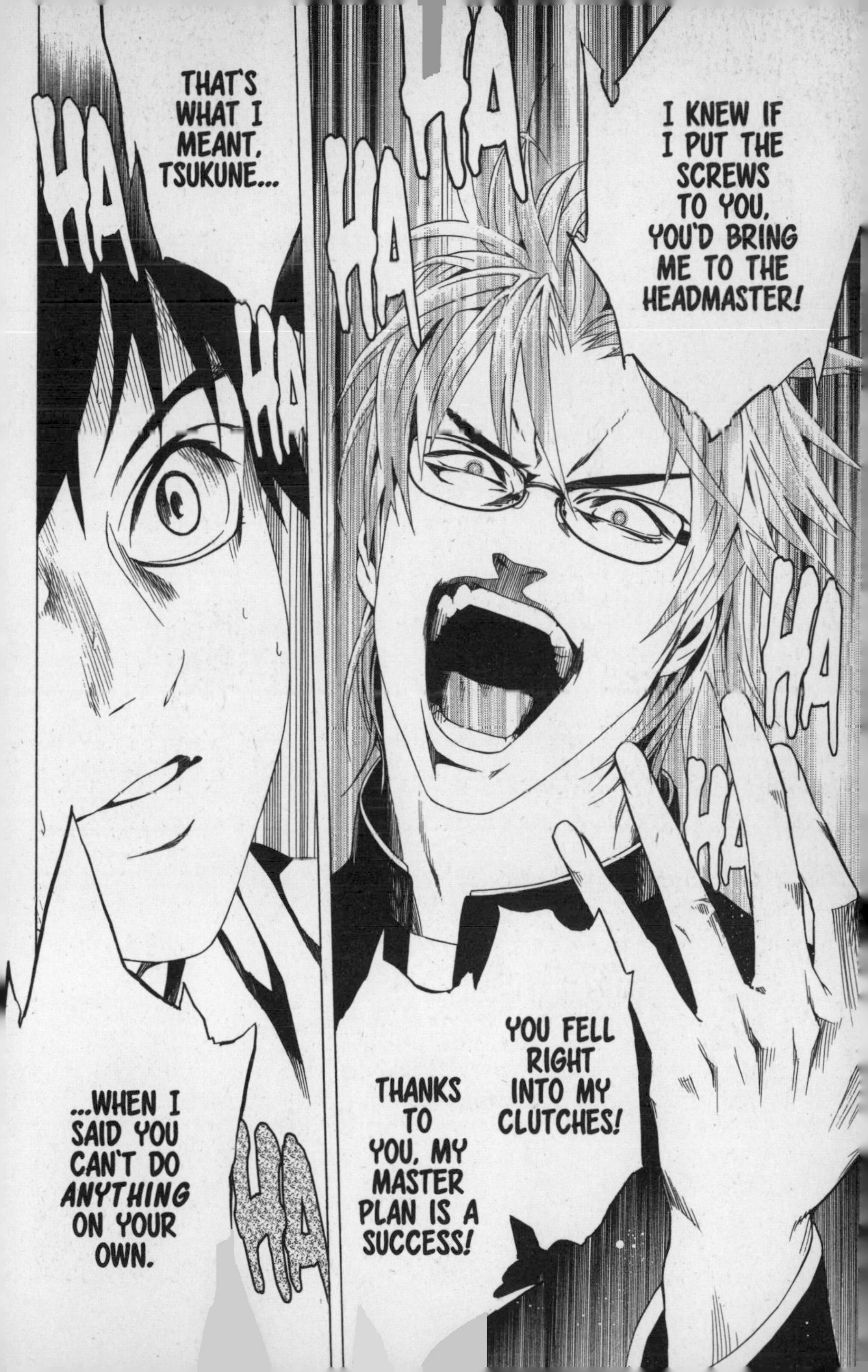
HA HA HA
I KNEW IF I PUT THE SCREWS TO YOU, YOU'D BRING ME TO THE HEADMASTER!
HA HA HA
YOU FELL RIGHT INTO MY CLUTCHES!
THANKS TO YOU, MY MASTER PLAN IS A SUCCESS!
THAT'S WHAT I MEANT, TSUKUNE...
HA HA
...WHEN I SAID YOU CAN'T DO *ANYTHING* ON YOUR OWN.
HA

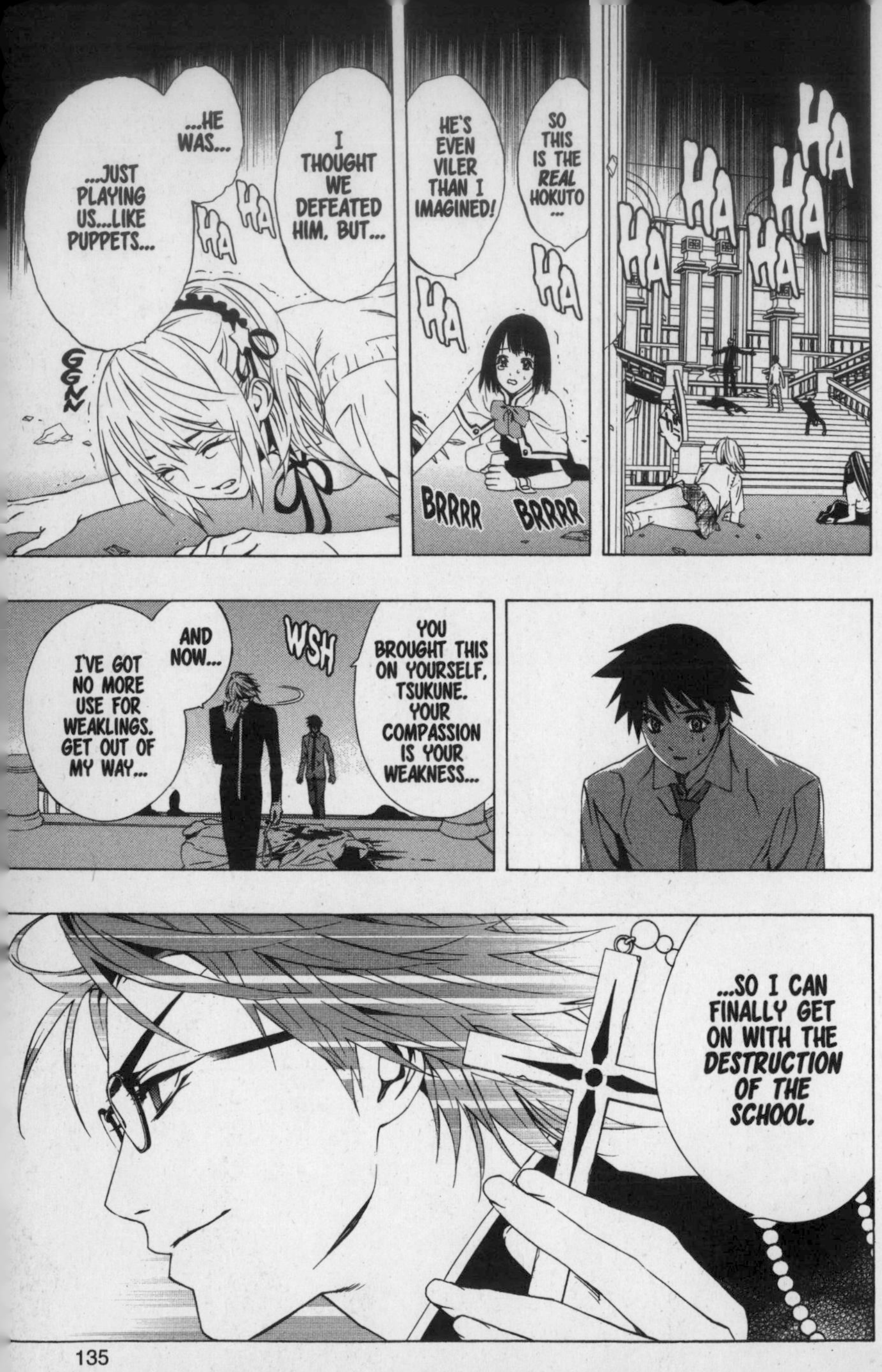
HA HA HA HA HA HA HA HA
SO THIS IS THE *REAL* HOKUTO...
HE'S EVEN VILER THAN I IMAGINED!
HA
HA
BRRRR BRRRR
I THOUGHT WE DEFEATED HIM, BUT...
...HE WAS...
...JUST PLAYING US...LIKE PUPPETS...
HA HA
GGGN
YOU BROUGHT THIS ON YOURSELF, TSUKUNE. YOUR COMPASSION IS YOUR WEAKNESS...
WSH
AND NOW...
I'VE GOT NO MORE USE FOR WEAKLINGS. GET OUT OF MY WAY...
...SO I CAN FINALLY GET ON WITH THE DESTRUCTION OF THE SCHOOL.

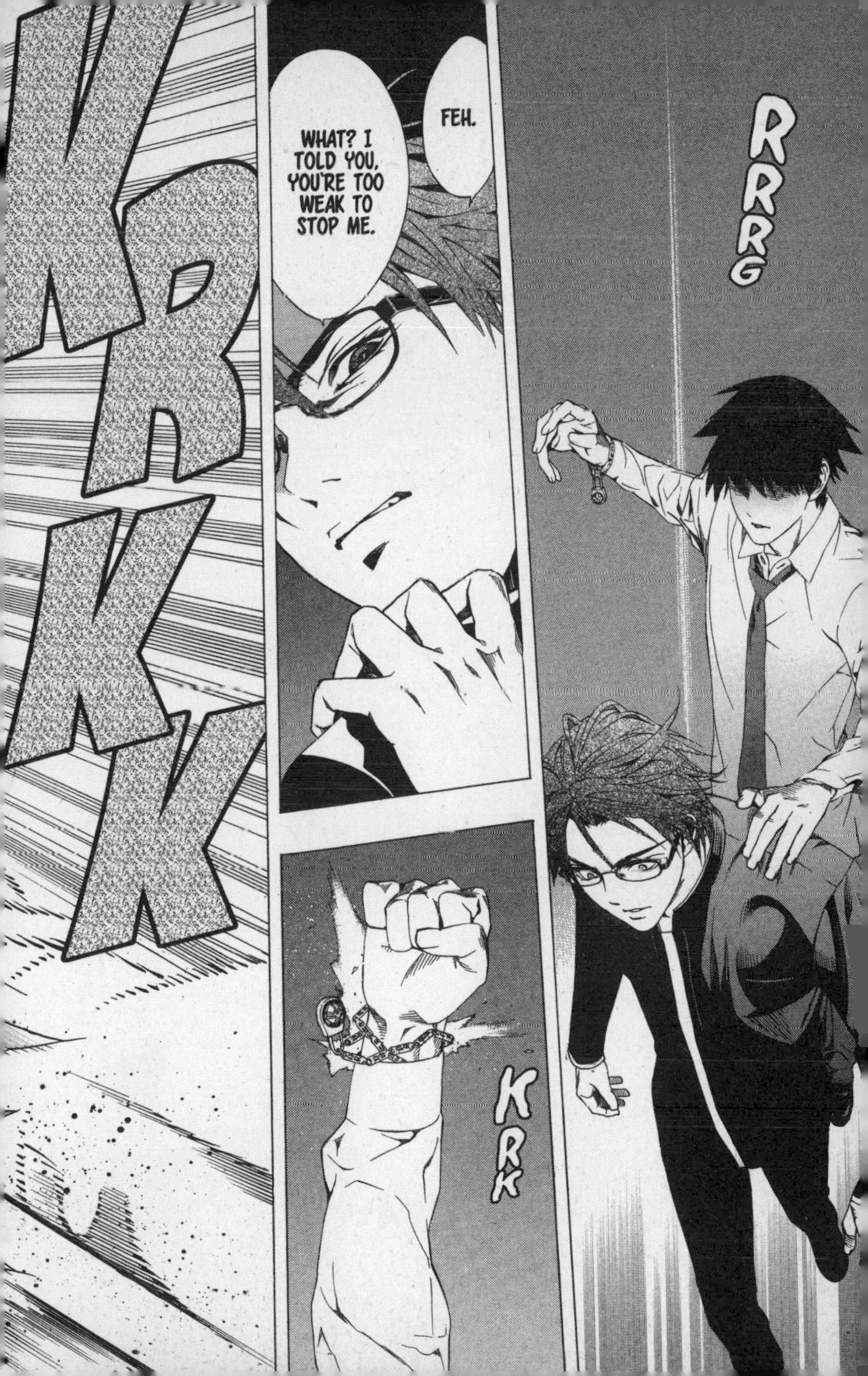
RRRG
FEH.
WHAT? I TOLD YOU, YOU'RE TOO WEAK TO STOP ME.
KRK
KRKKK

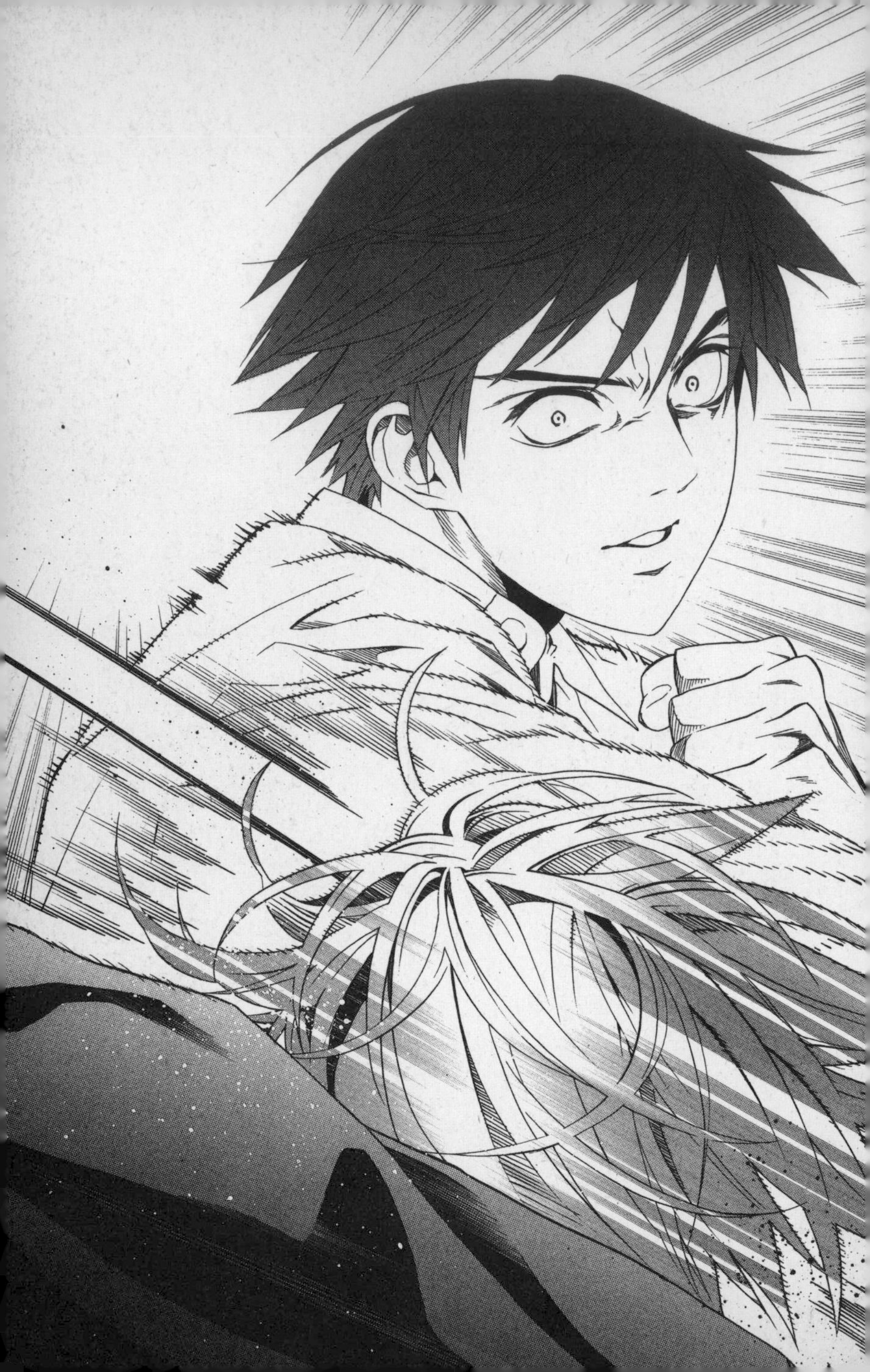

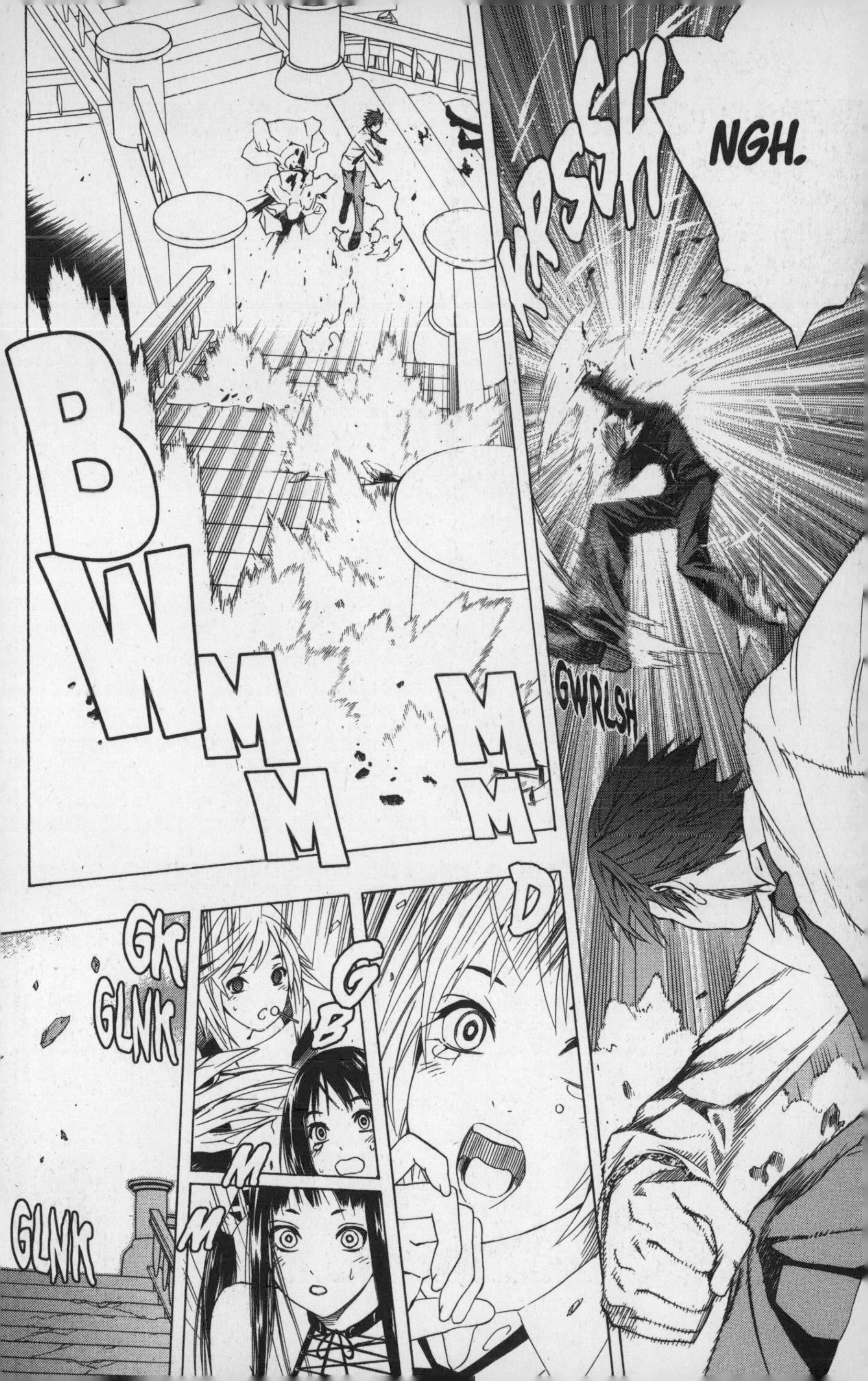
KRSSH
NGH.
GWRLSH
BWMMMMM
D
GB
MM
GK
GLNK
GLNK

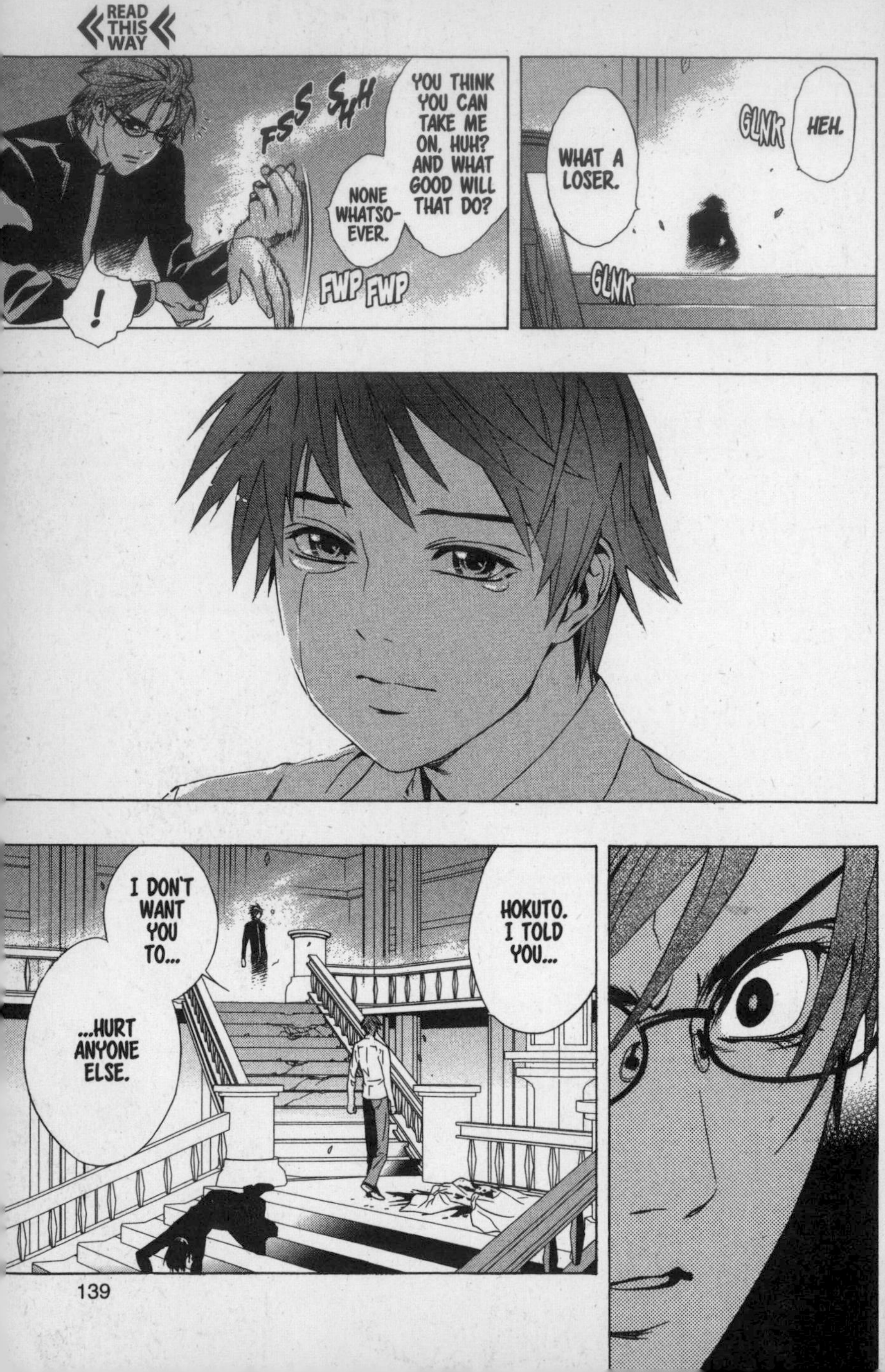
READ THIS WAY
HEH.
GLNK
WHAT A LOSER.
GLNK
YOU THINK YOU CAN TAKE ME ON, HUH? AND WHAT GOOD WILL THAT DO?
FSSSHH
NONE WHATSOEVER.
!
FWP FWP
HOKUTO. I TOLD YOU...
I DON'T WANT YOU TO...
...HURT ANYONE ELSE.

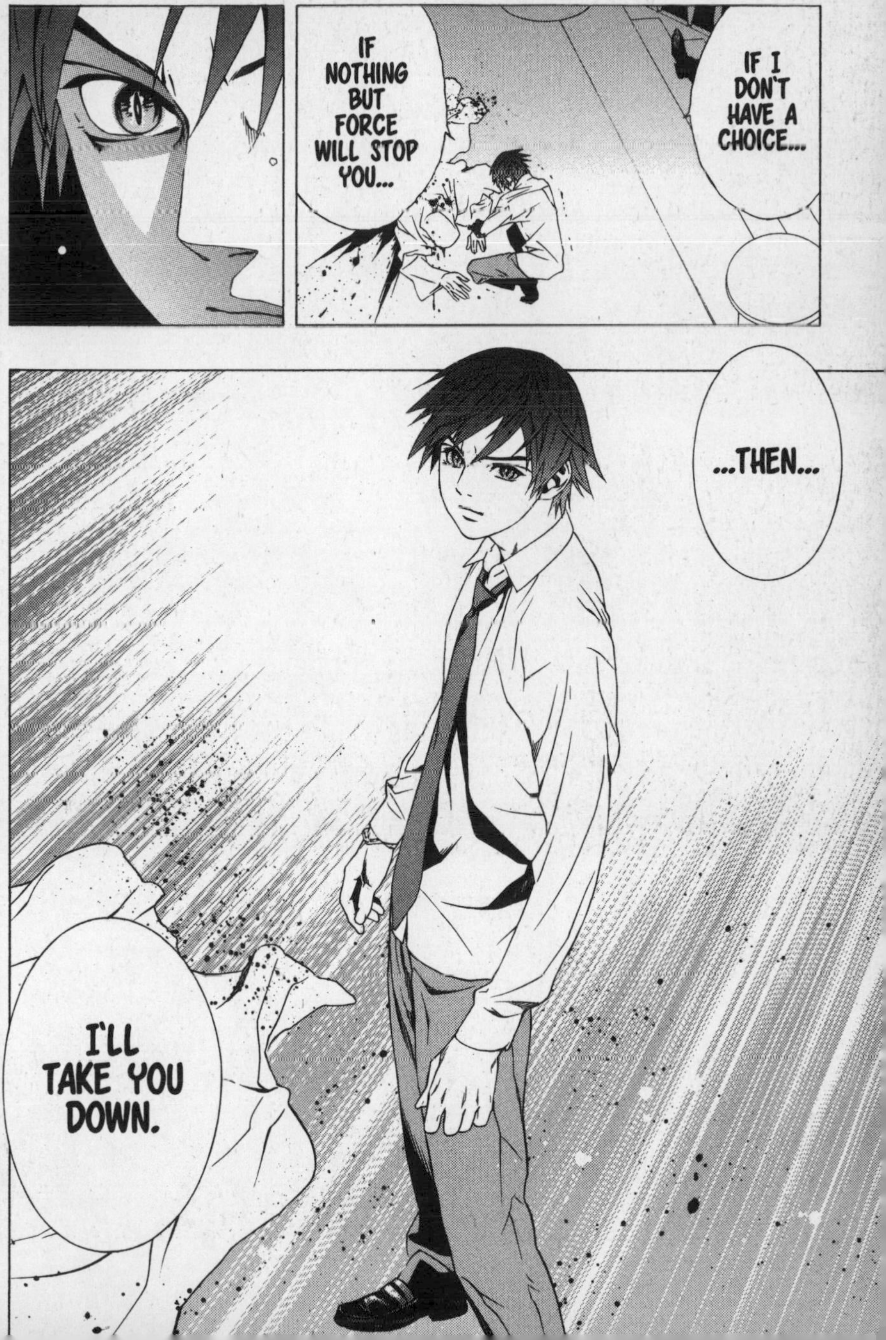
IF I DON'T HAVE A CHOICE...
IF NOTHING BUT FORCE WILL STOP YOU...
...THEN...
I'LL TAKE YOU DOWN.

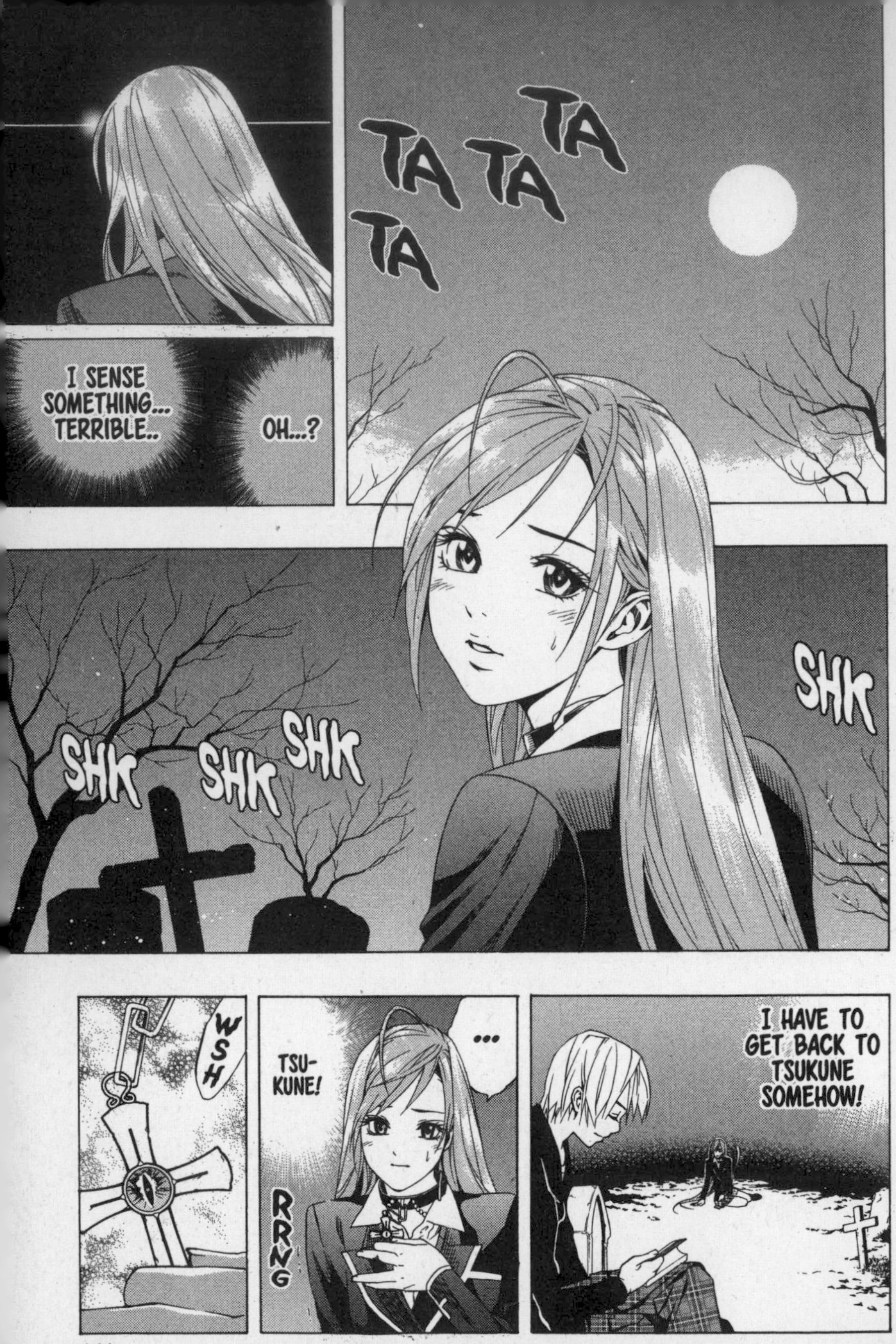
TA TA TA TA TA
OH...?
I SENSE SOMETHING... TERRIBLE..
SHK
SHK
SHK
SHK
I HAVE TO GET BACK TO TSUKUNE SOMEHOW!
...
TSU-KUNE!
RRRNG
WSH

32 : Key

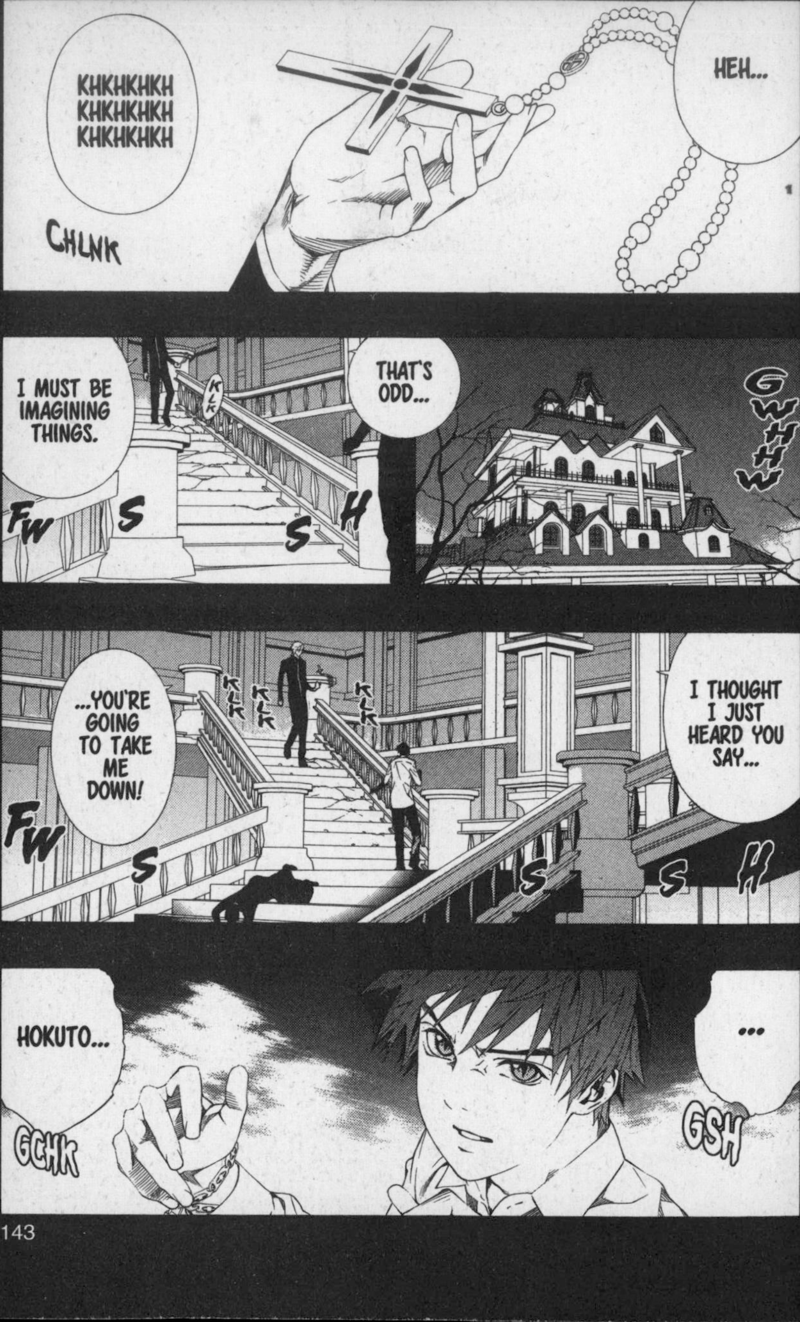
HEH...
KHKHKHKH
KHKHKHKH
KHKHKHKH
CHLNK
GWHHW
THAT'S ODD...
KLK
I MUST BE IMAGINING THINGS.
FWSSH
I THOUGHT I JUST HEARD YOU SAY...
KLK KLK KLK
...YOU'RE GOING TO TAKE ME DOWN!
FWSSSH
...
GSH
HOKUTO...
GCHK

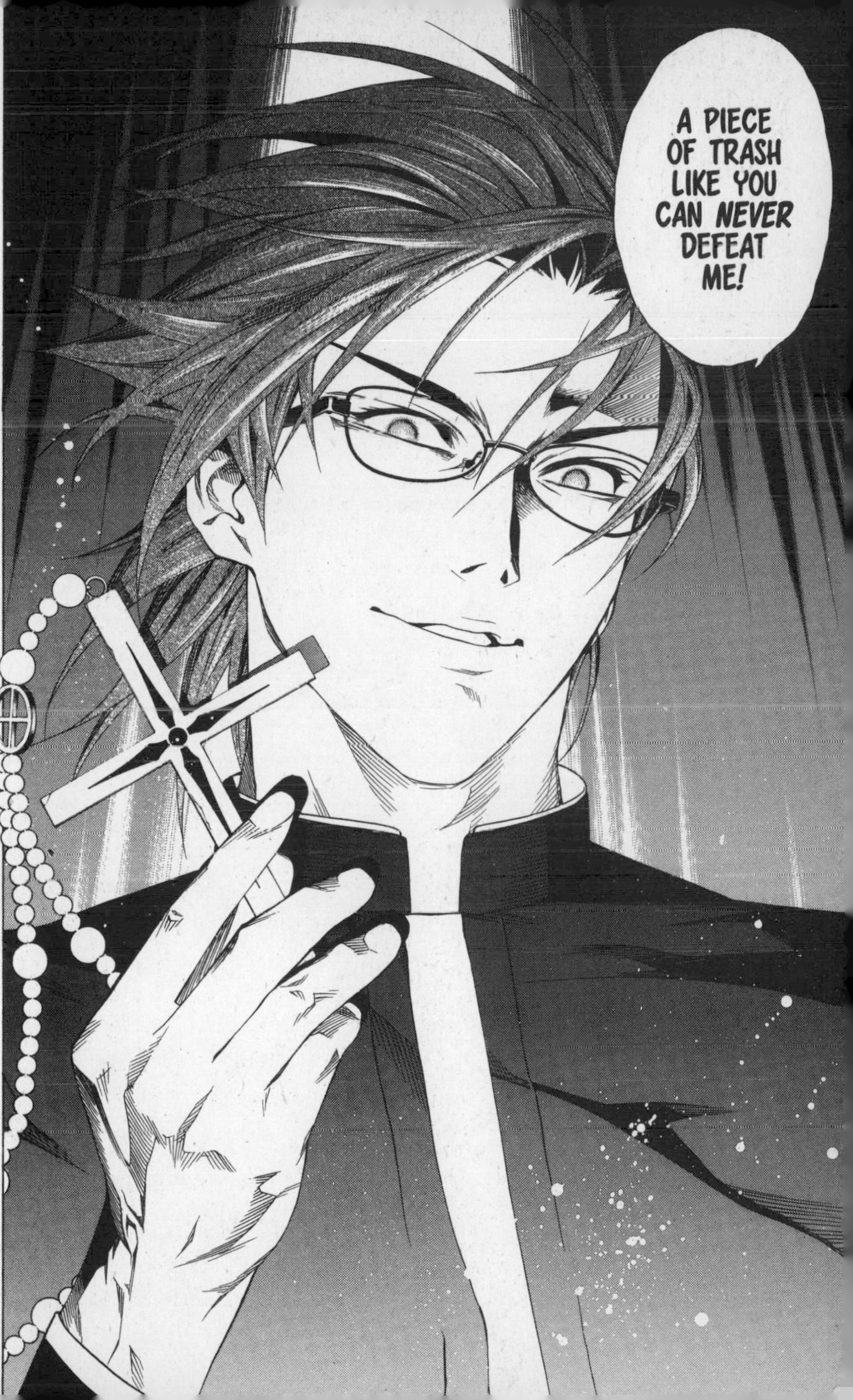
A PIECE OF TRASH LIKE YOU CAN NEVER DEFEAT ME!

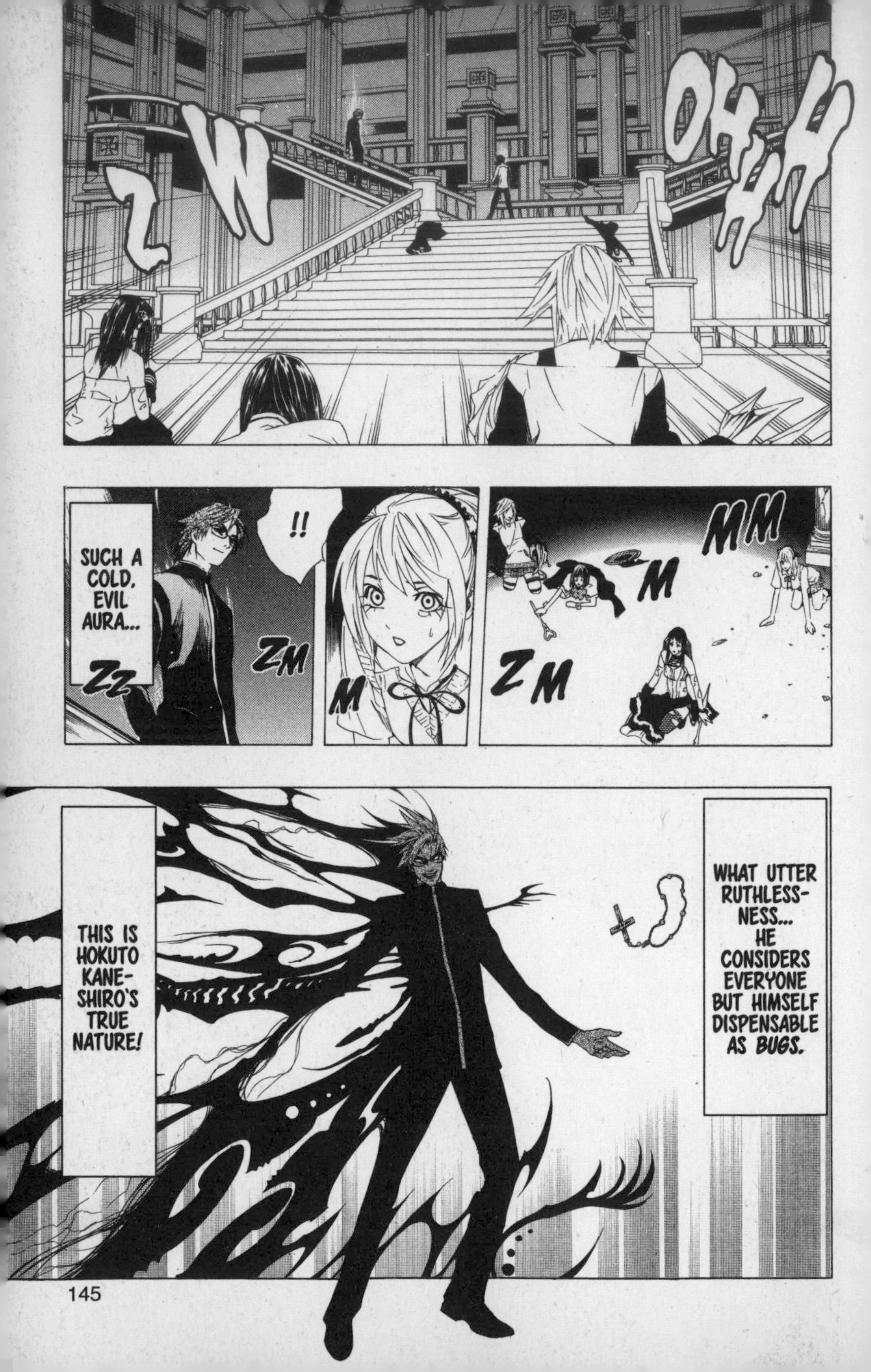
MM
M
ZM
!!
M
SUCH A COLD, EVIL AURA...
ZM
ZZ
WHAT UTTER RUTHLESS-NESS... HE CONSIDERS EVERYONE BUT HIMSELF DISPENSABLE AS BUGS.
THIS IS HOKUTO KANE-SHIRO'S TRUE NATURE!

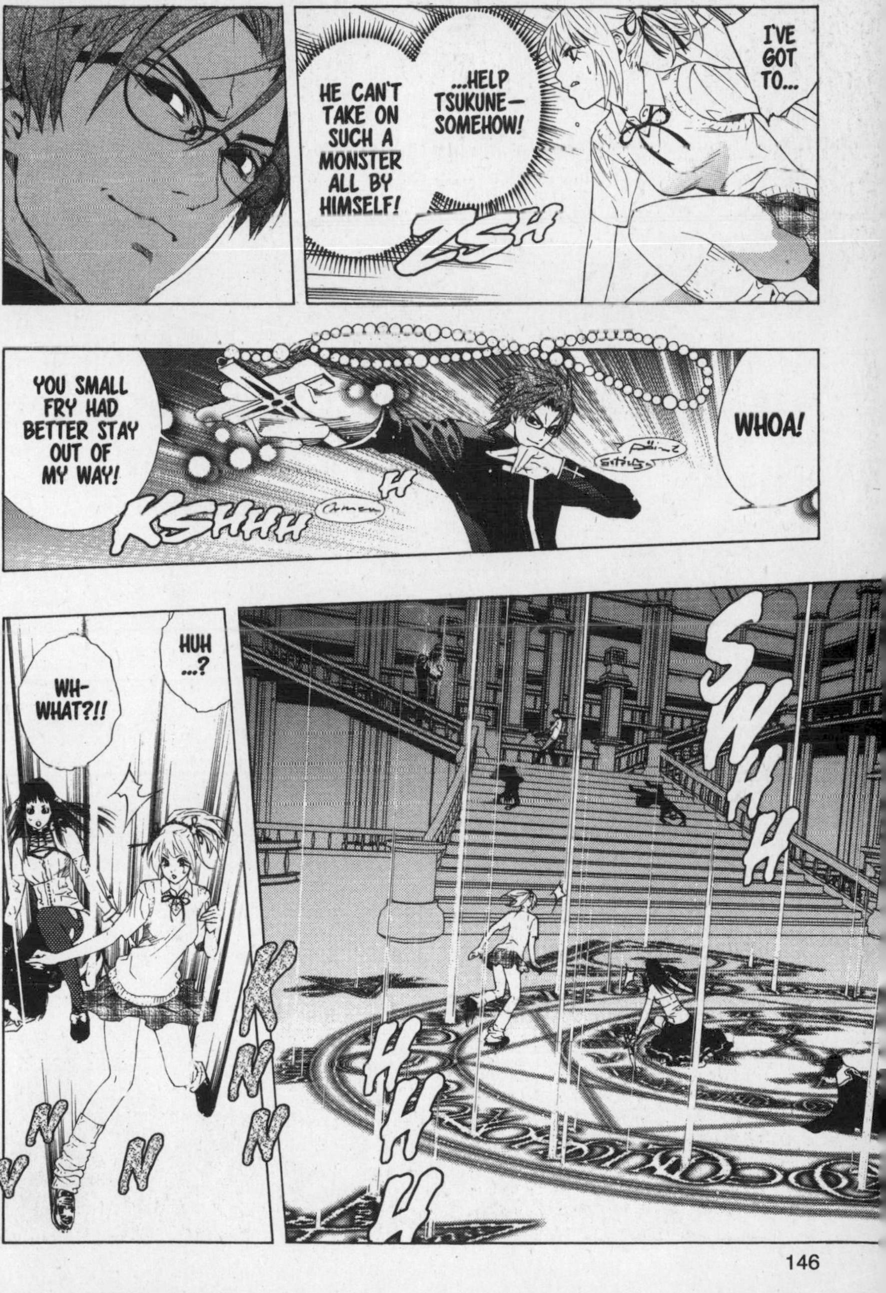
I'VE GOT TO...
...HELP TSUKUNE—SOMEHOW!
HE CAN'T TAKE ON SUCH A MONSTER ALL BY HIMSELF!
ZSH
WHOA!
YOU SMALL FRY HAD BETTER STAY OUT OF MY WAY!
KSHHHH
SWHHH
HHHH
HUH ...?
WH-WHAT?!!
KNNN
NNNN

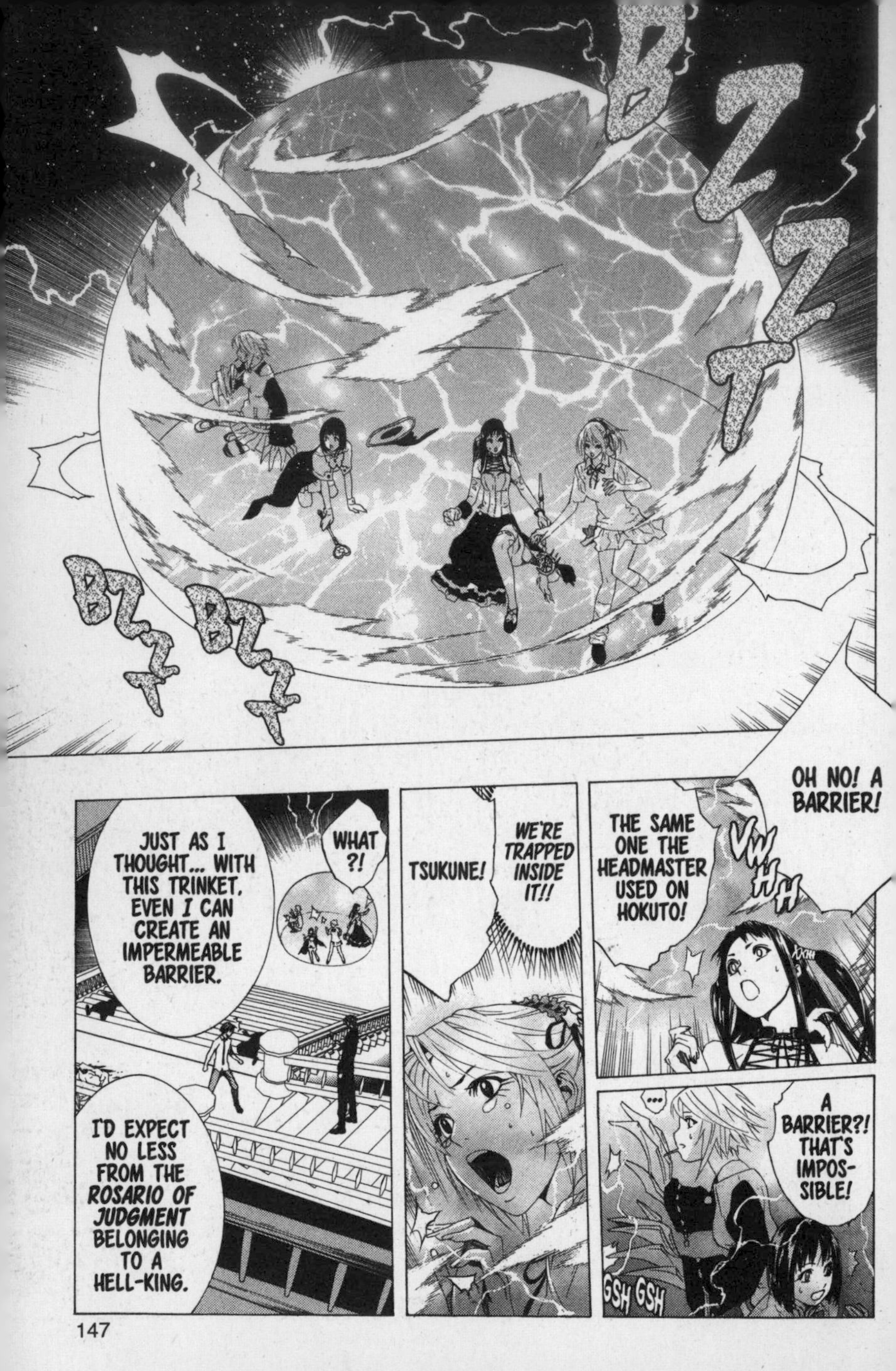
BZZZT
BZZT
BZZT
OH NO! A BARRIER!
VWHH
THE SAME ONE THE HEADMASTER USED ON HOKUTO!
A BARRIER?! THAT'S IMPOS-SIBLE!
...
GSH GSH
WE'RE TRAPPED INSIDE IT!!
TSUKUNE!
WHAT?!
JUST AS I THOUGHT... WITH THIS TRINKET, EVEN *I* CAN CREATE AN IMPERMEABLE BARRIER.
I'D EXPECT NO LESS FROM THE *ROSARIO OF JUDGMENT* BELONGING TO A HELL-KING.

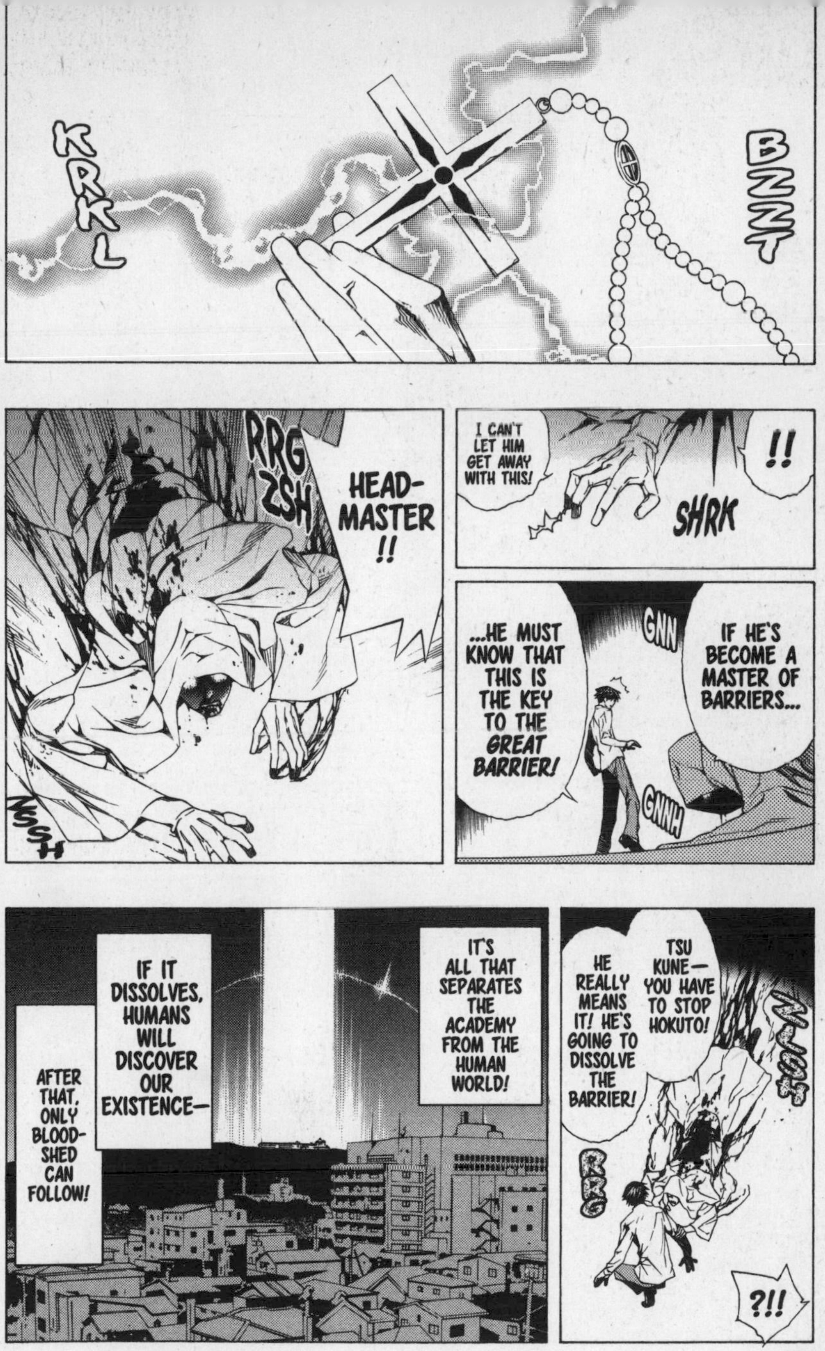
BZZT
KRKL
!!
I CAN'T LET HIM GET AWAY WITH THIS!
SHRK
IF HE'S BECOME A MASTER OF BARRIERS...
GNN
...HE MUST KNOW THAT THIS IS THE KEY TO THE GREAT BARRIER!
GNNH
RRG ZSH
HEAD-MASTER !!
TSU KUNE— YOU HAVE TO STOP HOKUTO!
HE REALLY MEANS IT! HE'S GOING TO DISSOLVE THE BARRIER!
RRG
?!!
IT'S ALL THAT SEPARATES THE ACADEMY FROM THE HUMAN WORLD!
IF IT DISSOLVES, HUMANS WILL DISCOVER OUR EXISTENCE—
AFTER THAT, ONLY BLOOD-SHED CAN FOLLOW!

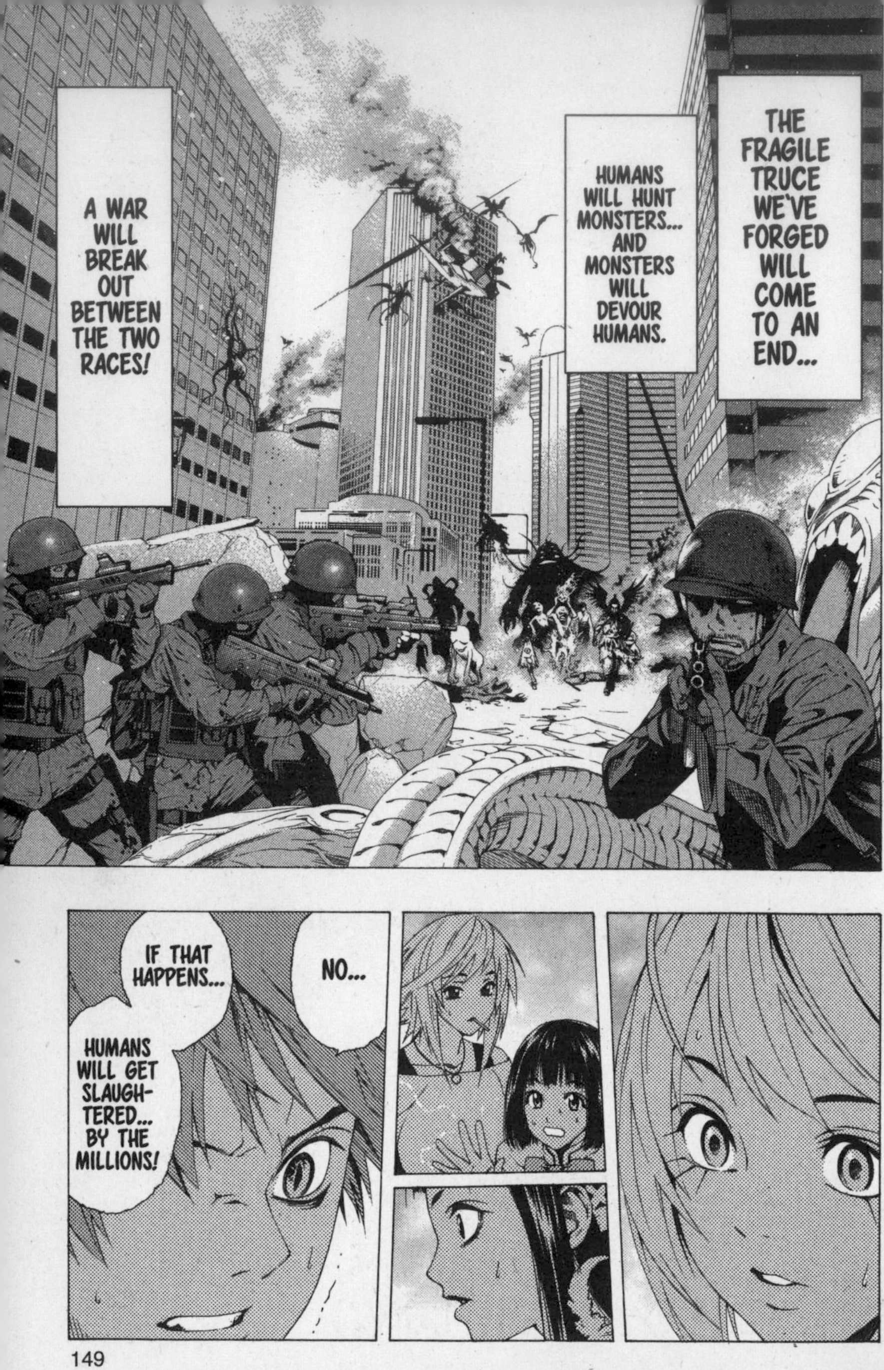
THE FRAGILE TRUCE WE'VE FORGED WILL COME TO AN END...
HUMANS WILL HUNT MONSTERS... AND MONSTERS WILL DEVOUR HUMANS.
A WAR WILL BREAK OUT BETWEEN THE TWO RACES!
NO...
IF THAT HAPPENS...
HUMANS WILL GET SLAUGHTERED... BY THE MILLIONS!

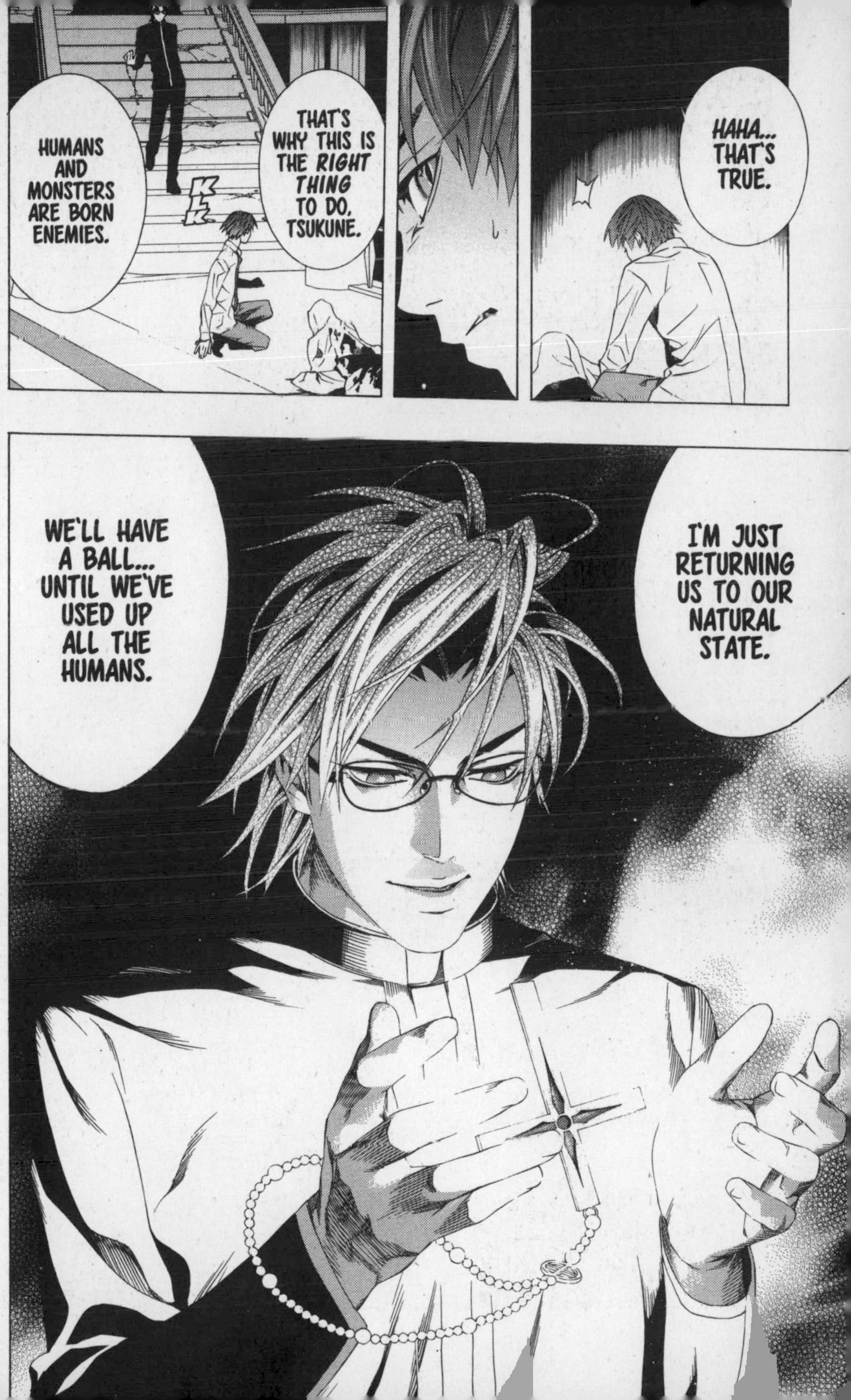
HAHA... THAT'S TRUE.
THAT'S WHY THIS IS THE RIGHT THING TO DO, TSUKUNE.
HUMANS AND MONSTERS ARE BORN ENEMIES.
KLK
I'M JUST RETURNING US TO OUR NATURAL STATE.
WE'LL HAVE A BALL... UNTIL WE'VE USED UP ALL THE HUMANS.

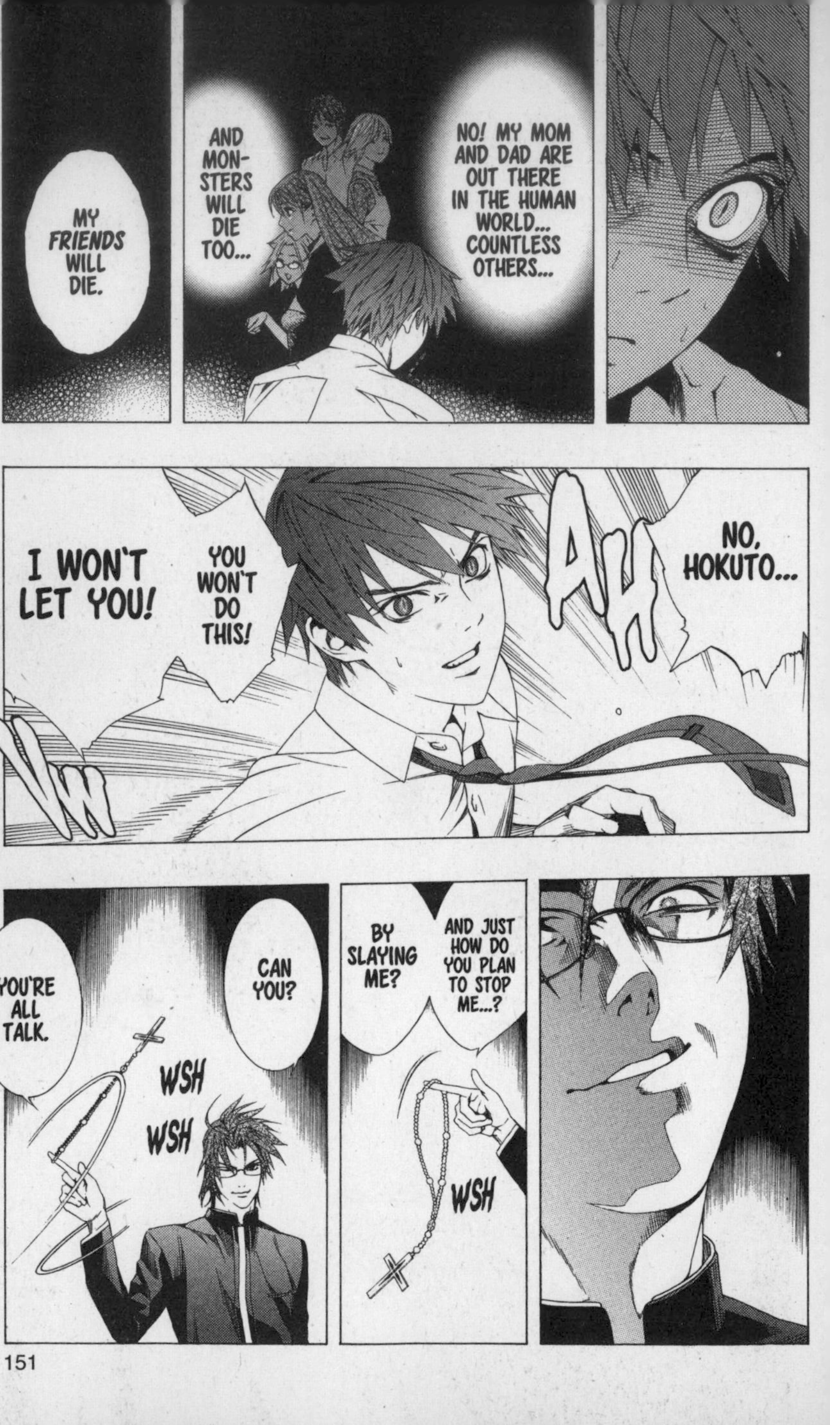
NO! MY MOM AND DAD ARE OUT THERE IN THE HUMAN WORLD... COUNTLESS OTHERS...
AND MONSTERS WILL DIE TOO...
MY FRIENDS WILL DIE.
NO, HOKUTO...
AH
YOU WON'T DO THIS!
I WON'T LET YOU!
VW
AND JUST HOW DO YOU PLAN TO STOP ME...?
BY SLAYING ME?
WSH
CAN YOU?
YOU'RE ALL TALK.
WSH
WSH

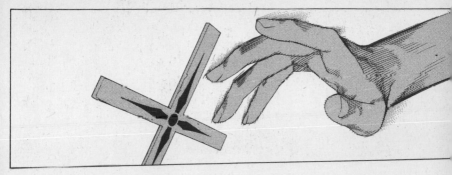

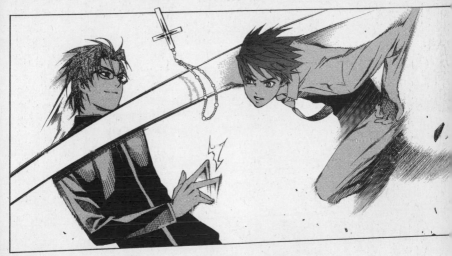

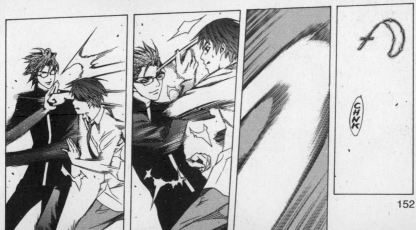

CHNK

READ THIS WAY

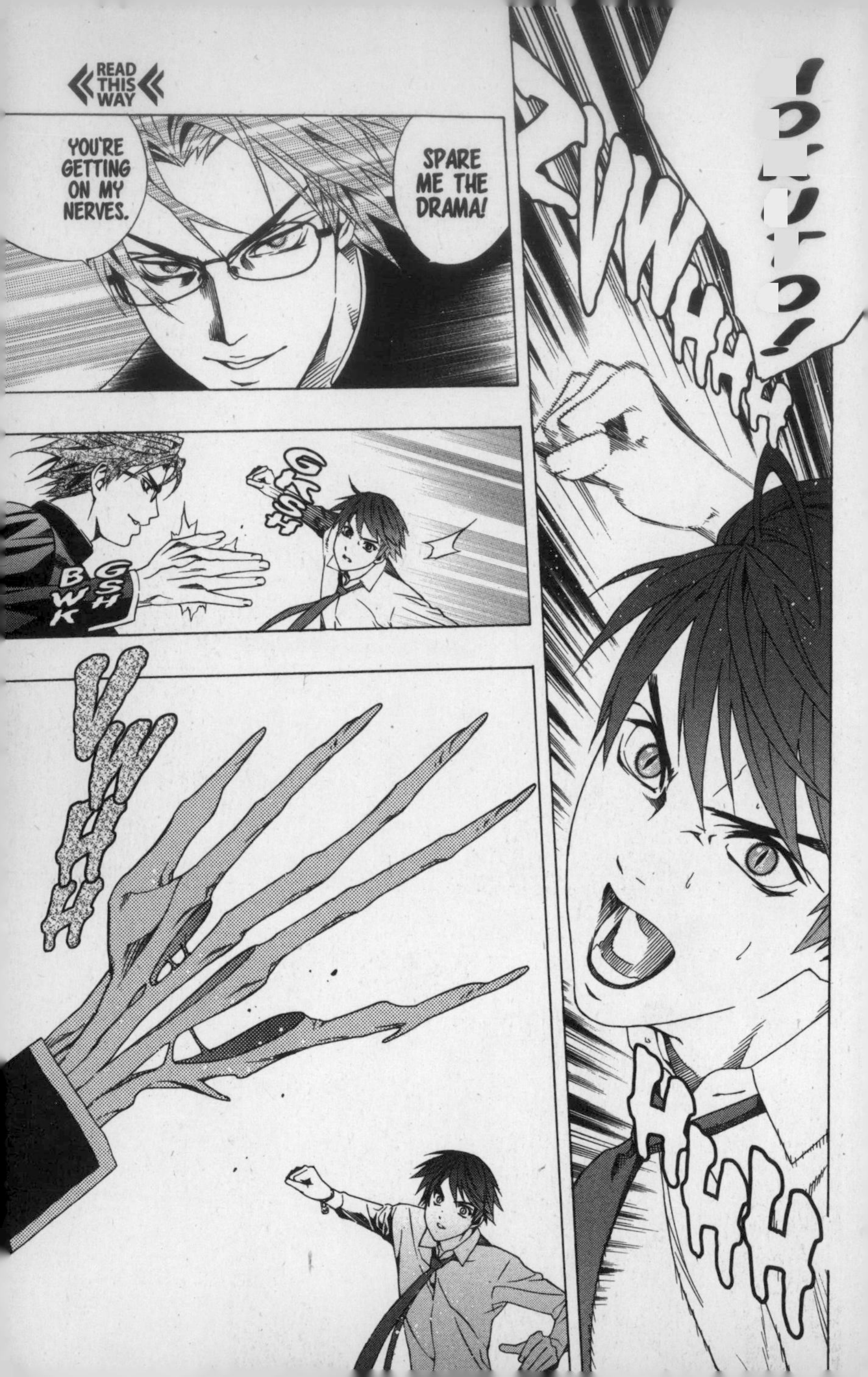
SPARE ME THE DRAMA!
YOU'RE GETTING ON MY NERVES.
GKSH
GSH
BWK

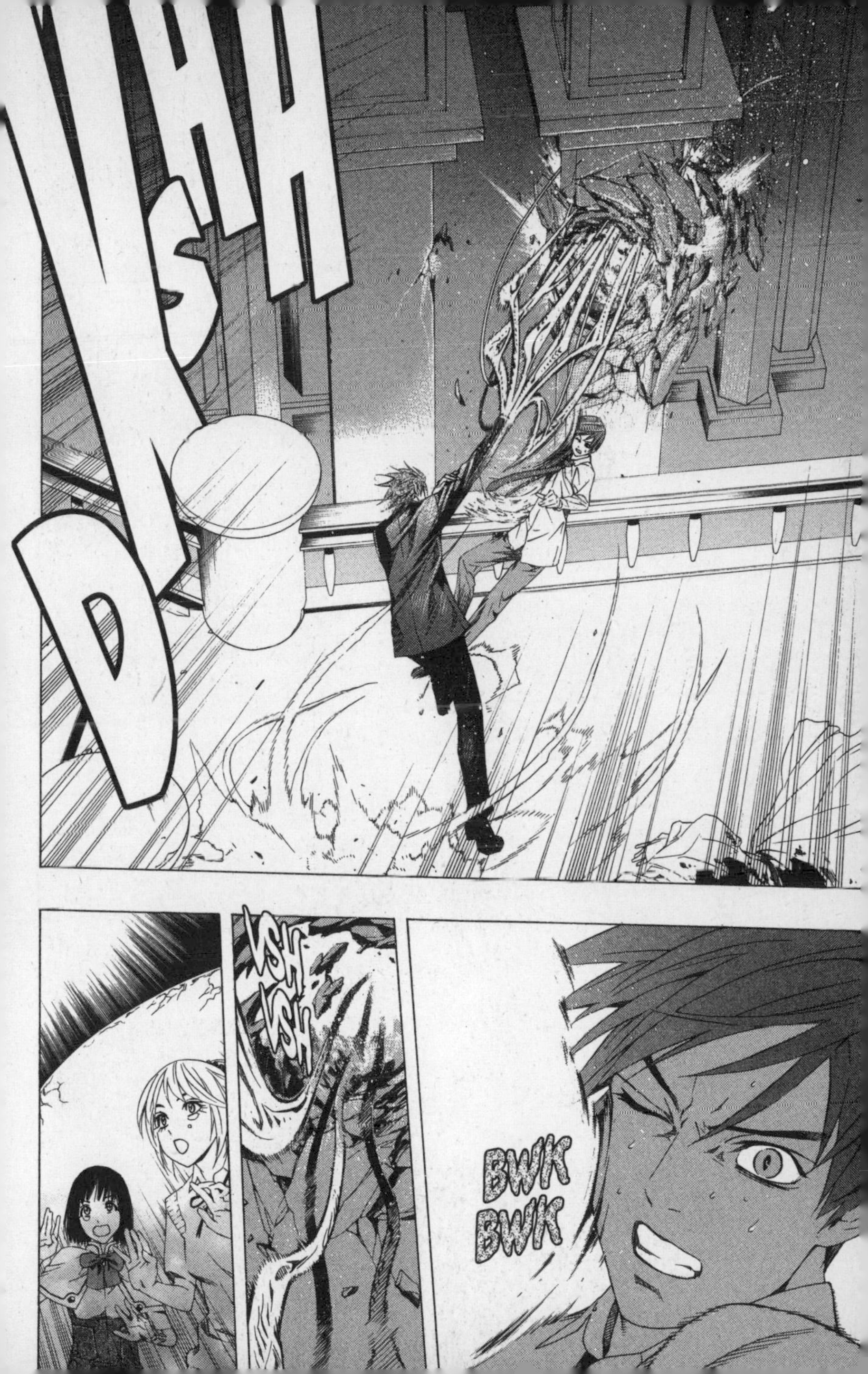
DVSHH
BWK BWK
VSH VSH

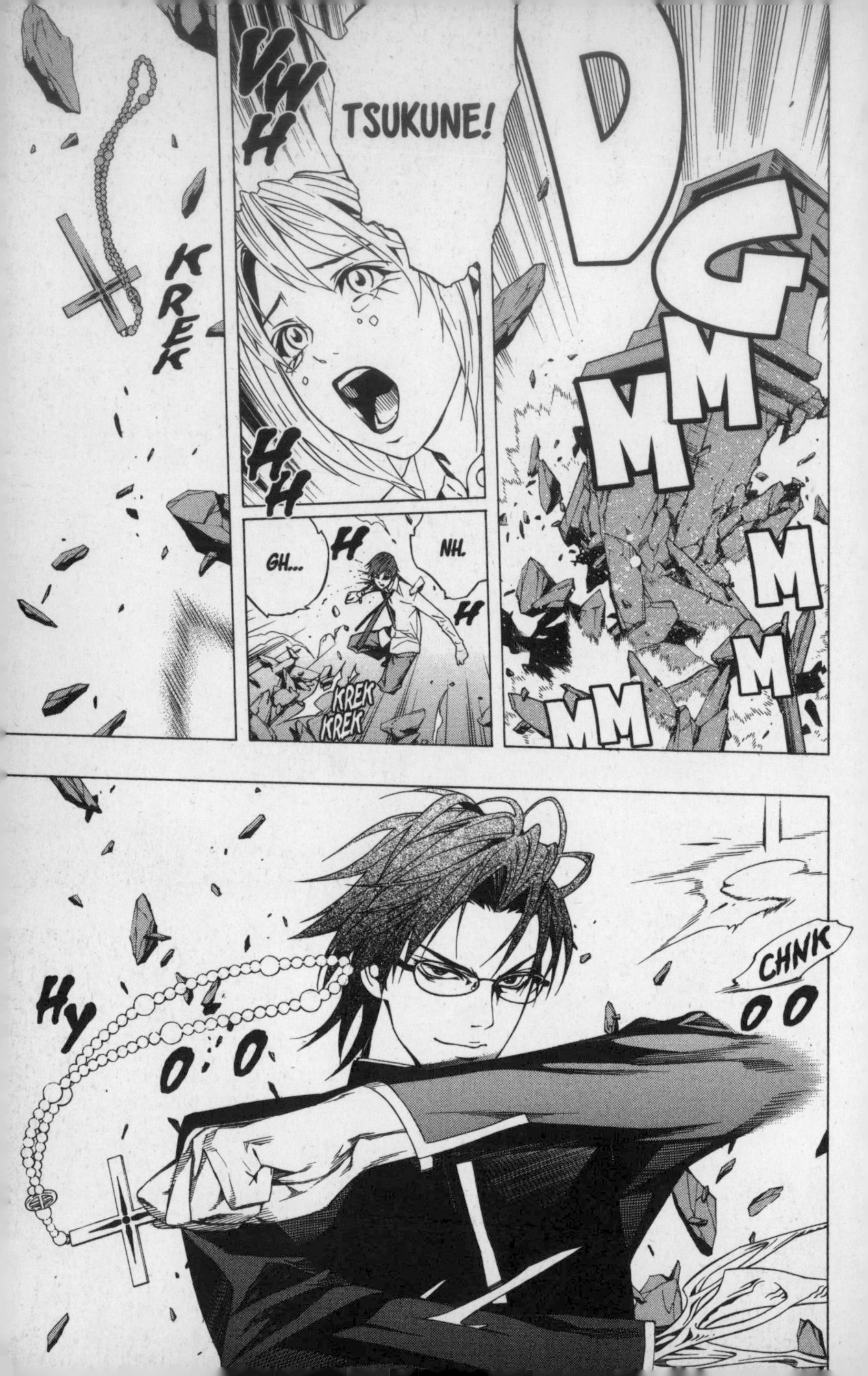

DG
MMM
MM
M
MM
VWH
TSUKUNE!
HHH
GH...
H
NH.
H
KREK
KREK
KREK
CHNK
OO
Hy
O O

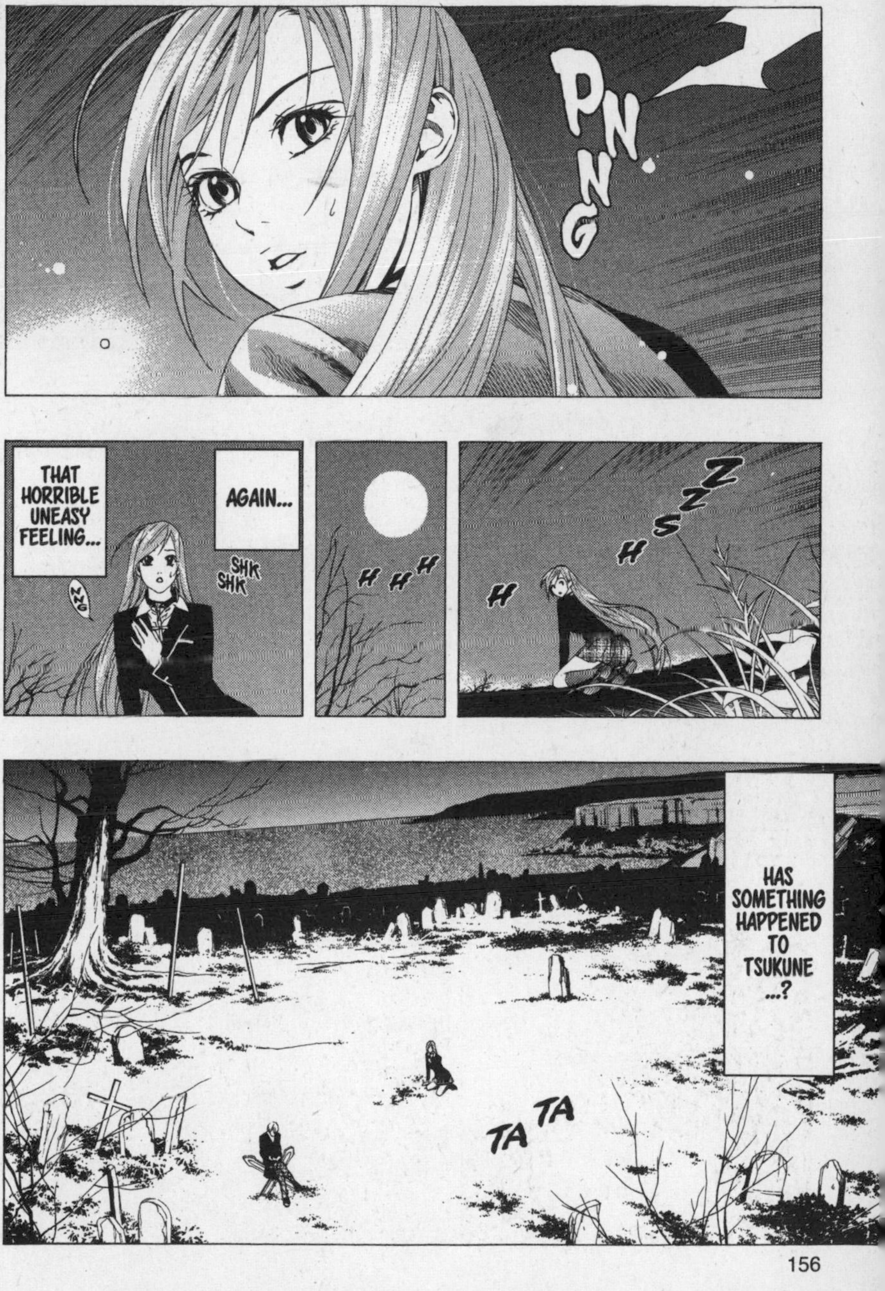
PNNG
HHSSZZ
HHH
THAT HORRIBLE UNEASY FEELING...
AGAIN...
NNG
SHK SHK
HAS SOMETHING HAPPENED TO TSUKUNE ...?
TA TA

READ THIS WAY

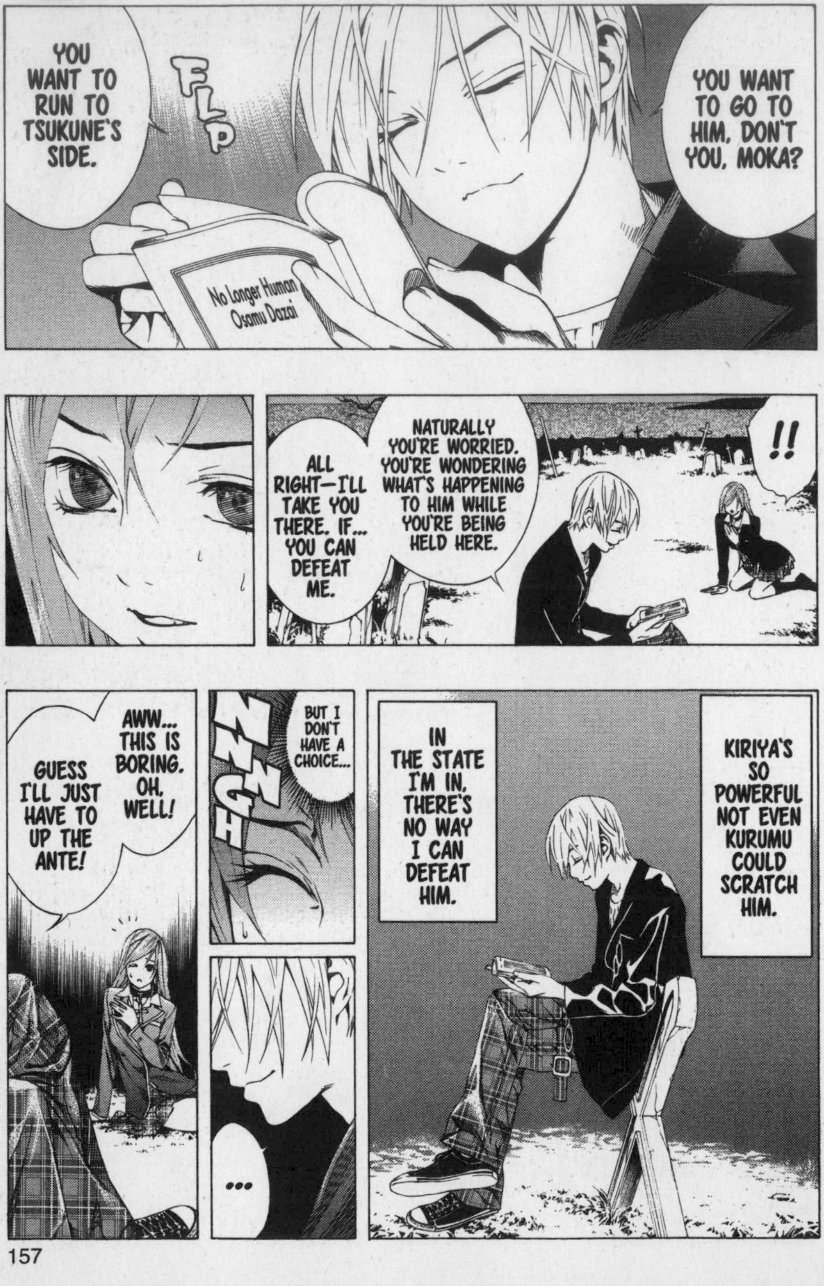

YOU WANT TO GO TO HIM, DON'T YOU, MOKA?
FLP
YOU WANT TO RUN TO TSUKUNE'S SIDE.
No Longer Human Osamu Dazai
!!
NATURALLY YOU'RE WORRIED. YOU'RE WONDERING WHAT'S HAPPENING TO HIM WHILE YOU'RE BEING HELD HERE.
ALL RIGHT—I'LL TAKE YOU THERE. IF... YOU CAN DEFEAT ME.
KIRIYA'S SO POWERFUL NOT EVEN KURUMU COULD SCRATCH HIM.
IN THE STATE I'M IN, THERE'S NO WAY I CAN DEFEAT HIM.
BUT I DON'T HAVE A CHOICE...
NNNGH
...
AWW... THIS IS BORING. OH, WELL!
GUESS I'LL JUST HAVE TO UP THE ANTE!

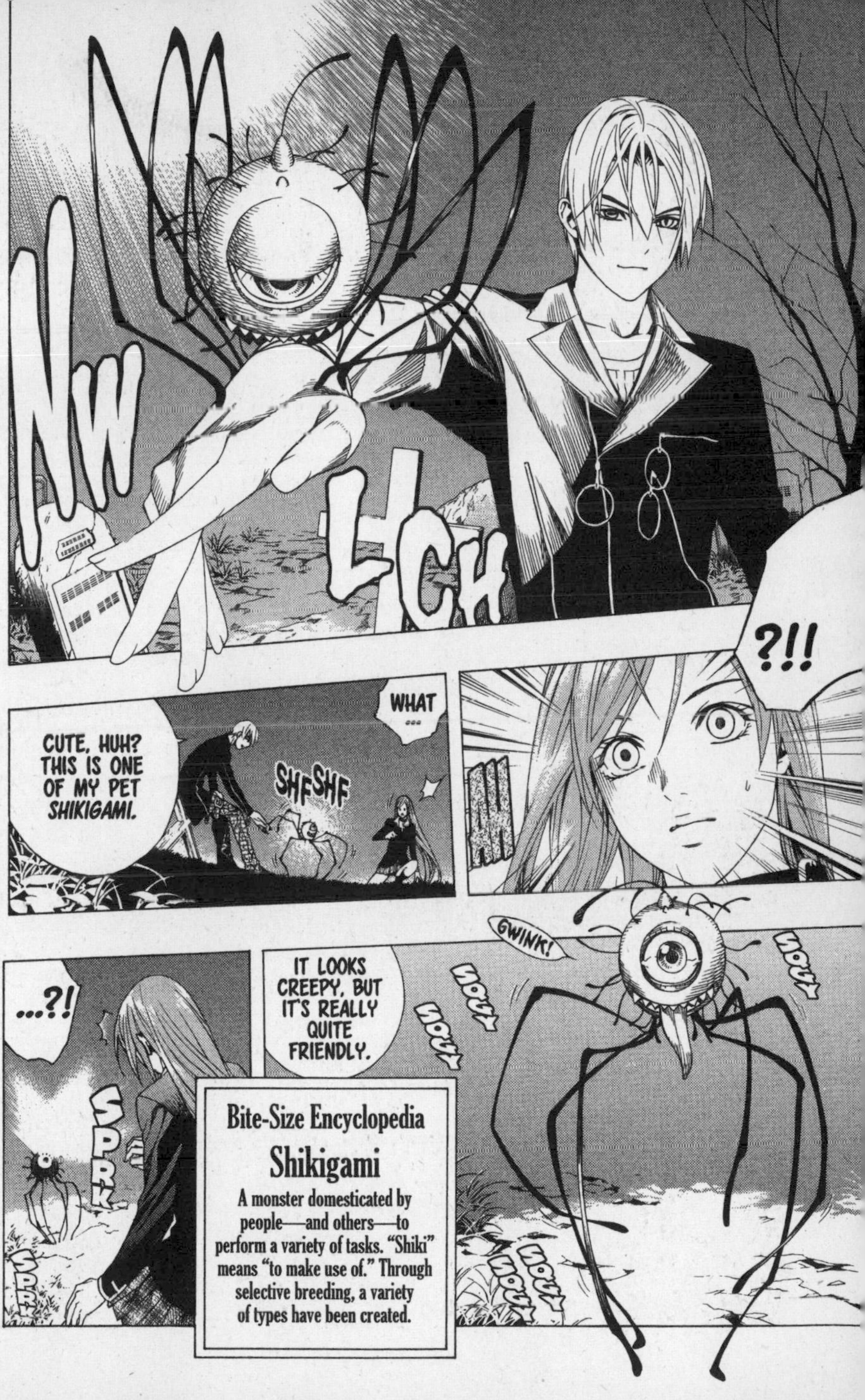
NW
LCH
?!!
WHAT...
CUTE, HUH? THIS IS ONE OF MY PET SHIKIGAMI.
SHF SHF
GWINK!
IT LOOKS CREEPY, BUT IT'S REALLY QUITE FRIENDLY.
...?!
SPRK
SPRK
Bite-Size Encyclopedia
Shikigami
A monster domesticated by people—and others—to perform a variety of tasks. "Shiki" means "to make use of." Through selective breeding, a variety of types have been created.

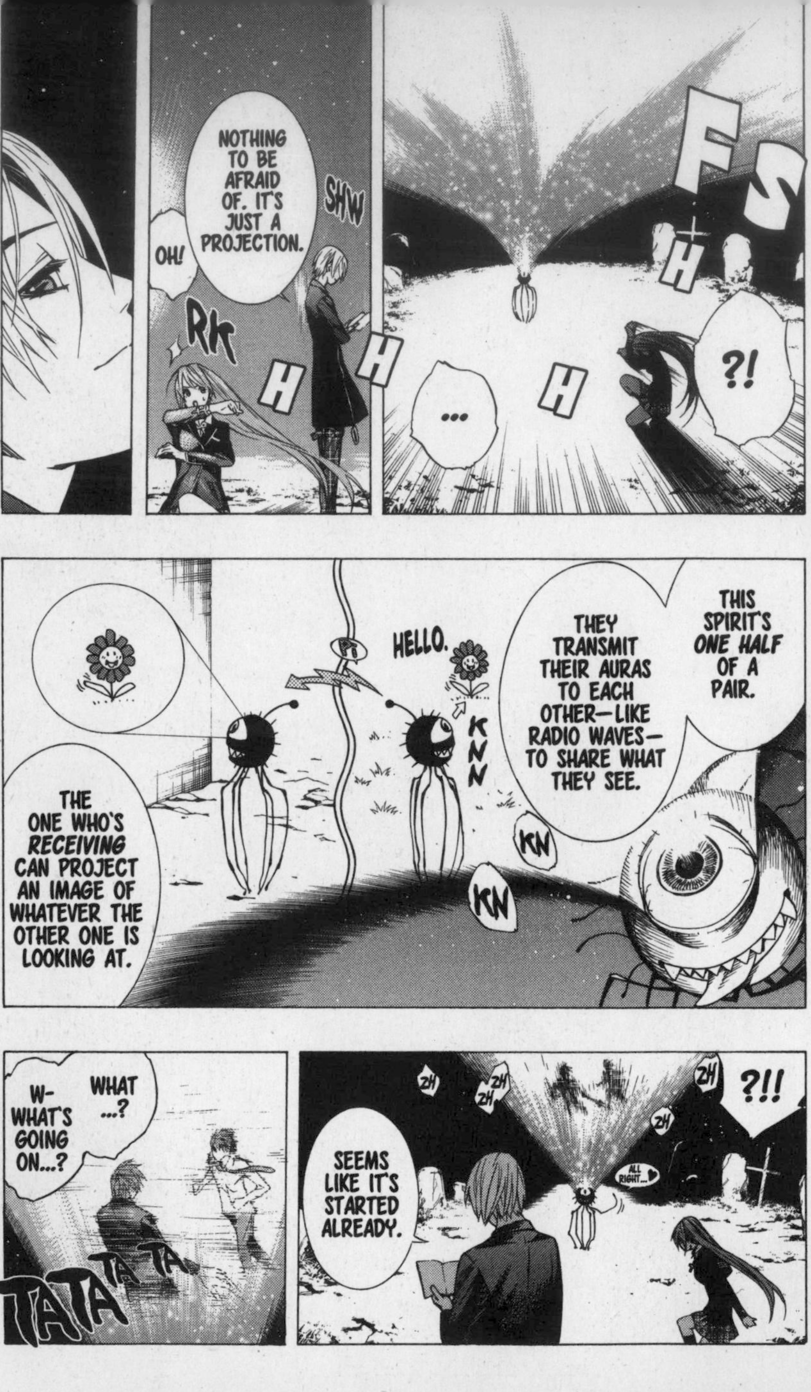
FS
H
?!
...
H
H
NOTHING TO BE AFRAID OF. IT'S JUST A PROJECTION.
SHW
OH!
RK
H
THIS SPIRIT'S *ONE HALF* OF A PAIR.
THEY TRANSMIT THEIR AURAS TO EACH OTHER—LIKE RADIO WAVES—TO SHARE WHAT THEY SEE.
KN
KN
KNN
HELLO.
PI
THE ONE WHO'S *RECEIVING* CAN PROJECT AN IMAGE OF WHATEVER THE OTHER ONE IS LOOKING AT.
?!!
ZH
ZH
ZH
ZH
ZH
ALL RIGHT...♥
SEEMS LIKE IT'S STARTED ALREADY.
WHAT ...?
W-WHAT'S GOING ON...?
TATATATA

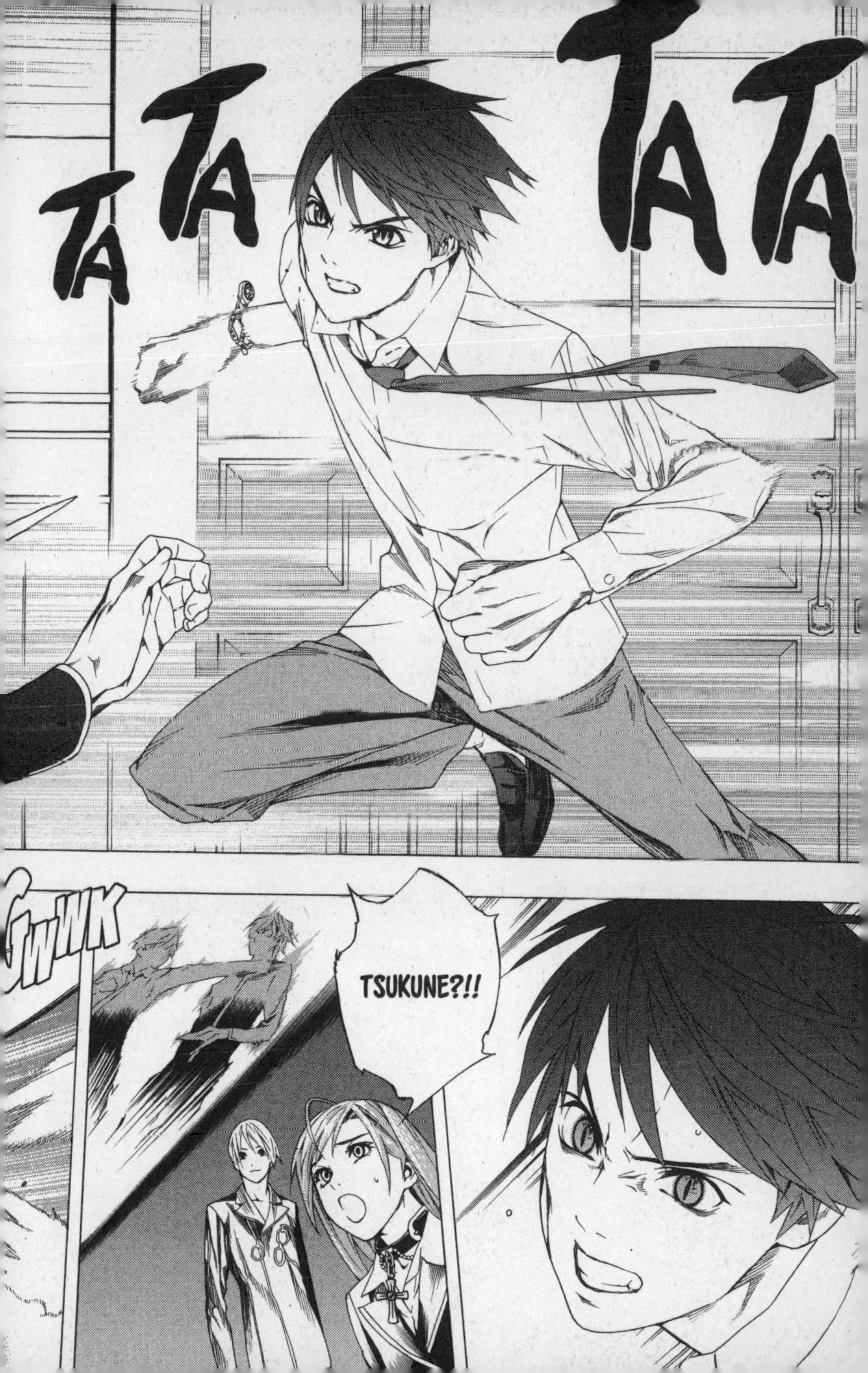
TATA
TATA
TSUKUNE?!!
GWWK

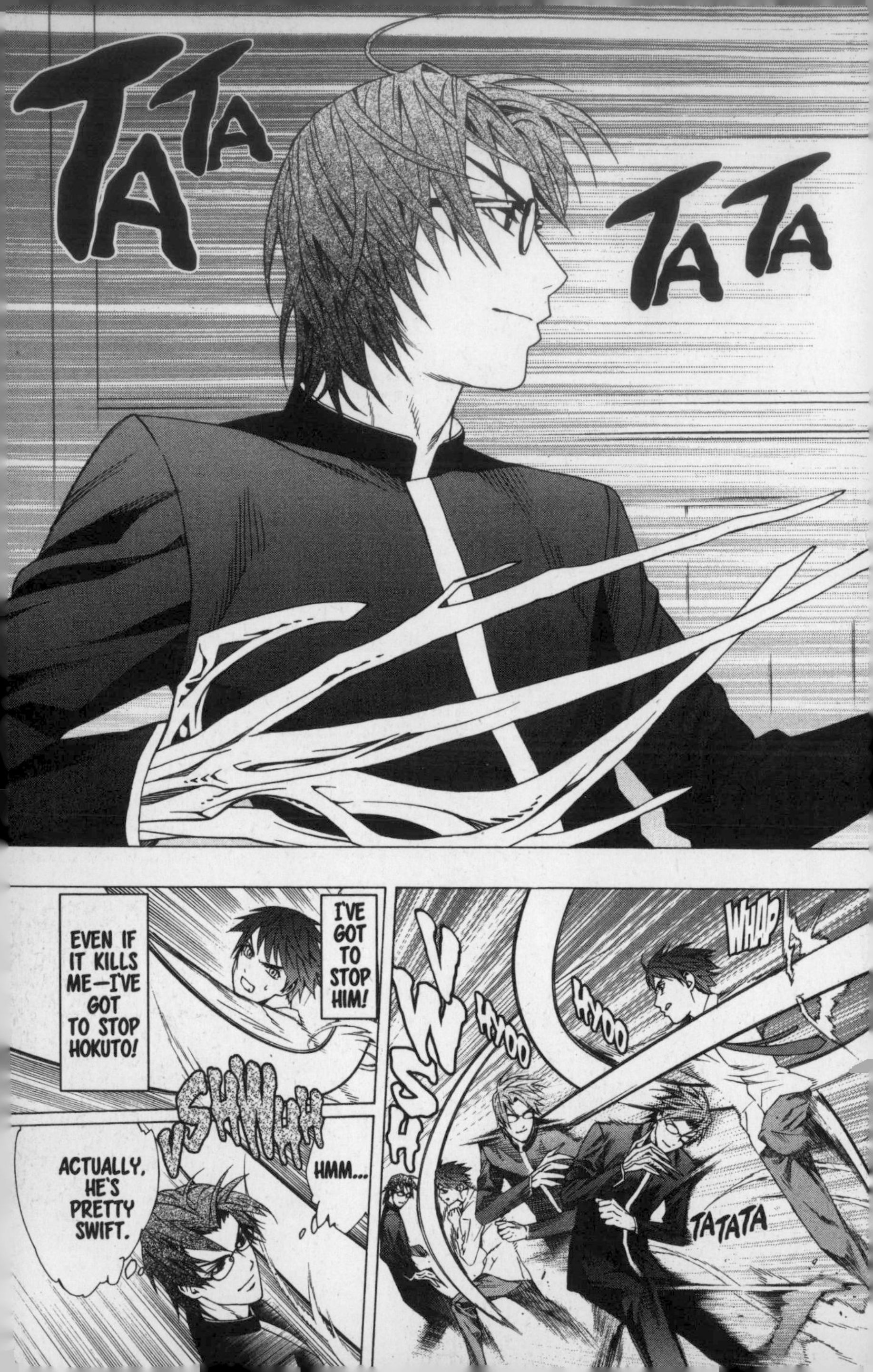
TATA
TATA
WHAP
HYOO
HYOO
TATATA
I'VE GOT TO STOP HIM!
EVEN IF IT KILLS ME—I'VE GOT TO STOP HOKUTO!
HMM...
ACTUALLY, HE'S PRETTY SWIFT.

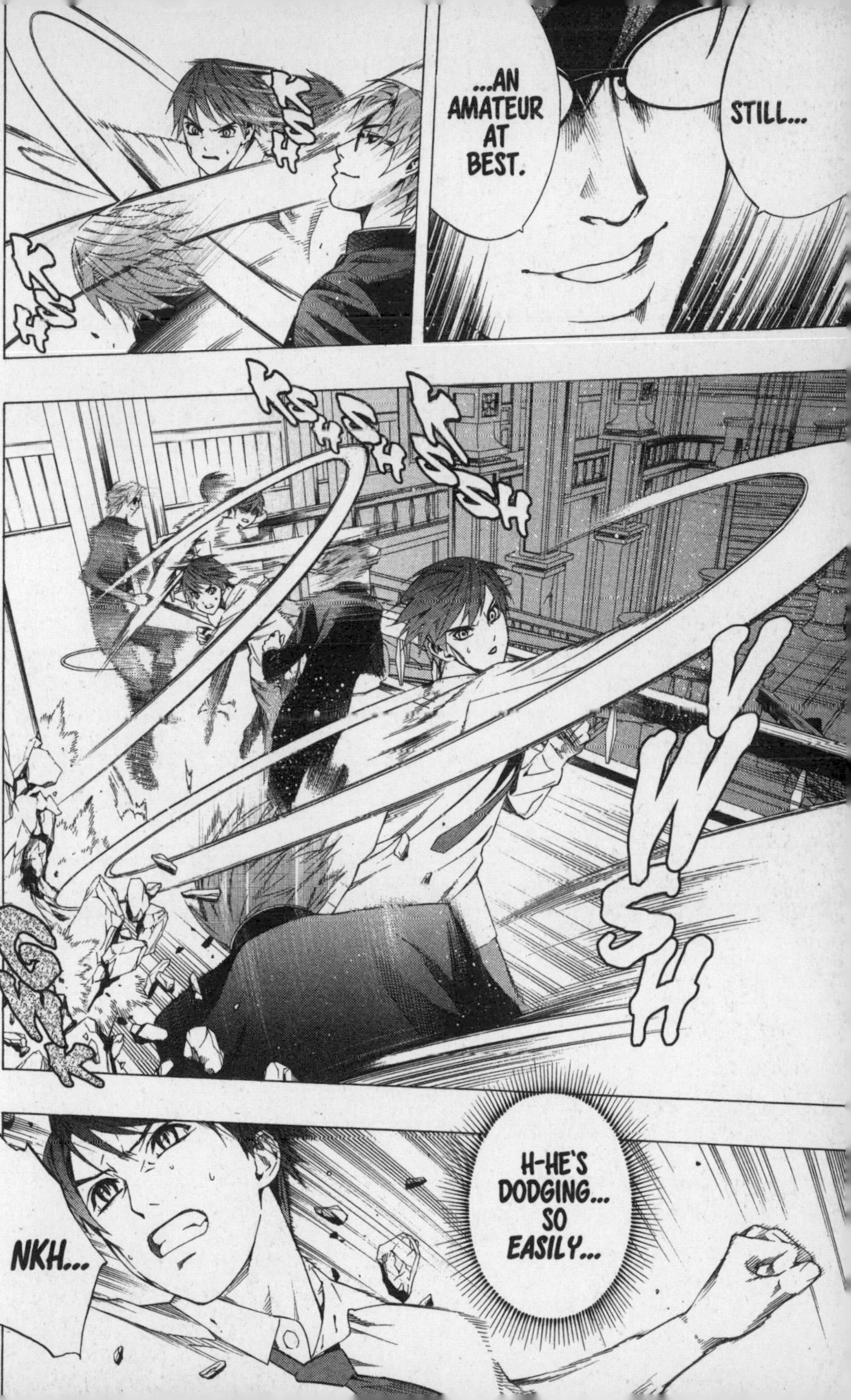
STILL...
...AN AMATEUR AT BEST.
KSH
KSH
KSHSH
KSSH
VWSH
GNK
H-HE'S DODGING... SO EASILY...
NKH...

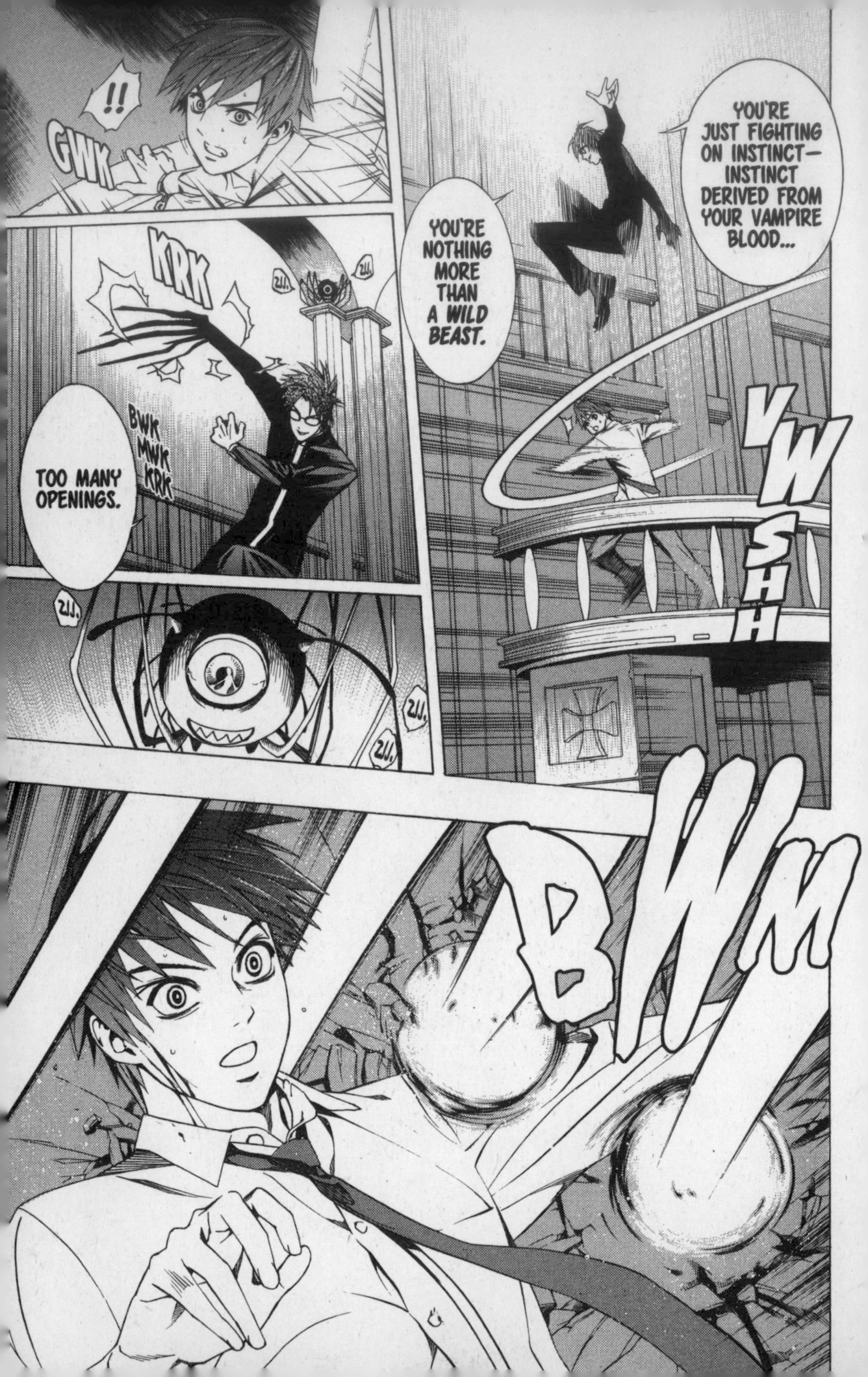
YOU'RE JUST FIGHTING ON INSTINCT— INSTINCT DERIVED FROM YOUR VAMPIRE BLOOD...
YOU'RE NOTHING MORE THAN A WILD BEAST.
VWSHH
!!
GWK
KRK
BWK MWK KRK
TOO MANY OPENINGS.
BWM

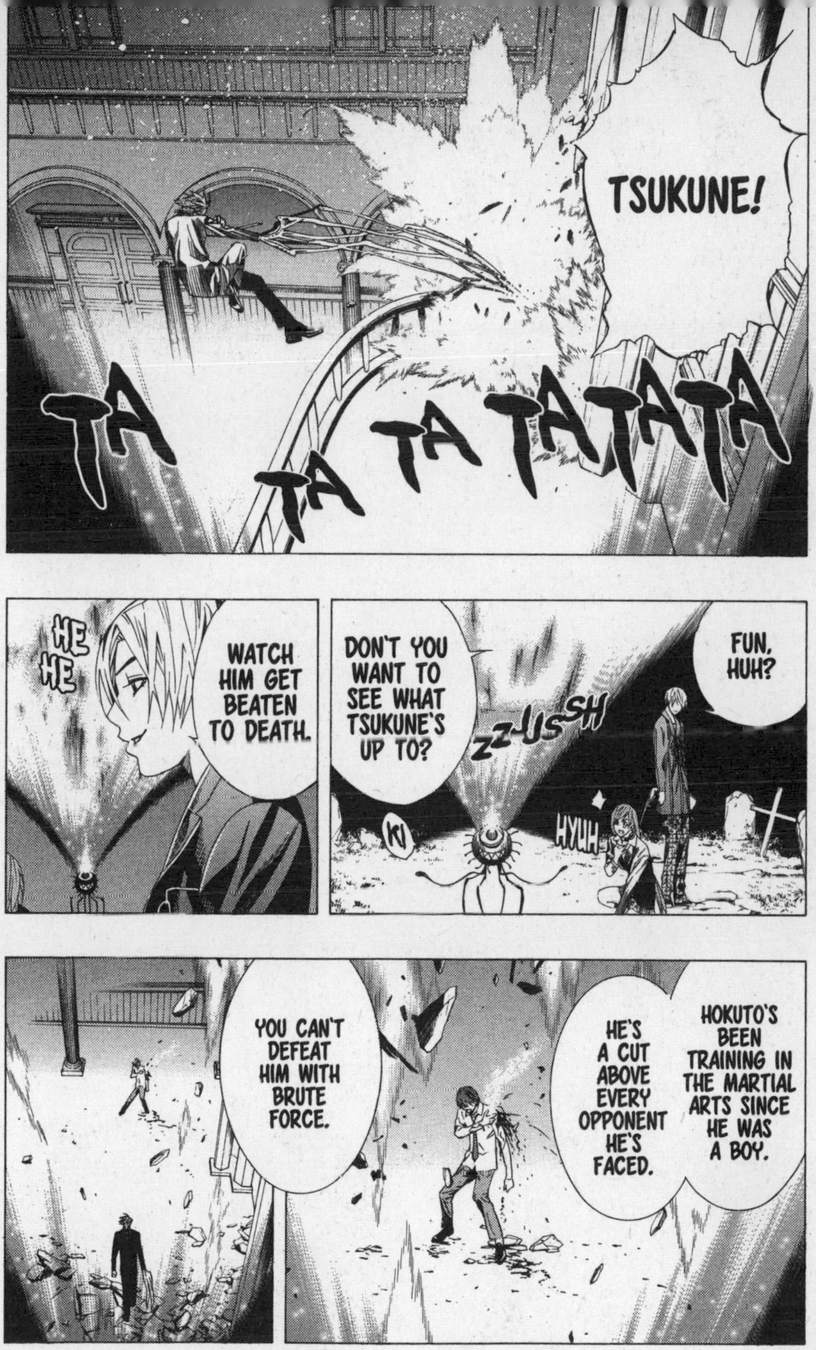
TSUKUNE!
TA TA TA TATATA
FUN, HUH?
DON'T YOU WANT TO SEE WHAT TSUKUNE'S UP TO?
ZZ-USSH
HYUH
KI
WATCH HIM GET BEATEN TO DEATH.
HE HE
HOKUTO'S BEEN TRAINING IN THE MARTIAL ARTS SINCE HE WAS A BOY.
HE'S A CUT ABOVE EVERY OPPONENT HE'S FACED.
YOU CAN'T DEFEAT HIM WITH BRUTE FORCE.

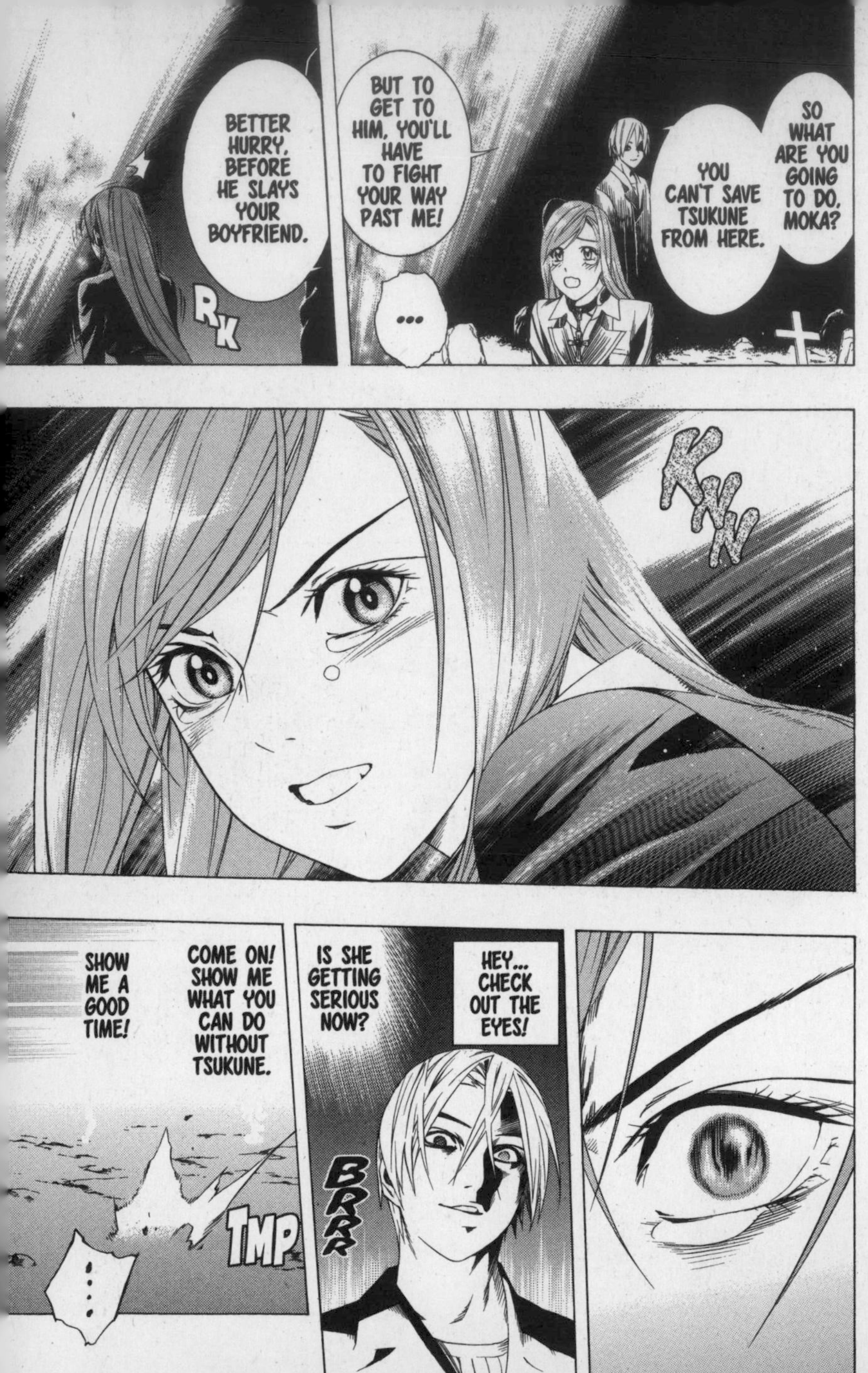
SO WHAT ARE YOU GOING TO DO, MOKA?
YOU CAN'T SAVE TSUKUNE FROM HERE.
BUT TO GET TO HIM, YOU'LL HAVE TO FIGHT YOUR WAY PAST ME!
...
BETTER HURRY, BEFORE HE SLAYS YOUR BOYFRIEND.
RK
KNN
HEY... CHECK OUT THE EYES!
IS SHE GETTING SERIOUS NOW?
BRRR
COME ON! SHOW ME WHAT YOU CAN DO WITHOUT TSUKUNE.
SHOW ME A GOOD TIME!
TMP
...

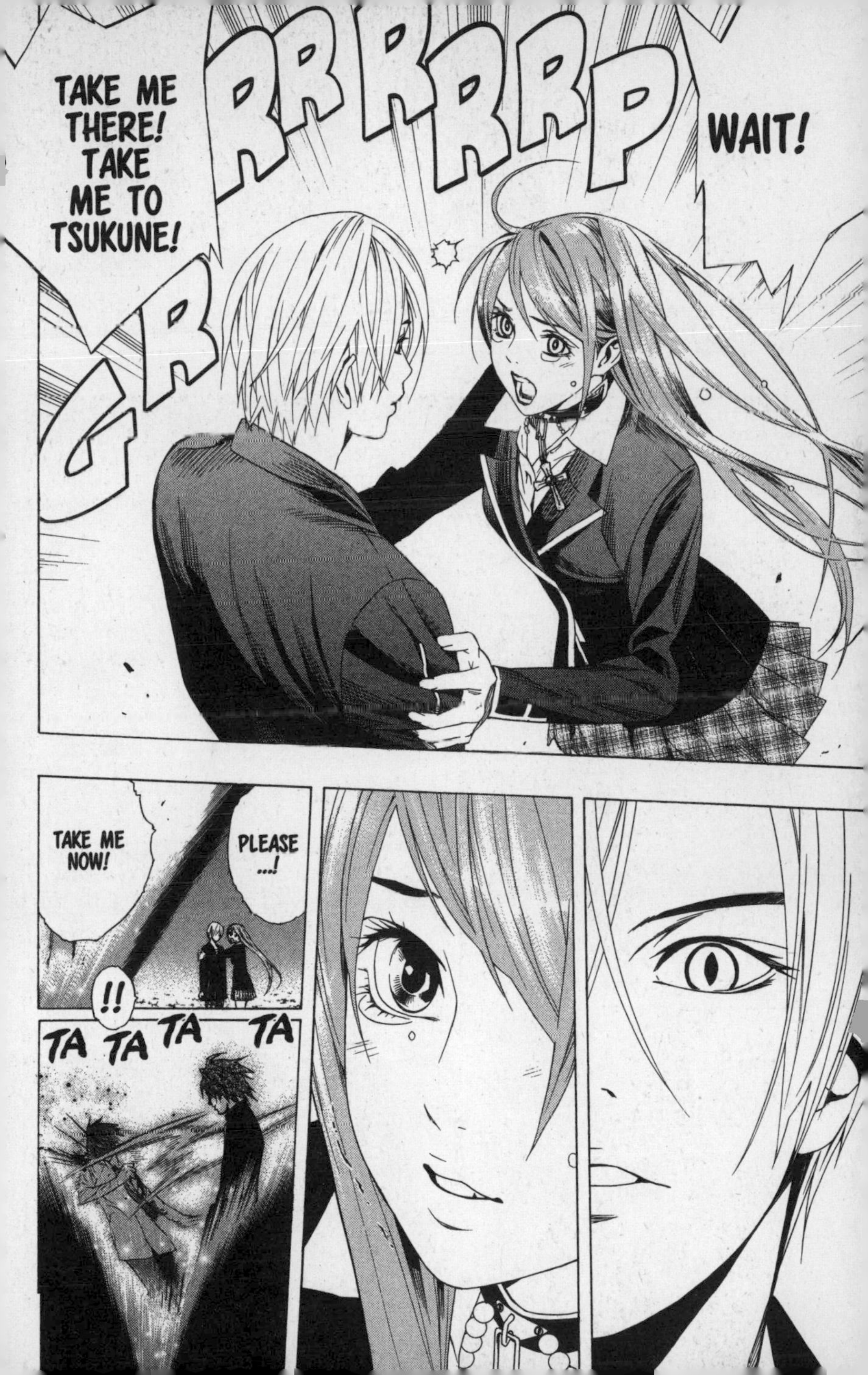
WAIT!
TAKE ME THERE! TAKE ME TO TSUKUNE!
GRRRRRP
TAKE ME NOW!
PLEASE ...!
!!
TA TA TA TA

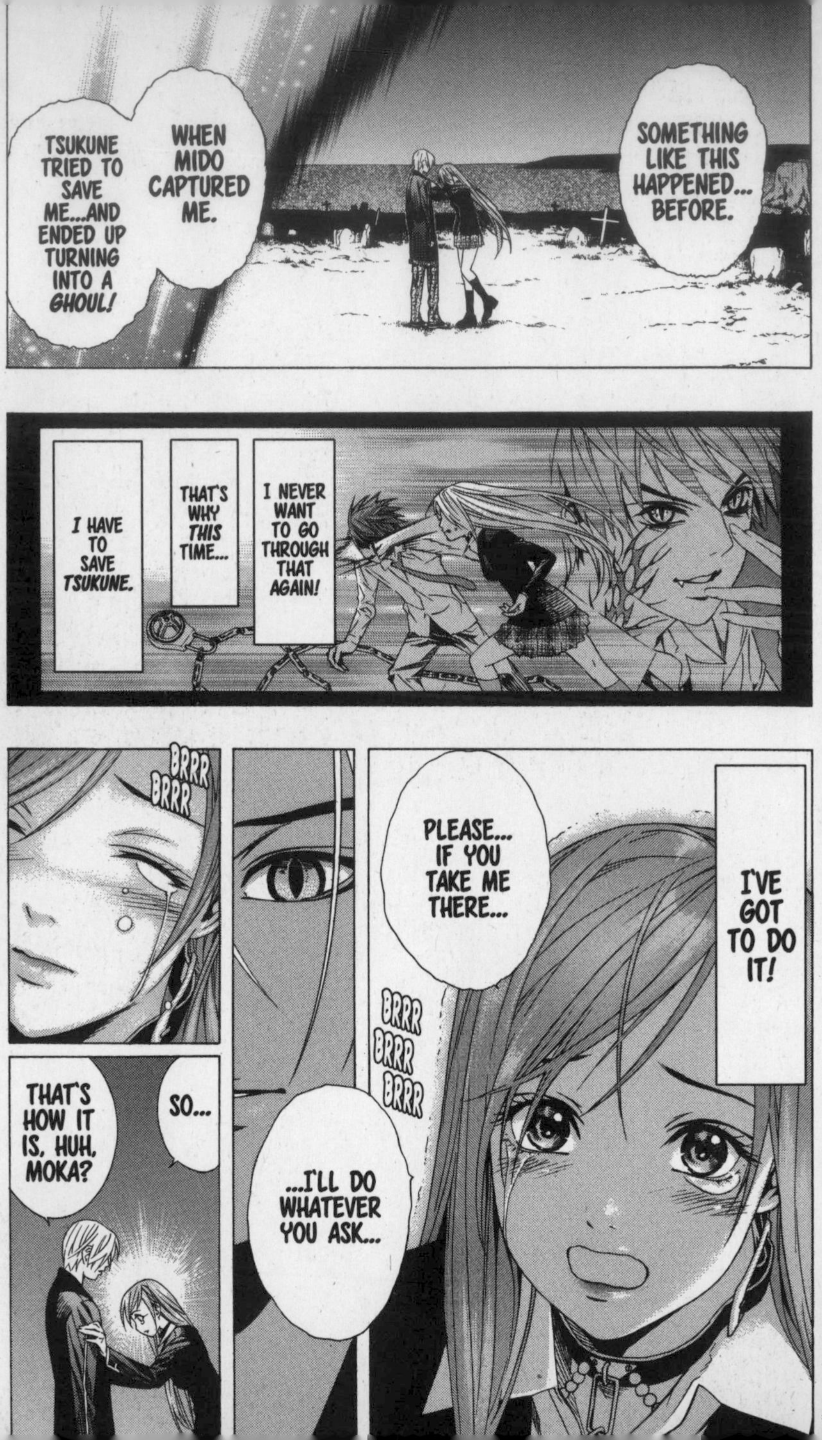
SOMETHING LIKE THIS HAPPENED... BEFORE.
WHEN MIDO CAPTURED ME.
TSUKUNE TRIED TO SAVE ME...AND ENDED UP TURNING INTO A *GHOUL!*
I NEVER WANT TO GO THROUGH THAT AGAIN!
THAT'S WHY *THIS* TIME...
I HAVE TO SAVE *TSUKUNE.*
I'VE GOT TO DO IT!
PLEASE... IF YOU TAKE ME THERE...
BRRR BRRR BRRR
...I'LL DO WHATEVER YOU ASK...
BRRR BRRR
SO...
THAT'S HOW IT IS, HUH, MOKA?

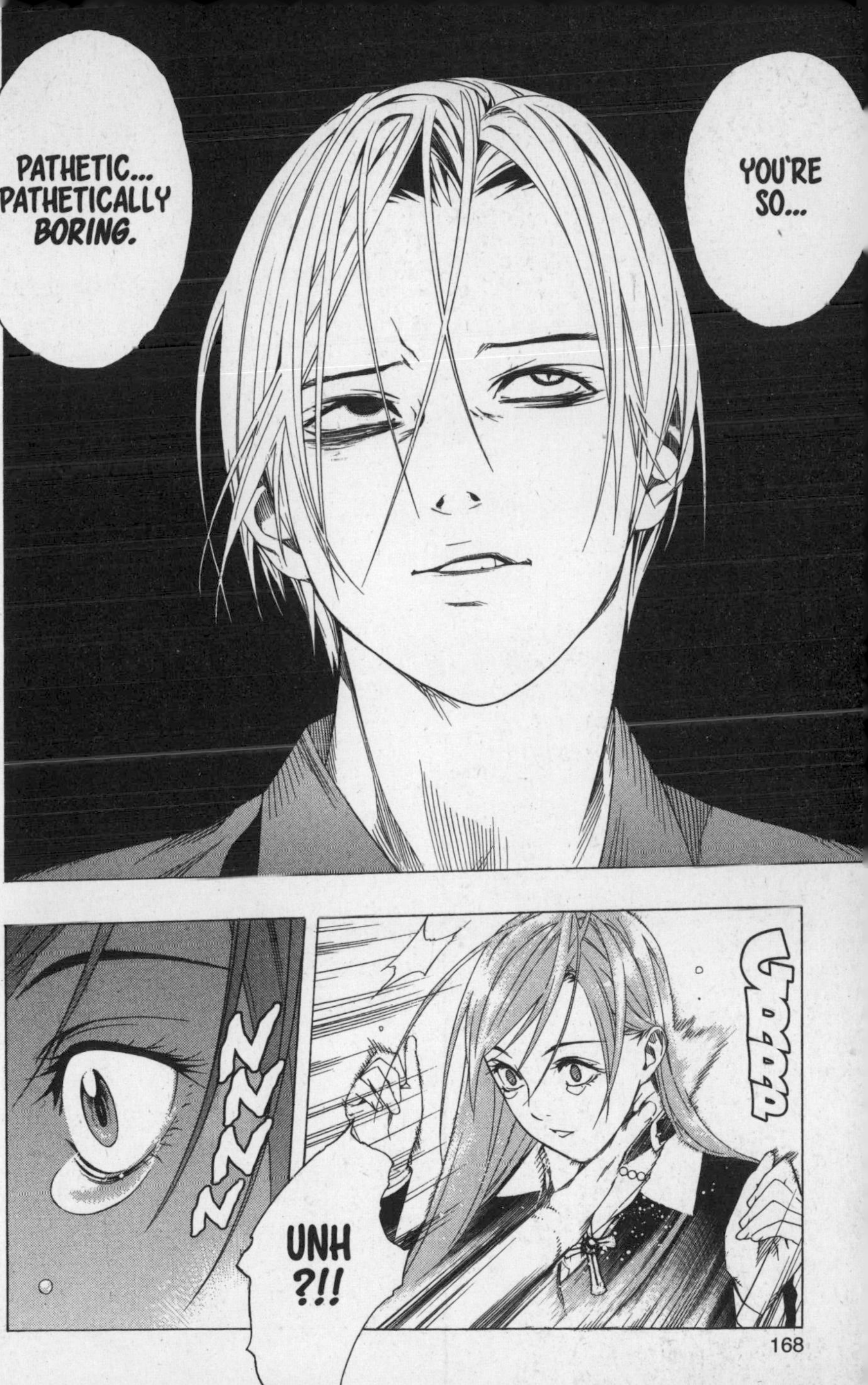
YOU'RE SO...
PATHETIC... PATHETICALLY BORING.
NNNN
UNH ?!!

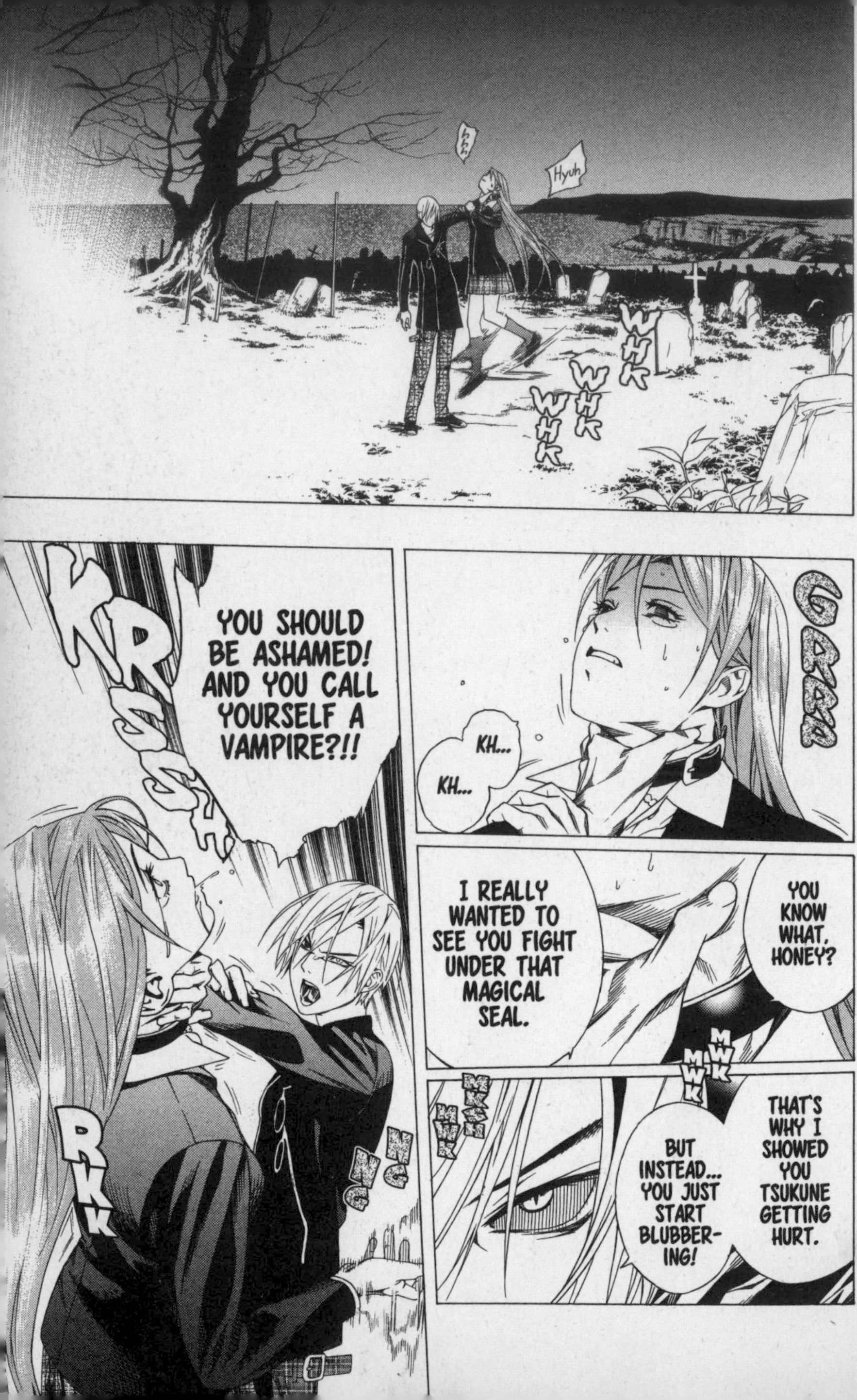
hhh
Hyuh
WHK WHK WHK
GRRP
KH...
KH...
YOU KNOW WHAT, HONEY?
I REALLY WANTED TO SEE YOU FIGHT UNDER THAT MAGICAL SEAL.
MWK MWK
THAT'S WHY I SHOWED YOU TSUKUNE GETTING HURT.
BUT INSTEAD... YOU JUST START BLUBBER-ING!
KRSH
YOU SHOULD BE ASHAMED! AND YOU CALL YOURSELF A VAMPIRE?!!
NG NG
RKK

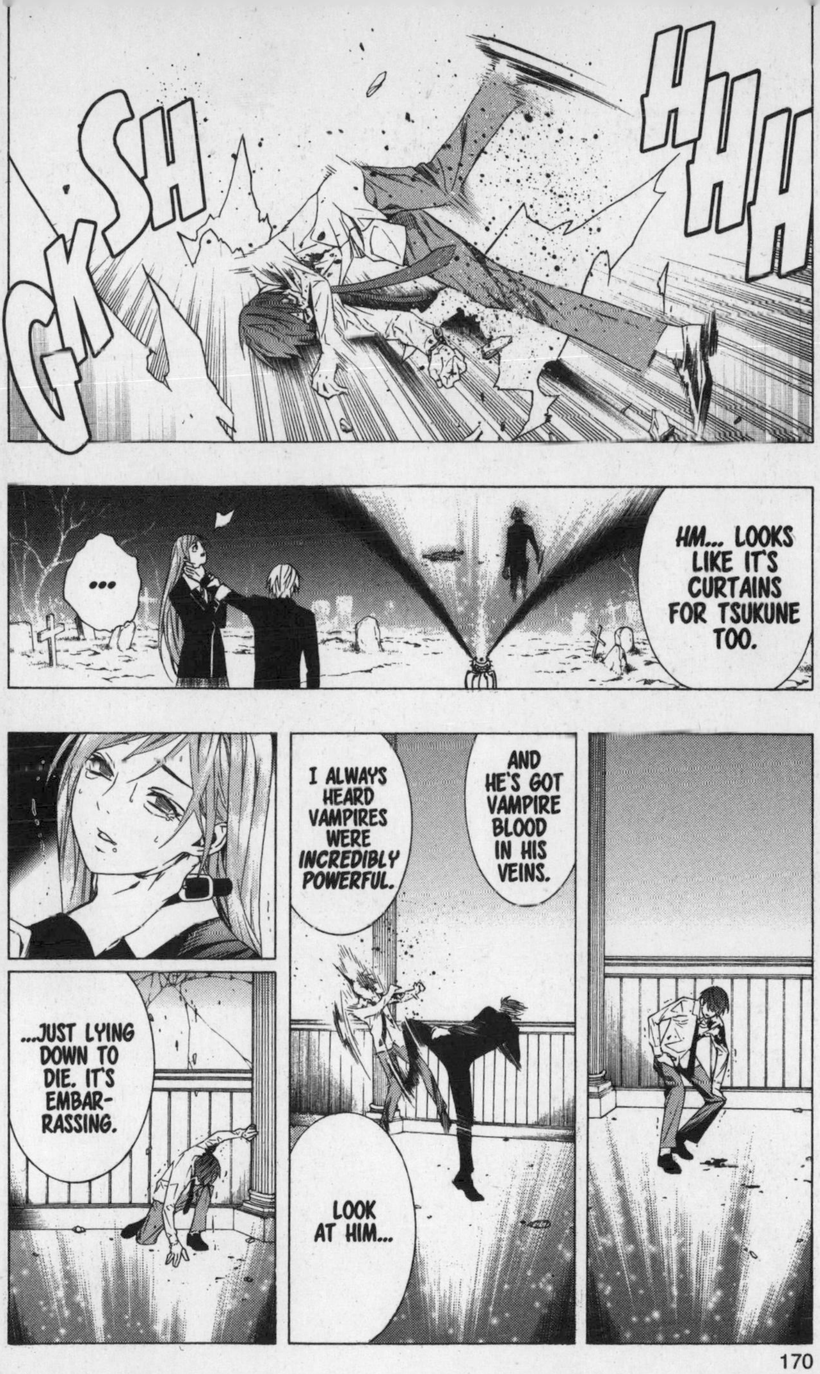
HHHH
GKSH
HM... LOOKS LIKE IT'S CURTAINS FOR TSUKUNE TOO.
...
I ALWAYS HEARD VAMPIRES WERE INCREDIBLY POWERFUL.
AND HE'S GOT VAMPIRE BLOOD IN HIS VEINS.
LOOK AT HIM...
...JUST LYING DOWN TO DIE. IT'S EMBAR-RASSING.

READ THIS WAY

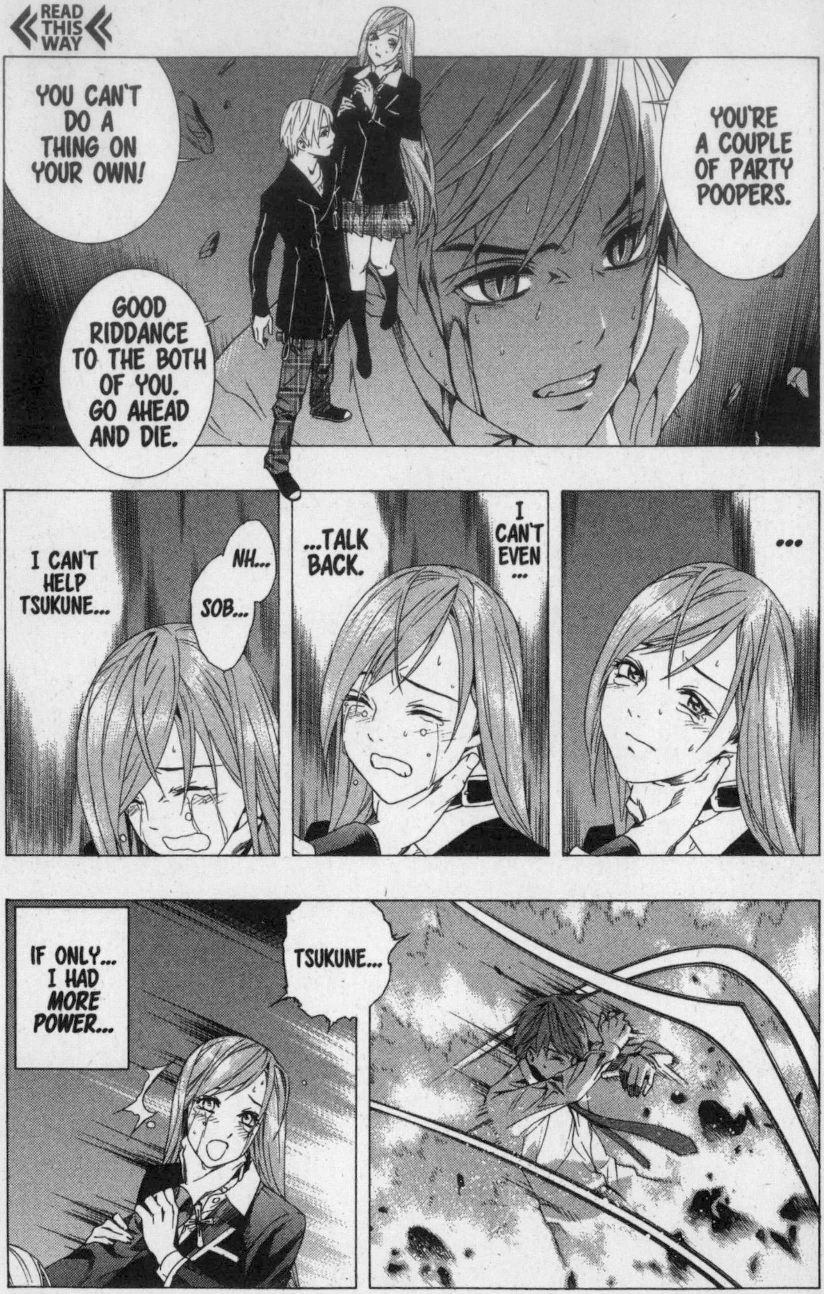

YOU'RE A COUPLE OF PARTY POOPERS.
YOU CAN'T DO A THING ON YOUR OWN!
GOOD RIDDANCE TO THE BOTH OF YOU. GO AHEAD AND DIE.
...
I CAN'T EVEN ...
...TALK BACK.
NH... SOB...
I CAN'T HELP TSUKUNE...
TSUKUNE...
IF ONLY... I HAD *MORE POWER*...

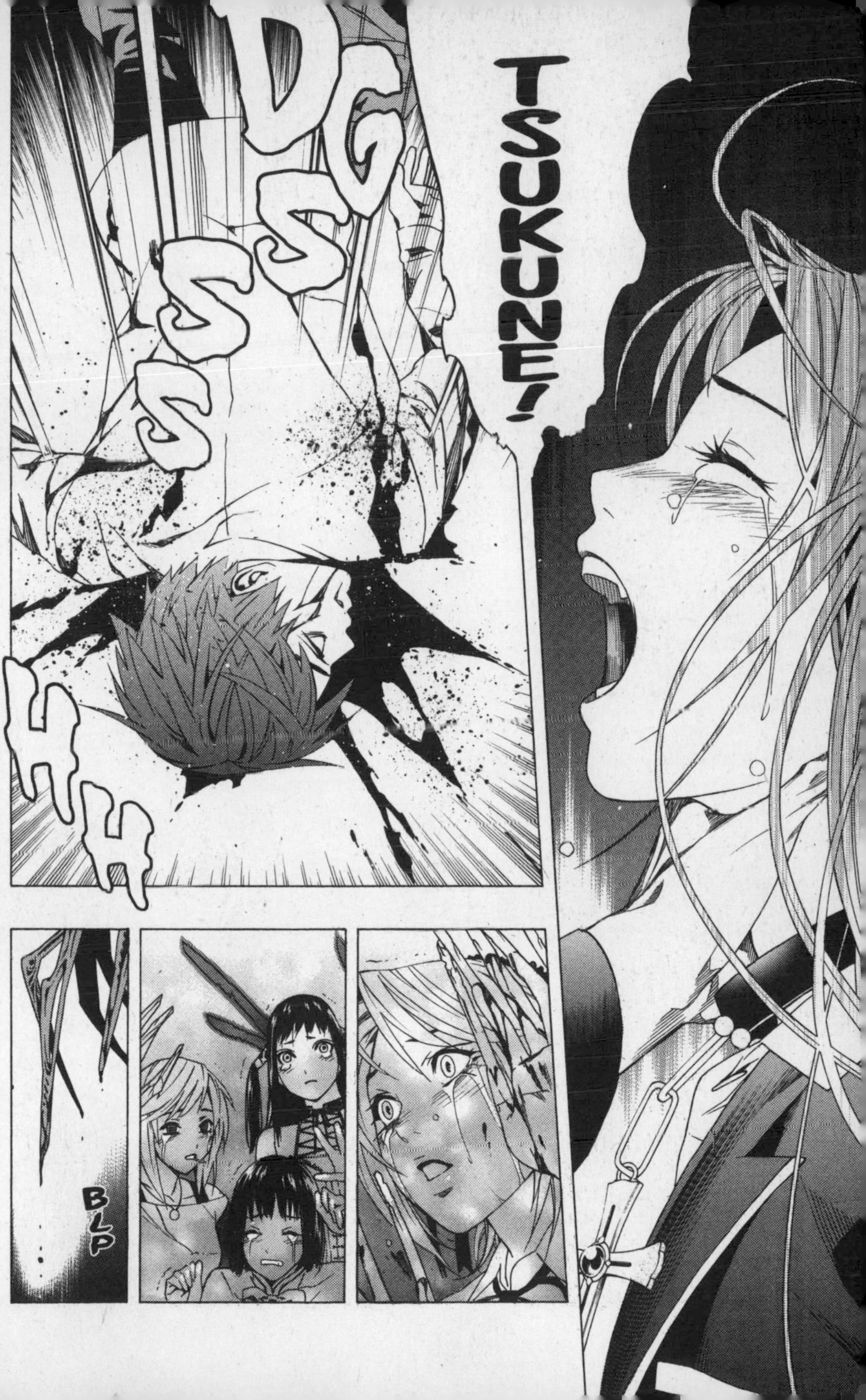
TSUKUNE!
DGSSS
HHH
BLP

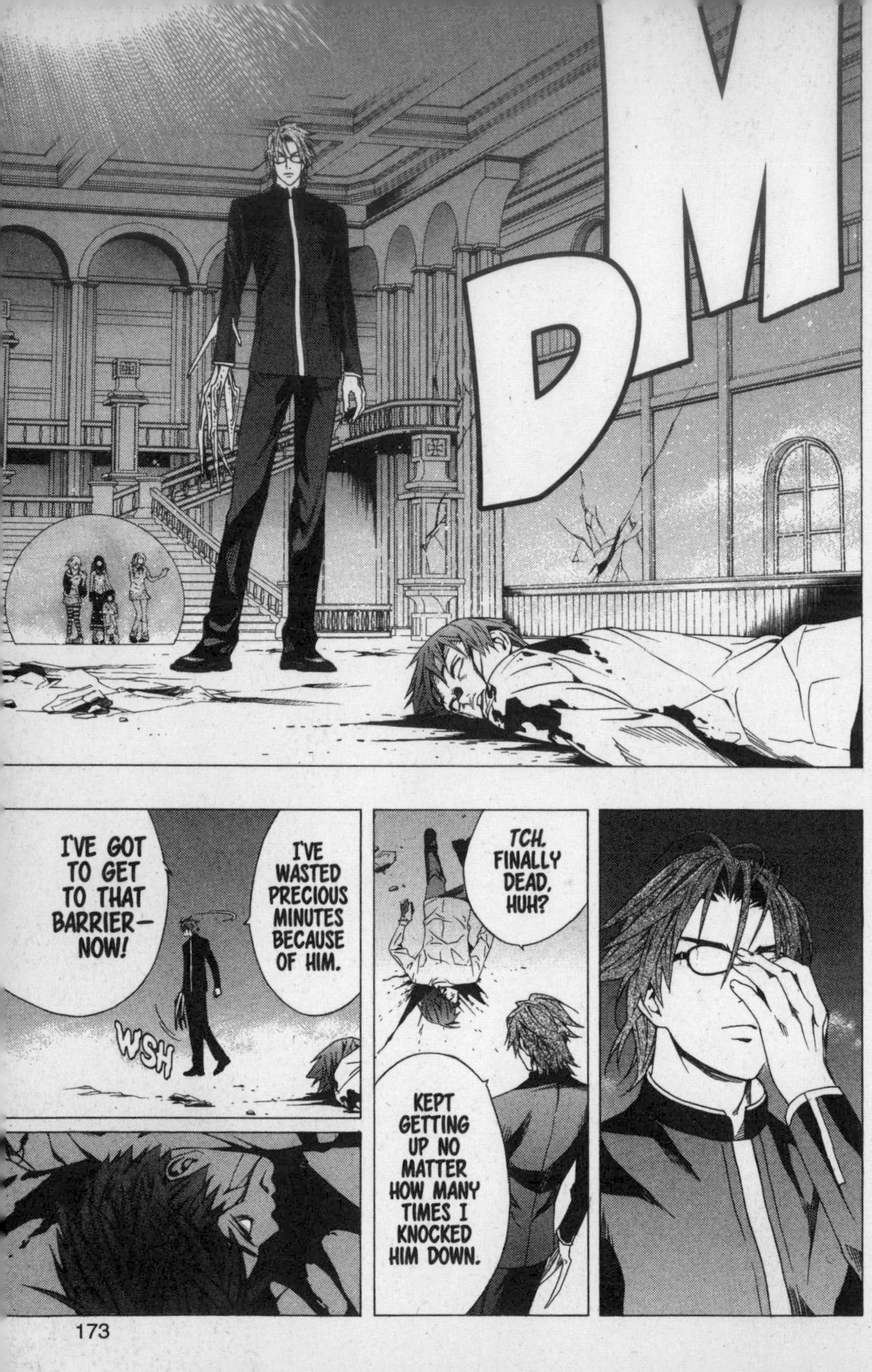
DM
TCH. FINALLY DEAD, HUH?
KEPT GETTING UP NO MATTER HOW MANY TIMES I KNOCKED HIM DOWN.
I'VE WASTED PRECIOUS MINUTES BECAUSE OF HIM.
I'VE GOT TO GET TO THAT BARRIER—NOW!
WSH

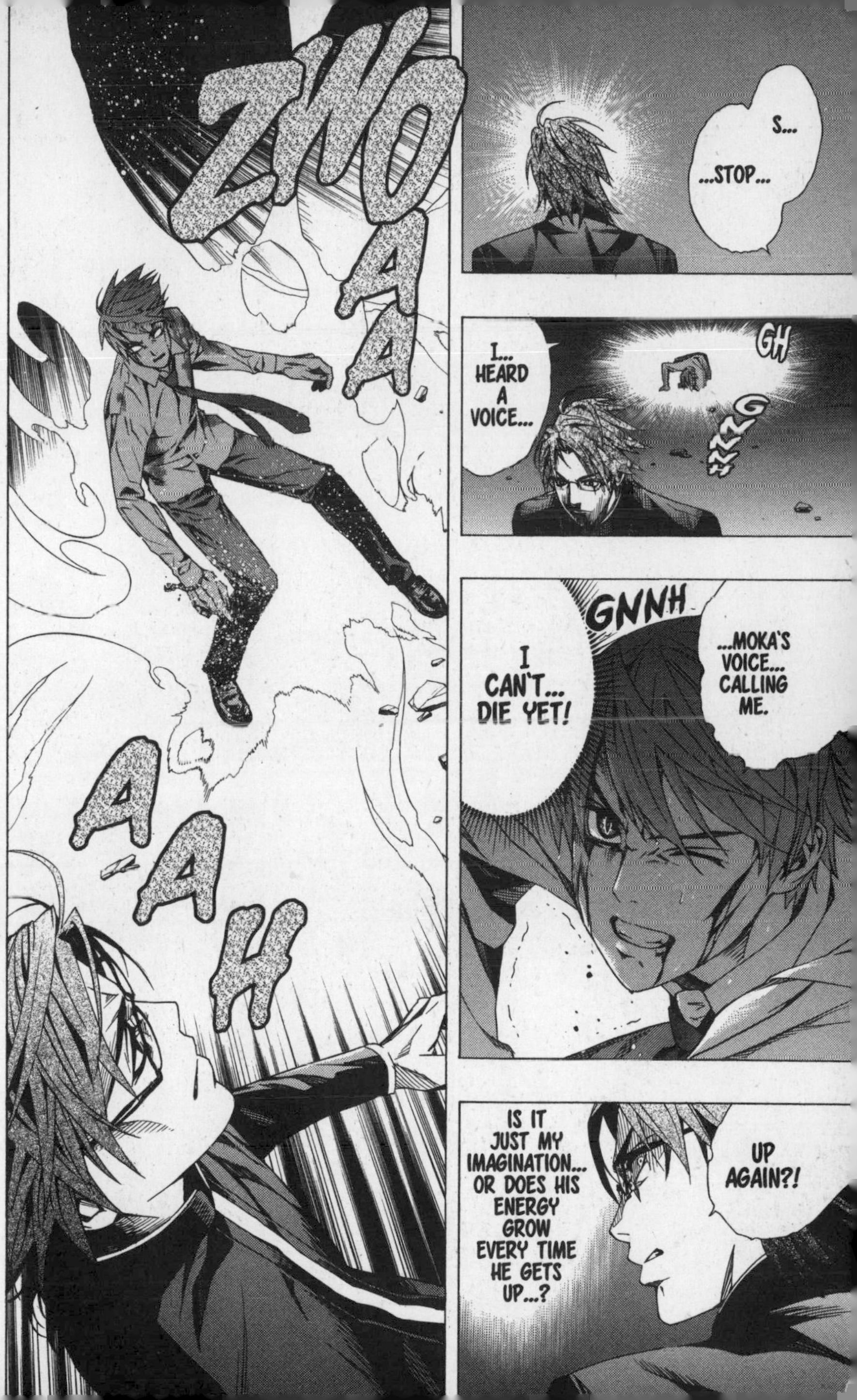
S...
...STOP...
GH
I... HEARD A VOICE...
GNNH
...MOKA'S VOICE... CALLING ME.
GNNH
I CAN'T... DIE YET!
UP AGAIN?!
IS IT JUST MY IMAGINATION... OR DOES HIS ENERGY GROW EVERY TIME HE GETS UP...?
ZWOAAA
AAAH

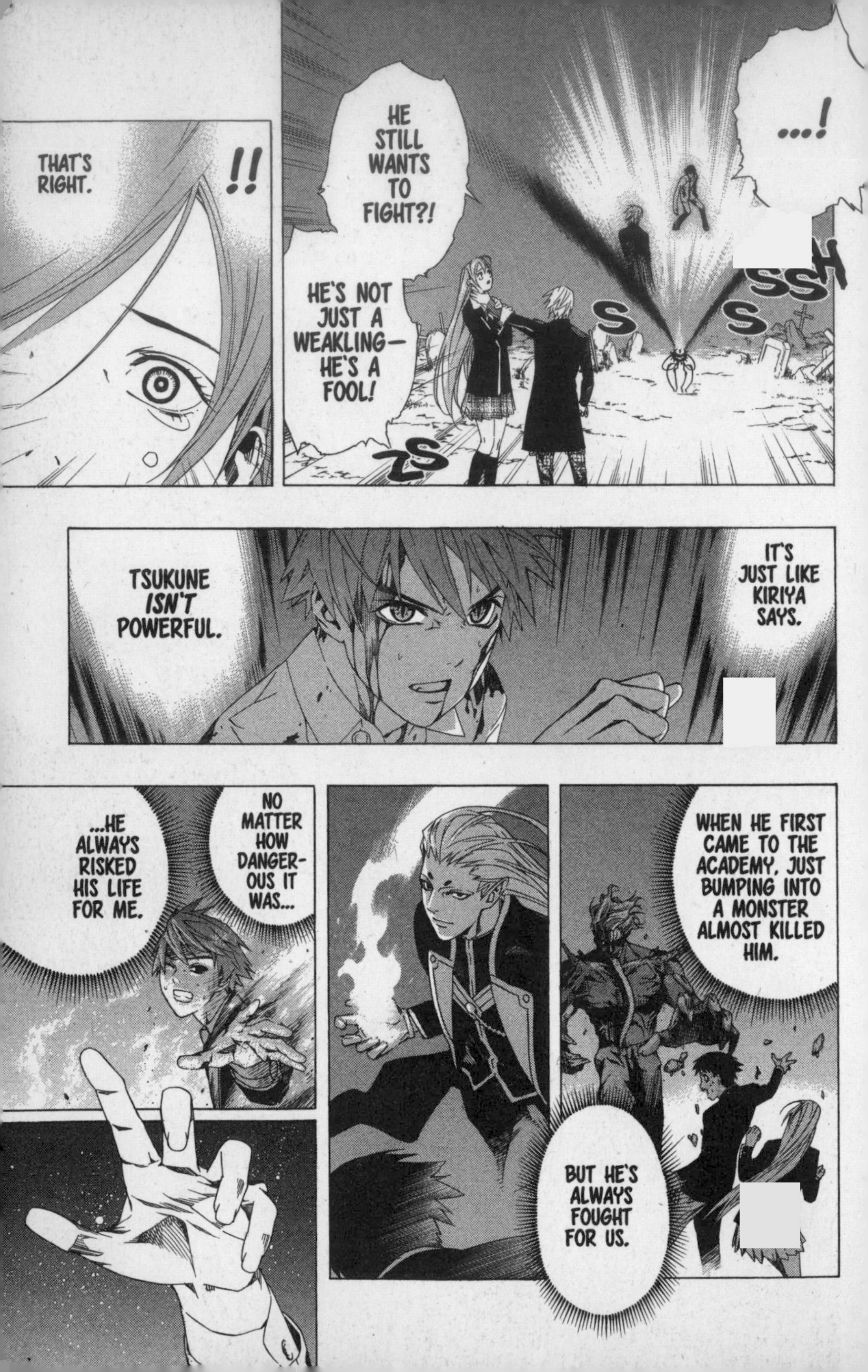
...!
HE STILL WANTS TO FIGHT?!
HE'S NOT JUST A WEAKLING— HE'S A FOOL!
S
S
!!
THAT'S RIGHT.
IT'S JUST LIKE KIRIYA SAYS.
TSUKUNE *ISN'T* POWERFUL.
WHEN HE FIRST CAME TO THE ACADEMY, JUST BUMPING INTO A MONSTER ALMOST KILLED HIM.
BUT HE'S ALWAYS FOUGHT FOR US.
NO MATTER HOW DANGER- OUS IT WAS...
...HE ALWAYS RISKED HIS LIFE FOR ME.

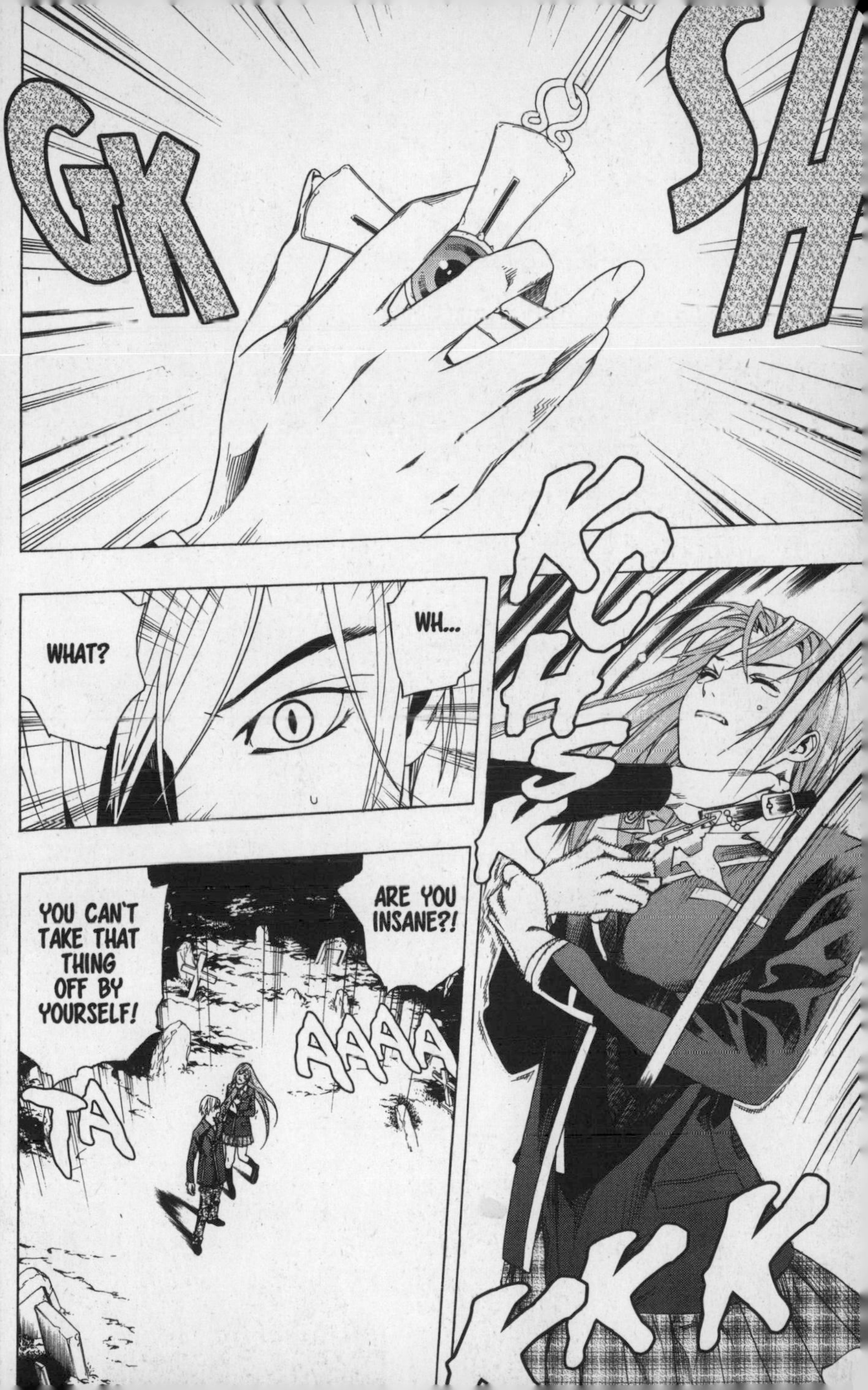
SH
GK
WH...
WHAT?
ARE YOU INSANE?!
YOU CAN'T TAKE THAT THING OFF BY YOURSELF!
AAAA
TA

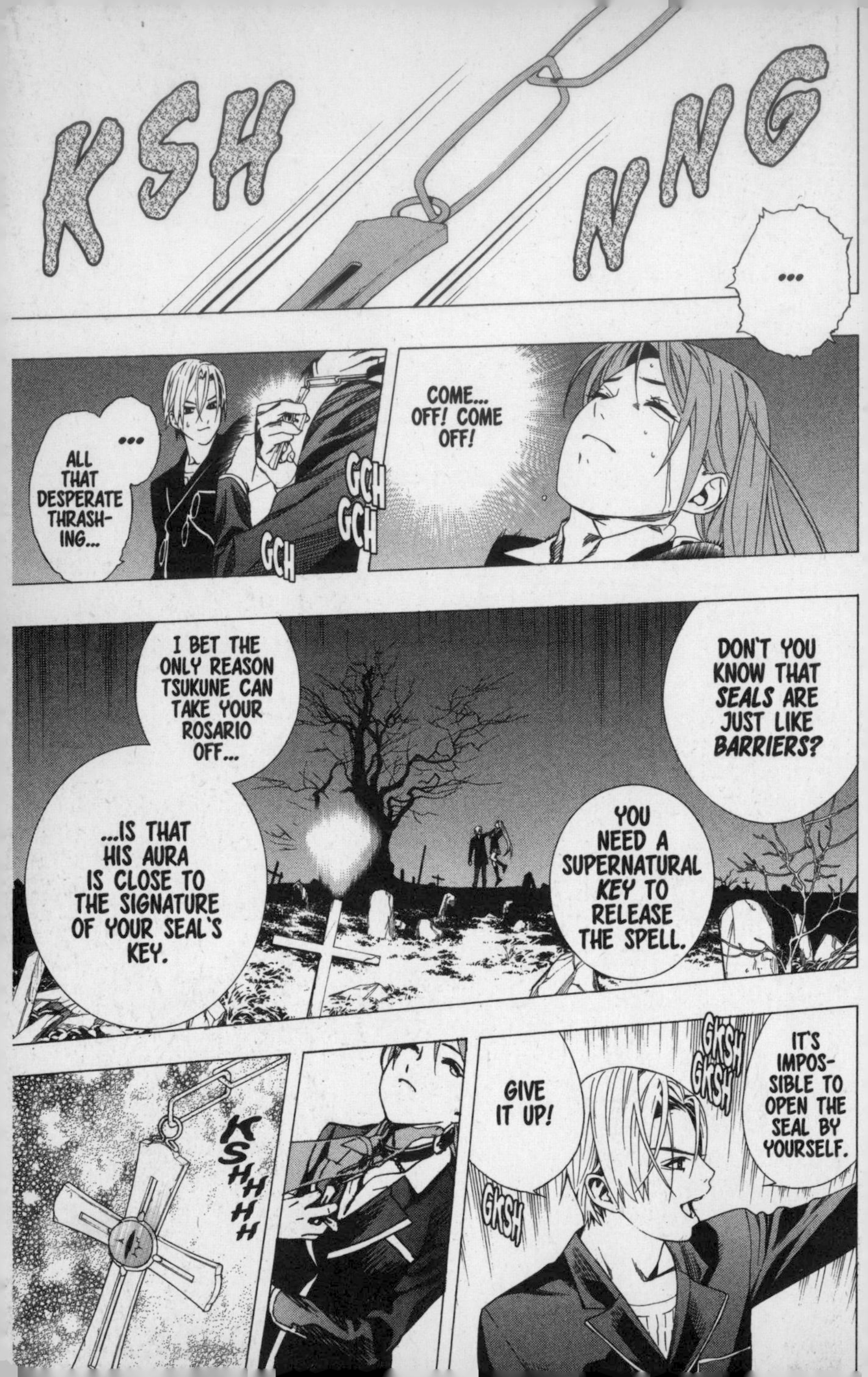
KSH NNG
...
COME... OFF! COME OFF!
...
ALL THAT DESPERATE THRASH-ING...
GCH GCH
GCH
DON'T YOU KNOW THAT SEALS ARE JUST LIKE BARRIERS?
YOU NEED A SUPERNATURAL KEY TO RELEASE THE SPELL.
I BET THE ONLY REASON TSUKUNE CAN TAKE YOUR ROSARIO OFF...
...IS THAT HIS AURA IS CLOSE TO THE SIGNATURE OF YOUR SEAL'S KEY.
GKSH GKSH
IT'S IMPOSSIBLE TO OPEN THE SEAL BY YOURSELF.
GIVE IT UP!
GKSH
KSHHHH

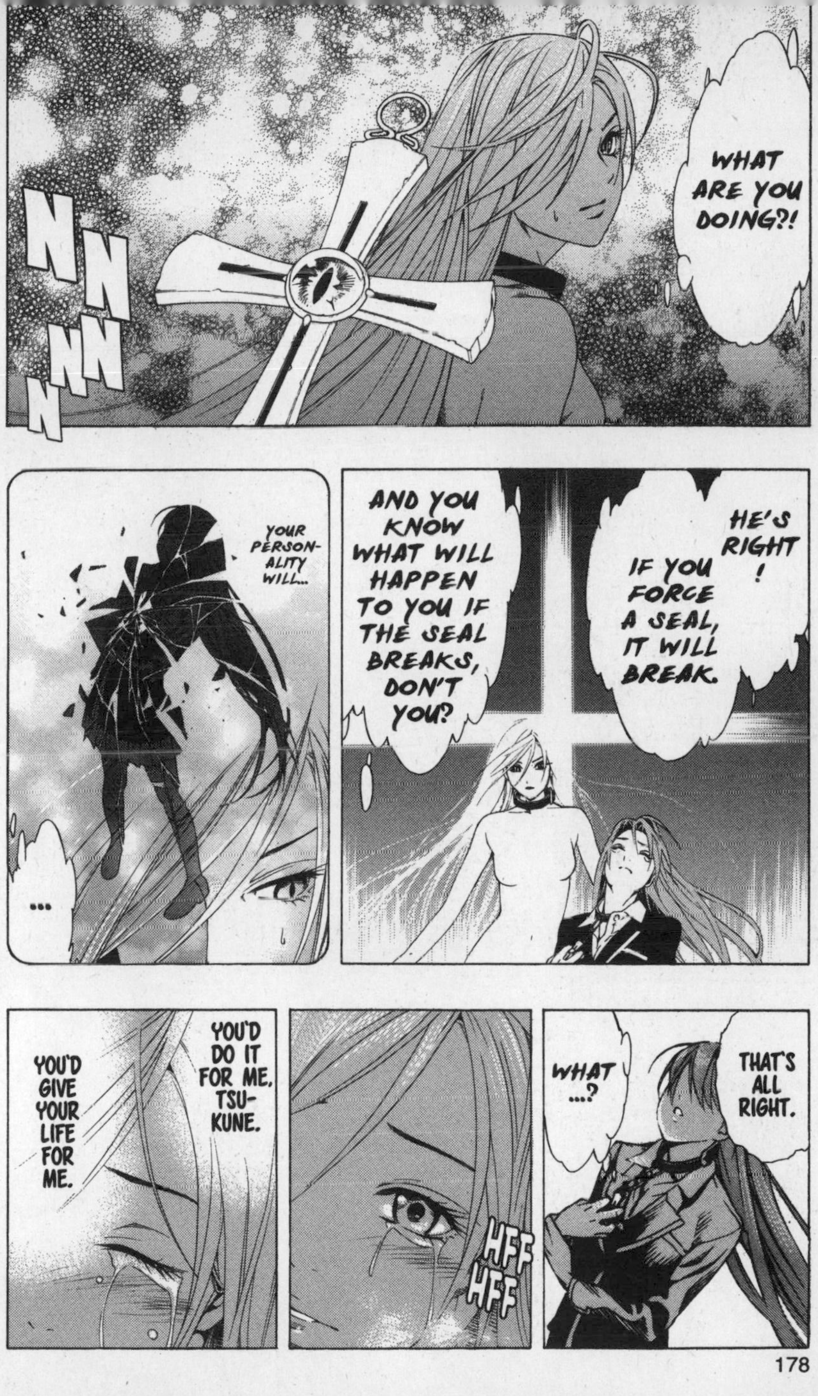
WHAT ARE YOU DOING?!
NNNNNNN
HE'S RIGHT!
IF YOU FORCE A SEAL, IT WILL BREAK.
AND YOU KNOW WHAT WILL HAPPEN TO YOU IF THE SEAL BREAKS, DON'T YOU?
YOUR PERSONALITY WILL...
...
THAT'S ALL RIGHT.
WHAT...?
HFF HFF
YOU'D DO IT FOR ME, TSUKUNE.
YOU'D GIVE YOUR LIFE FOR ME.

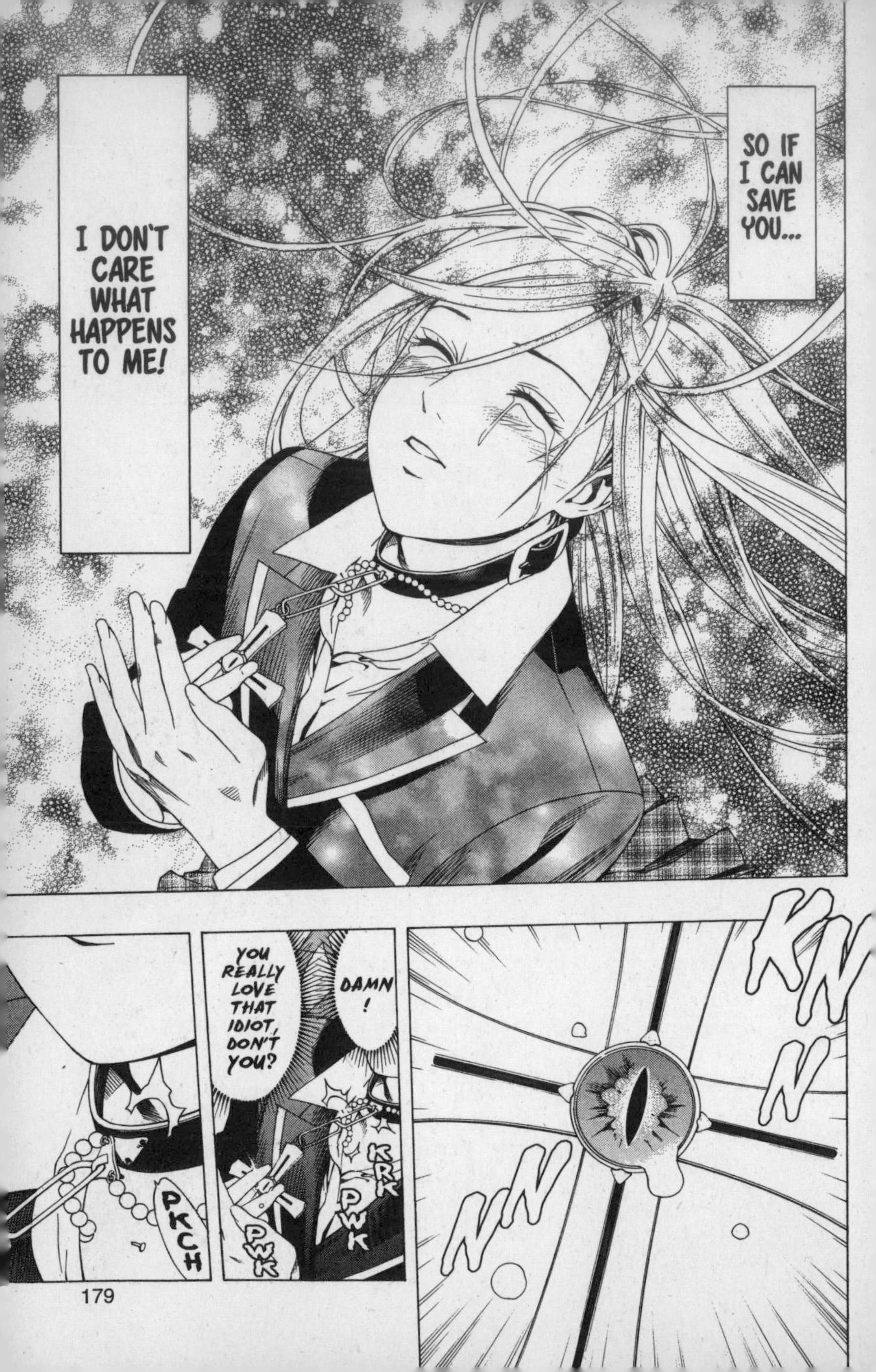
SO IF I CAN SAVE YOU...
I DON'T CARE WHAT HAPPENS TO ME!
KNNN
NNN
DAMN!
YOU REALLY LOVE THAT IDIOT, DON'T YOU?
KRK
PWK
PWK
PKCH

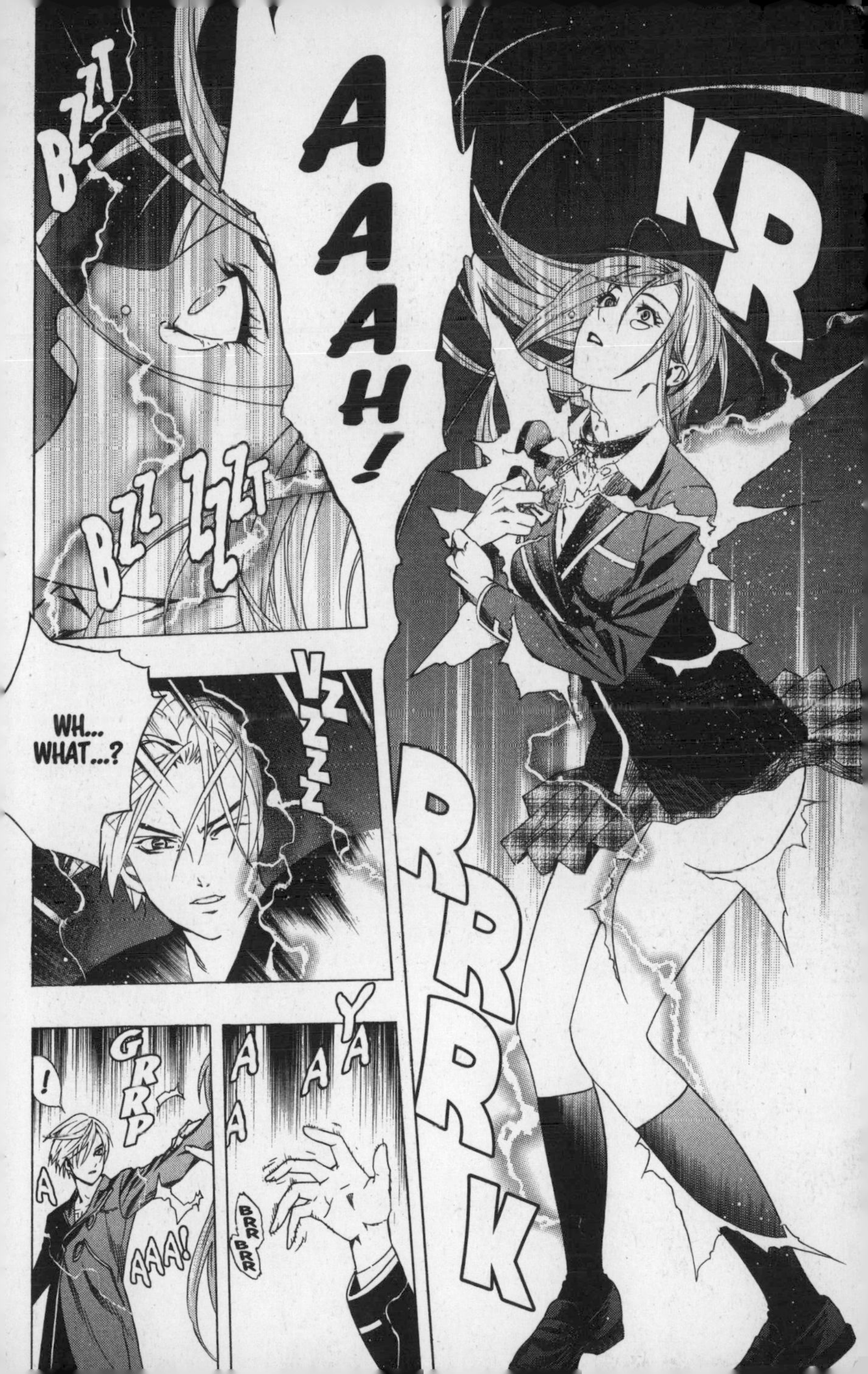
KR
AAAH!
RRRK
BZZZT
BZZ ZZZT
WH... WHAT...?
VZZZZZ
YAAAA
BRR BRR
!
GRRP
A
AAA!

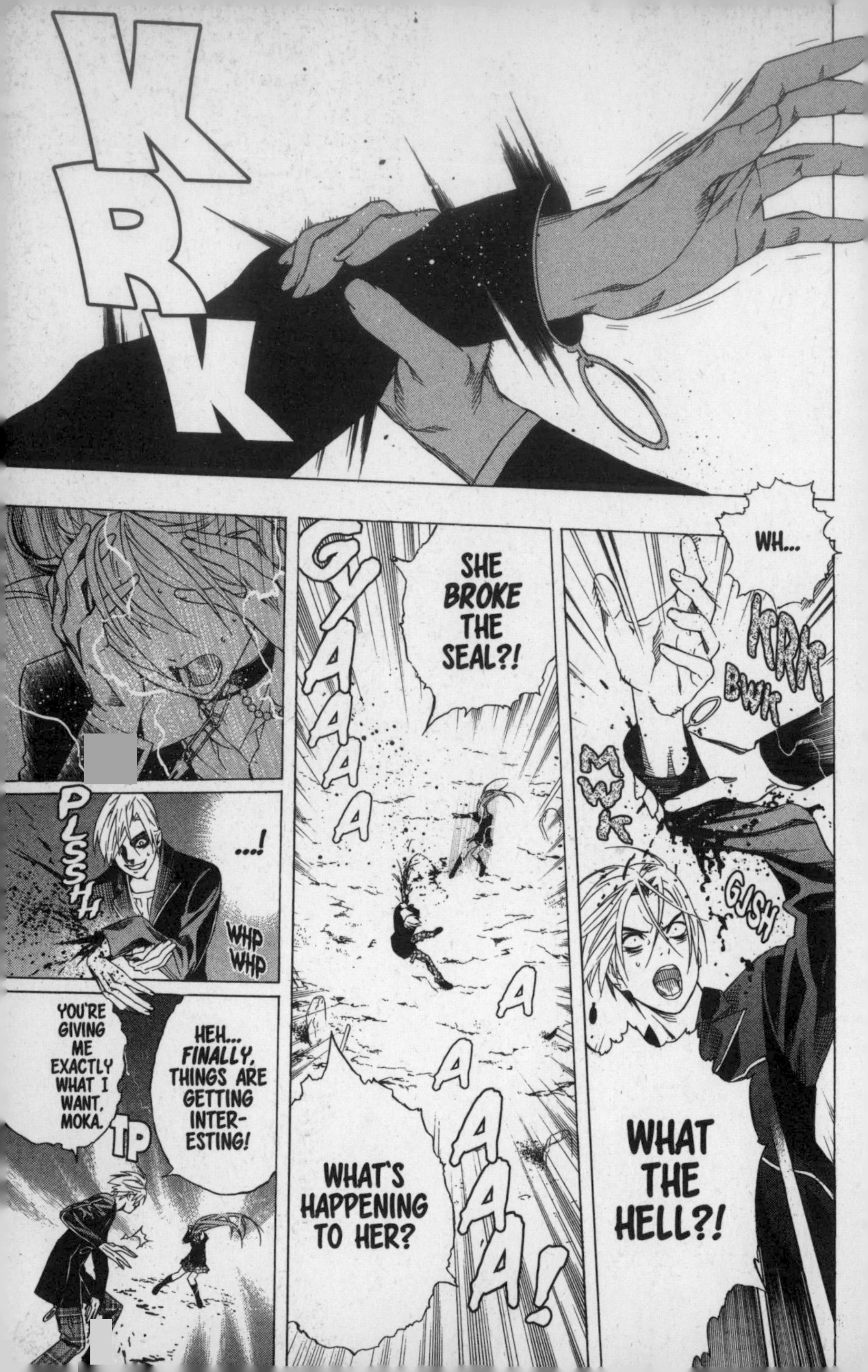
KRK
WH...
KRK
BWK
MWK
GJSH
WHAT THE HELL?!
SHE BROKE THE SEAL?!
GYAAAAAAAAAAA!
WHAT'S HAPPENING TO HER?
PLSSH
...!
WHP WHP
HEH... FINALLY, THINGS ARE GETTING INTER-ESTING!
YOU'RE GIVING ME EXACTLY WHAT I WANT, MOKA.
TP

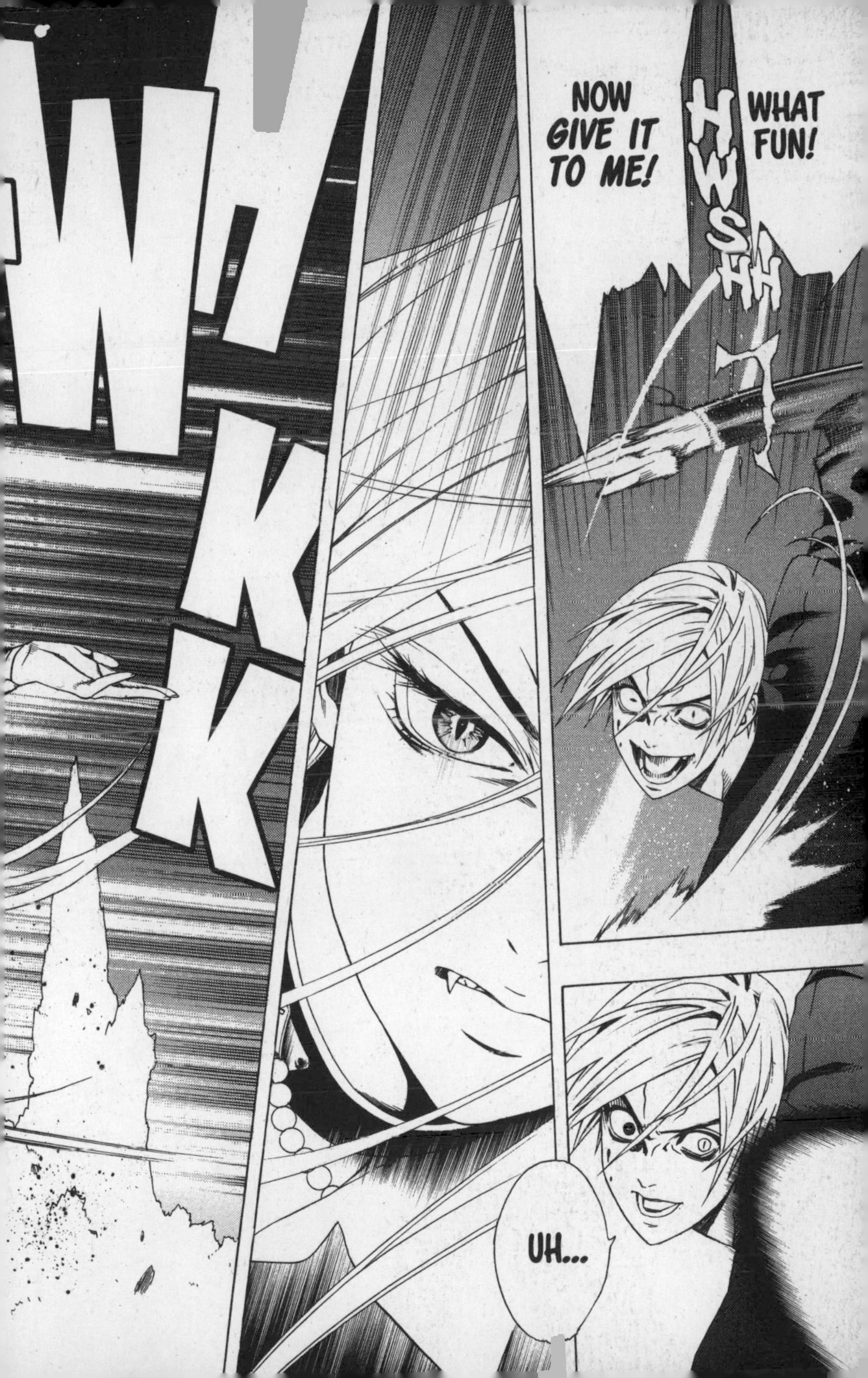
WHAT FUN!
HWSHH
NOW GIVE IT TO ME!
UH...

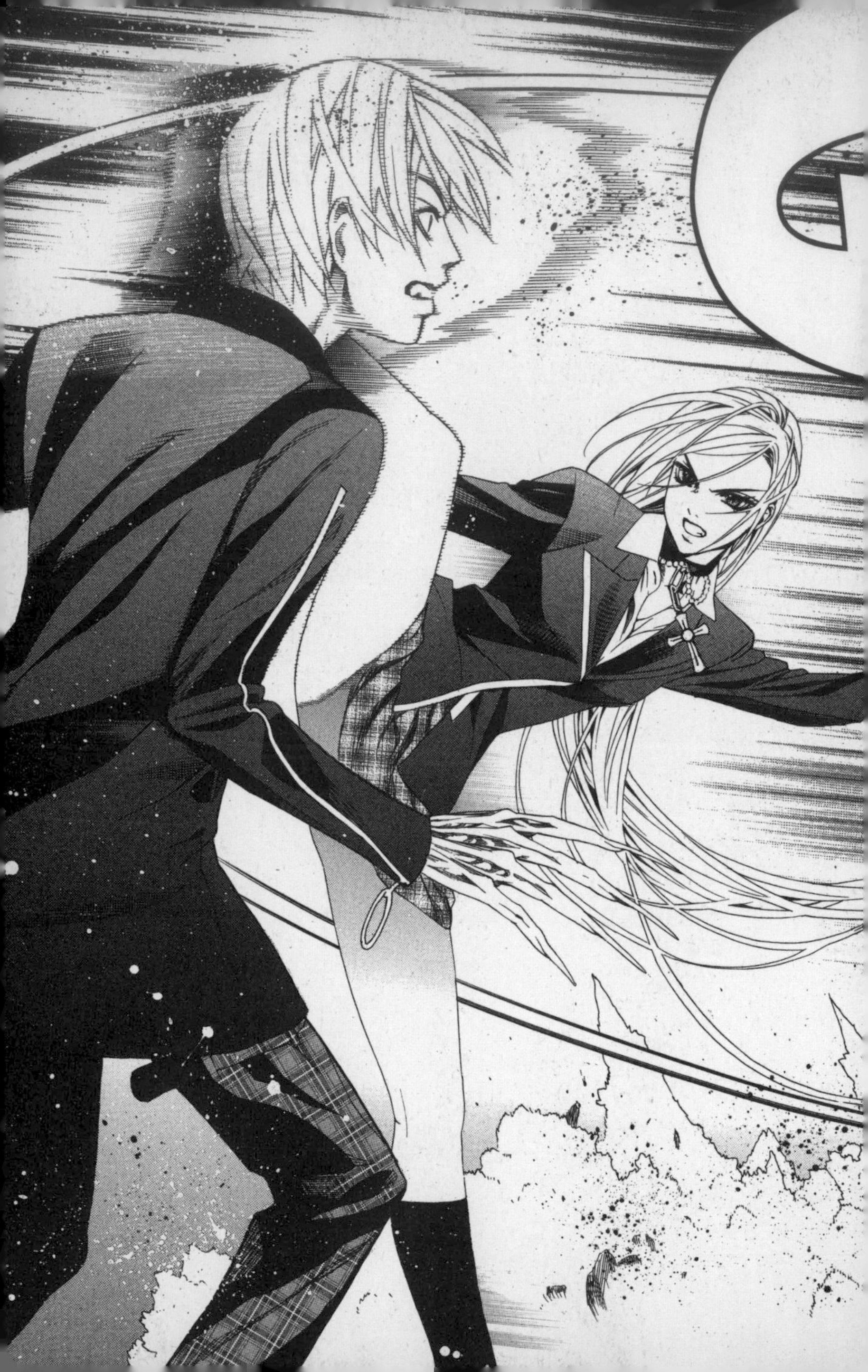

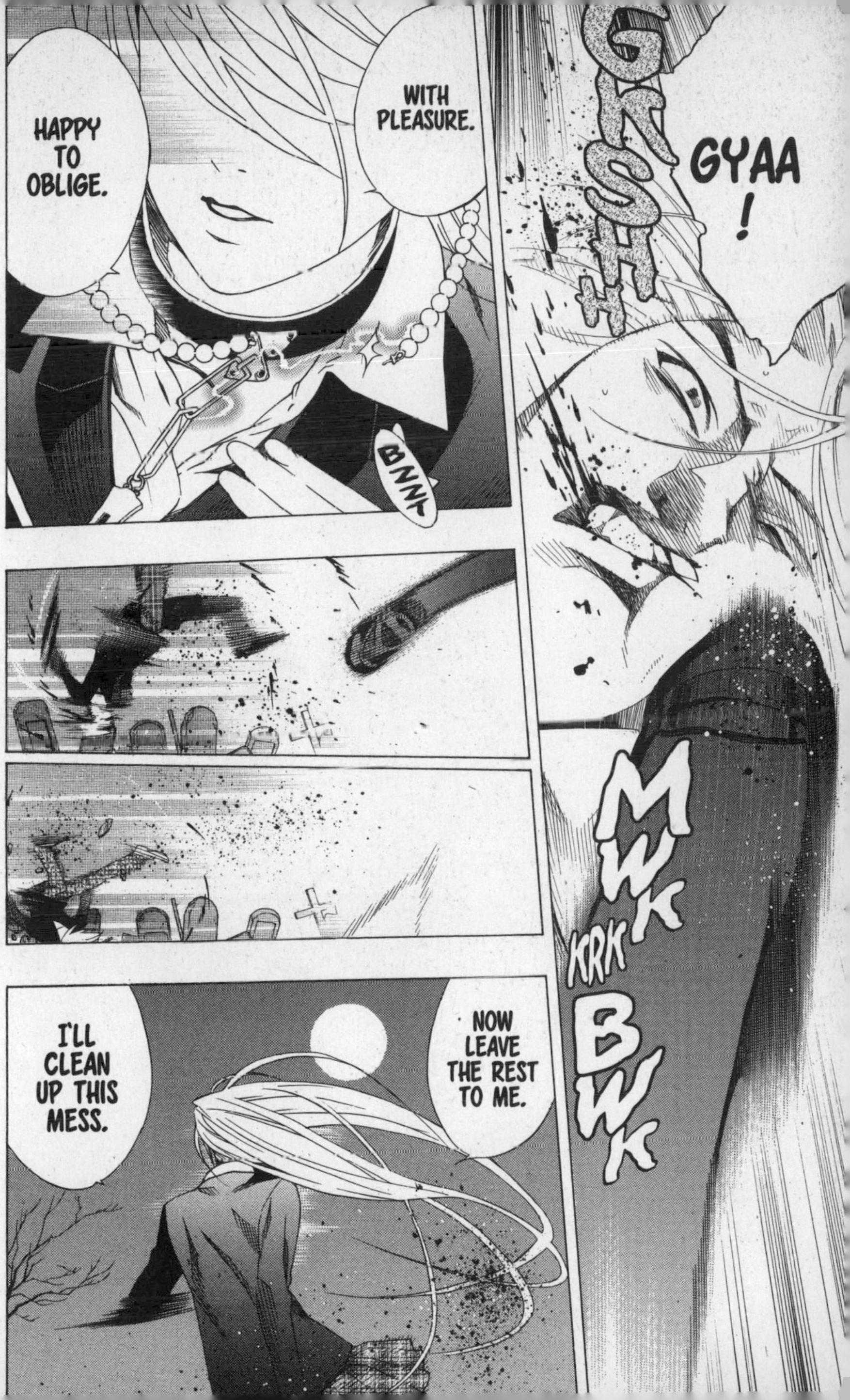
GKSHH
GYAA!
MWK
KRK
BWK
WITH PLEASURE.
HAPPY TO OBLIGE.
BZZT
NOW LEAVE THE REST TO ME.
I'LL CLEAN UP THIS MESS.

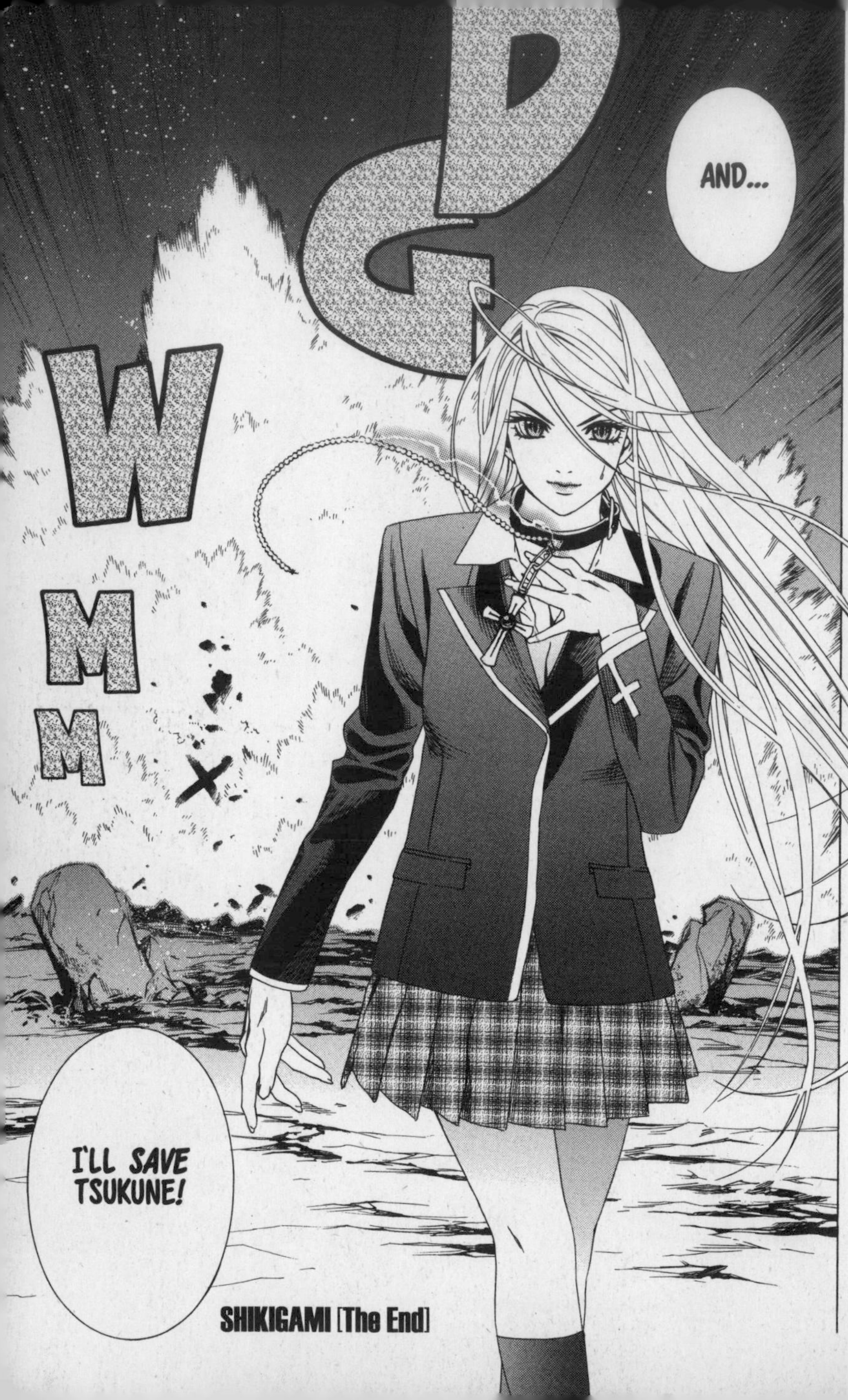
AND...
DG
WMM
I'LL SAVE TSUKUNE!
SHIKIGAMI [The End]

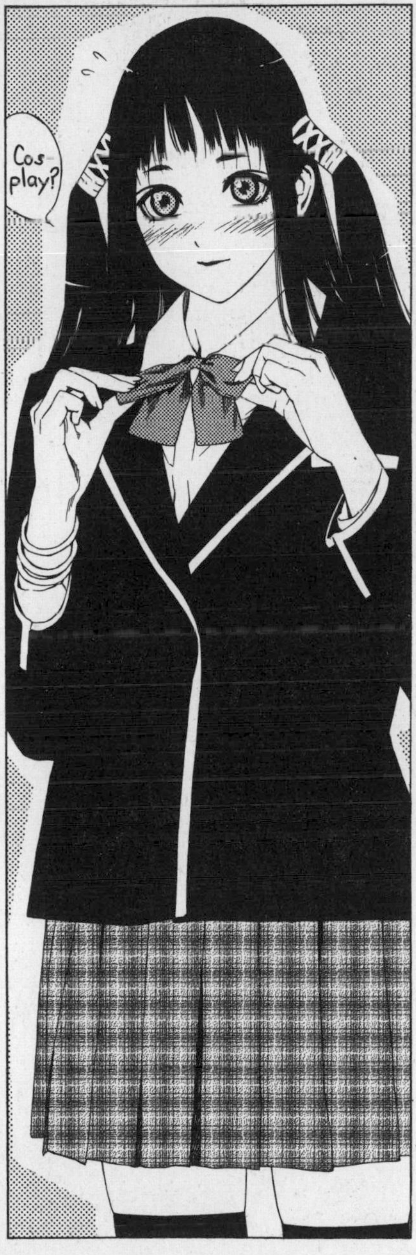
Cos-play?

ROSARIO + VAMPIRE

Meaningless End-of-Volume Theater

VIII

• The Name Is Ruby •

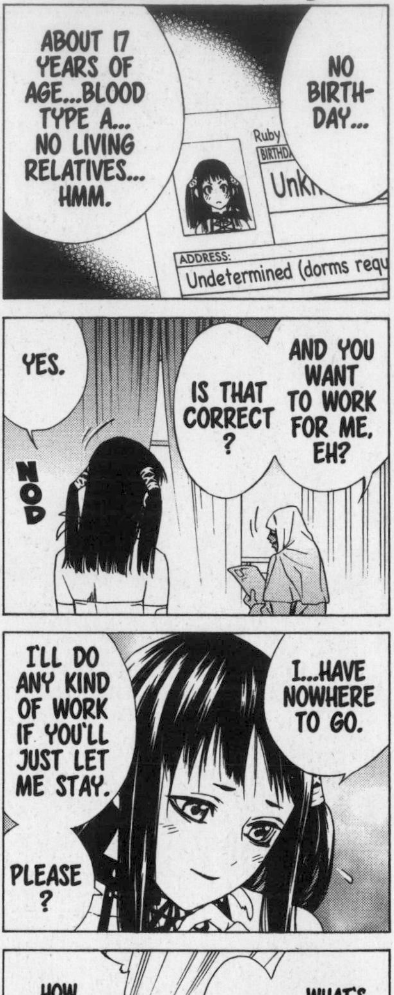
NO BIRTH-DAY...
ABOUT 17 YEARS OF AGE...BLOOD TYPE A... NO LIVING RELATIVES... HMM.
Ruby
BIRTHDA
Unkn
ADDRESS:
Undetermined (dorms requ
AND YOU WANT TO WORK FOR ME, EH?
IS THAT CORRECT?
YES.
NOD
I...HAVE NOWHERE TO GO.
I'LL DO ANY KIND OF WORK IF YOU'LL JUST LET ME STAY.
PLEASE?
WHAT'S YOUR *REAL* MOTIVE?
IS IT... TSU-KUNE?
WHA-?
HOW COULD YOU TELL?!
ACK

• Body & Soul •

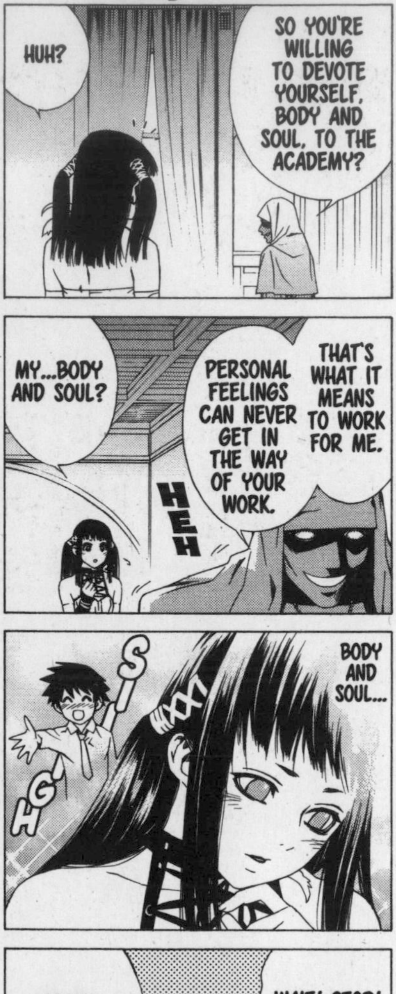
SO YOU'RE WILLING TO DEVOTE YOURSELF, BODY AND SOUL, TO THE ACADEMY?
HUH?
THAT'S WHAT IT MEANS TO WORK FOR ME.
PERSONAL FEELINGS CAN NEVER GET IN THE WAY OF YOUR WORK.
HEH
MY...BODY AND SOUL?
BODY AND SOUL...
S
HG
WAIT! STOP! THIS IS ALL MOVING TOO FAST!
WHAT ARE YOU TALKING ABOUT?
EEEEK!
B-DM B-DM
NO! NO!

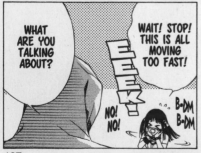

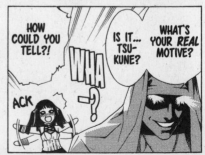

• I Even Practiced •

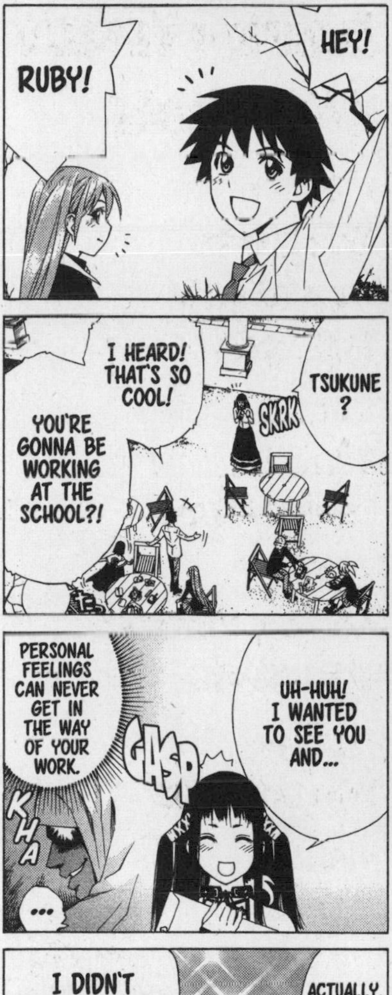
HEY!
RUBY!
TSUKUNE ?
SKRK
I HEARD! THAT'S SO COOL!
YOU'RE GONNA BE WORKING AT THE SCHOOL?!
UH-HUH! I WANTED TO SEE YOU AND...
GASP
PERSONAL FEELINGS CAN NEVER GET IN THE WAY OF YOUR WORK.
KHA
...
ACTUALLY, THAT'S NOT IT...
I DIDN'T COME HERE TO SEE YOU. NOPE. NO WAY, NO HOW. UH-HUH. (BY ROTE.)
NNG NNG
?

• Looking Good •

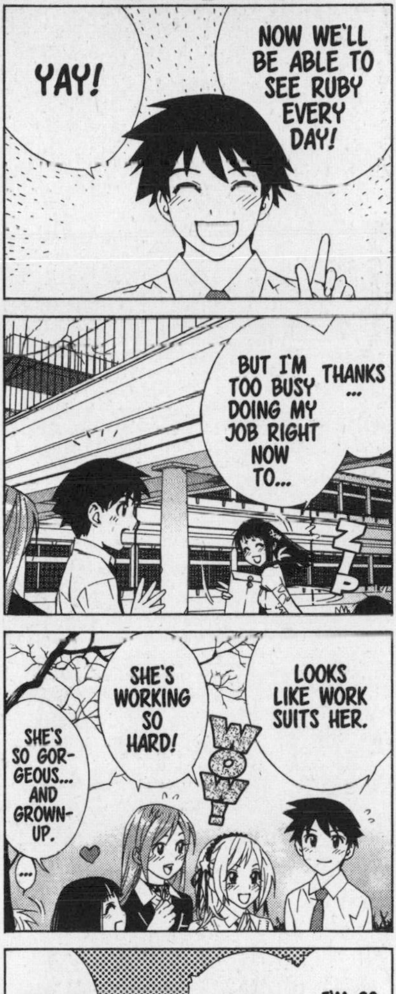
NOW WE'LL BE ABLE TO SEE RUBY EVERY DAY!
YAY!
THANKS ...
BUT I'M TOO BUSY DOING MY JOB RIGHT NOW TO...
ZIP
LOOKS LIKE WORK SUITS HER.
WOW!
SHE'S WORKING SO HARD!
SHE'S SO GOR-GEOUS... AND GROWN-UP.
...
I'M SO HAPPY!
SO HAPPY TO SEE YOU AGAIN, TSUKUNE!
GET TO WORK!
RRRG

Please send questions and fan letters to ➡ Rosario+Vampire Fan Mail, VIZ Media, P.O. Box 77064, San Francisco, CA 94107

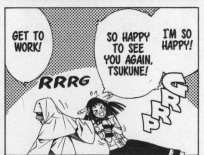

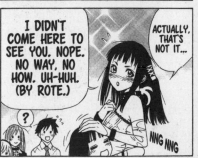

Rosario + Vampire
Akihisa Ikeda

• Staff •

Makoto Saito
Takafumi Okubo
Kenji Tashiro

• Help •

Satoshi Kinoshita
Yoshiaki Sukeno

• CG •

Takaharu Yoshizawa
Akihisa Ikeda

• Editing •

Tomonori Sumiya

• Comic •

Kenju Noro

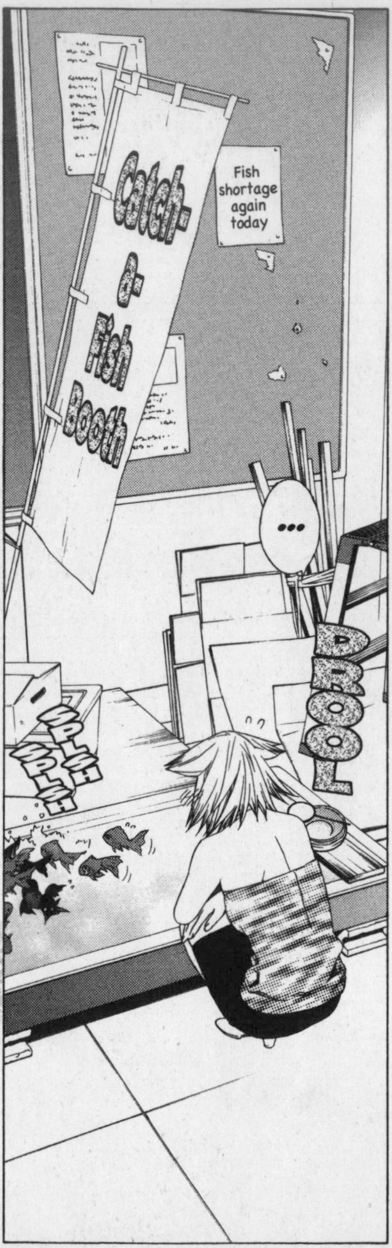
Catch-&-Fish Booth
Fish shortage again today
...
DROOL
SPLSH
SPLSH

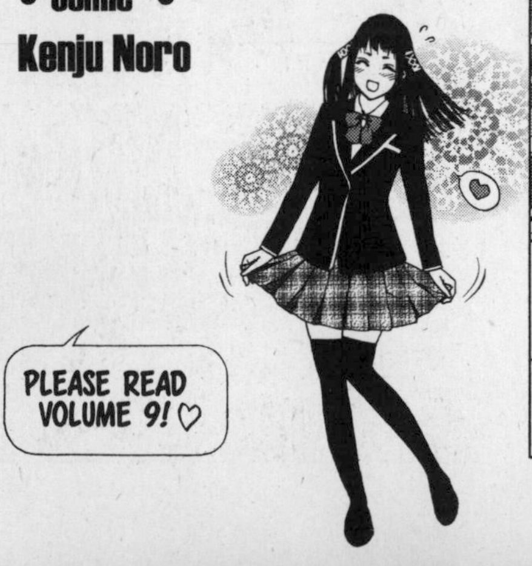
PLEASE READ VOLUME 9! ♡

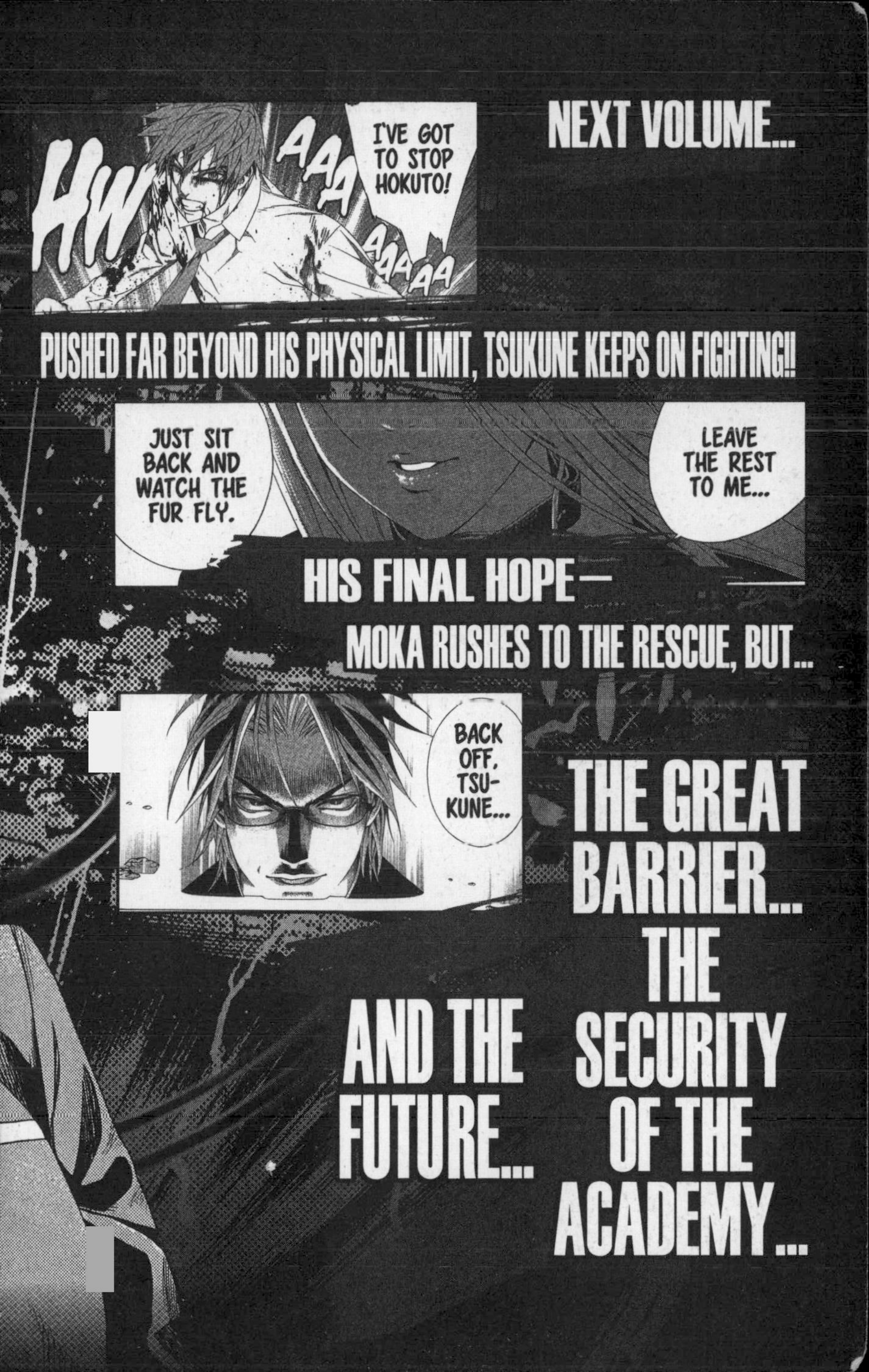
NEXT VOLUME...
I'VE GOT TO STOP HOKUTO!
HWAAAAAAAAA
PUSHED FAR BEYOND HIS PHYSICAL LIMIT, TSUKUNE KEEPS ON FIGHTING!!
LEAVE THE REST TO ME...
JUST SIT BACK AND WATCH THE FUR FLY.
HIS FINAL HOPE—
MOKA RUSHES TO THE RESCUE, BUT...
BACK OFF, TSU-KUNE...
THE GREAT BARRIER... THE SECURITY OF THE ACADEMY...
AND THE FUTURE...

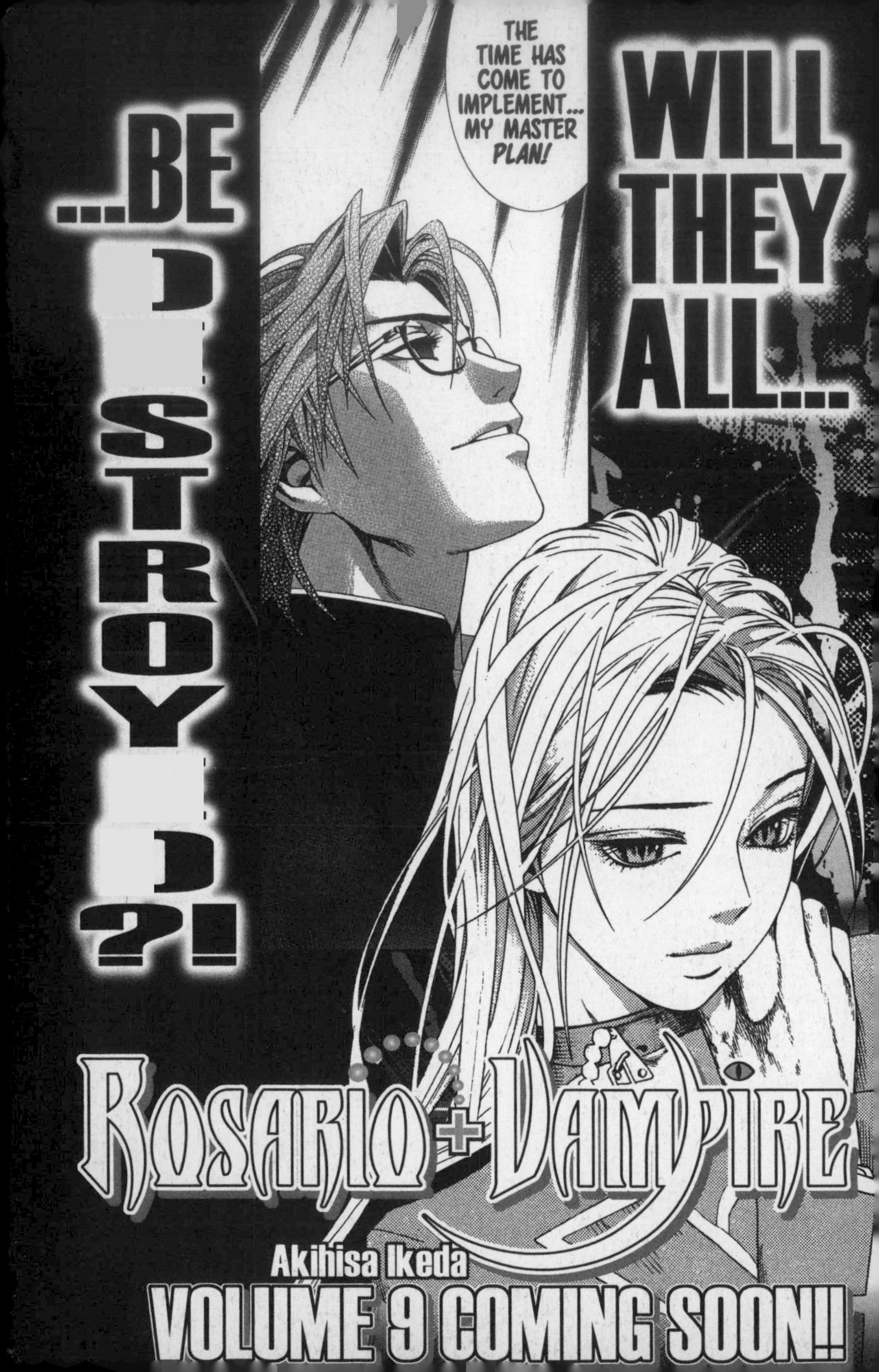
WILL THEY ALL...
THE TIME HAS COME TO IMPLEMENT... MY MASTER PLAN!
...BE DESTROYED?!
ROSARIO+VAMPIRE
Akihisa Ikeda
VOLUME 9 COMING SOON!!

Crypt Sheet for Volume 9: MONSTER MAMAS

QUIZ 9

WHEN TWO OF YOUR MONSTER FRIENDS' MOTHERS MISTAKE YOU FOR THEIR PRECIOUS DAUGHTERS' BOYFRIEND, ACT LIKE...

a. the perfect monster-in-law to be

b. you love to play the field

c. you never met their offspring before in your life

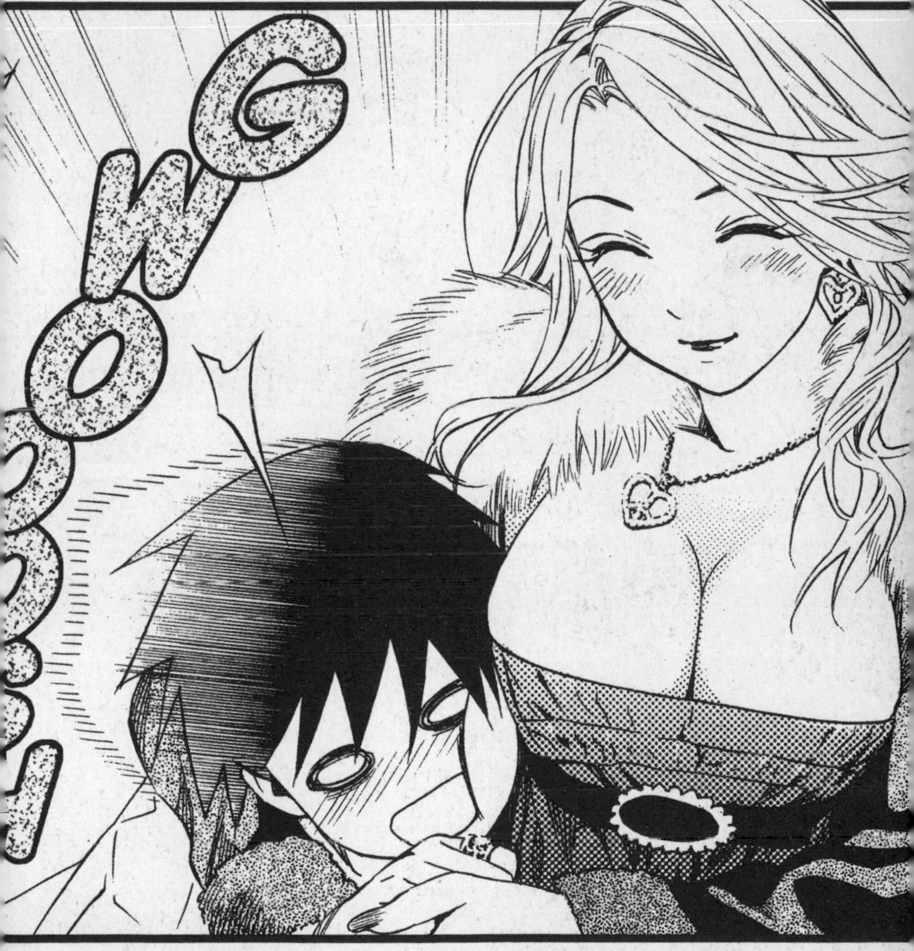

Available October 2009!

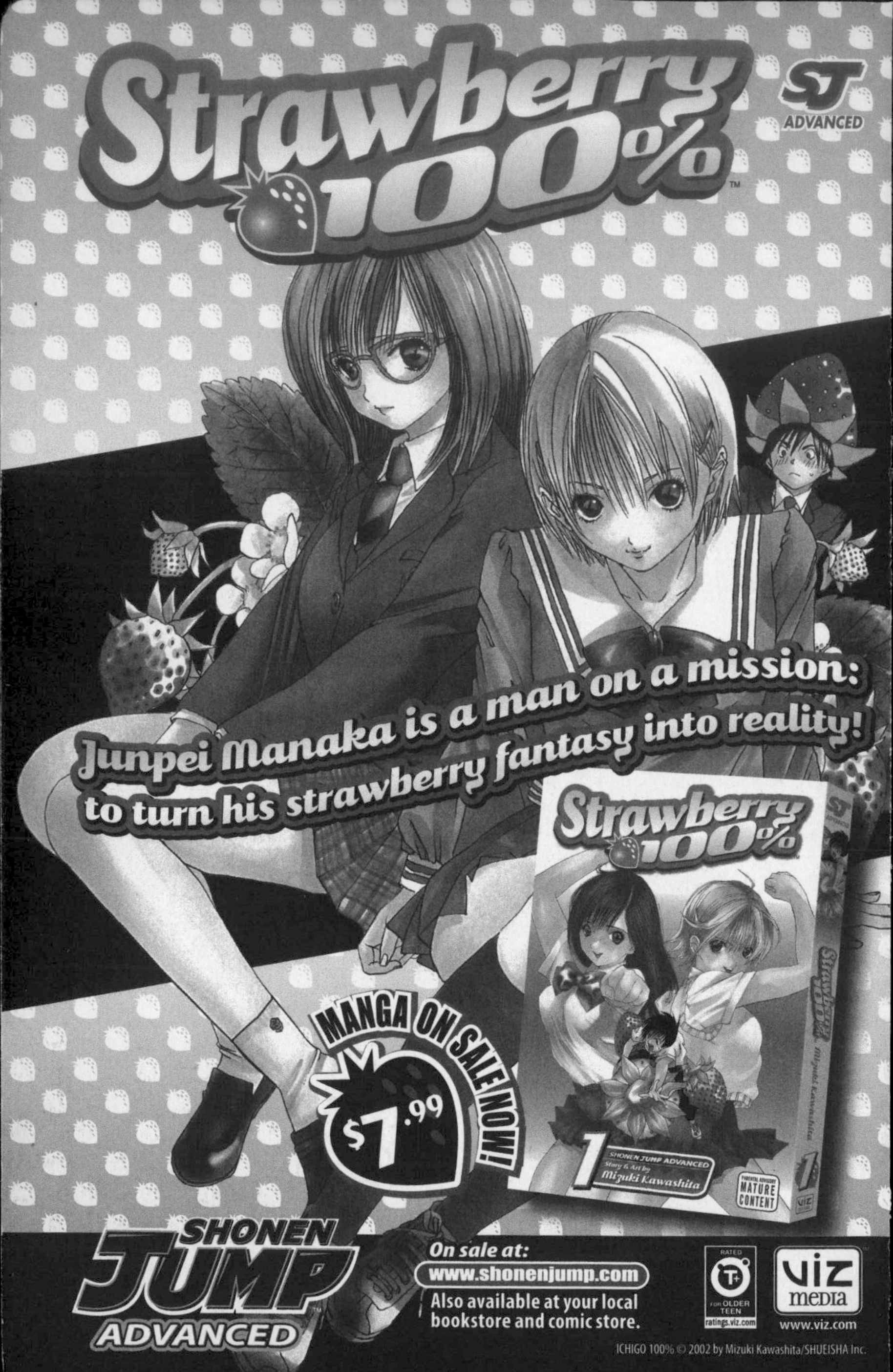
Strawberry 100%
SJ ADVANCED
Junpei Manaka is a man on a mission: to turn his strawberry fantasy into reality!
MANGA ON SALE NOW!
$7.99
Strawberry 100%
1
SHONEN JUMP ADVANCED
Story & Art by Mizuki Kawashita
PARENTAL ADVISORY MATURE CONTENT
SHONEN JUMP ADVANCED
On sale at:
www.shonenjump.com
Also available at your local bookstore and comic store.
RATED T+ FOR OLDER TEEN ratings.viz.com
viz media
www.viz.com
ICHIGO 100% © 2002 by Mizuki Kawashita/SHUEISHA Inc.

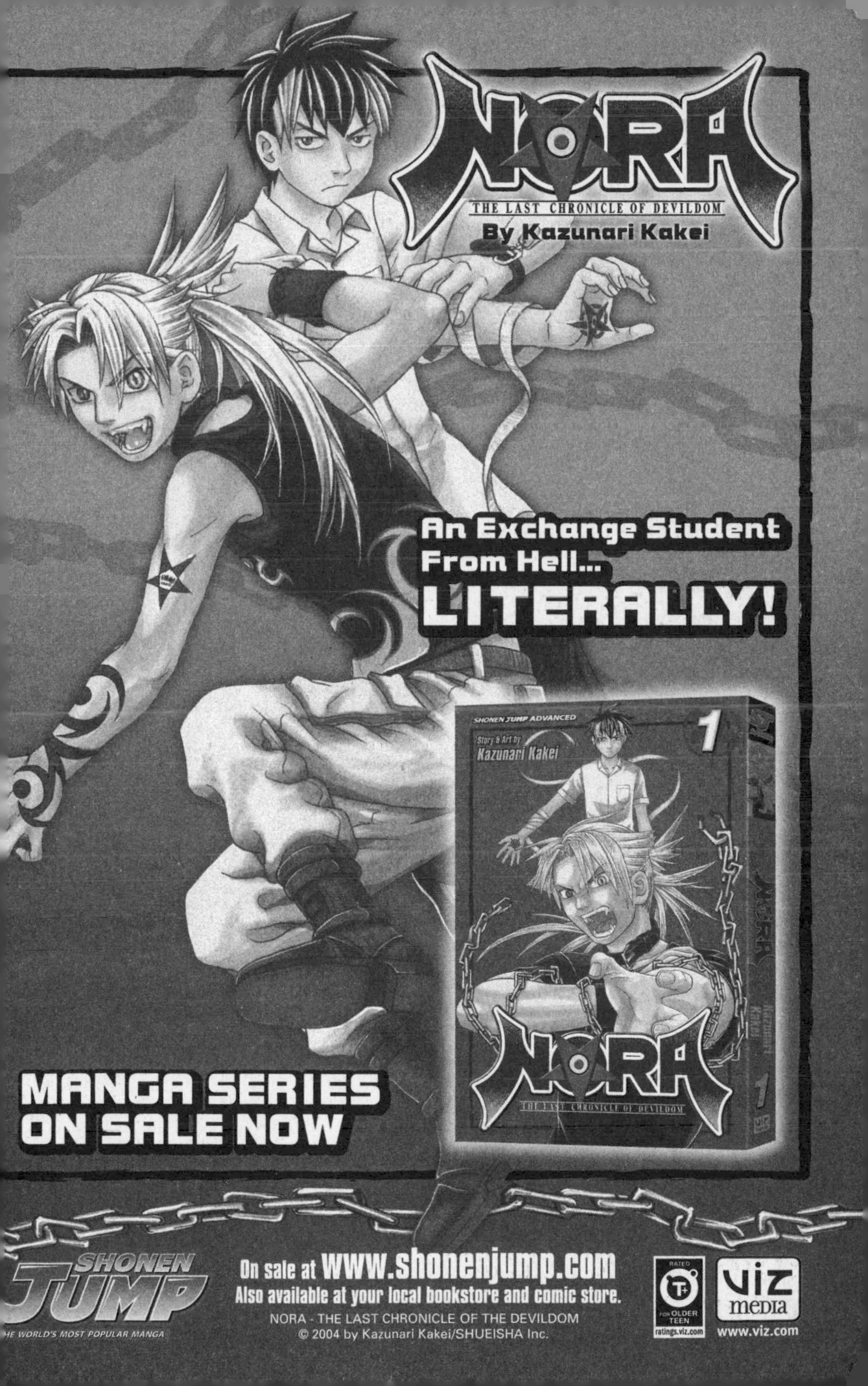

NORA
THE LAST CHRONICLE OF DEVILDOM
By Kazunari Kakei
An Exchange Student From Hell...
LITERALLY!
SHONEN JUMP ADVANCED
Story & Art by Kazunari Kakei
1
NORA
THE LAST CHRONICLE OF DEVILDOM
MANGA SERIES ON SALE NOW
SHONEN JUMP
THE WORLD'S MOST POPULAR MANGA
On sale at www.shonenjump.com
Also available at your local bookstore and comic store.
NORA - THE LAST CHRONICLE OF THE DEVILDOM
© 2004 by Kazunari Kakei/SHUEISHA Inc.
RATED T+ FOR OLDER TEEN
ratings.viz.com
viz media
www.viz.com

KUROHIME

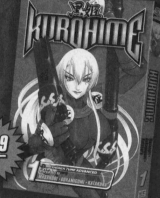
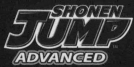

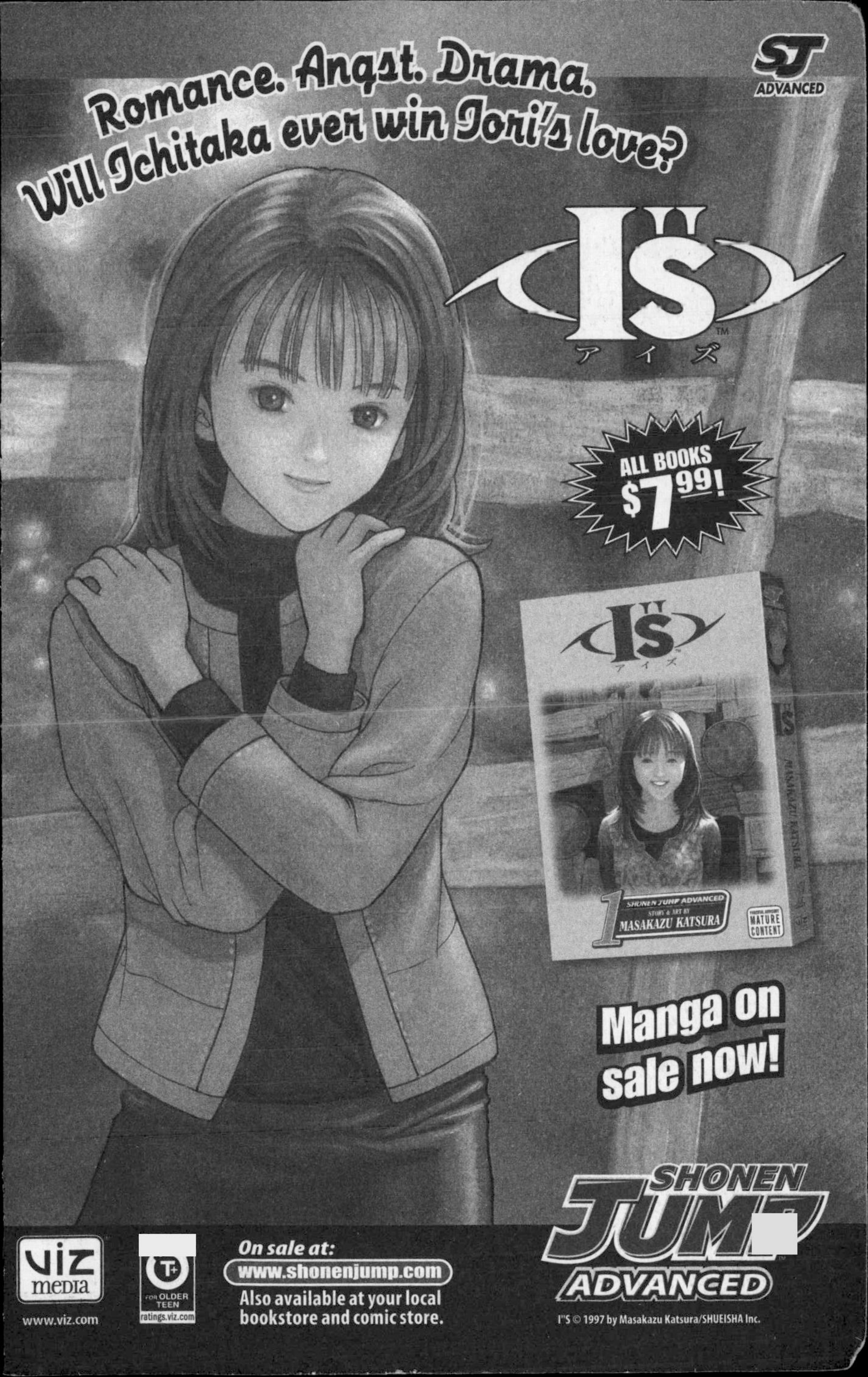

SJ ADVANCED
Romance. Angst. Drama.
Will Ichitaka ever win Iori's love?
I"S™
アイズ
ALL BOOKS $7.99!
I"S
アイズ
1
SHONEN JUMP ADVANCED
STORY & ART BY
MASAKAZU KATSURA
MATURE CONTENT
Manga on sale now!
SHONEN JUMP ADVANCED
viz media
www.viz.com
T+ FOR OLDER TEEN
ratings.viz.com
On sale at:
www.shonenjump.com
Also available at your local bookstore and comic store.
I"S © 1997 by Masakazu Katsura/SHUEISHA Inc.

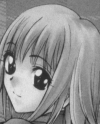
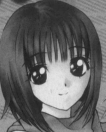
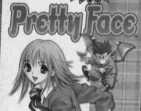

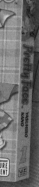
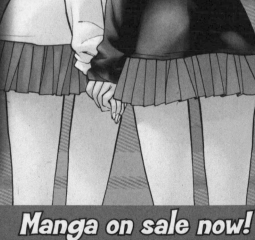

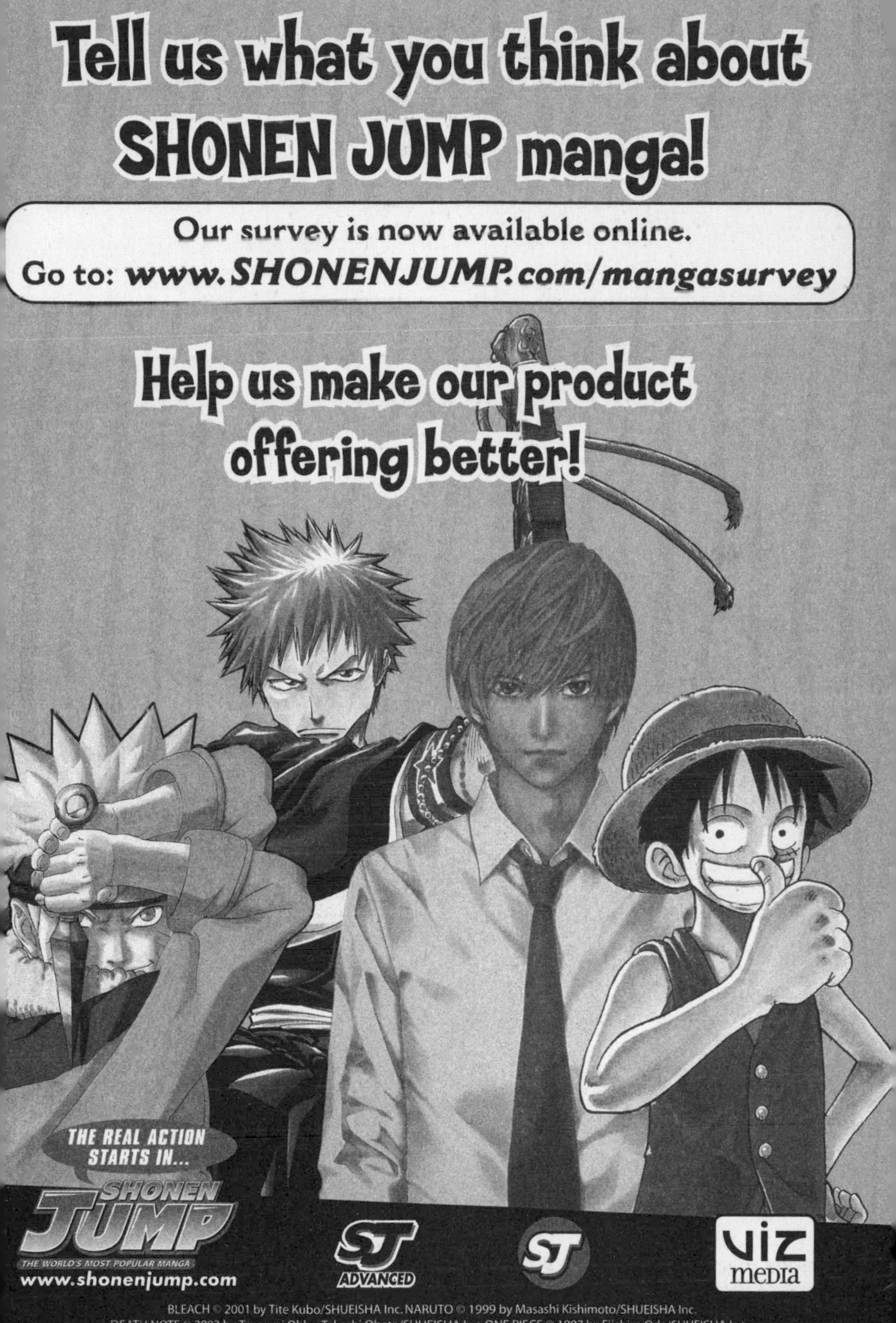
Tell us what you think about SHONEN JUMP manga!
Our survey is now available online.
Go to: www.SHONENJUMP.com/mangasurvey
Help us make our product offering better!
THE REAL ACTION STARTS IN...
SHONEN JUMP
THE WORLD'S MOST POPULAR MANGA
www.shonenjump.com
SJ ADVANCED
SJ
viz media
BLEACH © 2001 by Tite Kubo/SHUEISHA Inc. NARUTO © 1999 by Masashi Kishimoto/SHUEISHA Inc.
DEATH NOTE © 2003 by Tsugumi Ohba, Takeshi Obata/SHUEISHA Inc. ONE PIECE © 1997 by Eiichiro Oda/SHUEISHA Inc.

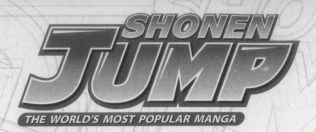
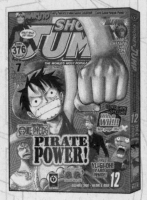
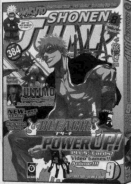
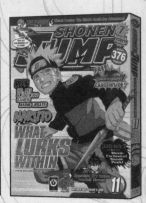

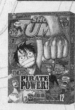
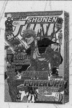
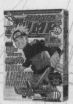